The Witness of the Synoptic Gospels to Christ

MacArthur Wagstaff

The Witness of the Synoptic Gospels to Christ

One volume combining The Witness of Matthew and Mark to Christ
and The Witness of Luke to Christ

Ned B. Stonehouse
Foreword by William L. Lane

BAKER BOOK HOUSE
Grand Rapids, Michigan

Copyright 1944 by
Ned Bernard Stonehouse

Reprinted 1979 by
Baker Book House Company
with permission of copyright owner
ISBN: 0-8010-8181-5

Foreword by William L. Lane
copyrighted 1979 by
Baker Book House Company

Formerly published in 2 volumes
under the titles,
The Witness of Matthew and Mark to Christ
and
The Witness of Luke to Christ

Originally published under the terms of
**THE HARRY A. WORCESTER
LECTURESHIP AND PUBLICATION FUND**
of Westminster Theological Seminary,
Philadelphia, Pennsylvania

FOREWORD

A man who is destined to make a permanent contribution to scholarship must be able to identify the crucial issues. He must also be committed to the disciplined exploration of those issues. The late Professor Ned B. Stonehouse was that kind of man. A graduate of Calvin College (A.B.) and Princeton Theological Seminary (Th.B. and Th.M.), he went to Europe in 1927 under the terms of a fellowship from Princeton to pursue graduate studies in New Testament at Amsterdam and Tübingen. The maturity of his scholarship in this early period is evident in his thesis, *The Apocalypse in the Ancient Church,* published in 1929, for which the Free Reformed University of Amsterdam conferred upon him the degree of Doctor of Theology. That year marked the foundation of Westminster Theological Seminary in Philadelphia, where from the beginning Stonehouse was associated with J. Gresham Machen in the field of New Testament, first as Instructor and then as Assistant Professor. When Machen died in 1937, his younger colleague became Professor of New Testament, a position he held with distinction until his untimely death at the age of sixty in November 1962.

The direction Stonehouse would pursue throughout his academic career was apparent already in his inaugural lecture upon his installation as Professor of New Testament on April 14, 1938. Speaking on the theme, "Rudolf Bultmann's Jesus in the Perspective of a Century of Criticism," he proposed to examine Bultmann's approach to, and estimate of, the testimony of the Gospels concerning Christ. He saw clearly that Bultmann was not an isolated figure. His view of Jesus possessed peculiar significance because in Bultmann there converged what Stonehouse regarded as the two most noteworthy developments in the study of the New Testament during the two previous decades, namely, the development of form criticism and the emergence of the theology of crisis. As a pioneer and advocate of form criticism, Bultmann had come to a position of radical skepticism concerning the testimony of the Gospels to the history of Jesus. Yet in his exposition of the message of Jesus he had sought to construct a positive theology based on Jesus' proclamation of the coming of the rule of God, the will of God, and God as the Remote and the Near.

Sketching the history of modern criticism as the background for an understanding of Bultmann's work as form-critic and theologian, Stonehouse identified the decisive issue as the estimate of the testimony of the Gospels. He amply demonstrated that in Bultmann's view the Gospels cease to be witnesses to the history of Christ, but are direct witnesses only to the history of early Christianity. This historical skepticism with respect to the Gospel records was bound up decisively with Bultmann's negative judgment on the historicity of the messianic consciousness of Jesus. What gave peculiar force to Bultmann's construction was his claim that at long last objective criteria had been discovered whereby the later strata of the gospel tradition could be eliminated and the primary stratum of historical fact could be recovered. These "objective criteria" were thought to be provided by the method known as form criticism, which Bultmann applied with unsurpassed thoroughness to the study of the Synoptic Gospels. Stonehouse's critical examination of the presuppositions, principles, and application of form criticism, undertaken to clarify Bultmann's approach to the history of Jesus, is distinguished by mature reflection and incisive judgment. It becomes clear that Bultmann does not seriously entertain the question of whether the content and form of the gospel tradition may not have been decisively determined by the impact of the person and message of Jesus upon the historical situation in which he lived.

Bultmann's radical historical skepticism concerning Jesus' person inevitably influenced his interpretation of the message of Jesus. Dr. Stonehouse protested:

> For Bultmann the gospel as Jesus proclaimed it has to do only with the God who is Remote and Near and not with the Son, and that is taken seriously to mean that the history and personality of Jesus are of no concern whatever. On this view Jesus is not the founder of historic Christianity and the religion which is attached to his message is a Christless religion.

In retrospect, that inaugural address exhibits remarkable foresight in its anticipation of the pervasive influence that Bultmann would exert over subsequent biblical studies. Indeed, Bultmann's legacy has proven to be a lingering radical historical skepticism regarding the authority and truth of the Gospel witness to Christ. The address was also programmatic for the direction Stonehouse would take for the remainder of his career. He devoted a lifetime to the study of the character of the Synoptic Gospels and the nature of their distinctive witness to Jesus Christ. He taught a course each year entitled "Gospel History: Jesus Christ in Modern Thought," in which his students were introduced to the history of modern thinking relative to the Gospels through exposure to the main figures in Gospel criticism from Reimarus to Bultmann. The complementary course, "Introduction to the Gospels," which was also taught each year, explored the question of Gospel origins and the distinctive character of the witness of each of the Gospels to the person and message of Jesus Christ.

Three years after his inaugural address Stonehouse was granted a leave of absence in order to engage in the research and writing which led to the publication of *The Witness of Matthew and Mark to Christ* (1944). As the preface makes clear, the task that he set for himself was to clarify "the character of the Gospels themselves" and "the nature of their testimony to Christ." His undertaking was motivated by the urgency of "the question of the authority and truth of the Gospel witness to Christ," which Stonehouse recognized as "a burning question for all who cannot escape the issue of their relation to him." In order to weigh the validity of the claims which the contents of the Gospels make upon us, Stonehouse addressed the question of "what the witness of the Gospels to Christ really is."

In his method of approaching the first two Gospels, Stonehouse broke new ground. At that time most synoptic studies concerned themselves with the recovery of the traditions behind the finished Gospels. In contrast, Stonehouse determined to focus his attention on the total witness of an evangelist to Christ with the conviction that an evangelist's distinctive interests and theological convictions are reflected in the composition of his Gospel as a whole. The validity of this approach has been acknowledged by virtually all biblical scholars today, but at the time when Stonehouse published his volume it marked a bold departure from both radical and conservative approaches to the Gospels.

The issues which Stonehouse addressed were those which had been thrust forward in the contemporary discussion of the Gospels. They were issues of primary importance precisely because they affected the interpretation of the text at a fundamental level. Stonehouse recognized the importance of critical research for a proper understanding of the Gospels, and his treatment is enlivened by constant discussion with scholars representing divergent points of view. He insisted, however, on "the primacy of exegesis," and brought exegesis into the service of an interpretation of the text that was consistently responsible.

After the publication of *The Witness of Matthew and Mark to Christ,* Stonehouse turned his attention to the Gospel of Luke. The invitation to give a series of public lectures under the auspices of the Free Church College at Edinburgh and at Sheffield University in 1949 provided the opportunity to formalize studies that had been initiated as far back as his leave of absence in 1941. In 1951 the sequel to the treatment of the first two Gospels appeared under the title, *The Witness of Luke to Christ*. Presented as studies in the interpretation of the third Gospel, the accent fell upon the exegesis of the text in order to exhibit "the witness of Luke to Christ in the context of certain modern interpretations of Christ and the Gospel." In the preface to his volume Stonehouse reveals that he had come to an even sharper appreciation of the importance of the diversity of expression within each of the Gospels. He wrote:

> In particular it has seemed to me that Christians who are assured as to the unity of the witness of the Gospels should take greater pains to do justice to the diversity of expression of that witness. It is a thrilling experience to observe this unity, to be overwhelmed at the contemplation of the *one* Christ proclaimed by the four evangelists. But that experience is far richer and more satisfying if one has been absorbed and captured by each portrait in turn and has conscientiously been concerned with the minutest differentiating details as well as with the total impact of the evangelical witness.

Writing clearly and forcefully, Stonehouse was able to lead others to experience the richness and satisfaction which he himself had so obviously experienced.

It is a pleasure to commend these two volumes, now combined under the title, *The Witness of the Synoptic Gospels to Christ*. They are models of solid scholarship, which compare favorably with more recent investigations of the Gospels. One cannot help but be impressed with Stonehouse's clear grasp of the issues and his solid marshalling of evidence. His discussion moves within the context of a thorough alertness to the contemporary investigation of critical issues. Professor Stonehouse's work is not out of date. It possesses a depth of penetration which continues to commend his scholarship to serious students of the Synoptic Gospels today.

WILLIAM L. LANE
Western Kentucky University

In Memory Of
MY MOTHER
1866-1943

And thus, like one of the heralds, I have endeavored, to the utmost extent that my ability allowed, to do honor to Christ riding magnificently in his royal chariot drawn by four horses.

JOHN CALVIN

A new face has been put upon life by the blessed thing that God did when he offered up his only begotten Son.

J. GRESHAM MACHEN

The Witness
of Matthew and Mark to Christ

PREFACE

For good or ill the momentous issue of the authority of Jesus Christ is bound up with the decisions which are reached regarding the authority and truth of the canonical gospels. Although many efforts have been put forth to discover a Jesus other than the divine Christ of the gospels to whom men might pledge fealty, the history of that search appears more and more clearly to have demonstrated its futility. The question of the authority and truth of the gospel witness to Christ, it accordingly appears, will continue to be a burning question for all who cannot escape the issue of their relation to him. But as one weighs the validity of the claims which the contents of the gospels make upon us, there emerges a more fundamental, although not more important and ultimate, question. That is the question of what the witness of the gospels to Christ really is. Much of the confusion and uncertainty that arises in connection with the efforts to resolve the former issue, the issue of authority, is due to erroneous conceptions of the character of the gospels themselves and of the nature of their testimony to Christ. In the interest of a partial clarification of this testimony, this study in the interpretation of the contents of the first two gospels has been undertaken. It is my plan to follow up this work with a similar treatment of the witness of Luke and of John, and thus to round out my consideration of the fourfold witness to Christ.

This volume is far from being intended, the reader will

please bear in mind, as a substitute for a commentary on Matthew and Mark. Judged by the comprehensive treatment which only a thorough commentary can provide, it will necessarily appear incomplete and inadequate. Many highly important questions of interpretation remain untouched. Those which have been selected for discussion, on the other hand, constitute some of the most important questions which have been thrust forward in the modern discussion of the gospels, and the method of treatment employed here offers the distinct advantage of permitting a far more thorough and detailed consideration than would be feasible in a commentary. I cherish the hope that this survey may serve the purpose of contributing to the clarification of these gospels in such a fashion that stimulus may be provided to further study on the part of many to whom their meaning is of pressing concern. Much of the popular knowledge of the gospels is, I fear, of a kind which detaches details from the broad gospel contexts, resulting in a blurred vision of the precise features of their testimony. If the method pursued here approves itself, it may encourage the study of the gospels themselves.

The reader who is abreast of modern critical developments in the study of the gospels may be disappointed that this work does not treat in any direct and explicit fashion the questions of literary relationship, and even less the debate concerning the oral transmission of the gospel before it received inscripturation in the writings of the evangelists. The silence concerning these matters is not due to any indifference to their importance. And, indeed, since the gospels do not permit one to come face to face with the testimony of any individual gospel without considering the others, questions raised by a comparison of the gospels have not been altogether avoided. Hence this study contains many observations that bear particularly upon the problem of literary relationships. In the main, however, I have been content to leave the questions of the origins of the gospel tradition to one side in order to concentrate attention upon the meaning of the documents that have come down to us. A conspicuous weakness of many modern studies is that, in their occupation with the issues of literary relationships and of the supposed original settings of the various sayings and incidents, there is a failure to deal adequately with the meaning of the gospels themselves. Whatever other questions may be legitimately raised as to the antecedents of the gospels, the first obligation of the scholar is to understand the testimony of the records. There cannot but be a disastrous degeneration in exegesis where there is not an awareness of the primacy of exegesis. Without anticipating that the individual conclusions of this study will receive approval everywhere, I trust that there will be little concern to dispute the legitimacy and value of this approach.

The recognition that the gospels are not isolated documents has significant bearing upon the disposition of the book as a whole. Although the plan adopted involves the treatment of Mark and Matthew under separate heads, four chapters being devoted to each, a measure of integration results from the rather frequent comparison of the testimony of one gospel with that of another. Hence there is much that bears upon the meaning of Mark, for example, in the chapters devoted particularly to Matthew. And the later chapters presuppose the earlier ones. Mark has been treated first, not as positively presupposing its priority to the others —on this question I am not convinced that the available evidence is sufficient to establish dogmatically either its priority or its secondary character—, but because it is the briefest, and, in some respects, the simplest of the gospels, and

PREFACE

because there are so few data which do not correspond more or less closely with materials in one or more of the other gospels. It serves therefore most admirably to disclose the essential features of this form of writing, and constitutes moreover a convenient standard of comparison in the analysis of the others.

In the interest of producing a work that might prove helpful to students of the gospels who are not trained scholars, the more technical aspects of the discussion have in the main been printed in smaller type and in footnotes. In the case of Mark, particularly in chapters II and III, however, it was found impossible to avoid the consideration of various aspects of certain modern hypotheses. On the basis of the judgment that Mark is the earliest gospel, and that the others presuppose Mark, it was inevitable that the study of that gospel should come to enjoy a unique place, and that students of the origins of Christianity should be busy with efforts to explain its message as an historical phenomenon. Accordingly, any discussion of the contents of Mark which takes notice of modern opinion is obliged to deal more or less directly with the most influential critical views concerning it.

The reader who has become accustomed to the capitalization of pronouns referring to the divine persons is perhaps owed an explanation of the employment here of lower case letters. The reason is not any lack of reverence, but, on the contrary, the consideration that the practice has apparently become largely formalistic, being retained, frequently, for example, even where Jesus is clearly regarded as a mere man. Actually of course, in view of the usage of the English versions of the Bible, the practice followed here is by no means an innovation.

It is a pleasure to acknowledge the contributions which

PREFACE xvii

others have made to the completion of this undertaking. My obligation to many scholars has been indicated in the footnotes. In the case of my own teachers in the New Testament, however, it is virtually impossible to intimate the extent of my obligations. Many things that I have learned from them, and especially from J. Gresham Machen, have become so inextricably intertwined with my own reflections as a student and teacher of the New Testament that I can no longer unravel the separate strands. It is far easier to express my indebtedness to others who have more immediately advanced the publication of this work. I wish to record here my thanks to the Board of Trustees of Westminster Theological Seminary for a year's leave of absence from my regular duties in order that I might engage in research and writing. I have become greatly obligated, moreover, to my colleagues in the faculty of that institution for their cordial encouragement of this project and their patient endurance of many inconveniences incidental to my absence, and especially to Paul Woolley, Professor of Church History, for his gracious and most helpful suggestions for the improvement of my manuscript. My hearty thanks are also hereby conveyed to Thomas R. Birch, Managing Editor of *The Presbyterian Guardian,* whose skillful services in connection with the publication of this book are too numerous to mention; to Miss Margaret S. Robinson for assistance in preparation of the typescript; and to my wife for aid both in the reading of the proof and in the makeup of the indexes. The defects of the work, I hardly need add, are to be charged to my account alone.

N.B.S.

PREFACE TO THE SECOND EDITION

The continued interest in this book, like the reception given it at the time of its publication in 1944, has been highly gratifying. And it is especially heartening that the Wm. B. Eerdmans Publishing Company and the Tyndale Press, who jointly issued the companion volume, *The Witness of Luke to Christ*, are uniting in the publication of this second edition.

The text remains substantially unaltered. I am thankful, however, for the opportunity of introducing on pages 91, 126 and 138 a number of minor changes. These clarifications and corrections are the result of comments and suggestions made by the Rev. Joseph C. Holbrook, Jr., Professor R. H. Lightfoot of Oxford and Professor Daniel S. Gage of Westminster College, Fulton, Missouri, which were gratefully received many years ago.

October, 1958   N. B. S.

CONTENTS

		PAGE
PREFACE		vii
ABBREVIATIONS		xv

THE GOSPEL ACCORDING TO MARK

I.	THE PREFACE OF MARK	1
II.	THE MARCAN OUTLINE OF THE PUBLIC MINISTRY	23
III.	THE DISCLOSURE OF THE MESSIAHSHIP	50
IV.	THE CONCLUSION OF MARK	86

THE GOSPEL ACCORDING TO MATTHEW

V.	THE STRUCTURE OF THE EARLIER CHAPTERS OF MATTHEW	119
VI.	THE RESURRECTION NARRATIVE IN MATTHEW	155
VII.	THE AUTHORITY OF THE OLD TESTAMENT AND THE AUTHORITY OF CHRIST	188
VIII.	THE SON OF MAN AND THE COMING OF THE KINGDOM	226
INDEXES		259

ABBREVIATIONS

AJTh	The American Journal of Theology
BC	Berliner Corpus: Die griechischen christl. Schriftsteller
BTS	Biblical and Theological Studies: Princeton Theological Seminary
DB	Dictionary of the Bible (Hastings)
DCG	Dictionary of Christ and the Gospels (Hastings)
EQ	The Evangelical Quarterly
ExT	The Expository Times
ExGT	The Expositor's Greek Testament
GThT	Gereformeerd Theologisch Tijdschrift
HB	Handbuch zum Neuen Testament (Lietzmann)
HC	Hand-Commentar zum Neuen Testament (H. J. Holtzmann)
HJ	Hibbert Journal
ICC	International Critical Commentary
ISBE	International Standard Bible Encyclopedia
JBL	Journal of Biblical Literature
JThS	Journal of Theological Studies

KNT	Kommentaar op het Nieuwe Testament (Grosheide and Greijdanus)
MNT	The Moffatt New Testament Commentary
PThR	The Princeton Theological Review
SBA	Sitzungsberichte der königl. preussischen Akademie d. Wissenschaften
S-BK	Kommentar zum Neuen Testament aus Talmud und Midrasch (Strack and Billerbeck)
SNT	Die Schriften des Neuen Testaments (J. Weiss)
TWNT	Theologisches Wörterbuch zum Neuen Testament (Kittel)
WC	Westminster Commentaries (Lock)
WThJ	The Westminster Theological Journal
ZNW	Zeitschrift für die neutestamentl. Wissenschaft

CHAPTER I

THE PREFACE OF MARK

SYNOPSIS

Introduction.

Brief survey of critical opinion concerning Mark. The need of attending to the distinctiveness of Mark's introduction of Jesus: its astonishing abruptness; its silence concerning historical origin and environment.

I. *The Superscription.*

Does it characterize the entire gospel or only the preface? Preference for the latter view: the gospel begins with the Baptist's ministry, which fulfills the divine word of prophecy. Implication that the gospel is in full view in the action of Christ.

The Gospel of Jesus Christ: "Gospel" as descriptive of contents of Mark, not as a name for the document. The glad tidings concern Jesus Christ: he is the one who constitutes in his very person and action the gospel itself. The name Jesus Christ recalls the confession of him as the Messiah who fulfills the hope of Israel.

Son of God: usage in Mark. Is it a gloss in 1:1? Argument against this reading not compelling.

II. *The Beginning with the Baptist.*

His significance in relation to Christ's coming. The abruptness of John's introduction. His place in the gospel by divine appointment in fulfillment of prophecy. No biographical traits. Concentration on John's witness to the person of Jesus.

III. *The Appearance of Jesus.*

Abruptness and silence. Central feature is heavenly witness to his divine sonship. Meaning of sonship: merely ethico-religious, or messianic, or ontological? Choice between the latter two. Criticism of the view that the words spoken to Jesus imply that he became the Son of God by virtue of his choice as the Messiah. Implication that Jesus is the Son apart from the divine utterance. Congruity of Mark's introduction of Jesus with the records of the virgin birth.

IV. *The Record of the Temptation.*

The divine direction and support of the Chosen One in his struggle against Satan.

FOR nearly a century now the question of Mark's understanding of Jesus of Nazareth has been in the foreground of critical discussion. It was inevitable, as the hypothesis of the priority and superiority of this gospel to the other canonical gospels became more and more widely accepted, that its witness to Jesus Christ should receive first consideration from those who were engaged in research and debate as to the origins of Christianity. If Mark is the earliest gospel, and the others are mere imitations, and even, to a considerable extent, mere editions of Mark, it follows that this work stands in a class by itself, not only as the original representative of a literary type, but also as the witness which stands nearest to the events of the life of Christ. Among those who have evaluated Mark in this fashion, however, there have developed two sharply variant judgments as to its fundamental character and value, judgments which may be conveniently distinguished as the Liberal and the radical estimates of this gospel.

The Liberals tended to regard Mark as a precious remnant saved from the fires of criticism, a source essentially historical rather than dogmatic. That Mark in the main contained history rather than interpretation was due, it was maintained, to the fact that its author based his work largely upon historical reminiscences of the preaching of Peter which he had attended. In spite of the presence of various features, such as eschatological perspectives and miraculous actions, which were admittedly irreconcilable with the historical presuppositions of Liberalism, it was insisted that such elements were so peripheral and irrelevant that they could easily be set aside, with the result that the powerful and moving personality of Jesus emerged into the full light of day. The Liberal lives of Jesus took for granted the Marcan outline as authoritative and, with some aid from sayings found in Matthew and Luke, proceeded to trace the development of the life of Jesus that was claimed to be psychologically intelligible to modern men.

At the very time, however, when this approach reached its high crest of popularity in the buoyant atmosphere of 19th century optimism, and there appeared to be certainty at long last as to the true personality of Jesus, there emerged new radical perspectives which were soon to spell the collapse of the Liberal point of view. Wrede and Wellhausen among others exposed the arbitrary and modernizing character of much of the Liberal treatment of Mark. While maintaining the priority of Mark, the radicals have insisted that Mark is essentially a theological construction rather than history, and consequently is only relatively superior to the other synoptic gospels and to John. On this view Mark is not a primary source for the life of Christ but rather for the historical situation out of which it arose, three or more decades after the crucifixion.

In their conclusion that Mark consists essentially of dogma rather than history the radicals may seem to present a far more destructive attack upon the trustworthiness and authority of Mark than the more mediating scholars. In our judgment this is not actually the case. Ultimately the Liberals agree with the radicals in denying that the supernatural figure with whom Mark is concerned can be historical. The radicals, moreover, must be credited with the advantage of perceiving the total witness of Mark in its unity to a far greater extent than the Liberals who arbitrarily characterized as history as much of the tradition as seemed to conform to their purely human experience. The radicals, on the other hand, went astray because of their presupposition that, since the facts of the gospel are everywhere interpreted, they are by that very token demonstrated to be unhistorical. But bare facts without interpretation are meaningless. The ultimate issue with respect to the gospels is therefore not whether they present facts alone or doctrine alone, but whether the meaning which they ascribe to the facts is their true meaning. While then we recognize that the radical approach has served to display the intrinsic fallacies of the Liberal method, and as well to center our thought upon aspects of the gospels which have often been neglected or misconstrued, our divergence from it is fundamental and thoroughgoing.

The goal of our investigation in the study of Mark, as of Matthew, is this, What does the evangelist think of Jesus Christ? What does he aim to have his readers think about him? Since however what he says about Christ is in the form, not of a systematic summary of belief, but of a narration of the life, death and resurrection of a person who appeared long ago in Palestine, we shall be required to approach the final question of the witness to Christ by way of an examination of the delineation of his historical career.

The Marcan outline appears indeed to be quite simple

and perspicuous. After a brief introduction which summarizes the preparatory ministry of the Baptist, including his baptism of Jesus, and which makes brief mention of a temptation in the wilderness, Mark describes in vivid fashion an extensive ministry of Jesus in Galilee and concludes with the narration of a journey to Jerusalem where Jesus is condemned to death and suffers crucifixion. Finally, he intimates briefly that Jesus did not remain in the tomb of his burial and was announced as having risen from the dead. The course of events from the time that he appeared publicly in Galilee until the crucifixion and resurrection appears to run swiftly and uninterruptedly to its great climax. Whether the disposition of the narrative of Mark is actually as simple as appears at first blush, and as it has often been supposed even by learned students of Mark to be, will be considered chiefly in the following chapter. In addition to these two comprehensive and interrelated themes, namely, the structure of the narrative of the ministry of Christ and the witness to the person of Christ, there remain two subsidiary features which, because of their extraordinary characteristics, demand separate treatment: the preface and the conclusion of Mark. Postponing the discussion of the intricate issues raised by the conclusion of the gospel to the fourth chapter, we shall proceed in the following pages to an evaluation of the introductory section.

If one contemplates the first thirteen verses of Mark through the spectacles of the birth narratives of Matthew and Luke, as most casual readers, consciously or unconsciously, probably do, there is a danger that the attention will not be arrested sufficiently long to notice the distinctive characteristics of this passage. Whether Mark was the earliest gospel or not, it must not be overlooked that it was not originally published as a part of the fourfold gospel canon. Moreover, even within the context of the completed New Testament this gospel must be recognized as possessing a unity and coherence of its own, as presenting, that is, an adequate and intelligible, if not exhaustive, publication of the gospel of Jesus Christ. Accordingly, the first requirement of the student of Mark's preface is that he examine it without the prepossessions gained from a knowledge of the manner in which the other gospels introduce Jesus to their readers, and only later relate its precise testimony to that of the other witnesses.

The most astonishing characteristic of Mark's introduction of Jesus is its meagreness, or, more pointedly stated, its silences. The silence of Mark at the very beginning is extraordinarily startling precisely because the person whom he introduces, as is widely admitted today, and as we shall observe in detail later, is not an ordinary person at all, but one no less than the Son of God, a supernatural being, who is declared by a voice from heaven to be the beloved Son, and who in the opening phases of his public activity provokes widespread wonder and astonishment by the singular authority of his teaching and the divine power which he claims and exercises in the performance of mighty works. Yet, for all that, Mark does not take time to satisfy curiosity as to the historical background and origin of this extraordinary person, as a biographer would have been compelled to do. Instead, in a few broad strokes, he associates Jesus with the preaching and baptizing activity of John the Baptist. He also mentions a temptation by Satan lasting forty days, this being the only specific reference to the lapse of time in the entire opening section. Mark is very far, therefore, from presenting a summary of the early life of Jesus. No attempt is made to provide an historical explanation of his appearance. The Son of God is simply there, surrounded from the very beginning with mystery. Nevertheless, for all of the mystery which envelops Jesus, the historical phenomenon of his life is not conceived of as essentially irrational. As Mark makes perfectly clear at once, the fact of Jesus Christ is full of meaning for men precisely because the meaning which it has in the divine plan has been made known.

Although Mark's introduction of Jesus is brief, and must leave completely unsatisfied one who is concerned primarily to draw upon it as a source for the treatment of the early life of Jesus, it demands for that very reason the most minute scrutiny. The opening words in particular require most careful evaluation if one is to estimate them at their true worth for the determination of Mark's own conception of the nature of his undertaking.

The opening words form a kind of superscription that is clearly intended to indicate the character of that which follows. But a question in dispute that demands investigation at once is this: how much of what follows? Is the phrase, "Beginning of the gospel of Jesus Christ," a description of the whole of Mark or only of the opening section? The former view has won vigorous support among exegetes representing widely divergent points of view. On this understanding Mark means to describe his work as a whole as setting forth the glad tidings of Jesus Christ. The qualification of this general characterization of his work as "the beginning" is understood then in two principal ways: (1) Mark is naively informing his readers that he is herewith beginning to set forth the gospel of Jesus Christ, or (2) Mark reflects upon the conviction that the gospel did not come to its complete expression in the delineation of the earthly career of Christ, but includes also its authoritative proclamation by the apostles, in line with Luke's characterization of his gospel in Acts 1:1, as also with the viewpoint of Hebrews 2:3. Mark, on the latter view, then intimates that there is a sequel to the aspect of the gospel to which his work is devoted, a sequel which he may or may not have been concerned to narrate.[1]

In spite of the weight of scholarly opinion favoring the reference of the opening words to the entire gospel of Mark, this view is not as satisfactory, in our judgment, as that which restricts the direct reference of the opening words to the account of the significance of the Baptist within the context of the gospel of Jesus Christ.[2] The gospel of Jesus Christ, it is here emphasized, was inseparably bound up with John's preparation for Christ, a preparation that served to thrust Jesus forward, as it were, upon the public scene. That John's work was an integral part of the divine action of salvation which the gospel sets forth is borne out by certain records of the apostolic preaching as that is summarized in the Acts (Acts 10:37f., 13:24f.; cf. 1:21f.) as well as by the consistent testimony of all four canonical gospels. Moreover, and this is the chief reason for insisting that the opening words of the gospel have the immediately following context specifically in view, it is difficult to escape the conclusion that the reference to prophetic testimony introduced in vv.2f. by the words,

---

[1] The former view finds expression in the discussion of this passage in the commentaries of J. A. Alexander, Wellhausen and J. Weiss (SNT, 1929); the latter in Menzies, *The Earliest Gospel*, 1901; Bacon, *Beginnings of the Gospel;* van Leeuwen, *Markus* (KNT); Zahn, *Geschichte d. ntl. Kanons*, II, p. 930.

[2] For various formulations of this conclusion see the commentaries of H. J. Holtzmann (HC); Klostermann (HB), Lohmeyer, Gould (ICC), Allen, Swete, Rawlinson (WC) and Branscomb (MNT). See also Grosheide, "Het Begin van het Evangelie," in GThT, 28 (1927-28), pp. 455ff.

"Even as it is written," is construed with the reference to the gospel in v.1. Even on the view that Mark 1:1 is meant to be a superscription to the whole gospel, the history of John would need to be understood as a part of the gospel, and it is altogether appropriate that Mark should reflect at the very beginning upon the nature of John's connection with the gospel. As Lohmeyer remarks in his comment upon this passage, the word "Beginning" (ἀρχή) has a "wundersamen klang" at the opening of Mark (as in Genesis and John), and serves to recall that God is the one who originates. It is the divine action for the salvation of men, then, rather than merely the Baptist's activity, that is in the foreground, and consequently Mark appropriately refers to the divine word of prophecy which finds its fulfillment in John's ministry. God began the redemptive action by sending forth the one who, in fulfillment of his divine word, would prepare the way for the coming of the Lord.

On the view which we have been defending, which finds the explanation for the opening word of Mark in the immediately following context rather than in some detached reflection of the evangelist, it remains true nevertheless that the significance of the opening words is not exhausted in their characterization of the opening section. As a part of the preface of the gospel, it implies that following upon John's ministry the full appearance of the gospel, not to say the gospel proper, would come in view. It is hardly a serious objection to this interpretation that Mark does not place independent headings above the body of the gospel and at other points of transition. Having been shown how the gospel began with the Baptist, the reader is adequately prepared to perceive when the gospel comes in full view with the appearance of Jesus himself. The emphasis falls then more upon the unity of the gospel in its unfolding than upon the stages of its progress which may be distinguished.

The word "gospel" as used here by Mark, it has been assumed in the foregoing discussion, does not refer to Mark as a written document but is descriptive of its contents. It was evidently not until the second century that this term came to be applied to the four gospels as a distinct kind of writing. The transition from the one usage to the other was not a radical one, however, for the second century evaluation of the gospels as authoritative proclamations of the single gospel of Christ finds its root in Mark's evaluation of the contents of his own writing.[3] The use of the term "gospel" in the opening verse of Mark, in agreement with its consistent employment in the rest of the New Testament, associates his work with the preaching of the early church. That he has in view the contents of the glad tidings, the message preached, rather than the active proclamation of good news, is evident from the character of the gospel as a whole, concerned as it is to set forth the Christian message, and this is confirmed by the other instances of its usage in Mark (*cf.* 1:14, 15; 13:10; 14:9; 8:35; 10:29).

The question of the manner in which Mark conceives of the relation of Jesus Christ to the gospel at this point is not in serious dispute today. Considering the vigorous and able support which has been offered in the past for the position that the genitive case in phrases like "the gospel of Jesus Christ" is *subjective*—implying that the phrase here means that Jesus Christ is proclaimer of the gospel—, there is a remarkable consensus of opinion that in Mark 1:1, as well as in most similar expressions, the *objective* relationship is

---

[3] On the meaning of "gospel" see especially Friedrich in TWNT, II, pp. 705ff., and on this point pp. 733f. *Cf.* also Klostermann *ad loc.*, Lohmeyer, *op. cit.*, p. 7, and Rawlinson, *op. cit.*, p. 251.

conspicuously in view, designating the glad tidings *concerning* Jesus Christ rather than the glad tidings *which he proclaimed*.[4] In Mark 1:14 indeed Jesus is described as proclaiming the gospel of God, and the New Testament at other points introduces Christ as the cause or originator of the gospel, for example, in Ephesians 2:17. In Mark 14:9, on the other hand, it is clear that "this gospel" is the gospel which centers in the proclamation of the death of Christ. The evidence of the usage of Mark is, accordingly, not unanimously in favor of the objective relationship, but the character of the gospel as a whole, occupied as it is with the story of the historical appearance of Jesus Christ, and concerned far less than the other gospels with the teaching of Jesus, demands the understanding that Christ is viewed in Mark 1:1 as *the content* of the proclamation—the one who constitutes in his very person and action the gospel itself.

The gospel of Jesus Christ has to do then with the meaning of the career of the person who had come to be known as Jesus Christ. This name brings to mind the Christian acknowledgment of him as the Messiah, the Anointed of the Lord. It is true of course that the name Jesus Christ tended to become a proper name whose use did not necessarily involve a conscious affirmation of Jesus as the Messiah of Old Testament expectation. In Mark, moreover, in striking contrast to Matthew, the emphasis falls upon the contemporaneous attestation of Jesus through the word and power of God rather than upon the attestation provided by the word of prophecy. Nevertheless, the Marcan usage of the designation Christ in 8:29; 12:35; 14:61 and 15:32 shows

---

[4] For the older treatment see Harnack, *Constitution and Law of the Church*, 1910, Appendix III, and Zahn, *Introduction to the N.T.*, II, pp. 459ff., 377ff.

that he is presupposing its traditional connotation. For Mark, too, the glad tidings proclaimed by Christian preachers was concerned with an individual whose historical career received its true explanation only when he was recognized as the Messiah. The gospel proclaimed the fulfillment of the hope of Israel, a hope which was distinctly eschatological in the sense that the coming of the Messiah spelled the arrival of the new age to which the prophets had looked forward. For this reason the transition from the opening words of Mark, which recall the fulfillment of the messianic hope, to the following verses which refer to the Old Testament proclamation of the Day of the Lord is not as abrupt or difficult as is often supposed. Isaiah particularly, whose reference receives special emphasis by the formula which introduces the quotation from the Old Testament, describes the new age as receiving its announcement from those bringing glad tidings of salvation, peace and the establishment of the rule of God.[5] Regardless of the difference of opinion which may exist among interpreters of the Old Testament concerning the relation of a distinctly messianic hope to the broad eschatological hope of Israel, there can be no doubt that the Christian church recognized in Jesus the one in whose person there came to realization the divine action in establishing the new age.

Whether or not the designation "Son of God" is viewed as a part of the original text of Mk. 1:1, no one today will seriously deny that Mark conceived of the messiahship of Jesus as involving a dignity and mission of transcendent character. If these words are a gloss, they represent the addition of a scribe who enjoyed a measure of real insight into the distinctiveness of Mark's portrayal of Christ. In

---

[5] Isa. 40:9; 52:7; 61:1. See Friedrich, *op. cit.*, pp. 706ff.

six other instances Jesus is designated as the Son of God. Besides his own acknowledgment before the high priest (14:62), Mark reports the divine witness at the baptism and at the transfiguration (1:11; 9:7), the supernaturally perceived recognition of the demons (3:11; 5:7), and the confession of the Gentile centurion at the cross (15:39). Adequate treatment of Mark's witness to Christ as the Son of God must await the consideration of the later portions of the gospel. Here one must be content to observe that it is widely admitted today that the figure of Jesus in Mark's gospel is altogether supernatural. So Lohmeyer, for example, declares: "The Son of God is not primarily a human but a divine figure. He is not merely endowed with the power of God, but is himself divine as to his nature; not only are his word and work divine, but his essence also."[6] The gospel does not at any point leave room for an interpretation of the messiahship of Jesus as representing a vocation to change the political or social scene by a purely human program. The gospel of Jesus Christ is the glad tidings of the appearance upon earth of God's Son, and that which the Son is concerned to accomplish on earth is a work which could have been done only by one who was divine. It would therefore have been quite congruous with Mark's total perspective to introduce at the very beginning of his work an acknowledgment of the divine messiahship of Jesus.

Although editors like Westcott and Hort and Nestle omit the reading "Son of God" from their texts of Mark, there have been not a few authorities who have favored its authenticity, including the recent commentators Rawlinson and Lohmeyer, as well as H. J. Holtzmann,

---

[6] "Der Gottessohn ist nicht zuerst eine menschliche, sondern eine göttliche Gestalt . . . Er ist nicht nur mit Gottes Macht ausgestattet, sondern selbst von Gottes Art; nicht nur sein Wort und Werk sind göttlich, sondern sein Wesen," *op. cit.*, p. 4. *Cf.* Rawlinson, *op. cit.*, p. 4, n. 2.

J. Weiss and Klostermann. Of interest also is the support of Turner in JThS, XXVIII (Jan., 1927), p. 150 and R. H. Lightfoot, *History and Interpretation in the Gospels*, p. 59, n. 2 and p. 85, n. 1. One is confronted here with an instance where the decision as to the early history of the text proves difficult because Codex Sinaiticus and Codex Vaticanus do not agree, the former omitting the epithet. The external evidence need not be reviewed here in detail. Suffice it to say that the evidence for the omission is not so powerful as to overbalance completely the evidence for its retention, and in such instances internal considerations must be allowed the preponderant weight. And it is fully as difficult to account for a scribal addition of the precisely appropriate words on the supposition that the shorter designation was original as, on the opposite supposition, to account for their being omitted intentionally.

The glad tidings begin with a proclamation of the activity of John the Baptist, not because of any independent significance attached to John, but only because of his preparation for the public ministry of Jesus Christ. This beginning is not related in any great detail. We hear nothing of John's origin and call, and much less of his message than in the other gospels, not indeed because Mark knows nothing more about him, for he clearly presupposes on the part of his readers a knowledge of the imprisonment of the Baptist (1:14). The brevity of his presentation of John's ministry serves to project into sharp relief the features which he is concerned to set forth to his readers, and the selection of his materials will accordingly illuminate the question of the purpose of the gospel as a whole.

John appears suddenly proclaiming a baptism of repentance unto remission of sins. The place of his activity is referred to vaguely as the desert, but the baptism in the Jordan and the concourse of people from the entire Judean country and Jerusalem mark the location more precisely as the southern part of Palestine. Yet these topographical references appear to be introduced only incidentally, not through any concern of the evangelist to write as a chronicler, a conclusion which receives corroboration from the absence of temporal notations. The physical appearance of the Baptist is alluded to, but again the motive is not biographical, but only evidently to recall the similar appearance of Elijah the prophet who was to come before the Day of the Lord (II Kings 1:8; *cf.* Mk. 9:11ff.; Mal. 4:5). Taken with the specific appeal to prophecy in Mark 1:2f. there is provided herewith an intimation of the perspective in which the Baptist appears. For all of the abruptness with which he is introduced, his witness is not conceived of in isolated fashion. The part which John's career occupies in the glad tidings concerning Jesus Christ is seen to be by divine appointment in fulfillment of prophecy.

Another highly significant feature of the description of John remains. It is the fact that Mark concentrates upon John's witness to the *person* of Christ, the Mighty One, whose power and dignity should cause men to turn from hearing John to hear Jesus himself. Not a suggestion is given as to how John received his prophetic message, how he came to his estimate of the person to whom he bears witness. The testimony itself, however, by the very fact of its remaining unexplained, serves to center attention upon the witness of John to the supreme dignity and power of Christ, a chord that is struck again and again in the gospel. The result is that, however much of the background and detail of the portrait one might not perceive, it would be impossible to remain unmoved by that overwhelming impression of transcendence and authority.

The appearance of Jesus in the gospel is no less abrupt and sudden. Only John's word is provided as a key to understanding Jesus. He hails from Nazareth, we are informed, but nothing is told concerning his earlier life. He leaves Galilee for the region of John's activity and there receives baptism. Thereupon he spends forty days in the desert enduring temptation. Nothing is intimated as to what follows immediately upon the forty days, but it is evident that Jesus continues for a time in Judea or its environs before going to Galilee after the imprisonment of John, which is otherwise not fixed chronologically.

What then is Mark chiefly concerned to set forth in this meager sketch of the pre-Galilean life and activity of Christ? It is evidently the witness from heaven to the person of Jesus. The Baptist in virtue of his prophetic gift has witnessed to Christ's exalted dignity and power. And now God himself declares that this person is none other than his own beloved Son. This two-fold witness, and especially the latter as the climax of the preface, provides a key to the understanding of the entire gospel. Jesus also appears unmistakably as a teacher and proclaimer of the kingdom of God, but he is preëminently God's well-beloved Son whose very presence and activity constitute the fulfillment of the messianic hope and whose proclamation must be received as glad tidings.[7]

In view of the specific context in which the name "Son" appears here, it is appropriate to advance our inquiry as to the sense in which Jesus is acknowledged to be the divine Son. Is the high view, which was noted above in connection with the discussion of the opening verse of the gospel, sustained here? Or is the sonship conceived in some subordinate sense, either as a designation of his messianic office

---

[7] That the chief interest of the evangelist Mark is not in the proclamation of the kingdom of God but in the person of Christ is observed by J. Weiss, *Das Urchristentum*, 1917, p. 540 (Primitive Christianity, p. 691) and R. H. Lightfoot, *History and Interpretation in the Gospels*, 1935, pp. 60f.

or as descriptive of "filial trust and fellowship with God which filled the soul of Jesus and which formed the sustaining ground of his consciousness"?[8] The flexibility of this name may be admitted so far as its comprehensive usage is concerned; yet the data provided here appear to require a specific meaning. The last view mentioned, which evidently conceives of the sonship as essentially ethico-religious, that is, as a relationship which does not transcend purely human religious and moral capacities, finds no real support in Mk. 1:11 in view of the absolutely unique appraisal of Jesus in the context. The decision, in our judgment, lies between the other two views: the view that the designation "Son" is merely the equivalent of "Messiah," and the view that it transcends messiahship as such, signifying a relationship that exists quite apart from any thought of official function in history (although, of course, for that very reason the messianic office of such a son must itself bear a transcendent character).

The former view is widely maintained. The commentary of Branscomb, for example, interprets the words, "Thou art my beloved Son," as referring to the appointment of Jesus as Messiah, the chosen representative of God, the second clause, "on thee my choice has fallen," expressing essentially the same thought. Of considerable interest in this connection is also the effort to find support in Mark for an adoptionist Christology. As Wellhausen interprets Mark, "the baptism of Jesus and not his birth is designated as the moment when Jesus becomes Son of God through the Spirit.... The essential significance of the baptism lies

---

[8] The formulation of Manson, *Luke* (MNT), p. 31. He appeals to Mt. 11:25-27 (Lk. 10:21, 22) but these passages, as we shall see later, even less than Mk. 1:11, allow for a merely ethico-religious estimate of the sonship of Jesus.

in the fact that it transforms him into the Messiah, that he descended into the water a simple man and comes out of it as Son of God." [9]

The conception that Jesus, according to Mark, became the Son of God at the moment of his baptism, that is, that he then received appointment as Messiah and underwent a certain transformation, presupposes that the reference to the fact of God's choice in the second clause, "on thee my choice has fallen," explains the appellation "Son" in the first clause, "Thou art my beloved Son." The divine voice declares then that Jesus becomes the Son of God because he has been chosen as Messiah. The chief difficulty of such an interpretation is, however, that the utterance then becomes tautological. It understands the first clause in the sense: "thou hast now become my Son," or "thy name has now become Son." But this presumes a past tense where the present is employed, and substitutes the idea of *becoming* for the expressed thought of *being*. As the text stands, however, there is a contrast between the two clauses, the former describing an essential relationship, a relationship conceived without reference to its origin, and the latter a past choice for the performance of a particular function. That the present tense cannot envisage an historical act receives powerful confirmation from the use of similar language in the transfiguration scene in Mark 9:7. Jesus did not any more become the Son of God at the baptism through the pronouncement of the words, "Thou art my beloved Son,"

---

[9] "Ganz im Sinne von Marcus wird damit die Taufe, und nicht die Geburt, als der Moment bezeichnet, wo Jesus durch den Geist zum Sohne Gottes wird . . . Auf alle Fälle liegt die wesentliche Bedeutung der Taufe Jesu darin, dass sie ihn zum Messias umwandelt, dass er als simpler Mensch in das Wasser hinabsteigt und als der Sohn Gottes wieder heraufkommt," *op. cit.*, p. 7. *Cf.* also Bultmann, *Geschichte der synoptischen Tradition*, 1931, p. 264, n. 1.

THE PREFACE OF MARK
19

than he became Son again at the transfiguration when the divine voice declared, "This is my beloved Son." He is seen to be the divine Son quite apart from the word spoken to him. The essential relationship, whether "beloved" is construed as adjectival or substantive, is clearly a completely distinctive relationship. The relationship of the second clause to the first in 1:11, while not expressed, is therefore by implication more properly viewed as resultative: *because of the unique filial relationship of Jesus he has been chosen to the task upon which he is about to enter.*[10] The Mighty

---

[10] *Cf.* Zahn *ad* Mt. 3:17; Vos, *The Self-disclosure of Jesus*, 1926, pp. 185-188. J. Weiss, *Urchristentum*, pp. 545f., E.T., pp. 698f., opposes the adoptionist interpretation.

Plummer, *Matthew*, 1910, p. 34, argues for a reference to messiahship rather than to divinity on the ground that "John was hardly ready for a revelation of the unique relation in which the Messiah stood to the Godhead, and we can hardly suppose that the Divinity of Christ, which was only gradually revealed towards the close of the Ministry, was at the outset made known to John at the beginning of it" (Briggs, *The Messiah of the Gospels*, p. 77)." But this is to apply a notion of development to the revelation of Jesus' person which is not derived from Mark or the other gospels, and in particular breaks down in the face of the parallelism of the disclosure at the baptism and at the transfiguration.

Matthew alone indeed intimates that the disclosure at the baptism was a disclosure to the Baptist, for the others report the divine announcement in the form, "Thou art my beloved Son" instead of "This is my beloved Son." This difference, however, may not be pressed to mean that Mark and Luke have in view a revelation which Jesus alone heard, for the Baptist's contact and understanding of Jesus, according to the context, are too intimate and self-assured to afford plausibility to the view that Mark conceives of him as unaffected by this disclosure. At any rate the high connotation of the name "Son" is not less plausible on the understanding that the words have primary reference to Jesus himself. Just as the disclosure of the sonship is introduced in Mk. 9:7 in order to ground the imperative "hear ye him," so the declaration to Jesus of his essential relation to the Father in Mk. 1:11 provides the indispensable background for the announcement of his messianic appointment.

One, upon whom the Spirit has fallen, will himself baptize with the Holy Spirit.

In a later chapter we shall have occasion to discuss the distinctive manner in which the evangelist Matthew introduces Christ to his readers. We cannot avoid, however, taking brief notice here of the conclusion sometimes drawn from the preface of Mark that he evidently knew nothing of the virgin birth of Christ, as reported by Matthew and Luke. Johannes Weiss, for example, has said that since Mark, like John and Paul, does not refer to a supernatural birth, his conception of the sonship of Jesus must have been conceivable apart from the idea of a divine conception.[11] The argument from silence is rather hazardous in the case of Mark, not to speak of John and Paul, in view of the extreme brevity of his account of the historical background of Jesus. Indeed, one might even say that Mark presents Jesus without any reference whatever to the origin of his historical life. It is God's voice that introduces Jesus as his beloved Son and as under appointment to perform a task upon the earth. The astonishing abruptness of the appearance of the Son of God in Mark's gospel leaves him far less explained than in the other gospels. It should also be borne in mind that, according to Matthew and Luke, Jesus does not any more become the Son of God at the time of or by virtue of his virgin birth than he becomes the Son of God at his baptism or transfiguration according to Mark. It is there-

---

In the consideration of the broad question of the meaning of the messiahship it must be borne in mind that, although the Old Testament antecedents clearly allow for the possibility that the name "Son" should signify messiahship, it is clear at many points that the Messiah is not a mere man. *Cf.* Warfield, "The Divine Messiah in the Old Testament" in PThR, xiv, 1916, pp. 379-416 (also in *Christology and Criticism*, 1929); Gressmann, *Der Messias*, 1929, pp. 245f., 272.

[11] In SNT, I, 1929, p. 73.

fore rash to affirm that Mark evidently knew nothing of the virgin birth or that his Christology is incongruous with the virgin birth of Christ. And even if it could be made out that Mark had not heard of the virgin birth, it still would not follow that his conception of Christ was any less transcendent or supernatural than that of the other evangelists.

After the high word of divine testimony to Jesus in Mark 1:11, the mention of the temptation in the two closing verses of the preface may seem anticlimactic. It may not be overlooked, however, that *divine* direction and support of the one who has been chosen introduces and concludes this brief account: it is the Spirit who initiates this interlude and divine messengers supply him with the necessary sustenance. The Spirit of God does not come into prominence in this gospel—perhaps because of its concentration upon the mysterious and meaningful appearance of the Son of God—, but Mark, too, associates the Spirit with Jesus at the baptism and in the temptation, and includes the broad characterization of his messianic work as baptizing with the Holy Spirit. The preface includes then brief indication that the Messiah has come, a Messiah who is divinely chosen, who is under divine protection, and has been charged with the performance of a supernatural task. But the accent falls upon the disclosure that Jesus the Christ is none other than the very Son of God. His conflict with Satan serves moreover to provide a background for the delineation of the struggle between the Son of God and the forces of Satan which is so prominent in the narrative of his ministry.

From the study of the preface we turn now to Mark's broad portrayal of the public career of Jesus Christ. We shall be concerned chiefly to inquire whether his witness to Christ bears the same stamp as appears in the preface or whether in the new contexts a somewhat divergent perspective comes to light. This undertaking can proceed, however, only as we have come to grips with the question of the method of the evangelist as disclosed by an examination of the disposition of the public ministry.

CHAPTER II

THE MARCAN OUTLINE OF THE PUBLIC MINISTRY

SYNOPSIS

I. *Indications of locality and time in Mark.*

Review of critical interpretation.
A. The Galilean Activity. Definition of its limits: Mk. 1:14 is the *a quo* limit, but provides no connection with the events of the preface; Mk. 8:26 is the most satisfactory limit *ad quem*.
References to locations within and outside of Galilee: "the Galilean ministry" is only an approximate description for the activity of this section; the indefiniteness of many references to the location of the action.
References to time within this period: the frequent absence of precise chronological connection of incidents; the positive value of the notices of time; data relating to the duration of the public ministry; the incidental nature of the references to time does not affect their reliability.
B. The Journey to Jerusalem and Subsequent Events.
Data relating to the journey to and the public activity in Jerusalem; the coherence of the passion narrative.
General conclusions as to the bearing of these considerations on the understanding of Mark.

II. *Mark's interest in Galilee and Jerusalem.*

The construction of Lohmeyer and R. H. Lightfoot.
The testimony of the preface: the revelatory action is not in Galilee but in or near Judea.
The supposed antithesis of activity in Galilee and Jerusalem: (1) the references to Galilean activity hardly appear schematic;

(2) the appeal to the verb "to proclaim": it is appropriate in describing public activity but not instruction of disciples which is in the foreground after arrival in Caesarea Philippi; the absence of this verb explained by controversial nature of public teaching in the broad narrative of the passion; moreover, in view of public teaching described in Mk. 10:1 and 12:35ff. no special significance can be attached to the mere absence of this word; (3) the infrequency of miracles in the area of Judea: possible explanations; their revelatory character; (4) Lightfoot's admission of "gleams of light" in the darkness of Judea; (5) the passion as glad tidings.

The Resurrection Narrative: the divine action and revelation in Jerusalem.

Some factors bearing upon Mark's interest in Galilee.

THE preface of Mark, we have observed, contains precious little information concerning the beginnings of the historical career of Jesus Christ. Nothing is told as to when and where he was born, little or nothing concerning the environment and development of his early years. Evidently Mark does not regard such matters as indispensable to the publication of the glad tidings of Jesus Christ. At the very beginning then Mark must prove disappointing to readers who approach the gospels primarily as sources for a reconstruction of the life of Christ, and particularly to those who are seeking to understand Jesus in terms of heredity and environment. One turns from the preface to the body of the gospel, nevertheless, with the expectation that now surely such a delineation of his historical life will be provided as will enable one to determine quite specifically when and where and how he lived. If his origins, so far as Mark's record goes, seem obscure, at least we shall hardly expect to remain in any uncertainty as to the progress of his public career through which he came to affect the lives and fortunes of great numbers of men, of thousands in his own lifetime and subsequently of uncounted millions. Still, with our eye upon the manner in which Mark has introduced Jesus in the opening section, we should be warned in advance not to prejudge Mark's treatment of the public ministry.

At first glance indeed it may appear that the narrative of the public life of Jesus is marked by close attention to change of scene and the passing of time. The reader may easily receive the impression that Mark conceives of the ministry as lasting only about a year, a year that begins with considerable success in Galilee and its borders but issues rapidly into a season of controversy and conflict that ends with his crucifixion at Jerusalem at the time of a Passover. The outline of the events in Mark, as we have noted, provided the structure for the scores of Liberal lives of Jesus which began to appear near the close of the nineteenth century. H. J. Holtzmann, who performed epochal work in expounding and developing the hypothesis of the priority, superiority and essential reliability of Mark, even supposed that it was possible, on the basis of Mark's outline, to distinguish seven stages in the Galilean ministry.[1] In spite of the drastic criticism of this view of Mark which has been forthcoming in the present century, advocacy and defense of it have not been completely wanting. F. C. Burkitt has perhaps been the most able English scholar to support the theory of the superiority of Mark and, supposing its dependence upon the reminiscences of Peter, to defend its trustworthiness as a primary source for the reconstruction of the historical career of Jesus.[2]

A new perspective in the study of Mark's framework has

---

[1] *Die synoptischen Evangelien*, 1863, pp. 479ff.
[2] *Earliest Sources for the Life of Jesus*, 1922; *Christian Beginnings*, 1924; *Jesus Christ*, 1932.

now emerged, following upon the radical and incisive criticism of the Marcan Hypothesis by Wrede, Wellhausen and others, through the application of the method of form-criticism to the study of the gospels. If the written formulation of the gospel is, as this method maintains, really the product of the transmission of isolated stories and sayings by the church, rather than primarily the record of personal reminiscences, the links which join the various units together may be, and actually are held by the advocates of this method to be, with the possible exception of the narrative of the passion of Christ, not integral and original elements of the proclamation of the gospel, but of later origin. These links, consisting for the most part of references to the temporal and geographical setting of the isolated stories and sayings, are thought to be most probably the creation of the evangelist who was responsible for weaving the separate stories and sayings into one continuous narrative. Credit for shattering the framework of the gospel history, and thus opening the way for the application of the form-critical method to the study of the gospels, is given in large part to K. L. Schmidt, whose book on *The Framework of the History of Jesus (Der Rahmen der Geschichte Jesu)* appeared in 1919. It now appears that, in undermining the confidence of the Liberal critics in Mark, this radical criticism has leveled a most destructive attack upon the reliability of the gospel story. The data need therefore to be examined afresh with a view to their bearing upon the question of the essential character of the Gospel according to Mark.

The activity of Jesus in Galilee which Mark describes begins with a return to Galilee, evidently from Judea, after the imprisonment of the Baptist (Mk. 1:9, 14). This entrance into Galilee, we must not fail to observe, is not fixed temporally nor is it associated in any specific way with the events recounted in the preceding context. The beginning of the Galilean ministry according to Mark, accordingly, is introduced without any effort to fix its precise place in the broader perspective of the life of Jesus. One gets the impression again that the glad tidings of Jesus Christ, though palpably concerned with the events of his life, do not aim to tell the story of that life as a continuous and closely concatenated whole.

Exactly where Mark locates the conclusion of the Galilean phase of the work of Christ is more difficult to ascertain. As late as Mark 9:30 mention is made of a journey through Galilee and in 9:33-50 the scene is Capernaum.[3] Only in the tenth chapter does the evangelist indicate that Jesus has arrived in "the borders of Judea" (Mk. 10:1). Nevertheless, it would seem to be a mistake to regard all of the section comprising Mk. 1:14-9:52 as properly descriptive of a public ministry in Galilee, particularly since the latter portion of this section is devoted to the narration of a journey to Jerusalem which ends at Mk. 10:52. The actual beginning of this journey appears to be found in Mk. 8:27ff., in connection with the confession at Caesarea Philippi and its attendant pronouncement of the approaching passion. The resultant division of the contents, according to our preference, is then as follows: I. Galilean ministry (Mk. 1:14-8:26); II. The journey to Jerusalem (Mk. 8:27-10:52); III. The ministry, death and resurrection at Jerusalem (Mk. 11:1-16:8).

But even the section including Mark 1:14-8:26 contains the narration of much that happens outside of Galilee

---

[3] The only later references to Galilee in Mark are found in 15:41, which recalls the earlier ministry, and in 14:28; 16:7 which refer to a future reunion.

proper. There is record of activity on the other side of the Sea of Galilee, first in the land of the Gerasenes (Mk. 5:1-20; *cf.* 4:35), and later in the region of Bethsaida (Mk. 6:45ff.). A ministry in Gennesaret is followed by his retirement to the borders of Tyre and Sidon, where the daughter of the Syrophoenician woman was healed (Mk. 7:24-30). On his return he is active for a time in the area of Decapolis, on the east side of the sea (Mk. 7:31-8:9), before crossing to Dalmanutha, which seems to be located on the western shore (Mk. 8:10).[4] The activity there is very briefly related; in 8:13 we hear of a crossing to the other side, and mention is made of arrival in Bethsaida in 8:22. There soon follows an account of the momentous teaching in the region of Caesarea Philippi. It appears from this survey that by no means all that Mark relates in the first main section actually took place in Galilee proper. Besides the stay described in 8:10-12, also 1:14-4:34; 5:21-6:44 and 6:53-7:23 appear to find their locale on the western side of the sea in the Tetrarchy of Herod Antipas. On the other hand, except for the withdrawal to Tyre and Sidon, the rest may be placed within the Tetrarchy of Philip, and most of this activity was evidently not far removed from the sea. The early ministry described in Mark is then Galilean in the sense that nearly all of it finds its setting in the areas about the Sea of Galilee.

The interest of the evangelist in the locality of Jesus' activity is therefore apparent. Yet it does not develop that Mark is concerned to fix precisely the location of every separate incident that he relates. Often the place of his ministry is referred to in the most indefinite terms. Galilee, without further restriction, is described summarily as the

---

[4] See Dalman, *Orte und Wege Jesu*, 1924, p. 124 (E.T., *Sacred Sites and Ways*, p. 128). *Cf.* also Swete *ad* Mk. 8:10.

area of his ministry in Mark 1:14f., 39. He is further said quite vaguely to be "at the sea" or "along the sea" (Mk. 2:13; 3:7; 4:1; 5:21), which is evidently the Sea of Galilee (1:16; 7:31), but in most instances no clear notion is given of the exact place of his activity. Moreover, he is described as being "in a desert" or "in desert places" (Mk. 1:35, 45; 6:31f., 35; 8:4). He is "on the mountain" (Mk. 3:13), which seems to be near Capernaum, and again he goes "into the mountain" (Mk. 6:46), but the context fails to indicate its location, except to note that the disciples left that area by boat to go to Bethsaida. Mark also speaks indefinitely of Jesus' coming "out from thence," that is, from a region referred to only as "by the sea," to "his own country," which, in view of Mark 1:9, is probably meant to be understood as Nazareth (6:1). The vagueness of many of these references, considered in connection with the specific character of others already noted, indicates that this evangelist cannot plausibly be charged with a tendency to fix geographically every detailed phase of the activity of Jesus.

The references to time are even more pervasively indefinite than those to place. Moreover, the several incidents are often joined in the loosest possible manner. For example, in chapter 1 the call of the disciples "along the Sea of Galilee" is not related chronologically to the entrance of Jesus into Galilee (*cf.* Mk. 1:16). The entrance into Capernaum (Mk. 1:21) is not marked as the first incident that occurred after the call, or even for that matter as the first entrance into Capernaum. It would be precarious in the extreme, therefore, to conclude from the position of this reference that Mark intends his readers to gather that Jesus began either his public ministry in general, or his Galilean ministry in particular, at Capernaum and at this juncture. The activity in Capernaum is indeed closely concatenated: Mark 1:29 tells what happened directly after their departure from the synagogue; 1:32, 35 what occurred "at even" and "in the morning."[5] But there follows a general reference to an activity "in the next towns . . . throughout all Galilee" (Mk. 1:38f.) the duration of which is left quite unspecified.

Observations of the kind presented in the preceding paragraphs militate powerfully against the effort to interpret the Marcan materials as presented in exact chronological order and as intended to set forth *the* chronological framework of the life of Christ. It may freely be recognized that the work of K. L. Schmidt contains a strong blow at the confident use which the Liberal biographers made of the Marcan arrangement. He is right, for example, in opposing the labored efforts of many scholars to interpret Mark 1:20f. so as to allow for Jesus' call of the disciples from their fishnets one day before the sabbath in Capernaum. On the other hand, his conclusion that the chronology of Mark is a "bare postulate" is, in our judgment, not established by the facts.[6] The absence of precise connections between many incidents by no means proves that the connections which exist are of the evangelist's invention. The recognition that Mark does not write with a strictly

---

[5] Dodd, in an article in ExT, 1932, pp. 396ff., describes this section as a travel document, and points to it as evidence that the form critics have exaggerated the indifference of the early church to the framework of the ministry of Christ.

[6] *Op. cit.*, p. 49. In fairness to Schmidt it must be observed that he does not regard all references to time and place as editorial. If they form an integral part of a single incident, for example, they are not forthwith rejected. Some references of this kind may have fallen away, he thinks; other may have been added. On the whole, however, connections between incidents of this kind are judged to be editorial. *Cf.* pp. 53f., 77, 181.

biographical interest, or as a modern historian, does not imply that he was indifferent to historical fact. Such temporal connections as he includes must in his judgment have been actually true to fact. Thus the use of "again" in Mark 2:1, in telling of a return to Capernaum, may well be a link provided by the evangelist, and the fact that he frequently employs this word not without significance; yet such observations by no means preclude a knowledge on the evangelist's part of a series of visits to Capernaum.

The story recorded in Mark 2:23-28, relating the disciples' plucking of grain on the sabbath, offers a good example of Mark's historical method. The references to time and place form an integral part of the story; "the sabbath" and "the grain fields" are part of the warp and woof of the narrative. But, as Schmidt says, Mark does not tell which sabbath nor where the field of grain was located.[7] There is then no special chronological or topographical interest at this point. Nevertheless, there is provided here quite incidentally a reference to the time of the year, inasmuch as the grain normally became ripe about the time of or soon after the passover. This datum in combination with the fact that the death of Christ took place at a passover has often been made the basis of definite conclusions as to the duration of the public ministry.[8] Schmidt, of course, finds himself completely out of agreement with such an inference from Mark since, on his view, Mark does not, strictly speaking, present the framework of the ministry of Christ, and his materials, being merely a treasury of anecdotes, cannot be fixed chronologi-

---

[7] *Op. cit.*, p. 89.

[8] *Cf. e.g.*, Turner, "Chronology of the N.T." in HDB, I, p. 406 and Armstrong, "Chronology of the N.T." in ISBE, I, p. 647.

cally and topographically.[9] On our part, without assenting to the general conclusions of Schmidt, we agree that the reference to the ripe grain is so purely incidental that Mark cannot be fairly regarded as intending to indicate that this incident took place approximately a year prior to the death of Jesus. Its incidental character, however, does not imply that it any less definitely affords the evidence that the ministry lasted at least a year. On the whole Mark's chronological intimations are so meagre, indeed, that, if it were not for the incidental inclusion of this incident, one might possibly compress all the happenings of his narrative within a few months, as Windisch sought to do.[10]

Another reference in Mark often interpreted as involving chronological implications may profitably be considered here. The narrative of the feeding of the five thousand refers in Mark 6:39 to the detail that the companies were commanded to sit on the *green* grass, and this is sometimes construed as evidence that Mark is referring to another spring. In the vicinity of the Sea of Galilee there is today, it is said, no sign of green grass except after the winter rains, in the months from January to March or April inclusive. If conditions in the time of Christ were similar, Mark would imply that this miracle occurred in the spring, and there would be a remarkable agreement with John who connects the incident with a passover (Jn. 6:4ff.). Ogg, who has presented the most thorough recent discussion of this question, concludes, however, that the evidence stops short of proof.[11] In allowing that the phrase

---

[9] *Op. cit.,* pp. 90f.
[10] "Die Dauer der öffentlichen Wirksamkeit Jesu nach den vier Evangelisten" in ZNW, xii, 1911, pp. 141ff. *Cf.* Schmidt, *op. cit.,* 12f.; Ogg, *Chronology of the Public Ministry of Jesus,* 1940, pp. 7f.
[11] *Op. cit.,* pp. 18ff.

"the green grass" may be only "a pictorial touch," as Rawlinson avers in his comment on this passage, or possibly an early interpolation into the text of Mark, Ogg does not appear to be on solid ground. However, when he points out the possibility that the green grass may have been on the bank of some stream, or at a spring at a site now unknown, he must be credited with showing that the appeal to 6:39 to support specific chronological conclusion is not well grounded. But even if one could be sure that the phrase implied the spring season, Mark's indication of time would appear once more to be quite incidental. Mark refers definitely to one passover only, and that reference too is introduced, not to indicate the duration of the ministry, but because of the background which it provides for the understanding of the meaning of the passion of Christ. Obviously, the observation that the reference to the passover is not dictated by an interest to indicate the duration of the public ministry does not detract in the slightest from the trustworthiness of that chronological datum.[12]

When one turns from a study of the temporal references employed in the depiction of the ministry in Galilee to those in the later sections, there appears to be a somewhat greater interest in temporal sequence. This phenomenon is clearly to be explained from the consideration that the journey to Jerusalem and the rapidly developing climax of the last days in the city were in Mark's estimation aspects of the gospel which for their very narration required

---

[12] Many students of Mark regard it as certain that various passages, including Mk. 11:2, 5f.; 14:3, 12ff., 49; 15:43, imply that Jesus had had contact with Jerusalem before the conclusion of his life. *Cf.* Schmidt, *op. cit.*, pp. 301ff., Lohmeyer, *Galiläa und Jerusalem*, 1936, p. 28; R. H. Lightfoot, *Locality and Doctrine in the Gospels*, 1937, pp. 125f.

indications of the passing of time and of changes of scene. No such necessity was present in the treatment of the earlier material since, as we shall see in our discussion in the next chapter, the Galilean ministry, with little or no employment of the concept of development, serves to confront the reader with Jesus Christ, the Son of God, whose presence and activity bring amazement and trust, but also a large measure of bewilderment and some vigorous opposition.

The story of the march from the regions of Caesarea Philippi to Jerusalem, "the way of the cross," is not, Mark makes clear, merely a convenient way of grouping together various isolated incidents. In this section also, indeed, Mark evidently does not desire to present a complete account of the journey. The itinerary is not depicted as so continuous that allowance may not be made for other incidents. The events recorded in Mark 8:27-9:29, to be sure, are so closely joined that this segment appears to be intended to relate a complete, or nearly complete, cycle of events. The following three verses, on the other hand, are in the nature of a summary of his instruction as he passed through Galilee (9:30ff.). There follows then an account, not necessarily complete, of happenings at Capernaum, and the teaching associated with the stay in that city may well be, in Mark's thought, characteristic of the entire journey (Mk. 9:33-50). The journey from Capernaum to the borders of Judea and beyond Jordan is not described at all (Mk. 10:1), and the teaching of Jesus at this stage is not provided with a precise temporal or geographical setting (*cf.* Mk. 10:2, 13, 17, 23, 32, 35).[13] Only as Jesus

---

[13] There is no adequate ground for regarding the framework of the final journey as a schematic construction of the evangelist around the pronouncements of the passion, as Schmidt, *op. cit.*, pp. 215ff. maintains.

draws near to Jerusalem do the topographical references become specific (Mk. 10:46; 11:1), but even then references to time are lacking and the account does not give the impression of being intended as exhaustive.

The activity in Jerusalem itself, however, is provided in Mark with a detailed chronological framework which notes the passing of separate days. But even then Mark nowhere, not even in the record of the events which immediately preceded the crucifixion, implies that he is aiming to set forth a chronicle of Jesus' movements on the separate days. Mark 11:1 points to the end of one day, but says little of its happenings. Only 11:12-19 treats of a second day. The larger section comprising 11:20-13:37, however, is concerned with a third day. The disparity in the extent of these sections is significant for our understanding of Mark's purpose. There is offered here no real substantiation for the judgment of Schmidt that Mark has placed within a scheme of three days many events and discourses which may well have taken place long before and in other localities.[14] Furthermore, the fact that Mark sets the events in such a specific framework indicates that he at least was not completely indifferent to chronology.

With regard to the Passion Narrative in the narrower sense, our discussion can be brief inasmuch as there is little difference of point of view on the framework of this account. It is commonly admitted, even by most proponents of the method of form-criticism, that the framework in this section is so much an integral part of the story that it cannot be shattered. The individual pericopes, it is held, would not have served to meet the needs of the church—liturgical, missionary and apologetic; such needs could only be satisfied by the narration of the story of the passion

---
[14] *Idem*, p. 301.

as a unit. The detailed chronological references, accordingly, are widely acknowledged to be essentially trustworthy.[15]

We may profitably pause to summarize our conclusions concerning Mark's interest in chronology and locality. On the basis of the evidence of his relative unconcern with the detailed course of the life and ministry of Jesus Christ, the inevitable conclusion follows that Mark was not writing as a biographer and that he does not provide adequate materials for the construction of a biography of Jesus of Nazareth. In an important sense he was not interested in presenting the history of Jesus' life, at least in the modern sense of historical writing. Even K. L. Schmidt still speaks of the *Geschichte Jesu* in the title of his book, and makes Mark responsible for the original construction of a framework of this history. But, as this writer himself demonstrates, Mark's writing discloses a remarkable indifference as to the time and place of the occurrence of many of the events which he records. Mark is far from claiming to offer a continuous history of Christ's life. He does not aim to recover and set forth the precise framework of the events. Nor does he intend his outline as an authoritative historical outline of his historical career. Accordingly, it is a gratuitous task to set out to shatter the Marcan framework.

On the other hand, the facts do not warrant the inference that Mark set no value upon his references to the time and locality of the activity of Jesus, and that he was merely fashioning a convenient outline into which he could fit the isolated stories and discourses which came to him through oral tradition. It is by no means clear

---

[15] *Idem*, pp. 303ff.; Taylor, *Formation of the Gospel Tradition*, 1933, pp. 44ff.; Dibelius, *From Tradition to Gospel*, 1935, pp. 178ff. Bultmann, *op. cit.*, pp. 297ff. is, however, an exception.

that in the period of the oral transmission of the gospel there was no interest in the historical course of Christ's life and the connection between various incidents and teachings. Only if the isolated details were observed in the perspective of their historical connection could the gospel be proclaimed as a single message.[16] The sharp contrast often drawn between the period of the oral transmission of the gospel and of its written transmission, as if the former could take place without any concern for chronology and the latter necessarily manifested a sudden new interest in the order of events, does not do justice either to the character of the oral gospel nor to the written records, and fails to reckon adequately with their continuity.

Moreover, and this consideration is of the greatest possible significance, Mark was constantly having to do with history, and could not but be dealing in terms of time and place. His interest in the history of Christ indeed is not that of the modern biographer or historian. It is rather that of one who has set as his goal the aim to present the glad tidings concerning Jesus Christ, the Son of God. The publication inevitably bore a stamp sharply at variance with that of a modern treatment of the life of "the historical Jesus." It had to do with the joyful significance of the appearance and action of the Son of God in Galilee and Jerusalem. Because of the place which the passion of Christ occupied in that message, the account at the end necessarily gave more minute attention to historical sequence, and the narrative became a more and more continuous story. In supplying the background for the story of the cross, however, Mark's account could properly be episodic, and, even in

---

[16] On this point see also Otto, *The Kingdom of God and the Son of Man*, 1938, pp. 83ff.; Filson, *Origins of the New Testament*, 1938, pp. 106f.

the last section, it was not imperative that all the events of his life should have been recounted and precisely connected.

The subject of the locality of the ministry of Jesus has also been thrust into the foreground of discussion in recent years in an entirely different fashion through the radical but brilliantly conceived theory of Lohmeyer and R. H. Lightfoot.[17] The doctrinal implications which they discover in certain contrasts between Galilee and Jerusalem recall the antithesis which Ernest Renan saw between Galilee and Jerusalem, between the serene and joyful moralist of the sunshine of Galilee and the sombre and repellent figure who came into conflict with the Jewish leaders in the barren and unattractive regions of Judea. Actually the views of Lohmeyer and Lightfoot have nothing in common with Renan's long-exploded construction except that they, too, appeal to geographical considerations to ground far-reaching doctrinal conclusions. The modern theory is not concerned, as Renan was, to understand the personality of Jesus through the study of geography but to explain the aim and methods of the evangelists, each approach being, accordingly, typical of the era of criticism in which it appeared.

In brief the theory of Lohmeyer and Lightfoot with respect to Mark (and to a certain extent also with respect to Matthew) is that this evangelist wrote in the belief that Jerusalem, the home of Jewish piety and patriotism, was the scene only of rejection and the centre of relentless hostility and sin, whereas Galilee, despised and more or less outlawed, was chosen by God as the seat of the gospel

---

[17] Lohmeyer, *Galiläa und Jerusalem*, 1936, and *Markus*, 1937; R. H. Lightfoot, *Locality and Doctrine in the Gospels*, 1937.

and of the revelation of the Son of God. The revelation in Galilee occupies the evangelist's attention at the beginning of his account, and then, after portraying the destruction of the Son of Man at Jerusalem, he looks forward to a new revelation in Galilee (Mk. 14:28; 16:7), so that the land where the divine fulfillment began is also conceived of as the land where it would receive its consummation. A subsidiary aspect of this theory, less positively argued by Lightfoot than by Lohmeyer, is that the consummation held in view at the end of his gospel is not strictly an appearance on earth of the resurrected Jesus but the coming of the Son of Man on the clouds of heaven. Moreover, it is maintained that Mark (as well as Matthew) presupposes a Galilean origin of the Christian church rather than its origin in Jerusalem.

The radical implications of this theory for the evaluation of the gospels are patent. In our judgment it cannot be dismissed with a word. If we are to understand the gospels we cannot remain indifferent to the subject of the scene of the historical career of Christ. Moreover, we are bound to admit that certain difficult problems have been raised. Every one must concede that the question of the locality of the appearances of the risen Jesus raises real issues. Why is the account of Luke confined to appearances in or near Jerusalem while Matthew relates only a reunion with the disciples on a mountain in Galilee, a reunion which Mark also appears to hold in prospect? Can it be that the preoccupation of Matthew and Mark with an appearance in Galilee is related to the phenomenon of the confinement of the public ministry, at least to a considerable extent, to Galilee? The judgment of Lohmeyer and Lightfoot that there is operative in Mark and Matthew an *a priori* estimate of the significance of Galilee deserves careful scrutiny because of its far-reaching significance for one's total conception of the gospels. Our examination of the evidence may well be undertaken in part in this chapter, in close connection with the study of the broad features of the topography and chronology of the public ministry; in part its consideration must be postponed until the special problem of the conclusion of Mark is reached.

It is fitting that we should begin to test this hypothesis by recalling the data of the preface of Mark. If the theory that, according to Mark, Galilee, and Galilee alone, is the scene of revelation, is examined in the light of the geographical data of the introductory section, which Lightfoot himself speaks of as the key to the understanding of the whole gospel, it will appear to be beset by severe, if not insurmountable, obstacles at the very start. For the action of this section, as has been observed, takes place not in Galilee but in Judea or its general vicinity. The preface presents chiefly, it will be recalled, two main features: (1) the prophetic witness of the Baptist and (2) the divine witness from heaven. Now both of these phenomena distinctly bear the character of revelation. Even if the heavenly word were conceived of as a purely private disclosure to Jesus, as it sometimes is among students of this gospel (although that is not distinctly implied in Mark), the disclosure would still be revelatory. In the face of these considerations it does not appear how Judea can be regarded as the scene only of hostility to Jesus. On the theory under discussion, furthermore, the story of the transfiguration is judged to be one of the most noteworthy instances of revelation in Galilee. If this is so, and we have no concern to challenge it, how can the revelation at the baptism in Judea be judged to be any less meaningful? Furthermore, the prophetic witness of John is unmistakably a public activity. John himself apprehended Christ and bore public testimony to the power and dignity of the one who was to come. Consequently, so far as the contents of the preface of Mark are concerned, not Galilee but Judea is the scene of the revelation and disclosure of the Son of God.

The only conceivable manner in which these considerations can be deprived of their force is by interpreting the preface merely as introductory to, but not as a part of, the divine action of salvation. Thus Lightfoot characterizes the preface as merely a prelude. It is "only with the coming of Jesus into Galilee that the destined hour strikes, the era of salvation draws near."[18] The superscription and contents of the preface, however, do not allow such an isolation from what follows. As we have seen, Mark explicitly includes the opening section as an integral part of the glad tidings concerning Jesus Christ.

When we turn to a survey of the Galilean activity itself, we should expect to find the clearest signs of the presence of the supposed scheme of the evangelist that Galilee is the seat of the gospel. The contents of this section, however, demand important qualifications of this thesis. In our review of the locality of Jesus' activity during this period, we observed that it is not Galilee in the narrow sense that is the scene of the ministry so much as the area immediately surrounding the Sea of Galilee, and that special notice is taken of activity in Tyre and Sidon. Moreover, Caesarea Philippi, the scene of the first solemn pronouncement concerning the approaching passion and of the momentous disclosure on the mount of transfiguration, is not strictly in Galilee. Lightfoot says, indeed, that "Tyre and Sidon,

---

[18] *Idem*, p. 115. He has spoken of the preface as the key designed to unlock the meaning of the book in *History and Interpretation*, p. 61.

Decapolis, Bethsaida, the villages of Caesarea Philippi, all these stand on the circumference of Galilee and are thereby brought within the orbit of salvation," and refers to Mark 1:28 as indicating "the district round about Galilee as the area of Jesus' activity."[19] It is doubtful, however, that the phrase translated in the American Revised Version "all the region of Galilee roundabout" can plausibly be stretched to comprehend any districts outside of Galilee proper. The activity of Jesus that is in view is clearly in Capernaum, before any extensive journeys have been undertaken, and the phrase most naturally refers to the whole area in Galilee surrounding Capernaum. In any case Mark is describing merely the extent of the spread of reports concerning Jesus' work, not the actual scene of his activity. Moreover, if Galilee is properly understood as including the regions on its circumference, as Lightfoot supposes, it would be difficult to include, for example, Tyre and Sidon, and exclude the regions to the south (*cf.* Mk. 3:7f.). In our judgment, therefore, the geographical references in this first period do not in any clear fashion point to the presence of a doctrinal interpretation of Galilee as the scene of revelation.

The chief argument advanced to support the hypothesis is that Mark presents a striking contrast between the activity of Jesus in Galilee and that outside of Galilee, a contrast that is observed in the fact that in the latter period (1) Jesus is not described as "proclaiming" the gospel or demanding repentance, and (2) Jesus never exorcises demons and works but two miracles.[20] Without doubt Mark intended to present a vivid impression of the appearance of Jesus, the Son of God, in Galilee. Through the authority

---

[19] *Locality and Doctrine*, p. 121; *cf.* Lohmeyer, *Gal. u. Jer.*, p. 27.
[20] Lightfoot, *idem*, pp. 117f., 123ff.; Lohmeyer, *idem*, p. 30.

with which Jesus spoke and by means of his mighty works he was revealed to be the very Son of God to those who had ears to hear and eyes to see. Moreover, it may be granted that there is a change in the activity of Jesus after he left Galilee. But the question at issue is whether the difference between the two phases is so great and of such a kind as to support the theory that Galilee and Jerusalem are seen as antithetical so far as the revelation of the Son of God is concerned.

Lightfoot appeals especially to the Marcan use of the verb "to proclaim" (κηρύσσειν) to support his theory. Since Mark does not employ this verb beyond 7:36, that is, beyond a point near the end of the Galilean ministry, while he uses it eight times within this period, the claim is made that "there is no present proclamation of the gospel at Jerusalem, or elsewhere than in Galilee and its environs."[21] This argument is, however, not impressive when the evidence is analyzed. The word "to proclaim" is used of Jesus' own preaching only three times. These occur in two contexts which characterize his activity (Mk. 1:14, 38f.), and perhaps are sufficient proof that Mark regards Jesus' mission in Galilee as being concerned chiefly with the proclamation of the divine gospel. Nevertheless, it would seem that the mere absence of this terminology in the description of his mission after he left Galilee is not in itself of great weight. The other instances of the verb "proclaim" are either used in telling how persons who were healed by Jesus heralded abroad what he had done for them (Mk. 1:45; 5:20; 7:36) or are descriptive of the preaching of the disciples (Mk. 3:14; 6:12). With regard to the former group, we may well ask how much is proved

---

[21] *Idem*, p. 118.

by the fact that in the single record of healing activity in the closing period, the healing of blind Bartimaeus at Jericho, we fail to read that he published abroad what Jesus had done for him (Mk. 10:46-52) since similar statements are found in only three of the several stories of healing in the Galilean period (*cf.* Mk. 1:31; 2:12; 3:5f.; 5:34, 42). Why should it be considered significant that Bartimaeus is not represented by Mark as publishing the action of Jesus when nothing similar appears in the record of the restoration of sight to the blind man at Bethsaida (Mk. 8:25f.)? The references to the preaching activity of the disciples may indeed have in view a mission in Galilee and its environs, but it is exceedingly doubtful that the reference to the appointment of the twelve by Jesus "that they might be with him and that he might send them forth to preach" (Mk. 3:14) did not in Mark's thought include their subsequent preaching mission. Moreover, if so much weight is to be given to the use of the verb "proclaim" as the advocates of this theory insist, how shall we account for its employment to describe the preaching of the Baptist at or near the Jordan in Judea (Mk. 1:4, 7)?

The question remains why Jesus does not appear as a preacher in the latter sections of Mark, why so little place is given to his mighty acts. Obviously, the distinctive contents of these sections must be kept in view as one estimates the force of this inquiry. Of decisive moment is the consideration that the disciples now are the center of Jesus' interest rather than the general public. In the story of the passion and of the events preliminary to it, Jesus is not so much carrying forward a public program of teaching and healing as preparing his intimate disciples for the events to come. The whole of the section devoted to the stay in Caesarea Philippi and the journey to Judea

(Mk. 8:27-9:30) is occupied only with the instruction of the disciples who themselves had been appointed that they might preach. Consequently, no appropriate place is evident where the terminology employed in connection with the preaching to the people could have found appropriate use. Some of the public teaching in Judea is indeed recorded, but, after his arrival in Judea also, most of his time seems to have been spent in the company of his disciples.

In so far as Mark relates the contact of Jesus with the larger public in the closing periods, he is so much occupied with the story of the passion that he limits his narrative, to a very considerable extent, to a record of Jesus' conflicts with the Jewish authorities (Mk. 10:2-12; 11:15-18, 27-35; 12:1-35). There are, however, two significant references of a positive character to his public discourses. The first occurs in Mark 10:1, and states that when Jesus came into the borders of Judea (that is, when he clearly had left Galilee behind), and multitudes came together to him again, *"as was his custom* he taught them again." If the evangelist intended to contrast Galilee and Judea in the matter of the character of his public discourses, he could hardly have done so in a more obscure fashion. The use of the verb "to teach" rather than "to proclaim," we venture to declare, cannot be seriously regarded as indicating a significant change in the perspective of the evangelist. The second passage, Mark 12:35-44, is the only section in the final chapters specifically dedicated to his public teaching activity, and the samples of his instruction presented are far from suggesting any departure on Jesus' part from his characteristic teaching. And it is noteworthy that Mark reports that "the common people heard him gladly" (Mk. 12:38), a reaction which is the very antithesis of the hostility which is said to be the mark of the final division of the gospel.

The absence of many mighty works from the record of events after the departure from Galilee may be due to a variety of factors. It may be partially due to the fact that Jesus actually performed few mighty acts in the last days when the cross was immediately before him. Another factor may be that Mark is concentrating his attention deliberately upon the contacts of Jesus with his disciples and upon the actual development of the great climax in the passion and death of Christ. Just as the public teaching is included only summarily or by way of example, the deeds of power may be included as indicative of a larger exercise of his might. Moreover, the miracles in the latter part of Mark, however few, serve as well as the many associated with Galilee to bring to men a revelation of his supernatural power (Mk. 10:46-52; 11:12-14, 20ff.).

The case for the theory of Lohmeyer and Lightfoot is seriously weakened, moreover, by the admission that Mark relieves the darkness of the passion narrative by sudden gleams of light. These are: (1) the anointing at Bethany, which points to the meaning and issue of the passion; (2) the assertion of his messiahship before the sanhedrin; and (3) the confession of the gentile centurion at the cross, "Truly this man was the Son of God."[22] These gleams of light add up to an impressive series of disclosures! If the significance of his messiahship is disclosed in such striking fashion within the passion narrative, it is impossible to allow that Mark conceives of Jerusalem only as the scene of hostility and sin.

Here in fact we encounter what is ultimately the greatest weakness of the entire theory under consideration. While

---

[22] *Idem,* pp. 53f.

it is true that the passion of Christ may be seen from the point of view of man's action as spelling darkness, Mark's own understanding as a Christian evangelist is surely that it' is powerfully luminous. It is a part, in truth the most meaningful part, of the glad tidings concerning Jesus Christ which Mark publishes in his gospel. One may not fairly maintain that in the perspective of Jesus' teaching his death appears as an "altogether incredible fate" (Lightfoot's phrase),[23] however paradoxical it might appear from some points of view that the exalted Son of Man should suffer and die. This gospel is not preëminently concerned with the teaching of Jesus, as every one knows, but with the divine action of salvation which came to expression in the history of Jesus Christ. The gospel resounds with the note that the death of Christ was a divine necessity (*e.g.*, Mk. 8:31, 33). We are not confronted here with an obscure and baffling fatalism but with the divine redemptive purpose, the utterances concerning the meaning of the messianic mission reaching their high point in the saying that the Son of Man came to give his life a ransom for many (Mk. 10:45). Thus in Mark's thought Jesus continues as the transcendent Messiah even in his march to the cross.

The contents of the final section in Mark (16:1-8) receive their true perspective only when they are viewed in connection with the discussion of the larger questions bound up with the conclusion of Mark. This is preëminently true of the mention of a future reunion in Galilee (Mk. 16:7). So far as the record of historical events takes us, however, we may observe at once that this section also centers our thought upon the divine action of salvation, not in Galilee, but in Jerusalem. The empty tomb is eloquent of the

---

[23] *Idem*, p. 122.

divine activity in fulfilling the words of Jesus concerning his resurrection (Mk. 8:31; 9:31; 10:33f.), and there accompanies it the witness of angels to the glorious fact concerning Christ. This then is also part, indeed the climax, of the glad tidings concerning Jesus Christ.

If the question be pressed why Mark is absorbed to the extent he is with the public activity of Jesus in Galilee, one must admit that the answer is not easy, chiefly because Mark does not himself intimate the reason or reasons. Clearly it suited his purpose in describing the appearance of Jesus to sketch the historical background of the passion on a Galilean canvas. The entrance into Galilee is left unmotivated (Mk. 1:14). Jesus appears there without explanation. It was appropriate enough that he should have been active in the area with which he was most familiar, and the journeys across the sea may be connected with the fact that some of his disciples must have been exceedingly familiar with it through their occupation as fishermen, and besides must have been competent navigators. Moreover, it was in Galilee that Jesus was relatively free from interference. Even there indeed he sometimes found it necessary to retire for a while and he encountered increasing opposition; still the threat to his continued activity was considerably less than it would have been in Jerusalem. So Galilee served well to portray the impact which Jesus made upon men before the conflict reached its climax. We do not mean to suggest that the foregoing represents a complete answer. There may have been other factors which shaped the disposition of Mark, such as, for example, the form which the oral proclamation of the gospel had taken. In any case we are not prepared to dismiss the subject altogether, and shall return to it in connection with the discussion of certain features of Matthew in Chapter VI.

We must now proceed to inquire more precisely as to the witness of Mark, his witness to Christ. We may not overlook the fact that in presenting Jesus Christ as the content of the glad tidings the gospel never ceases to publish the *history* of Christ. Hence the questions we have been considering, the questions relating to the scene of Jesus' historical career and to its temporal setting and development, bear in significant fashion upon the estimate to be formed of his total portrayal of the person of the divine Messiah. In the following discussion we will not attempt any abstractly systematic treatment of what Mark has to say about Christ; since the history of Christ is of the very essence of the gospel, as Mark (and the other evangelists) conceives of it, we could not remain faithful to its witness if we sought to isolate Christ from the historical framework in which he comes to us. Nevertheless, since the history of Christ, in spite of its mystery, is altogether meaningful because it constitutes divine action and speech towards men, we may expect to apprehend something of its essential coherence and unity. We must ask, accordingly, what Mark tells us chiefly as to the impact which Jesus made upon men by his deeds and words.

CHAPTER III

THE DISCLOSURE OF THE MESSIAHSHIP

SYNOPSIS

Introduction.

History and doctrine; theory of the messianic secret.

I. *Disclosure through the mighty acts of Jesus.*

The demonic recognition of Jesus and the injunctions to silence: survey of the data; the perception of Jesus as the Son of God and of his coming to destroy the power of Satan; the injunctions to silence characteristic of exorcisms by Jesus, but are directed to demons, not to persons set free (Mk. 1:25; 5:19, 20); the view that Jesus was both active and passive in the disclosure of his messiahship satisfies data in a manner that the theory of secret messiahship does not.

Revelation and secrecy in connection with other mighty acts: emphasis falls upon fact of positive revelation; the isolated instances of injunctions to silence; these commands themselves presuppose far greater degree of recognition and understanding of Jesus than theory of secret messiahship allows; the motivation for the commands provided in narratives of healing of a leper (Mk. 1:40ff.) and of the resurrection of Jairus' daughter (5:22ff., 35ff.); supposed impracticability of command in latter story.

II. *Disclosure to the disciples.*

A. The cycle of events in Caesarea Philippi: the confession of Peter is not occasioned by a fresh disclosure, and is evidently regarded as the result of the revelation during the entire preceding period; the epochal significance of these events is to be found in the new teaching concerning the consummation of the ministry which includes stress on the passion; the injunction to silence in Mk. 8:30; significance of the revelation in the episode of the transfiguration is not that a new, epochal disclosure is given, but that Jesus receives divine attestation as the Messiah in the face of the program of suffering, and must be believed and obeyed; the injunction to silence in Mk. 9:9 refers to what they saw; the accent in the account upon bewilderment and fear in the presence of the transcendent Son.

B. Before and after Caesarea Philippi.

Evidence of the relationships of Jesus and the disciples in Galilee stresses their apprehension and trust; but elements of bewilderment, astonishment and fear are also conspicuous; illustration by accounts of the storm and of the walking upon the water; the problem raised by the hardness of heart attributed to the disciples in the latter narrative; note on the parabolic teaching: interpretation and historicity of Mk. 4:10ff.

The attitude of the disciples after Caesarea Philippi: evidences of dullness, confusion and disloyalty; possibility that the distinctive tone of failure in the crisis derived from Peter's own experience as reflected in his preaching; elements of Mark congruous with tradition of dependence upon Peter; the reticence toward Peter; prominence given to Peter's obtuseness and denial in the story of the passion; Peter as typical of trust and disloyalty.

Mark's notice of the human, emotional life of our Lord.

Résumé.

SINCE Mark's explicit aim is to set forth the glad tidings concerning Jesus Christ, it is necessary to proceed with our inquiry as to the witness which his gospel as a whole bears to the person who has been introduced in the opening words. That witness to Christ is not offered in dogmatic form, not in a systematic consideration of the person and work of Jesus, as we have had occasion to observe, but in a concrete, historical setting. Without manifesting the least concern to treat that historical life from a biographical point of view, in terms of historical origins and development and of psychological motivation, the author nevertheless purposes to let the reader come to an apprehension of the true nature and meaning of Christ's person and work as that was disclosed in his life in Palestine at a particular, though undesignated, time. To accomplish this end he selects and presents vividly various phases of the historical appearance of Christ, both where Jesus was active shaping the course of events and where his actions called forth decisive reactions on the part of others, the whole presentation of Christ being conceived of as possessing the character of good news because of the significance of his history for human destiny.

On this understanding the antithesis often drawn between history and doctrine is not valid. The Liberals viewed Mark as essentially "historical," or at least as offering adequate data for the recovery of a knowledge of "the historical Jesus." The more radical criticism, which has been characteristic of the present century, on the other hand, conceives Mark to be essentially doctrinal or theological, and as, on this account, unhistorical. However, on a Christian-theistic understanding of history, which we think was Mark's own, all of history is viewed as *sub specie aeternitatis*, and the history of Christ, the Son of God, is regarded as God's decisive, miraculous action. The proclamation of the meaning of that divine action in history is necessarily doctrinal without ceasing to be historical.

Mark's doctrinal view of the life of Christ then did not in the estimation of the evangelist constitute it any less a part of history, and any effort to understand Mark, accordingly, which presupposes such an antithesis is proceeding on a false principle. Nevertheless, it remains true that the radicals must be credited, through their attack upon the Liberal approach, with centering attention upon Christological data in Mark which demand the closest possible

DISCLOSURE OF THE MESSIAHSHIP

attention if his witness to Christ is to be comprehended.

Of all the facets of criticism that are significant at this point that which concerns the theory of "the messianic secret" is easily of the most decisive bearing upon the interpretation of the Marcan witness to Christ. That this approach, which received its classic formulation in Wrede's work on *The Messianic Secret in the Gospels (Das Messiasgeheimnis in den Evangelien, 1901)*, is still an influential factor in the study of the gospels appears from the observation that it is presupposed by the leading exponents of form-criticism, like Bultmann and Dibelius. Moreover, its leading features reappear in the recent studies of Lohmeyer and R. H. Lightfoot. In his book, entitled *History and Interpretation in the Gospels* (The Bampton Lectures of 1934), the last named writer presents what is perhaps the ablest and most lucid exposition and defense of the leading features of the theory that is available in the English language. Since our present concern is with Mark's witness to Christ rather than with this theory as such, we shall not attempt to expound or examine it here in any comprehensive fashion. For our purpose it will be of chief importance to concentrate upon the evidence which is appealed to by its protagonists.

In the interest of clarity of perspective, however, a word may be added concerning the modification which the theory has undergone in its development from Wrede to Lightfoot. Both writers center attention upon phenomena in the gospels connected with the narratives concerned with demons, the miracles, the attitudes of the disciples and the parabolic teaching of Jesus, which seem to include the element of secrecy. Both interpret these data as involving the doctrinal notion that the messiahship of Jesus, according to Mark, was a secret, a notion which when closely examined is seen to be a dogmatic conception of the evangelist which Mark (perhaps in dependence upon the church) used in shaping into the form of a gospel the tradition which had come into his hands. Wrede and Lightfoot differ, however, as to the period in which, according to Mark, the messiahship was conceived of as a secret. Wrede, who minimized the position commonly held in his day that the confession of Peter at Caesarea Philippi represents a sharp turning point in the history of Christ, understood Mark, as indicated by Mk. 9:9, to mean that the messiahship was regarded as secret before the resurrection and to be revealed thereafter. Lightfoot, on the other hand, in connection with the contrast which he finds between the Galilean and Judean aspects of the ministry of Jesus in Mark, maintains that the secrecy applies preëminently to the period before the events of Caesarea Philippi, and that Mark means to say that the messiahship was no longer secret after that.[1] Wrede accordingly puts a far greater stress upon continuity in the entire public ministry than is possible on the construction of Lightfoot which draws a clear line between the earlier and later phases. Our attention is directed forcibly to the consideration of the place which the confession of Peter and the transfiguration scene occupy in Mark's total presentation of Jesus as well as the differences which may exist between the earlier and later phases of the ministry. If, as has been shown, Lightfoot's sharp antithesis between the Galilean and Judean ministries cannot be maintained, the question would still remain open whether Wrede's accent upon continuity wholly accounts for the transitions which Mark underlines.

The glad tidings of Jesus Christ, in Mark's thought, find expression in the account which he publishes of the life of Jesus in the midst of men. The reader evidently is supposed to come to an understanding of the meaning of Jesus, not through an apocalypse of his heavenly glory, not by way of an ecstatic or mystical exaltation, not through contact with a supra-historical, noumenal realm beyond the dimensions of human history, but through an apprehension of the significance of the truly historical life of a truly human person. Hence one could not, if he would, set forth Mark's witness to Christ in isolation from the reactions which his deeds and words called forth on the part of the men to whom he disclosed himself. It would seem to follow that the most significant disclosures would be made to those who were his most intimate associates, and we shall accordingly

---

[1] *History and Interpretation,* pp. 66f.; *cf.* pp. 119, 127.

be concerned in this discussion above all with the relations of Jesus and his disciples. If his messiahship was a secret for a considerable time, that should appear most indisputably in the record of his contacts with them. If there was a disclosure of his messiahship from the beginning, we should expect to find the most perspicuous evidence of it in the accounts of his dealings with them and of their responses to his activity. Before coming to grips with the evidence of the disclosure of the messiahship to the disciples, however, we shall first consider the manner in which Jesus affected a wider circle through his mighty works. The advantage of treating the disclosure of Jesus in his mighty works at once is that in these narratives, and especially in the accounts of the exorcism of demons, the feature of secrecy is most conspicuous and the implication of supernatural revelation is most obvious.

I. Disclosure Through the Mighty Acts of Jesus

Mark's record of the witness of the demons to Christ, according to Wrede, introduces the element of secrecy in a twofold manner: (1) the demons possess a supernatural, that is, a secret, knowledge of Christ, and (2) they are commanded to keep silent, that is, not to divulge this secret.[2] Since Wrede, as a matter of course, regards the former as mythical, the latter is judged also to be obviously unhistorical. This feature of double secrecy then, taken with other similar phenomena, is held to point to the presence of a dogmatic scheme. Lightfoot, who observes that exorcisms are not related in the latter portion of Mark, concludes from a survey of the references to Jesus' relation to the demons as follows:

---

[2] Wrede, *op. cit.*, pp. 23ff., 47ff.

"The messiahship, as understood by the evangelist, continually and inevitably expresses itself in both word and deed. But it is not, cannot, and must not be recognized as yet by any man, and therefore the witness to it can only be given by those who have more than human insight, in other words, the demons. For others the only result of what they hear and see is astonishment."[3]

That the exorcism of demons filled a prominent place in the public ministry of Jesus is clearly borne out by the Marcan references. It is a feature that receives special mention in the general descriptions of his work (Mk. 1:32, 34, 39; 3:11f.). Its prominence is further presupposed by the charge of the scribes that Jesus had acted through the power of Satan in casting out demons (Mk. 3:22-30). Moreover, we learn that the disciples were likewise appointed and equipped to exorcise demons (Mk. 3:15; 6:7, 13; cf. 9:18, 38). Four particular instances of exorcisms on Jesus' part are reported: (1) of the man in the synagogue at Capernaum (Mk. 1:23-37); (2) of the Gerasene demoniac (5:1-20); (3) of the daughter of the Syrophoenician woman (7:25-30); and (4) of a boy after the descent from the mount of the transfiguration (9:15-29).

According to Mark the demons knew Christ (1:34) (or, as many mss. read, "knew him to be the Christ"); moreover they were capable of making him known (3:12). They acknowledged him as the Holy One of God and as the Son of God (Mk. 1:34; 3:11; 5:7). They recognize the irreconcilable conflict that existed between themselves and the Son of God, for they sense that he has come to destroy and torment them (Mk. 1:24; 5:7; cf. 3:23, 27). The very presence of the Son of God in the world then evoked recognition on the part of the demonic world, and his presence was understood as spelling the defeat and destruction of the world of evil. From Mark's point of view, as the preface

---

[3] *Op. cit.*, p. 70.

already shows, Jesus was from the beginning the Son of God who was divinely appointed to engage in conflict with the world of Satan, and there was therefore for him no intrinsic difficulty in the notion that demons as supernatural beings should have enjoyed an apprehension of him as the Son of God. The messiahship of Jesus, transcending purely human categories, could be perceived only on the basis of a supernatural discernment. Nevertheless, Mark clearly implies that it was revealed and that it was recognized.

The commands to keep silent, on the other hand, seem to point to secrecy, to non-revelation of his messiahship. These commands specifically accompany only the first two examples of exorcism noted above, but in view of the general reference in Mark 1:34 and 3:11f., it may be inferred that Mark regards such commands as characteristic of the reaction of Jesus. Nevertheless, in our judgment, these phenomena do not provide adequate support for the theory that Mark is here presupposing a dogma of secret messiahship.

In seeking to evaluate the evidence of the commands to keep silent, it is commonly overlooked that *these commands are directed, not to those who benefited from Jesus' releasing acts, but to the demons within these persons.* They are thus essentially different from the commands to keep silent in the instances of certain persons who were healed or in the case of disciples who witnessed a revelation, which are considered below. In the account of the man in Capernaum, for example, the demon is silenced by the very act of exorcism, but no such command is directed to the man himself. Instead, we immediately hear, without any intimation of reproach, of the spread of the fame of Jesus in that area (Mk. 1:25).

In the case of the Gerasene demoniac, similarly, a sharp distinction is observed between the witness of the demon (Mk. 5:7) and of the one who had been possessed (5:18). In the former instance, although there is nothing said of silence, the demon is in fact silenced by the word of Jesus. But no restriction is placed on the man. He is refused permission to remain with Jesus, but instead receives the command: "Go to thy house unto thy own and tell them whatsoever the Lord hath done for thee and how he had mercy on thee." And we read further that he went his way and began to publish in Decapolis how great things Jesus had done for him, and all men marvelled (Mk. 5:19, 20). Here then the accent falls upon the apprehension of the divine action and its publication abroad rather than upon secrecy and silence.

> This passage accordingly creates considerable difficulty for the advocates of the theory of messianic secrecy. Wrede attempted to meet the difficulty by drawing a sharp distinction between v. 19 and v. 20 *(op. cit.,* pp. 140f.). The command of Jesus limits the man's report, it is said, *to his own house* and it concerns only God's *(cf.* "the Lord's") action, and thus involves silence as to Jesus himself, whereas the man published in *a broad area*, in Decapolis, the things *Jesus* had done. This is surely a tortuous exegesis, for, as a matter of fact, in both cases the object of the proclamation is not the person of Christ directly, but *what had been done* to the man by Jesus. Moreover, even if a contrast between "his own house" and Decapolis is implied, it is impossible to allow that the charge to tell his own people what the Lord had done for him implied that he was to keep silent about Jesus. Lightfoot, rejecting Wrede's solution, suggests that Mk. 5:18-20 may be an editorial addition, and offers an allegorical interpretation to the effect that in the mission to the Gentiles the great things done by Israel's God in the person of Jesus must be told *(History and Interpretation,* pp. 89f.). This latter approach has at least the merit of recognizing the incongruity of the Marcan text with the theory of secret messiahship at this point.

The evidence concerning the witness of the demons to Christ accordingly fails to support the hypothesis that Jesus did not wish to be recognized as the Son of God who came exercising divine authority and power, and that his activity was not adequate for such apprehension. To admit that the recognition of the messiahship of Jesus required more than human insight is not to allow that only demons could recognize him. The more than human insight could be given to men. Jesus was active in manifesting himself as the Messiah, yet, awaiting the quickening of human insight in order that his disclosure might be comprehended, his positive action of disclosure was united with passivity and reserve. This tension between action and passivity in the disclosure of his person, rather than a dogma of secret messiahship, controls Mark's portrayal, as will be shown more fully below. In view of his passivity, as he awaited God's action, it was highly incongruous that Jesus should have allowed the kingdom of Satan to be the agent of his revelation to men.

Several of the other accounts of mighty works, other than exorcisms, bear directly upon the issue of the nature of the Marcan witness. We have observed that Mark does not contain a single instance where a person set free from demonic control by Jesus' action, as distinguished from a demon, was commanded to keep silent; indeed, there is even express exhortation to tell others what had happened. The situation is similar with respect to the other beneficent acts of Jesus which are recorded in Mark—with a few striking exceptions. The general descriptions of his healing activity (Mk. 1:32ff.; 3:10; 6:54-56; 7:37) as well as most narratives of particular acts (Mk. 1:29-31; 2:2-12; 3:1-6; 5:25-34; 10:46-52) contain no suggestion that the mighty deeds of Jesus are not to be proclaimed abroad. This observation, it may be noted in passing, applies also to the mighty acts of Jesus other than acts of healing (4:35-41; 6:32-44; 6:47-52;

8:1-9; 11:12-14, 20ff.). One miracle of healing, the cure of the paralytic, was in fact so public that it became the occasion of controversy with the scribes, and led to an explicit avowal of messianic power: "the Son of Man hath authority on earth to forgive sins" (Mk. 2:10). Similarly, the healing of the withered hand (Mk. 3:1-6) is intimately associated with a sabbath controversy in which there is a further highly significant claim of messianic authority: "the Son of Man is lord even of the sabbath" (Mk. 2:28).[4]

The problem of the isolated instances of commands to keep silent in connection with certain miracles remains. These commands are found in the following narratives: (1) the healing of a leper (Mk. 1:40-45); (2) the raising of the daughter of Jairus (5:22-24, 35-43); (3) the cure of a deaf mute (7:32-37); and (4) the restoration of sight to a blind man in Bethsaida (8:22-26). The leper was severely charged to say nothing to anyone (1:43f.); those who witnessed the raising of the girl were charged much that no one should know this (5:43); those who brought the deaf mute were commanded that they should tell no one (7:36); and the blind man was sent home with the injunction that he should not even enter into the village, or, as the textual variant reads, that he should not speak to anyone in the village (8:26).[5] Are these various commands to be explained

---

[4] Lightfoot, *idem,* p. 73, n. 1, admits that the element of secrecy does not enter into the cycle of events narrated in Mk. 2:1-3:6, which he apparently regards as dependent upon a separate source from the tradition as a whole. But the question arises why, if such a distinctive source existed and was used by Mark, the evangelist failed to apply his dogmatic scheme to this source material. Moreover, the other evidence which precedes and follows this section, as noted above, does not state or imply that there was any injunction to secrecy with reference to Jesus.

[5] On the text *cf.* Turner, JThS, XXVI (Oct., 1924), p. 18; Lightfoot, *op. cit.,* pp. 72, 91.

by appeal to a doctrine of secret messiahship even though no specific reference is made to the messiahship in these particular narratives? Lightfoot, in affirming this question, takes the position that in Mark's thought the messiahship was inevitably expressed by Jesus' acts, and therefore, even though these persons do not recognize the messiahship, the commands to keep silent apply to the messiahship.[6]

The question presses itself forward, however, whether these commands receive adequate motivation if, on Mark's view, men cannot have any inkling as to the truth concerning Jesus, at least not during the Galilean stage. If what one has to say concerning Jesus cannot disclose his messiahship, how can these prohibitions be judged to have reference to the disclosure of the messiahship? Where recognition is excluded from the sphere of possibility, injunctions to secrecy are hardly sensible. A major error of this hypothesis emerges at this point. The injunctions to silence must presuppose a far greater degree of recognition and understanding concerning Jesus than this theory allows. Those who appealed to Jesus for supernatural aid and were rewarded in their quest could hardly fail to receive at least some inkling of the truth concerning him.[7] The answer to this theory then, in our judgment, is not to be sought in a sharp dissociation of messiahship from these contexts, simply because no specific recognition of messiahship is mentioned. These mighty acts are assuredly to be associated with the disclosure of Jesus' messiahship, but they nevertheless fail to support the theory of secret messiahship. The account in Mark makes clear that Jesus' disclosure of himself through his mighty works produced

---

[6] *Op. cit.*, p. 71.
[7] Lightfoot, *ibid.*, says that "no human being has at present any inkling of the truth."

apprehension, at least in some degree, and consequent inevitable communication to others. At the same time Jesus remained reserved and to a considerable extent passive in the disclosure of his person and mission.[8] Although he went about doing good, he did not desire the acclaim that the deeds of a mere thaumaturgist would have received. In a few instances the reserve of Jesus was so dominant that he even enjoined silence.

In the story of the leper a hint is given as to why Jesus on occasion went to the extremity of commanding silence. Except for restraint on his own part and on the part of others, the situation might easily have gotten out of hand and his public ministry brought to an untimely end. The disclosures concerning his authority and power were so stupendous that even those who received his severe commands could not contain themselves. Consequently, there were times when he had to seek retirement from the public eye (Mk. 1:45; cf. 7:24, 36).

A special problem is raised by the narrative of the resurrection of the daughter of Jairus (Mk. 5:35-43). As evidence of the schematic, arbitrary character of Mark's conception of the messiahship, Wrede pointed to the impracticability of the injunction to silence as most strikingly displayed in this case of the resurrection of the dead. How could Jesus have contemplated the possibility of silence on this matter in view of the fact that it was well-known that the girl had died?[9] The girl could not stay permanently in isolation.

---

[8] On the subject of the passivity of Jesus cf. Schlatter, *Die Zweifel an der Messianität Jesu*, 1907; Vos, *The Self-disclosure of Jesus*, 1926, pp. 56ff., 71, 98ff., and the present writer in an article in WThJ, II, 2 (1939-40), pp. 136f.

[9] Wrede, *op. cit.*, pp. 48f.; Lightfoot, *op. cit.*, p. 73.

In the interest of elucidating this problem it is necessary first of all to observe that, apart from the question of the alleged impracticability of the command, the narrative lends no more support to the theory of secret messiahship than the others. It is incorrect to say, as Lightfoot does, for example, that the story implies that at the time the meaning of Jesus' mighty work was veiled of set purpose from the eyes of all who witnessed them.[10] It is of the essence of the narrative that a wonderful disclosure is made to a small group of persons, the parents of the girl and the three most intimate disciples, while the others are excluded. The five witnesses possess a knowledge which they are not to convey to others. The impression given therefore is that these five received the privilege of an esoteric disclosure, which they were not to communicate to others. That which is to be kept secret is to be kept secret by those who witnessed Jesus' action; the secret is to be kept from those who did not witness it. The revelation and the veiling of the messiahship proceed hand in hand. Neither is unqualified nor unrestricted.

If special motivation for the injunction to silence at this point is sought, it may perhaps be found in the fact that the people have ridiculed Jesus. Outspoken unbelief did not provide the most suitable atmosphere for the disclosure of his divine power and authority, as the story of the unbelief and inaction in his home city illustrates (Mk. 6:5, 6). His passivity and reserve evidently were most conspicuous where unbelief was most blatant.

The notion that, since the girl obviously could not remain permanently in isolation, Mark is guilty of attributing to Jesus a command which was quite impracticable, conceives of the evangelist as an exceedingly naïve writer.

---

[10] *Ibid.*

Can a writer who has been credited with the elaboration and application, if not the creation, of an involved dogmatic scheme like that of the secret messiahship of Jesus be quite so clumsy as to introduce ridiculous situations into his narrative? The words in question may hardly be pressed so as to require that judgment, and indicate the need of deeper scrutiny. On the understanding that Jesus revealed his messiahship only with reserve, one can comprehend that he should not have wished to make himself known to the raucous, unbelieving crowd that had gathered. He did not permit them to witness his miraculous act and he directed that it should continue to remain unknown to those on the outside. Nevertheless, the responsibility of the parents in this regard could perhaps not continue indefinitely. The child would soon appear in public, and the facts would speak for themselves. Meanwhile, however, the parents could withhold from them what had happened, and so fulfill the charge of Jesus in its evident intent. When the facts became known, the immediate purpose of the charge might have been fulfilled, for Jesus himself would have departed (Mk. 6:1) and would not have been subject to their ostentatious acclaim.

II. Disclosure to the Disciples

On the theory of a secret messiahship even the intimate disciples of Jesus do not grasp the significance of the messianic consciousness. On Wrede's understanding of Mark the disciples were blind until after the resurrection.[11] And Lightfoot, who allows that in the central section there emerges a disclosure to a chosen few, describes the disciples as being in darkness during the Galilean ministry.

---

[11] *Op. cit.*, pp. 101f., 114; *cf.* pp. 93ff.

"The disciples themselves remain in darkness, they do not understand the truth and are not meant to understand it; and yet from time to time they are blamed (4:40; 8:17) because they fail to understand. For the present the only results produced by Jesus' acts are astonishment, bewilderment, amazement."[12]

If these judgments are supported by the evidence, it would be a misnomer, at least so far as a considerable portion of Mark is concerned, to speak of Jesus' disclosure of himself to the disciples.

Before proceeding to a study of the pertinent evidence, we can perhaps gain a clearer perspective for the reader if we set down at once our chief objection to the views of Wrede and Lightfoot on this matter, and indicate briefly the conclusion which, in our judgment, is demanded by the evidence. Wrede errs especially in failing to observe that the evidence of apprehension of the messiahship on the part of the disciples runs parallel to that of their bewilderment. Lightfoot, while improving upon Wrede here in recognizing a measure of apprehension in the period beginning with the events of Caesarea Philippi, shares the former's view that unrelieved darkness dominates the story of the relations of the disciples with Jesus in Galilee, and by his contrast between the Galilean and subsequent ministry fails to mark the continuity of the gospel story. In our judgment the disciples, according to Mark, never stand in total darkness nor do they ever emerge into cloudless light. Rather the portraiture of the disciples makes a pervasive and arresting use of light and shadow. Their responses move back and forth between faith and doubt. That the presence of unbelief does not necessarily point to a complete absence of faith finds striking expression in the cry of the father of the lad with a dumb spirit: "Lord,

---

[12] *Ibid.*

I believe; help thou my unbelief" (Mk. 9:24). The fact of the presence of divine power and divine authority was so stupendous and overwhelming that bewilderment and astonishment, and even fear, could well be wedded to apprehension and trust.

A. THE CYCLE OF EVENTS IN CAESAREA PHILIPPI

Nothing is as crucial for the elucidation of this subject of the relations between Jesus and the disciples as the cycle of events introduced by the confession at Caesarea Philippi (Mk. 8:27-9:29), and there is therefore an advantage in studying this section before we proceed to a comparison of the periods divided by this episode. Wrede has stood almost alone in modern times in perceiving nothing epochal in the confession of Peter, the meaning of the story being exhausted, in his opinion, in the command to keep silent (Mk. 8:30).[13] On the view of Lightfoot, however, and in accordance with the trend of the less radical criticism, the significance of this event as a part of the disclosure of Jesus' messiahship is, we think, exaggerated, and its true place in the Marcan narrative misconstrued. According to Mark (and Matthew as well) the epochal character of this episode is to be found in the fact that Jesus now begins to insist emphatically upon the fact that the messianic office demands his passion, death and resurrection at Jerusalem (Mk. 8:31; *cf.* Mt. 16:21). Contrary to the usual interpretation we think that there is nothing to suggest that Peter's apprehension of Jesus originated at that moment, through a sudden revelation as to who Jesus really was. No such revelation is recorded or even implied as taking place at that time. The account tells rather of a retirement into Caesarea Philippi where, without the benefit of new acts or new

---

[13] *Op. cit.*, pp. 115ff.

teaching on Jesus' part, and without any dependence upon a voice from heaven, Peter for the disciples expresses faith in Jesus as the Christ. What is new is not their recognition of Jesus but an open acknowledgment which is elicited by Jesus, and the recognition is evidently thought of as *the result of the disclosures of the person of Jesus during the entire preceding period of their association with him.* Jesus elicits the confession at this time, accordingly, not because now for the first time the disciples had emerged from the darkness of total ignorance into the light of knowledge of and faith in Jesus but because, on the background of open avowal of his messiahship, he wishes now to set forth the consummation of his messianic ministry and what it required of his followers. The subsequent action and discourse at this point, in which Peter protests Jesus' word concerning the future and is rebuked as a spokesman for Satan, confirms this approach, for Peter's second rôle shows that alongside of exultant faith there remains profound misunderstanding (Mk. 8:29, 33). To sum up: the confession in Caesarea Philippi does not represent an apprehension of the messiahship of Jesus on the basis of a fresh disclosure; the disclosure there is rather, preëminently, that the messiahship, previously recognized and now openly acknowledged, involves for Jesus the march to the cross, a march that would not end in the defeat or in the destruction of the Messiah since he is to be vindicated through resurrection from the dead.

There is indeed an injunction to silence concerning Jesus in this context (Mk. 8:30). Since it is here unmotivated, one is left to infer from the total picture of Jesus' attitude towards his messiahship why at this juncture he enjoins such a command. When viewed in conjunction with other similar commands, which have been scrutinized above, it appears to be fully as plausibly construed as due to Jesus' continued reserve in disclosing his messiahship, and the demands of the momentous situation that was developing, as to an artificial scheme of the evangelist.

That Mark is concerned here with the narration of Jesus' insistence that his vocation as Messiah demanded his passion at Jerusalem, rather than with a dogma of secret messiahship, receives significant confirmation in the account of the transfiguration, which is set forth as a feature of the cycle of events introduced by the confession. Here indeed there is a fresh disclosure of the transcendent messiahship of Jesus, which finds its only parallel in the utterance at the baptism of Jesus. If the disclosure at the transfiguration stood alone, and especially if it preceded the confession of Peter, it might be construed as a completely new and epochal revelation of the person of Jesus.[14] Following the confession as it does, and finding its setting in the midst of the solemn utterances concerning the approaching passion, it must be interpreted as an integral element of the account of the way of the cross. A supernatural confirmation is provided that the one who has spoken of the necessity of his passion, to the consternation of Peter, and has also declared the subsequent necessity of their self-denial and self-sacrifice and loyalty (Mk. 8:34-38), must be believed and obeyed (Mk. 9:7). He remains the messianic Son of Man in the face of the cross.

The command to keep silent which follows the transfiguration scene (Mk. 9:9) also points to the reality of revelation to a chosen few. This command does not indeed

---

[14] A striking feature of Schweitzer's reconstruction of the life of Jesus is that he transposes the order of these events. *Cf. Quest of the Historical Jesus*, 1926, pp. 381, 394. If this transposition of the order were justified indeed, the theory of secret messiahship would gain greater plausibility.

refer to the messiahship as such, as Wrede maintained in regarding this passage as the key to the interpretation of the secrecy phenomena in Mark. The silence is concerned with "what they saw." The resurrection to be sure is indicated as introducing a new phase of activity on the part of the disciples. But Mark lends no support to the conception that before the resurrection there was to be no witness to Christ whatsoever, much less that before that event the disciples remained in total darkness.[15] The accent in the narrative, however, falls fully as much upon fear and bewilderment as upon comprehension, and it again appears that the episode is far from being in Mark's mind a transition from a stage of darkness to one of light. The light which shone from the mount of transfiguration was too bright to behold. There is an overwhelming sense of awe and inarticulateness in the presence of the transfigured Jesus (Mk. 9:6, 10).

The events connected with the stay in Caesarea Philippi presuppose therefore both too much comprehension and too much misunderstanding to allow for either Wrede's or Lightfoot's interpretations. Faith and stumbling, insight and bewilderment keep company, and neither the notion that the disciples are represented as being in complete darkness nor the theory that they are conceived of as emerging now from darkness to a measure of comprehension is compatible with the data of Mark.

B. BEFORE AND AFTER CAESAREA PHILIPPI

In the interest of a further clarification of Mark's understanding of the manifestation of Christ to his disciples, we must now proceed to an examination of the other data, those which precede and those which follow the episode

---

[15] On Mk. 9:11-13 *cf.* Lightfoot, *op. cit.*, pp. 92ff.

that marks transition from one phase of his ministry to another. As our review advances we shall continue to bear in mind the representations of the theory of secret messiahship.

In the period of activity in Galilee which Mark describes, the disciples appear as a group who have become the intimate companions and confidants of Jesus, and who themselves have acknowledged his leadership and authority. They leave their secular occupations to follow him (Mk. 1:16-20; 2:14) and acting under his authority and endowed with his power they preach and cast out demons (3:13ff.; 6:7ff., 12f., 30). Their relation to Jesus results in distinctive practices which Jesus himself defends by appeal to his messianic authority (2:18f., 23ff.; cf. 7:1ff.). They receive private instruction and are admitted to witness miracles from which the crowds are excluded (4:14ff., 33f., 36ff.; 5:37; 6:45ff.; cf. 8:1ff.). Everywhere there is presupposed a measure of apprehension of and trust in Jesus.

Astonishment, bewilderment and fear, on the other hand, are also conspicuously present in the Galilean ministry. After the silencing of the storm the disciples are rebuked for their previous fright and lack of faith, and they are further described as filled with great fear and questioning as to who he might be (Mk. 4:40f.). Yet even in this connection it does not follow that Mark conceives of the disciples as walking in total darkness and in stark unbelief. Their fright was evoked by the storm, and the rebuke may point to nothing more than a momentary lapse of faith. Moreover, the fear which followed the rebuke is by no means obviously a mere continuation of their fright. It was a fear called forth by a stupendous miracle and therefore is not so much terror as awe in the presence of the divine action. The questioning as to who he might be likewise is not the inquiry which proceeds from total ignorance but from dawning apprehension of the transcendence of Jesus' person.

In similar fashion we may understand the amazement which follows Jesus' act of walking on the sea (Mk. 6:45ff.). Their amazement is not of one piece with the terror which characterized the disciples when they thought that they had seen a ghost. Amazement at the performance of a miracle is not a sign of lack of apprehension or of faith; in fact, Mark in one instance specifically links such an attitude with a readiness to glorify God (2:12; *cf.* Lk. 5:25f.). Amazement in such a context then appears to be a religious attitude which, while not necessarily implying deep insight or steady trust, is different essentially from sheer ignorance and unbelief.

The question of the attitude of the disciples towards Jesus in this narrative is complicated, however, by the reason attached to their astonishment. The conclusion of the story reads as follows: "And he went up with them into the boat, and the wind ceased; and they were sore amazed in themselves, for they understood not concerning the loaves for their heart was hardened" (Mk. 6:51f.). Here amazement is definitely associated with lack of understanding and hardness of heart, and the disciples thereby seem to be placed in the same class with the Jewish enemies of Jesus (*cf.* Mk. 3:5). Nor does this reference to the hardening of their hearts stand alone, for the same, or a similar, state of mind is ascribed to the disciples a little later. When Jesus speaks of the hunger of the multitude, in the narrative of the feeding of the four thousand, the disciples, apparently not allowing for the possibility of a miracle, ask in matter of fact fashion: "Whence shall one be able to satisfy these men with bread here in a desert place?" (Mk. 8:4).[16] And almost immediately a situation is presented when the disciples themselves, being greatly agitated because of their own lack of bread, are questioned in terms that suggest that Jesus regards their misunderstanding and lack of faith as approaching, if not identical with, the hardness of heart which characterized "those who were without" (*cf.* Mk. 4:11f.), for Jesus says:

"Why reason ye because ye have no bread? Do ye not yet perceive neither understand? Have ye your heart hardened? Having eyes, see ye not, and having ears, hear ye not? And do ye not remember, when I broke the five loaves among the five thousand, how many baskets full of broken pieces ye took up? (They say unto him, Twelve.) When the seven among four thousand, how many basketfuls of broken pieces ye took up? (And they say, Seven. And he said unto them) Do ye not yet understand?" (Mk. 8:17-21).

If the lack of discernment, the obtuseness, ascribed to the disciples in these contexts were typical of Mark's delineation of their responses to Jesus, we should indeed be compelled to admit that the disciples dwelt in the same total darkness as those who were not his followers. In view of all of the evidence to the contrary, however, the absoluteness

---

[16] This query does not point to the presence of a doublet in Mark, as Rawlinson, *op. cit.*, p. 85, n. 3, contends. It is entirely consistent with, and evidently presupposes, Mk. 6:51. As Mk. 8:19f. shows, it is not necessary to conclude that the disciples are represented as having forgotten the former miracles of the loaves, and therefore as manifesting an "incredible dullness." The words imply only that at that time the disciples lacked adequate faith as to the power of Jesus. An eclipse of understanding at one point does not justify the conclusion that an eclipse under similar conditions is unhistorical or incredible. The query would be shown to be incredible in the second instance only if it could be proved that hardness of heart in the face of the first stupendous miracle was inconceivable.

of ignorance attributed to them at these junctures must be understood as exceptional and temporary. As we have observed, while Mark is far from offering an idealizing picture of the faith of the disciples in contrast to Jewish unbelief, he does maintain unmistakably a qualitative distinction between the acknowledgment of Jesus' authority on the part of the disciples and the unrelieved unbelief of others. Hence even the exceptional ignorance in view here can hardly be taken to mean a total eclipse of faith and understanding, for the reproaches of Jesus assume their continuous adherence to him rather than an apostasy from him.

But two questions remain: (1) Can the exceptional character of their dullness be accounted for? (2) Is any light shed upon the connection between the ignorance with respect to the loaves and their state of mind at the time of their encounter with Jesus as he walked upon the sea? With regard to the former question, we must confess that data for a positive answer are not provided in the narratives. Their dullness in this apparently absolute form appears indeed only in the contexts where the actuality or possibility of the miraculous supply of bread is in view. Perhaps there was something in the transaction or circumstances of these wonders which contributed to their lack of apprehension. Swete suggests, in commenting on Mark 6:51, that the administration of the food may have diverted their thoughts from the work of the Lord. Whatever degree of plausibility may inhere in a conjecture of this kind, however, there remains an inscrutable element. For the hardening in view is not described as originating in connection with the miracles of the loaves but as affecting their apprehension of what took place. We must admit therefore that the cause of the hardening is left unexplained. The mystery here is a part of the mystery of the working of sin upon the human heart. Clearly no optimistic or idealizing or perfectionist conception of human nature is presupposed.

On the second question we can perhaps speak with greater certainty. How can an ignorance that is restricted to the miraculous supply of bread be construed as a ground for their astonishment after Jesus had walked upon the water and quieted the wind? It seems clear at least that Mark implies that if the state of their mind at the time had been different, that is, not under the impact of a hardening influence, their response to Jesus' appearance would have been more favorable (Mk. 6:51f.). They might possibly have perceived the identity of Jesus at once, without giving way to extreme terror, and there would have been no occasion for their exceeding astonishment as to his identity. The astonishment then is seen not to be complete lack of comprehension but an emerging apprehension which remains blameworthy because it points back to a state of heart-hardened dullness.

This discussion provides a background for the study of the place occupied by Jesus' teaching in the disclosure of his meaning in Mark and of the response of the disciples to his teaching, and we shall take brief notice of the issues. The discussion centers naturally enough largely about the parabolic teaching of Jesus recorded in Mark 4, and especially about the relation of Mk. 4:10-20 to the record of the parables as such, the common critical opinion being that this section, because of the antithesis set up between the disciples and those who were outside, because of its implication that Jesus did not contemplate that the parabolic teaching would truly inform his hearers as a whole, and because of supposedly allegorical traits in the interpretation given, cannot be referred back to Jesus but must be taken as the construction of the evangelist. Assuming that this account, and especially Mk. 4:10-12, constitutes an unmistakable composition of the evangelist, the advocates of the theory of secret messiahship have appealed to it as a confirmation of their judgment that the evangelist has introduced the secrecy phenomena in the interest of a dogmatic reconstruction of the historical tradition (Wrede, *op. cit.*, 54ff.; Lightfoot, *History and*

Interpretation, pp. 74ff.; *cf.* Bultmann, *Geschichte der synoptischen Tradition*, pp. 215, 202, 351; Dibelius, *From Tradition to Gospel*, pp. 227f.). Wrede sums up his judgment as follows: "Geheimnis ist die ganze Lehre Jesu, weil sie der Menge ganz verborgen wird. Geheimnis ist der Sinn der Parabeln im Speziellen, da er nur den Jungern erschlossen wird und auch ihnen nicht ohne Deutung" (p. 80).

It is highly important to distinguish sharply between the questions of interpretation and those relating to historicity. So far as the former are concerned, we fail to see that Mark introduces here any feature that is inconsistent with the other representations of the relations between Jesus and his disciples. In view of the double advantage which the disciples enjoy, namely, that theirs is the mystery of the kingdom, that is, apprehension of its revelation, and that they alone have the benefit of private exposition of the meaning of the parables, this context clearly accents emphatically the reality of the disclosure to the disciples during the Galilean ministry, and points clearly to the untenability of a consistent theory of secrecy. That, on the other hand, the disciples appear here as requiring elucidation of the parables, that they are blamed for their dullness of apprehension (Mk. 4:13; *cf.* 7:18; 8:17ff.), while qualifying in decisive fashion the degree of their understanding of the message of Jesus, does not by any means place them in the category of those on the outside, with whom in fact they are placed in antithesis.

Regarding the historicity of the statements attributed to Jesus in Mk. 4:10-12, a few observations must suffice. The basic assumption of those who take the negative view appears to be that Jesus was essentially a humanitarian rabbi, a conclusion sharply at variance with the conviction of Mark and the other evangelists. On that presupposition indeed one might perhaps not be able to justify the antithesis set up in Mk. 4:11f., and one might insist that the parables had to be perspicuous in their intent. The fact is, however, that Jesus himself and his message were not perspicuous to most who heard him, and the lack of understanding is bound up with the essential mysteriousness of the person of Jesus. To remain unsettled on the ultimate question of the meaning of Jesus, as the negative critics do, and yet to claim that the meaning of the parables is perfectly plain, is, in our judgment, to resort to an atomistic method of exegesis which radicals like Wrede have condemned as unscientific. And who can say that Jesus the Messiah could not have taught the antithesis between his disciples and those on the outside, that he could not have foreseen the rejection of his claims on the part of the Jewish people as a whole, that he could not have been unwilling to intrust himself to all men? The suggestion of Lightfoot that Mark, like Paul in Romans 9-11, is grappling here with the problem of the unbelief of Israel presupposes that Jesus could not have presented such an explanation of the negative attitude towards himself by appealing to a word of Isaiah. We do not mean to imply that these considerations will settle the question of historicity, but we venture to state that they serve to show that isolated questions of this kind cannot be settled without a decision on the broad question of the historicity of the witness of the gospels to Jesus Christ.

The Marcan portrait of the disciples during the Galilean ministry accordingly represents them as enjoying a considerable measure of understanding of the purposes of Jesus and as manifesting on the whole confidence and allegiance towards him. There are indeed no halos about their heads. Darker hues are freely employed. And yet for all their dullness and imperfect vision they never appear, even in the most unfavorable circumstances, as standing in total darkness. The question must now be put how this picture compares with that found in the latter part of the gospel. Does the polarity of faith and unbelief, of understanding and dullness, continue in evidence? Or does there emerge a more constant and stable attitude? As our study of the section which introduces the new period has shown, the earlier tension continues to be present: Peter who has confessed Christ has to be rebuked for his misunderstanding almost at once, and on the mount of transfiguration there is bewilderment in the face of their awesome experience. In the rest of the history of the consummation of the life of Christ also, we shall see, the same features are reëchoed again and again. Although the disciples enjoy the privilege of instruction concerning the meaning of the messianic task and of their discipleship, the accent in this section, at least so far as their own responses are concerned, falls at least as emphatically upon their confusion and dullness as in the earlier period.

The pronouncements concerning the passion and resurrection continue to leave the disciples in uncertainty (Mk. 9:32) and unaware of its implications for their discipleship (10:35-45). Even Jesus' steadfastness in going to Jerusalem brought amazement and fear to those who followed (10:32). The disciples had to be corrected and rebuked for their misconception of the terms of admission to the fellowship of Christ (9:38; 10:13f.). His teaching concerning the burden of riches produced amazement and astonishment (10:24, 26). There is indignation at his anointing which betrays a failure to understand the meaning of his death (14:8f.). Judas, one of the twelve, shall betray him (14:10, 17f.) and when he is taken, all shall be offended and scattered abroad (14:28). The climax of the story in Mark finds the disciples, in spite of all the instruction that had been lavished upon them, and in spite of their previous manifestations of loyalty and faith, in a state of confusion approaching panic. The cross, both in anticipation and in actuality, proved a stumblingblock to them, a stumblingblock which, in order that it might be removed, required the reappearance of Christ (14:28; 16:7).

Is this uncomplimentary portrayal of the disciples the product of a dogmatic scheme of the evangelist or does it represent actual history? The high place which the apostles held in the esteem of the early church excludes the possibility that this story of failure would have been tolerated, even if it could have been invented, unless it rested securely upon tradition which came from the apostolic circle itself.[17]

It is profitable in connection with our study of the relation of the disciples to Christ to examine the tradition which connects the Gospel according to Mark with the preaching of Peter. Does the story of failure which we have been reviewing perhaps proceed from Peter's reminiscences? Can

---

[17] *Cf.* Vos, *op. cit.*, p. 78.

the distinctive tone of Mark be accounted for, to some extent at least, as reflecting the intense personal experience of one who was painfully conscious of his own shameful disloyalty and unworthiness?

There are many details in the gospel story as published by Mark that are remarkably congruous with the tradition of his dependence upon the preaching of Peter. The story of the reviving of the daughter of Jairus, for example, contains many details not found in Matthew and Luke: the presence of the father and mother of the child and of the intimate disciples, the Aramaic words addressed to the child, her walking about after she had been raised up, and her age (Mk. 5:40-42; *cf.* Mt. 9:25; Lk. 8:53ff.). Now since Peter, along with James and John, was present to witness the miracle, these vivid details may well be explained from the supposition that he was wont to recall them in his preaching. Similarly, his presence at the transfiguration may plausibly account for the fact that, in Mark alone, the story of the reunion with the other disciples and of his approach to the crowd about them, is told from the point of view of those who had been in Jesus' company, Mark alone distinguishing sharply between the intimate group about Jesus and the larger circle of disciples, and reporting that when they came to the disciples "they," that is, Jesus and the three intimates, "saw a great multitude about them," that is, about the other disciples, "and scribes disputing with them" (9:14; *cf.* Mt. 17:14; Lk. 9:37). Other instances of possible dependence upon Peter's reminiscences are found in Mark 1:29, and 3:16, as well as in the somber story, interwoven with the delineation of the passion of Jesus, of Peter's unfaithfulness in the face of strong protestations of loyalty (although the last is not especially distinctive of Mark) (*cf.* Mk. 8:32f. and 14:37, 66-72 with 8:29; 10:28 and 14:29).

The argument for dependence upon Peter, as developed by both orthodox and liberal scholars, has sometimes been subjected to criticism on the ground that Mark, when compared with the other evangelists, is far from showing any special regard for Peter.[18] But this criticism is based on a basic misconception of the real nature of Mark's supposed dependence upon the preaching of the apostle. The argument is not to the effect that, if the tradition of Papias concerning Mark's use of Petrine reminiscences is true, Mark's gospel would be bound to exhibit a greater interest in and regard for the course of Peter's life as a disciple of Christ than the other evangelists. As Eusebius long ago observed,[19] Mark does not tell more about Peter than the others; in fact he is more reticent about Peter, and especially in matters that might seem to reflect credit upon him. There is nothing disconcerting in such reticence, however, if only it is not forgotten that Peter was preaching, and Mark was publishing, the gospel of *Christ,* which was, properly speaking, not biographical even of Christ, and much less biographical of the preacher of the gospel. It is necessary therefore to maintain a precise division between evidences of reserve about Peter's life and signs of dependence upon Peter's preaching.

The most striking instance of reticence on Mark's part is noted by comparing his account of Peter's confession in Caesarea Philippi with Matthew's, for the former contains nothing concerning the blessing pronounced upon Peter

---

[18] *Cf. e.g.,* Bacon, *Beginnings of the Gospel Story,* p. xxv. Burkitt, *Earliest Sources,* pp. 89f., provides an effective reply.

[19] *Demonstratio Evangelica* III, 5: ed. BC, XXIII, p. 128.

and the significance attached to his new name as a disciple of Christ (Mt. 16:17-19; *cf.* Mk. 8:29ff.). Another remarkable proof that Matthew rather than Mark centers the readers' attention upon the career of Peter is found in the parallel accounts of Jesus' walking upon the sea, for Matthew alone includes the extraordinary detail of Peter's departure from the boat to meet Jesus upon the water (Mt. 14:28-31; *cf.* Mk. 6:50).

It appears then that vivid personal reminiscence of Jesus and reserve concerning his own person might both have characterized Peter's proclamation of Christ. Why, however, would Peter's reserve also not extend to his own sad experiences during the days of Jesus' journey to the cross? Mark, it has been observed, is preëminently the gospel of the passion of Christ. The opening chapters may well be regarded as serving principally as a necessary introduction to the narrative of the way of the cross. Because of this absorption with the passion, the story of Peter's obtuseness and denial, interwoven into the texture of the story of the way of the cross, stands out most conspicuously in this gospel. In astonishing contrast to the submission of Christ to the death of the cross, compelled by the self-conscious purpose to give his life as a ransom for many, stand the insensibility and faithlessness of Peter, which are underscored by his impetuous and impudent confidence in his own discrimination and stability. This individual experience of Peter, a profound experience of forgiveness and of gratitude for his restoration after his conspicuous failure, has left its impress upon the whole of the gospel tradition, but nowhere does it stand in as bold relief as in Mark. Here the gospel of the passion of Christ is set in sharper focus because of the background provided by Peter's pride and fall. What is more plausible than that this pattern is not of Mark's conception but rather reflects the peculiar emphasis which Peter's preaching received from his own personal experiences? His personal recollection of failure would contribute to the proclamation of the unique Saviour from sin.[20]

On the broader question of the nature of Mark's representation of the attitude of the disciples towards Jesus, the question of the disclosure and the secrecy of the messiahship, the evidence of Peter's faith and failure does not require any modification of the general conclusion reached above. Peter is typical of the disciples both in his apprehension and trust and in his insensibility and disloyalty. If he is distinctive it is only because in him these contrasting attitudes reach their zenith and their nadir. The accent at the end indeed is on Peter's failure, and yet it is obvious to the reader of Mark that the story does not end with failure. Peter's prominence in the establishment of the Christian church must have been a matter of common knowledge and that his career was not to be one of continued denial of Jesus is indicated by his penitence (Mk. 14:72) and the intimation of an approaching appearance to Peter after the resurrection (16:7). To Peter, too, might well have been attributed the words: "Lord, I believe, help thou my unbelief."

---

[20] *Cf.* R. O. Hall, "Accuracy in the Gospel Records," in HJ, xxxiv (1935-36), pp. 278ff., who speaks of Mark as the "deposit of Peter's vivid experience, particularly of his own misunderstanding of Jesus' way." Lightfoot, *Locality and Doctrine*, pp. 27f., declares: "It may be part of St. Mark's purpose to emphasize the uniqueness and solitariness of Jesus Christ . . . in the work of man's redemption; he wishes perhaps to exclude altogether the possibility of any human claim, apart from the work of Jesus Christ, to merit before God, even in respect of those who had formed the first and most intimate body of disciples and subsequently had given up everything for Christ."

Although Mark's witness to the person of Christ is preeminently to one who appears as the transcendent Son of God, who is understood ultimately only if his divine origin and nature is apprehended, we should be dealing inadequately with the evidence if we failed to observe that he is none the less a true man. His human, emotional life comes indeed to conspicuous expression in Mark. This evangelist includes references to the anger of Christ (3:5; *cf.* 1:43; 10:14), his compassion (1:41), his wonder (6:6), his sighing in his spirit (8:12).

Such data, together with other passages in Mark reflecting the truly human character of the life of Jesus, which likewise find no parallel in corresponding sections in Matthew, have often been appealed to as evidences of the priority and superiority of Mark's witness to Jesus.[21] Mark, it is held, represents an earlier stage of Christological reflection, and provides more data for the reconstruction of his life as a man. If there were some truly objective method by which these data could be separated from the context of Mark, and could be referred to an earlier stratum of tradition about Jesus, this evaluation might be justified. It appears, however, that such a sifting of the Marcan data can be carried through only by beginning with the *a priori* assumption that Jesus was a mere man. Moreover, the problem would remain of the meaning which these data had for Mark whose proclamation of Jesus was completely unconcerned with historical origins and development; evidently his own thought of the humanity of Jesus was far removed from modern notions on this subject.

---

21 *Cf.* Allen, *Matthew* (ICC), p. xxxi; Hawkins, *Horae Synopticae*, 1909, pp. 117ff.; Moffatt, *Introduction*, 1918, p. 249; Enslin, *Christian Beginnings*, pp. 394f. On the subject of the emotional life of our Lord see the article of B. B. Warfield in BTS, pp. 35-90.

If, in spite of his portrayal of Jesus as the supernatural and transcendent Son of God, Mark includes vivid details of Christ's emotional life, the explanation must be sought in the origin and purpose of his account. Here the tradition of the Petrine background of the gospel again appears to offer help. Peter, one of the most intimate of Jesus' associates, had a capacity for deep feeling and strong emotional reactions, and these may have left an impression upon his proclamation of the gospel, as we have observed. The result for Mark's record would be that it would often provide a more intimate and vivid narrative than the other gospels, an account more personal and subjective and experiential. The other gospels also witness to the human character of the life of Jesus, but as we shall see in later chapters the others recognize this fact in a manner which agrees with their own distinctive aims and methods.

Looking back upon our investigation of Mark it is profitable to pause for a résumé. How does Mark conceive of his record? What is the nature of the testimony which he bears to Jesus Christ? That he was not writing a chronicle or biography has become sufficiently plain. He is publishing the glad tidings of Jesus Christ, and this presupposes something different from the interest which a biographer has in his subject. He writes as a believer in the one whose history signifies the action of God for the salvation of men. In Mark's thought the truth of his history is bound up with the truth of his presuppositions as a believer; likewise, these presuppositions are judged to have found their demonstration in his witness to the historical life of Jesus Christ. Hence, his record cannot be shown to be unhistorical merely by pointing to his presupposition of faith; fact and meaning, the divine meaning and the divine action in deed and word, cannot be isolated with a view to separate evaluation.

The gulf that separates Mark's historical method from the typical modern one is seen most clearly in the almost complete absence of the notion of development. This is true even of the form of the narrative, for in place of a continuous, closely concatenated story, he presents with considerable abruptness a series of sharply delineated pictures and impressions of Christ at work and on the march, and as he receives both acclaim and condemnation. That Jesus was perfectly clear from the very beginning as to who he was and what he was to do is written so large that one wonders today how anyone could ever have associated with this gospel the notion of a development on Jesus' part into a consciousness of messiahship. Indeed, the evangelist feels no need to account for the presence of this consciousness at the beginning of the public ministry; it is sufficient that the divine voice from above, seconded by the testimony of the Baptist, reveals his transcendent character. There is, moreover, very little evidence of a gradual disclosure of his messiahship to the disciples. His power and authority as the Son of God and the Son of Man from the beginning produce overwhelming impressions upon the disciples, impressions so stupendous that faith and loyalty are never completely separated from amazement and fear and lack of understanding in the presence of divine mystery. Only when Jesus insists that they must associate in their minds the way of the cross with his transcendent messiahship does the reader become sharply aware of progress and movement in the account. Looking forward one sees only the cross, and looking backward one realizes that the hostility of the Jewish leaders must issue in their utter repudiation of Jesus. Meanwhile, however, the redemptive purpose of the cross becomes clear as the whole approaches its climax.

Although then the disclosure of the full meaning of the

messiahship is not without a definite forward movement, the evangelist by no means represents the disciples as responding to the fuller disclosure with ever clearer apprehension. The overwhelming impression created by his acts and words could not be denied, but the insistence that suffering was the path to glory, for the Messiah as for them, proved a stone of stumbling. Their attachment to him and his cause which was fashioned in the early days was so powerful that they did not forsake him until the very end, but then their repudiation was so complete that the element of hope can remain present, not because anything in their attitude suggests the possibility of a change of heart and mind, but only because of the prospect of Jesus' own action on their behalf through and after the resurrection.

CHAPTER IV

THE CONCLUSION OF MARK

SYNOPSIS

I. *The Defense of the Long Ending.*

Apparent preponderance of external testimony in favor of it; the evidence for the abrupt conclusion; analysis of the history of the text demonstrates that the long ending, in spite of its early origin, was not contained in the earliest types of text; the decisive weight of intrinsic considerations: its distinctive style and lack of continuity with Mk. 16:1-8; efforts of defenders of the long ending to overcome these external and internal arguments weighed and found wanting.

II. *The Problem of the Abruptness of Mark. 16:8.*

A. The view that Mark is incomplete, either because the evangelist was interrupted or because the end was lost: intrinsic weakness of this view in its various forms.

B. The view that Mk. 16:8 represents the intended end of the gospel:

    1. Consideration of the form of Mk. 16:8: stylistic parallels from classical and Hellenistic Greek show that it need not be supposed that the gospel ends in the middle of a sentence; similarities to the Marcan style.

    2. Consideration of the meaning of Mk. 16:8 in the light of vv. 1-8 and the gospel as a whole:

        a. The "silence" of the women considered as an aspect of their astonishment, trembling and fear; confirmation from the study of the Marcan use of the same terminology in other contexts.

        b. The event provoking overwhelming awe is the resurrection attested by the empty tomb and the angelic disclosure; consideration of the hypothesis that the event is the eschatological consummation: the eschatological perspective of Mark as shown by his use of "the Son of Man"; the place of the resurrection in his perspective; the expectation of the end in Mk. 13; the meaning of Mk. 16:7.

c. The silence of Mark concerning the fulfillment of the prophecy of a reunion in Galilee: necessity of emancipation from the spell of Liberal presuppositions concerning the gospels; the abruptness and "incompleteness" of the conclusion compared with similar features in the preface of Mark; the conclusions of the other gospels and the publication of the glad tidings of Jesus Christ.

ALTHOUGH the distinctive character of Mark's portrayal of Jesus Christ may be gauged with considerable certainty from a survey of the first fifteen chapters, it would be foolhardy to suppose that the conclusion of the gospel may be lightly passed over without serious loss. The very brevity of the preface served to center attention in an arresting fashion upon Mark's distinctive approach, and a similar advantage might be anticipated from the study of the conclusion, especially since there we are concerned with the witness to the momentous event of the resurrection which, as various pronouncements of Jesus demonstrate, is the consummation of the life and ministry.

The problem of the conclusion is, however, a very complex one. The complication is due primarily to the necessity of determining exactly where Mark ends. Most scholars since the days of the epochal work of Westcott and Hort in the field of textual criticism have agreed that the last twelve verses printed in our English Bibles, with or without benefit of spacing and footnotes, are not original, although it may not be overlooked that there has been some vigorous defense of the traditional text, not only from the side of

Roman Catholicism, but also from representatives of Anglican, Reformed and Lutheran churches.[1] Even if the question of the extent of the Marcan text might be regarded as settled, however, the problem of its interpretation emerges as one of peculiar difficulty; indeed, the historical and exegetical questions are so inextricably intertwined with the strictly textual considerations that the latter cannot be treated in isolated fashion. Textual criticism, it clearly emerges here, is not a neutral science; it involves far more than a mechanical weighing of the value of certain manuscripts. Apart from an evaluation of the disposition of Mark 16:9-20, and especially of 16:1-8, in relation to the gospel as a whole, there can be no adequate treatment of the form and meaning of the resurrection narrative in Mark.

The originality of the long ending has indeed seemed to many to be settled by the mass of manuscript evidence which may be cited in its favor.[2] All of the extant Greek manuscripts except Codex Sinaiticus and Codex Vaticanus, and all of the Latin mss. except Codex Bobiensis, contain it. Moreover, it clearly formed a part of the New Testament

---

[1] The most exhaustive treatment and defense of the long ending were presented by J. W. Burgon in *The Last Twelve Verses of the Gospel according to St. Mark*, 1871. See also *The Revision Revised*, 1883, and Burgon and Miller, *The Traditional Text of the Gospels*, 1896, Appendix VII. Recent defenders include the Reformed scholar van Leeuwen, *Markus* (KNT), 1928, pp. 294-316; the Lutheran R. C. H. Lenski, *The Interpretation of St. Mark's and St. Luke's Gospel*, 1934, pp. 471ff.; and the Roman Catholic P. Dausch, *Die drei älteren Evangelien*, 1932, pp. 17f.

[2] We are content here to provide a bare summary of the evidence. The student who is prepared to examine the question for himself may readily find the details in Tischendorf, Legg or Souter. For important discussions see Hort, *The N. T. in the Original Greek*, II, 1882, Appendix, pp. 335-360; Swete, *Mark*, pp. ciii-cxiii; Streeter, *The Four Gospels*, 1930, pp. 335-360; Rawlinson, *Mark* (WC), 1936, pp. 267ff.; Zahn, *Geschichte d. ntl. Kanons*, II, 2, 1892, pp. 910-938.

THE CONCLUSION OF MARK

of Irenaeus (c. 185) and of Hippolytus (c. 200), as well as of the gospel text of Tatian (c. 170) and possibly of Justin Martyr (c. 155). Nevertheless, such a summary, without significant qualification, would leave an entirely erroneous impression as to the actual history of the text of Mark. Such a summary, quite apart from the all-important matter of the evaluation of the evidence in terms of quality rather than of quantity alone, does not take into account a considerable body of external evidence that bears upon the decision.

Although there are only two of all the Greek mss. that we possess, the two great uncials mentioned above, which end at Mark 16:8, there were undoubtedly many others which have not been preserved. This fact is established by the testimony of the well-informed historian Eusebius, c. 325, who in answering a question that had been raised about the harmony of Mt. 28:1 and Mk. 16:9, states that "the most accurate copies" and "almost all the copies" known to him ended with the words "for they were afraid." Moreover, four extant Greek uncials, including the highly-respected Codex Regius, as well as certain cursive mss. and versions, clearly presuppose the presence of the abrupt ending in exemplars which they followed, for, while they contain Mark 16:9-20, they insert between v.8 and v.9 the so-called "Short Ending," which no one today is prepared to defend as an original part of Mark and which was unmistakably composed in an effort to overcome the seeming abruptness of v.8. In addition to this weighty evidence, which proves that the long ending was missing from far more than a few isolated mss., there is to be joined the direct testimony of the Old Syriac version in its most accurate witness (the Sinaitic ms.), the Georgian and Armenian versions, and apparently also the Sahidic Coptic version.

When now the external evidence is placed in the perspective of time and place, the apparent preponderance of testimony for the long ending disappears. If one sets aside the mass of evidence which characteristically supports the type of text which did not emerge before the fourth century and became predominant in the middle ages, the type commonly known as the Syrian or Byzantine text, the long ending fails to retain the unanimous support of any single earlier type of text. No doubt it was current at an early time in the west, and came to occupy a secure place in the Latin Bible; yet it is highly significant that Codex Bobiensis, which is judged to be the best exemplar of the earliest African gospel text, ends at Mk. 16:8, and it is therefore doubtful that the earliest form of the Latin Bible contained the long ending. This fact combined with the evidence that evidently the earliest forms of the Greek New Testament to reach Alexandria, Caesarea and Antioch ended at Mk. 16:8 provides a far-reaching correction of estimates of the external evidence which have been formulated by some defenders of the traditional text.[3]

Even if the manuscript evidence for the long ending were far more weighty than it in reality proves to be when it is placed in historical perspective, the decision as to its right to a place in the gospel could hardly longer remain in doubt when intrinsic considerations are taken into account. There are two impressive phenomena which weigh heavily against the supposition that Mk. 16:9-20 was written by the author of Mk. 1:1-16:8: (1) its distinctive style, and (2) its lack of continuity with that which precedes.

The simple, paratactic style which is found as far as Mk. 16:8 is absent from the long ending, where instead one finds a more complex sentence structure and distinctive

---

[3] See especially Streeter, *op. cit.*, pp. 88 and 335f. on the Caesarean text and on the character of the other early evidence.

connecting links. καί ("and") commonly serves to introduce sentences or clauses before Mk. 16:9, appearing, for example, ten or more times in the thirteen verses of the preface and seven or more times in the eight undisputed verses of chapter 16, but it occurs only once in the long ending (16:15). On the other hand, "after these things" (16:12), which occurs frequently in John, and "afterward" (16:14), which is common in Matthew, do not appear at all in the earlier text of Mark. However precarious arguments from language and style admittedly are, it is difficult to deny that the style of Mark 16:9-20 is far from offering any corroboration to the general proposition of its unity with the rest of the gospel.

The second consideration mentioned, pointing to lack of continuity between Mk. 16:8 and 16:9 is still more difficult to set aside. Mark's previous narrative, as shown by 14:28 and 16:7, points forward to a reunion in Galilee, but instead of fulfilling this expectation, as Matthew does (*cf.* 26:32; 28:7, 16ff.), the long ending presents a summary of appearances none of which is specifically localized. Moreover, Mk. 16:9 does nothing to relieve the abruptness of the end of v. 8. Although the abruptness of this verse, as we shall show in some detail below, has often been exaggerated, no one can deny that at this point Mark leaves some things unsaid which the narrative clearly holds in prospect. It may be disputed whether Mark necessarily had to go on to relate in his gospel what had actually happened after the development of v. 8, but on the assumption that Mark did continue the narrative beyond v. 8, which the supporters of the traditional text maintain, it is inconceivable that he should have broken off the thread of his narrative, and begun to summarize various other appearances.

Those who continue to defend the long ending fail, in

our judgment, to do justice to these external and internal considerations. If they do not undertake a broad defense of the Textus Receptus against the text of the great uncials, as Burgon and Miller did, they seek substantiation of their position by appeal to supposedly suspicious traits in the leading mss. which omit the text in dispute. For example, the fact that Codex Vaticanus leaves a column blank after concluding the gospel at 16:8 and subscribing the phrase "According to Mark" is held to weaken the testimony as a whole, and perhaps even to betray that the omission of the long ending was due to none other than the scribe of this manuscript.[4] Exactly why this space was left blank is indeed unknown. It could possibly point to the scribe's familiarity with a copy or copies which contained a longer text. In view of the early currency of the long ending, it is plausible enough that a fourth century scribe should have known of its existence, but this is not to suggest that his exemplar must have contained the long ending or that he was betraying the insecurity of the abrupt text. Only if the scribe of Codex Vaticanus constantly went out of his way and was habitually given to arbitrary omissions would such conjectures possess a degree of plausibility. It may not be overlooked, moreover, that the external evidence as a whole presupposes that the abrupt ending was known considerably before the origin of this codex.

The support of Codex Sinaiticus for the abrupt ending has been criticized on a different score.[5] On the basis of Tischendorf's judgment that the scribe of the New Testament portion of Codex Vaticanus was one of the scribes of

---

[4] See, *e.g.*, Miller in *The Traditional Text*, pp. 298f.; Dausch, *op. cit.*, p. 18.

[5] See Miller, *ibid.*

Codex Sinaiticus, in fact the scribe of the portion under discussion here, it has been held that these two mss. do not represent two independent witnesses but only one, and this scribe is then made responsible for the origin of the shorter text. Miller even states that the scribe of this portion of Codex Sinaiticus, designated as "D," cancelled the sheet originally written by scribe "A" containing the long ending, and substituted for it the sheet as we now have it, written by himself. That Tischendorf's thesis is untenable, and that the hypothesis concerning the editorial activities of scribe "D" necessarily falls to the ground, has been demonstrated by Milne and Skeat who have had the opportunity of a minute examination of this codex since its arrival in the British Museum.[6] These scholars show that all of the affinities of scribe "D" of Sinaiticus are with another scribe of Vaticanus than the one who was responsible for the New Testament portion, and even these affinities, while sufficient to prove a single scribal tradition, are not adequate to prove beyond all doubt their identity. Scribe "D" of Sinaiticus indeed was responsible for sixteen columns at the end of Mark and the beginning of Luke (Mk. 14:54-Lk. 1:56), in a context where scribe "A," the normal scribe of the New Testament, was judged to be in error. Did then scribe "D" possibly "correct" the text of scribe "A" by rewriting these columns so as to exclude Mark 16:9-20? Milne and Skeat, on the basis of detailed computations of the amount written in the sixteen columns of the two sheets that were substituted by scribe "D," and comparing these data with typical writing of scribe "A," show that

---

[6] *Scribes and Correctors of Aleph*, 1938, pp. 9ff., 87ff. *Cf.* also Kenyon, *Our Bible and the Ancient Manuscripts*, 1940. pp. 140, 132 and Zahn, *op. cit.*, pp. 911ff.

there could not have been room for the more than nine hundred letters of Mk. 16:9-20 (approximately a column and a half of the normal writing of scribe "A") in the exemplar which scribe "D" modified.

> Inasmuch, moreover, as Luke would have been begun on the top of a new column, and since at the normal rate of 635 letters per column scribe "A" would have required rather considerably more than six columns, and rather considerably less than seven, for Lk. 1:1-56, it is highly probable that scribe "D" was correcting a somewhat longer text of Luke rather than a longer text of Mark, a text which probably then took seven columns as originally written, and which had to be rewritten simply because "A" had been guilty of an instance of dittography. Scribe "D" decided to compress the Lucan text within six columns, but this required him to average c. 690 letters per column, whereas he had written at the rate of less than 600, apparently his normal rate, in copying the last portion of Mark. If "D" were in the process of shortening the text of "A" to the extent of a column and a half, it would be extraordinary indeed if he decided to take less space than "A" had done for the Lucan passage. Accordingly our knowledge of the writing of both "A" and "D" excludes the possibility that we have to do here with a deliberate omission of the long ending.

In discussing certain intrinsic aspects of the text of Mark we expressed the judgment that, even if the external evidence were indecisive, the scales become decidedly unbalanced in favor of the abrupt conclusion when the style and contents of the long ending are considered in relation to what precedes. It is precisely here, we think, that the advocates of the long ending betray most glaringly the weakness of their own case. In comparing the language of the long ending with the body of the gospel, for example, there is indeed a comparison made in terms of diction, and the proper enough conclusion is drawn that the vocabulary is not so strikingly different as to demand that a later writer must have been responsible for the twelve verses in question. There may be some allusions to stylistic considerations also, and yet the main point, namely, that of sentence structure, is overlooked.[7]

Nor is the problem of the lack of continuity met in any impressive fashion. Miller works out a solution that saves Mark as the author of the twelve verses by virtually denying that he was the author of all that precedes. He conceives of Mark as a purely mechanical amanuensis of Peter whose dictation, interrupted either by Peter's arrest or death, went only so far as 16:8. He says:

> "He would not alter a syllable that had fallen from St. Peter's lips. It would be the conclusion composed by one who had lost his literary illuminator, formal, brief, sententious, and comprehensive. The crucifixion of the leading Apostle would thus impress an everlasting mark upon the Gospel which was virtually his. Here the Master's tongue ceased: here the disciple took up his pen for himself." [8]

Such a mechanical use of the materials at his disposal is not borne out by the gospel itself, greatly exaggerates the dependence of Mark upon Peter, and does not account for the readiness of Mark, on this hypothesis, to add anything on his own authority. Moreover, even the tradition which associates Mark's gospel with Peter, as set forth by Papias and others, views Mark, and not Peter, as the real author. And it is inconceivable that the other evidence of Marcan authorship, including the witness of the title which is very ancient, could have originated if the gospel were conceived of as being as fully Peter's as the conjecture of Miller presupposes.

Van Leeuwen deals somewhat more solidly with the realities of Mark.[9] He seeks specifically to account for the failure of the conclusion to include an appearance to Peter

---

[7] Cf. Burgon, *The Last Twelve Verses*, pp. 142ff.; van Leeuwen, *op. cit.*, pp. 296-299; Lenski, *op. cit.*, pp. 471ff.

[8] *Op. cit.*, p. 306; cf. pp. 305ff.

[9] *Op. cit.*, pp. 314f.

which seemed clearly to be in prospect by making specious use of Mark's restraint concerning Peter, which has been observed to be a distinctive mark of this gospel. His supposition is that due to his reticence towards Peter, just when the narrative calls for the recording of an appearance to this apostle, he breaks off, and concludes the book with a résumé which corresponds to the preface. Is not this a misuse of the phenomenon of Mark's restraint concerning Peter? If he was not so reticent towards Peter as to allow the inclusion of the prophecy of the approaching appearance to Peter (Mk. 16:7), it does not appear what would have dictated the omission of the fulfillment of the prophecy. Moreover, the account foretells a particular meeting with *the disciples* as well as Peter *in Galilee,* and no studied reserve with respect to Peter will explain the silence of the conclusion as to its fulfillment. Nor does it explain why, if Mark actually wrote vv. 9-20, he did not provide a smoother transition from v. 8 to v. 9.

So far as the supposed similarity of the long ending, conceived of as the conclusion of the gospel, and the introduction in Mk. 1:1-13 is concerned it is quite superficial. The contents are actually no more similar than the style. The preface does not offer a summary of things known concerning Jesus Christ before his appearance in Galilee, in particular it tells nothing of his entrance into the world, but in a few broad strokes, through the testimony of the prophet and the utterance of the divine voice, introduces him to the readers as the Son of God. The long ending is, however, properly a summary of appearances, and the concluding verses, referring to both the ascension and the session at God's right hand, take far less abrupt departure from Jesus than the concluding passages of the other gospels.

In our judgment then no really solid case can be built up

in the defense of the genuineness of the long ending. On the view that the text of Mark ends at 16:8, however, the problem of its abruptness still remains. Some attention must be given here to the various efforts to explain this phenomenon. Can this difficulty be overcome? Most scholars have maintained that the abrupt ending of Mark can be accounted for only on the assumption that the gospel is not complete as it is, either because the author was interrupted in his composition, and never resumed his writing, or because, having completed it, a leaf or more was lost almost immediately. Streeter's discussion of the conclusion of Mark represents one of the ablest expositions of this approach. He does not make a final choice between the two possibilities in his conclusion:

> "We conclude, then, *either* that Mark did not live to finish his Gospel —at Rome in Nero's reign this might easily happen—*or* that the end of the Gospel was already lost when it was used by Matthew and Luke."[10]

Zahn is perhaps the strongest defender of the view that the gospel was never completed; while he allows for the possibility that death interrupted Mark's labors, he regards the supposition more plausible that some other factor, such as a flight from Rome necessitated by Roman persecution, prevented Mark from completing his work, which, it is held, in all probability involved far more than the addition of a few lines since Mk. 1:1 holds in prospect a comprehensive work similar to Luke-Acts.[11] Burkitt [12] and Good-

---

[10] *Op. cit.*, p. 344. Hort, *op. cit.*, p. 47 and Branscomb, *Mark* (MNT), pp. 310f. also allow for both possibilities, although they seem to incline to the latter.

[11] *Op. cit.*, pp. 93of. See also Rawlinson, *op. cit.*, p. 270.

[12] *Two Lectures on the Gospels*, 1901; "The historical Character of the Gospel of Mark," in AJTh, XV (Apr., 1911), pp. 171ff.; *Christian Beginnings*, 1924, pp. 83f. See also E. F. Scott, *Literature of the N.T.*, 1932, pp. 6of. (who says that "the breaking off of Mark in the very

speed,[13] on the other hand, are representatives of the view that Mark suffered accidental mutilation, the latter maintaining as against the former that Matthew presupposes a completed form of Mark and provides the materials from which the original conclusion can be reconstructed.

Obviously none of these proposals can claim any finality as solutions of the problem raised by the abrupt ending of Mark. They are too highly conjectural for that. The least plausibility attaches to the last view mentioned for it presupposes that, in spite of a rather extensive circulation of Mark with the hypothetical longer ending, not a trace of that ending has been preserved in any manuscript and no knowledge of it is intimated in any patristic document. The view represented by Burkitt likewise lacks any positive confirmation whatever. It must assume *either* that, though Mark circulated for a brief time, it managed to survive only in a single mutilated manuscript,[14] a supposition that ill agrees with the evidence of the wide circulation of Mark, *or* that the loss of the final portion occurred before it began to circulate, a supposition that has the advantage of accounting for the uniformity of the early tradition of the gospel, but which itself raises new problems. For Mark clearly was intended for the public, and if the last sheet or more was

---

middle of one of the cardinal passages is perhaps the worst disaster that has befallen the New Testament"), K. and S. Lake, *Introduction to the N.T.*, 1937, pp. 35ff.; and Filson, *Origins of the N.T.*, p. 158, for recent support of this position.

[13] *New Solutions of New Testament Problems*, 1927, pp. 116ff.; *Introduction to the N.T.*, 1937, p. 156. For criticism of the judgment that Matthew provides a basis for reconstructing Mark *cf.* especially Streeter, *op. cit.*, pp. 342ff.

[14] A particular feature of Burkitt's view which Streeter refutes in his discussion on pp. 339ff. Burkitt's opinion also receives support from J. Armitage Robinson, *The Study of the Gospels*, 1928, pp. 5f. and A. S. MacLean in DCG, II, p. 133.

THE CONCLUSION OF MARK

lost before it began to circulate, the question arises why Mark himself did not supply what was lacking before it was made available for wider reading. Unless one is ready to insist that publication was delayed for some time after the completion of the gospel, one must conjecture that Mark was prevented by death or some other interruption from amending the defect. There is nothing intrinsically impossible in the latter supposition, as there is not likewise in the view of Zahn and others that some external cause prevented Mark from completing the work which he had left unfinished. On the other hand, these conjectures make no positive contribution to the settling of the issue raised. Nor do we think that the theory that Mark had in view a second section or a second book, similar to the Acts, offers any appreciable aid. If our exegesis of Mk. 1:1 is correct, the word "Beginning" is much more obviously explained by reference to the witness of the Baptist than by the supposition of a plan to write a continuation of the gospel beyond the earthly career of Christ. Moreover, on the supposition that Mark contemplated such a broad and comprehensive treatment of the career of Christ, it remains difficult to suppose that he could have regarded Mark 16:8 as comprising a suitable end to the section devoted to the earthly career of Jesus. While then some of these suppositions must be admitted to possess a degree of plausibility, they should be envisaged as serious possibilities only if, after Mark 16:1-8 is studied in connection with the evident aim and method of this evangelist, one is compelled to conclude that it could not have been intended as the conclusion of the gospel.[15]

As we have observed above (pp. 38f.), in presenting an out-

---

[15] This survey takes no notice of the theory that the original ending of Mark was suppressed deliberately because of its supposed contra-

line of the theory of Lohmeyer and Lightfoot with reference to Mark's occupation with Galilee, these critics understand Mark as bringing his gospel to a close with an intimation of a glorious consummation in Galilee, a consummation which they conceive of as the eschatological appearance of the Son of Man on the clouds of heaven. As a matter of fact, however, there were many isolated but vigorous instances of support for the view that the evangelist regarded Mk. 16:8 as the proper conclusion of his work, not indeed in connection with the drastic approach to Mark set forth in the theory of Lohmeyer and Lightfoot, but nevertheless with radical implications for the meaning of Mark and its relation to Matthew.[16] In spite of the untenability of the

---

diction of accounts of the resurrection in the other gospels, either with respect to the location of the appearance of Jesus or the nature of the resurrection. *Cf.* Harnack, *Die Chronologie*, I, 1897, pp. 696f.; Lake, *The Resurrection of Jesus Christ*, 1907, pp. 70f., 88ff., 143ff., 224ff.; Bultmann, *Geschichte d. syn. Tradition*, 1931, *pp.* 308ff.; Bacon, *Beginnings of the Gospel Story*, 1909, pp. 234ff. and *The Gospel of Mark*, 1925, pp. 187ff. For criticism see W. P. Armstrong, "The Place of the Resurrection Appearances of Jesus," in BTS, 1912, pp. 324ff.; Streeter, *op. cit.*, pp. 341f.; Branscomb, *op. cit.*, p. 310. Among the chief objections to this theory are the considerations that no trace whatever has been preserved of the suppressed ending, though it is presupposed that Mark had been circulating for some time, and that, on the assumption that Mark originally went on to say what took place after the situation reached in v. 8, the excision was not taken at a point, say a verse earlier, which would have made the operation less conspicuous.

[16] For Lohmeyer's discussion of the end of Mark, see *Markus*, pp. 358ff.; for Lightfoot's, see *Locality and Doctrine*, pp. 1-48. Wellhausen was apparently the first to maintain that Mk. 16:8 was the contemplated end of the gospel: *Das Evangelium Marci*, 1903, p. 146. Among others who have supported this view are E. Meyer, *Ursprung u. Anfänge des Christentums*, I, pp. 17f.; Bousset, *Kyrios Christos*, 1913, pp. 78f.; Creed in JThS, 1930, pp. 175ff. and *Luke*, 1930, p. 314; Jülicher-Fascher, *Einleitung in das N.T.*, 1931, pp. 309ff.; Goguel, *La Foi a' la Resurrection de Jesus*, 1933, pp. 176ff.; Enslin, *Christian Beginnings*, pp. 387f. Brun, *Die Auferstehung Christi*, 1925, is less decisive than the above.

Lohmeyer-Lightfoot hypothesis in general, and the unsoundness of many particular aspects of the arguments advanced by them and others who have insisted that Mk. 16:8 represents the intended conclusion of the gospel, we are convinced that this approach has been far from receiving the consideration which is due it. These radical interpretations have the merit of seeking to understand the single aspects of Mark in the light of the whole, and have moreover in particular brought to light certain data which show that Mk. 16:8, at least from a formal point of view, is not nearly as abrupt and unfinished as commonly supposed.

The advocates of the theory of accidental mutilation have frequently maintained that the concluding words of Mark 16:8, "for they were afraid," cannot possibly be conceived of as a complete sentence, much less as the conclusion of a paragraph or a book, and there have been conjectures that Mark originally wrote that "they were afraid of the Jews" or "they were afraid lest they should be thought mad" or the like. The Greek words, it may be admitted, easily leave an impression of incompleteness due to the position of "for" at the end, an impression which the English renderings seem largely to overcome.

If a Greek sentence demonstrably could have ended as Mk. 16:8 does, however, we consider that any objection, on formal grounds, to the interpretation of these words as the proper end of the paragraph and book would likewise disappear. And the fact is, as parallels from both classical and Hellenistic Greek demonstrate, that this construction, however unusual, by no means represents an impossible Greek sequence. No exhaustive survey of the stylistic parallels to the Marcan language is necessary here.[17] A few

---

[17] The best survey of stylistic parallels is to be found in Lightfoot, *op. cit.*, pp. 10-18. It draws chiefly from an article by R. R. Ottley in

examples will serve to illustrate the strength of the case against the supposed "impossible Greek" of Mk. 16:8. Perhaps the most striking parallel is found in the Septuagint rendering of Gen. 18:15. There Sarah's denial that she had laughed (when she heard the divine word to Abraham that she would bear a child) is motivated in the clause "for she was afraid," the Greek clause being ἐφοβήθη γάρ. Two of the clearest instances which indicate that a sequence like Mark's might end a paragraph as well as a sentence are found in the writings of Plato and of Justin Martyr. In Plato's *Protagoras* the last paragraph of an extensive speech offers as a reason for not laying a certain charge against two men that they were young, the final words of the discourse being νέοι γάρ.[18] Similarly Trypho concludes an indictment of the Christian confession of Christ with the words ἐσταυρώθη γάρ. The crucifixion was evidence, Trypho maintained, that the curse of the law had fallen upon him, for it was irreconcilable with the prophetic expectation of a glorious appearance of the Messiah.[19]

There is indeed no exact parallel in Mark, or in any other part of the New Testament, to the combination found in Mk. 16:8, but it is noteworthy that Mark often uses similar short clauses introduced by the postpositive γάρ ("for") to explain declarative statements. For example, after the transfiguration Peter is described as not knowing what he should answer, and this is motivated by the clause ἔκφοβοι γὰρ ἐγένοντο, which may be rendered "for they became afraid," and this is remarkably similar to the concluding clause of Mark both in form and meaning (Mk. 9:6). Less

---

JThS, July, 1926, and articles or notes by C. H. Kraeling, H. J. Cadbury and M. S. Enslin in JBL, 1925 and 1927.

[18] Protagoras, 328C; ed. Hermann, 1856, III, p. 158.
[19] Dial. c. Trypho 32:1, ed. Goodspeed, p. 126.

striking but significant instances of brief clauses introduced by γάϱ are found in Mk. 1:16; 3:21; 10:22; 16:4. Bearing upon the judgment that to be complete the final sentence would have required a complement of some kind, whether a direct object or a dependent clause, is the observation that Mark uses the verb "to fear" absolutely on five different occasions (Mk. 5:15, 33, 36; 6:50; 10:32). The final clause of Mark, accordingly, judged purely from a formal point of view, rather than requiring amplification, appears to be completely in keeping with Mark's style.

In view of these considerations, and the difficulties attached to the other hypotheses, it must be admitted that considerable attractiveness attaches to the judgment that Mark regarded 16:8 as constituting the conclusion of his work. Apparently insuperable obstacles appear, however, when one turns from the merely formal to the material aspects of the question, for this judgment has been associated with radical presuppositions as to the nature of the gospel of Mark, and with radical implications as to the meaning of the final section. The position developed by Lohmeyer and Lightfoot, for example, conceives of Mark's perspective as being sharply at variance with that of the other gospels, for it is maintained that the event to which Mark looks forward at the end is not an appearance of the resurrected Jesus but the eschatological consummation on the clouds of heaven, an event which, it is said, could only take place there. Earlier proponents of the view that Mark properly ends at 16:8, like Wellhausen, Meyer and Creed, have insisted that Mk. 16:7 disturbs the unity of the final section and must be understood as an interpolation into the tradition, and regard Mark as presupposing a quite different sequence of events from Matthew and Luke. The question remains then whether the view that Mk. 16:8 was the intended end of Mark can be dissociated from its radical implications, and be integrated with the witness of the gospel as a whole.[20]

The fear and silence of the women, with which Mark concludes his narrative of the resurrection, appears to place his account in violent opposition to that of Matthew which, after the command of the angel to the women, relates that they departed from the tomb with fear and great joy to inform the disciples as the angels had charged them (Mt. 28:8). If Mark ends on the notes of terror and disobedience, moreover, there is added to the difficulty of harmonizing Mark with Matthew the problem of explaining how a Christian writer could have been satisfied to conclude his publication of the glad tidings of Jesus Christ on this distressing note. Perhaps, however, to understand Mark in this fashion is radically to misunderstand him. With regard to Mark's statement that the women said nothing to anyone, due caution must be exercised lest more be read into this characterization than it will properly bear. In particular the conclusion is extreme that Mark implies that they were disobedient to the angelic command. No particular stress is placed upon this detail. Their silence is a subordinate feature of Mark's description of the emotional reaction which overcame the women in the face of a stupendous miracle and a startling revelation. Mark reaches a striking climax in depicting the state of their minds: looking into the tomb and seeing the angel, "they were amazed" (v. 5), but after the marvelous disclosure they fled, overwhelmed by trembling, astonishment and fear (v. 8). No hint is given that their silence continued indefinitely; Mark is not con-

---

[20] For treatments of the apparent conflict between Mk. 16:8 and Mt. 28:8 see especially Swete in his comment on the former passage and McNeile on the latter. *Cf.* also Rawlinson, *op. cit.*, p. 268.

cerned here to depict the later course of events but only to describe the over-powering immediate impression created by these stupendous events. What is more plausible then than that Mark's reference to their silence is included as a particular, subordinate aspect of the impact which these events made upon them, that he means to say that they were so overwhelmed by trembling, astonishment and fear that they were struck dumb? If this feature is viewed in the perspective of its immediate context, it does not appear necessary to regard it as anticipating the narration on Mark's part of the breaking of their silence on their arrival at the abode of the disciples, and much less to resort to the radical conjecture that the silence of the women was a detail included in the story of the empty tomb, in the period of its oral transmission, to disguise its late origin, and that Mark has awkwardly interpolated v. 7 into this story so as to obscure its original intent.

The conclusion that Mark intends to fasten the reader's attention upon the overwhelming experience of the women is entirely in keeping with his manner in the gospel as a whole. Amazement, astonishment and trembling often serve to express an attitude of awe, of godly fear, of obeisance in the presence of a manifestation of divine power or of a disclosure of divine authority. The verb translated "they were amazed" (ἐκθαμβεῖσθαι) (16:5) occurs only four times in the New Testament, and all of these are in Mark (9:15; 14:33; 16:5, 6); and the form without the prefix (θαμβεῖσθαι) likewise occurs only in Mark (1:27; 10:24, 32). In one of these instances Jesus himself is described as being amazed, in the garden of Gethsemane (14:33), but in all the others it serves to indicate a reaction of wonderment that Jesus' acts and teaching did not conform to a human pattern.

The word "trembling" (τρόμος) (v. 8) is used only here

in the gospels, but a cognate form is used in Mk. 5:33 and Lk. 8:47 to describe the fearful confidence of the woman who in the crowd behind Jesus came to avail herself of his divine power.

The word "astonishment" (ἔκστασις) (v. 8) is confined to Mark and Luke, the same being true of the cognate verb except for single instances in Matthew and II Corinthians. With the exception of its use to denote a divinely-produced trance (Acts 10:10; 11:15; 22:17), it is commonly employed to characterize reaction to divine actions or disclosures (Mk. 5:42; Lk. 5:26; Acts 3:10; *cf.* Mt. 12:23; Mk. 2:12; 6:51; Lk. 2:47; 8:56; 24:22; Acts 2:7, 12; 8:9, 11, 13; 10:45; 12:16). The positive connotation of the word appears most clearly perhaps in the records of the healing of the paralytic because of the amplification of the description of the manner in which the people responded to the action of Jesus. Luke describes the result most fully: "And astonishment took hold upon all, and they glorified God, and they were filled with fear, saying, We have seen wonderful things today" (Lk. 5:26). Mark likewise joins the glorification of God to the expression of astonishment (Mk. 2:12), while Matthew, not using the word "astonishment," says that "they were afraid and glorified God" (Mt. 9:8). The astonishment which accompanied amazement and trembling does not signify, therefore, any want of trust or any readiness to disobey; rather it converges with the other terms to convey the thought of overwhelming awe and reverence.

The term "fear" (φοβεῖσθαι) (v. 8) expresses various shades of meaning in Mark and the other gospels. It is frequently employed of the rulers' cowering fear of the people (*e.g.*, Mt. 21:26, 46; *cf.* Mk. 11:18) and of the selfish fear which is blameworthy because it points to lack of trust (*e.g.*, Mk. 4:41; 5:33; 6:50). But it is also used of reverential fear (*e.g.*, Mt. 10:28; Lk. 1:50; 18:2; 23:40; *cf.* Rom. 11:20; Col. 3:22). In the body of Mark apparently it is not found in the last sense, except perhaps in the instance of the woman who approached Jesus with fear and trembling (5:33). That reverential fear is in view in Mk. 16:8, however, seems to be demanded by its association with amazement, astonishment and trembling, which, as the survey of Marcan usage indicates, characteristically point to an attitude of deferential awe. The linking of these terms with fear then, like Matthew's conjunction of joy and fear (Mt. 28:8), shows that deep religious prostration, rather than terror or slavish fear, marks the women's response to the stupendous events of the early resurrection morning.

Impressive confirmation of the correctness of this conclusion is provided, in our judgment, in the Marcan account of the transfiguration. For there Mark uses an intensive form of the adjective "fearful" (ἔκφοβοι) to describe the response of Peter, James and John to the overwhelming transformation of Jesus and the appearance of Moses and Elijah, and further grounds the bewildered speech of Peter in the awe which overcame him and the others: "he knew not what to answer, for they became exceedingly afraid" (Mk. 9:6). This statement, in spite of certain formal differences, is remarkably parallel to Mk. 16:8 where we read that the women "said nothing to any one, for they were afraid." Peter indeed does not become completely inarticulate, but the implication is nevertheless present that the experience was so awesome as to preclude any fitting response.[21]

---

[21] Lightfoot, *op. cit.*, pp. 26ff., maintains that the women, in contrast to the failure of the disciples, appear in a very favorable light in Mark, as witnesses of the death, burial and resurrection of Jesus. Perhaps there is a measure of truth in this point of view, but, in view of the

If it be true that there is nothing incongruous in bringing a narrative to a conclusion on the note of reverential awe, the question still remains whether Mark's account adequately grounds such an overwhelming reaction on the part of the women. In the story of the transfiguration the sheer supernaturalism of what appeared before their eyes accounts fully for the response of the three intimate disciples. What event or what disclosure does Mark have in view in the final section as properly calling forth the overpowering experience of the women? The context indicates that this event is none other than the resurrection of Jesus, not a description of the resurrection itself nor yet of any appearance of Jesus to men, but the doubt-shattering witness of the empty tomb. Mark then is content to end his gospel with the story of the empty tomb. Now it should not be overlooked that Mark is not satisfied to present the phenomenon of the empty tomb as a bare fact. As an isolated fact it would have been powerless to bring conviction as to the resurrection of Jesus. The distinctive feature of the story is found in the consideration that this event is accompanied by its interpretation, not a human interpretation of the supernatural event but a divine explanation, for Mark undoubtedly regarded the angelic presence and disclosure as constituting a divine witness to the meaning of what had occurred. Their first response of amazement at the presence of the angel in the tomb of "Jesus, the Nazarene, who was crucified" elicits

---

large measure of parallelism which has been observed in the comparison of the transfiguration and resurrection narratives, it appears to be somewhat overdrawn. The women, moreover, occupy a subordinate position in the resurrection account since they, though afforded the first knowledge of the resurrection, serve as messengers to the disciples, whose epochal significance in the future has been suggested in various ways. *Cf.* Mk. 4:11ff.; 9:9; 14:28; 16:7.

the disclosure: *"he has risen; he is not here. Behold the place where they laid him!"* (v. 6). This stupendous fact in conjunction with its divinely-disclosed meaning was clearly adequate to ground the response of the women as indicated by Mark. The angelic message proceeds, indeed, to charge them to report to the disciples, and to recall the promise of Jesus that he would go before them to Galilee (v. 7). This charge and the message are also of momentous meaning, and remain to be considered below, but to seek to account for the response of v. 8 wholly or principally upon the basis of the contents of v. 7 is to fail to observe the disposition of the section as a whole. The reference to the future in Galilee is subordinate to the disclosure of what has just happened in Jerusalem. It is the fact of the resurrection itself, as evidenced by the empty tomb and the angelic interpretation, together perhaps with the presence of the divine messenger, which arouse astonishment, trembling and dumbness. When once the fact of the resurrection struck home, the intimation of his appearance to his disciples would hardly come as a new and baffling source of wonder.

Since then Mark 16:1-8 is disposed in such a manner as to place the emphasis squarely upon the awesome event of the resurrection of Jesus, there is no compulsion or warrant to seek to account for the awe of the women by reference to some other event. In particular, the view of Lohmeyer, supported with considerable reserve by Lightfoot, that the event Mark has in mind is nothing less than the eschatological consummation ushered in by the appearance of Christ on the clouds of heaven is far from being well grounded. This theory appeals to the general consideration that the gospel of Christ, as understood by Mark, must necessarily have included the proclamation of the eschatological consummation. Assuming that the expectation of the coming of Christ on the clouds of heaven formed a fixed element in the faith of the early church, and that a comprehensive publication of the Christian message would, and a brief summary might, include this element, it does not yet follow that Mark would have felt compelled to refer to it at the end of his gospel. This general question of Mark's conception of the elements of the gospel of Christ, in any case, cannot be dealt with except as one considers the particularities of Mark's plan for his own gospel as disclosed by its contents.

The eschatological perspective of Mark is to be observed, it is said, in the three-fold instruction of Jesus concerning his coming passion and resurrection (Mk. 8:31; 9:31; 10:33). On our part there is of course agreement that these references give unity and meaning to the entire passion narrative, which, as has been observed, receives singular emphasis in Mark's gospel. If now we ask how these references, which say nothing of the coming again of Christ, are indicative of the prospect of eschatological consummation, the answer that is forthcoming is that, in spite of the absence of mention of the return on the clouds of heaven, it is not to be overlooked that the suffering and resurrection are predicated of *the Son of Man*, and these events would therefore be regarded as forming the prelude to his forthwith manifestation as the Son of Man with great power and glory.[22] The claim is further made that this expectation of the

---

[22] Lightfoot, *op. cit.*, pp. 32, 41, 62. It may be noted here that Lightfoot virtually admits that this view of the gospel is not set forth unambiguously in Mark, for he frequently asserts that this evangelist had not yet achieved a perfect adjustment of the various notes or moments in the accomplishment of man's salvation, which he and his readers had found in Jesus Christ. Cf. *op. cit.*, pp. 30, 35, 42; *History and Interpretation*, p. 104.

consummation is in view in the eschatological discourse of Mk. 13, "which brings the reader to a topmost peak of expectation"; but since according to the gospel the passion of Christ must be fulfilled as a necessary prelude to his glory, it is not until Mk. 16:7 that "the reader once more finds himself on the heights of expectation."[23] And the intimation of Mk. 16:7: "there ye shall see him" points, in view of the future form of the verb "to see" (ὄψεσθε), precisely to the eschatological consummation rather than merely to an appearance of the resurrected Christ.[24]

There is, we think, a basic error in this whole approach to an understanding of Mark's eschatological perspective: it judges Mark's outlook more in terms of Jewish apocalyptic than in the light of indications provided by Mark himself. For Mark, while including definite intimations of a future manifestation of the Son of Man with great power and glory on the clouds of heaven, clearly underscores in his gospel the significance of the historical manifestation upon the earth of the heavenly Son of Man. There is an unrealized eschatology but also a realized eschatology. In three passages an appearance of the Son of Man which is still future to Mark and his readers is described (Mk. 8:38; 13:26; 14:62), but the ten other references to the Son of Man clearly imply that in his historical appearance Jesus was already the Son of Man. Moreover, the meaning which this title bears is not narrowly eschatological; it points to the heavenly, transcendent character of his person. His avowals of his right to forgive sins "upon the earth" and to exercise lordship over the sabbath spring from his consciousness of being the Son of Man (Mk. 2:10, 28). And

---

[23] Lightfoot, *Locality and Doctrine*, p. 75.
[24] *Cf.* Mk. 13:26; 14:62. See Lightfoot, *op. cit.*, pp. 39f., 63ff., 73f., but also 75f.; Lohmeyer, *Gal. und Jer.*, pp. 35f.

the whole of the record of the final journey to Jerusalem is pervaded by the teaching, not that he was to become the Son of Man by his appearance on the clouds after an interlude of suffering, but that the necessity of his suffering was found in the conviction that he, the Son of Man, had come for this very purpose.

> "The Son of Man came not to be ministered unto, but to minister, and to give his life a ransom for many" (10:45).
> "The Son of Man goeth as it is written concerning him; but woe to that man through whom the Son of Man is betrayed" (14:21).
> "The hour has come; behold, the Son of Man is betrayed into the hands of sinners" (14:41).

These passages, together with the references to his instruction concerning his death in Mk. 8:31; 9:31 and 10:33, establish unmistakably the conclusion that Mark describes Jesus as acting, not out of a consciousness of prospective dignity as the Son of Man, but as the one who in his entire historical life possesses the authority and power and dignity of the Son of Man, and yet is called upon to give up his life. In view of the transcendence of his person it was inconceivable that death should be the end; final vindication must come through the power of God. But the striking feature of the whole story is that the vindication in prospect is the resurrection on the third day. The final glory of the Messiah will indeed appear at the consummation, but the element of vindication that forms a part of the very warp and woof of the fabric of the passion narrative is the resurrection rather than the return of Christ (Mk. 8:31; 9:31; 10:33; *cf.* 9:9). Accordingly, the brief witness to the resurrection in Mk. 16:1-8 not only is completely congruous with the entire disposition of Mark's narrative but also provides the very climax which the attentive reader would have expected.

While therefore in Mark's perspective the resurrection is the event which forthwith will bring vindication and which consummates the earthly career of Christ, the coming on the clouds of heaven is set down in more isolated fashion. The disciples are warned to be watchful, but that warning is joined precisely to the consideration that they have no knowledge of the time of his coming (Mk. 13:32, 35). Two of the notices of the future coming are quite without temporal setting (Mk. 8:38; 14:62), and the context in the thirteenth chapter does not permit one to be much more definite as to the time when the prediction of Mk. 13:26 is to be fulfilled. Jesus warns against deception by false Christs and against supposing that wars and catastrophes in the earth are more than the beginning of sorrows (13:5-8, 21-23). Other signs are definite precursors of the end, but no intimation is given of the time when the gospel shall have been proclaimed to the nations and when "the abomination of desolation" shall be manifested (Mk. 13:10, 14; *cf.* 13:24 "in those days"). It is unwarranted to conclude therefore that the height of expectation to which Mark brings his readers, and without a reference to which the narrative would not be complete, is the coming on the clouds of heaven. The disclosure of the resurrection at the empty tomb brings the entire gospel to its awaited climax.

Brief attention must still be given to the argument on the basis of Mk. 16:7:

"But go, tell his disciples and Peter, He goeth before you into Galilee. There ye shall see him, just as he told you."

Although, apart from this verse, the future tense of "to see" is found in Mark only in two passages that refer to the coming of the Son of Man on the clouds of heaven

(13:26; 14:62),[25] the mere fact of formal coincidence is inadequate to ground the theory that Mark does not have in mind an appearance of the resurrected Jesus. The use of aorist passive forms of this same verb in I Cor. 15:5-8; Lk. 24:34; Acts 13:21 and 26:16 and of perfect and aorist active forms in I Cor. 9:1; Jn. 20:18, 20, 25, 29; Mt. 28:17; and Lk. 24:39, as Lightfoot himself admits, raises doubt whether the words "there ye shall see him" in Mk. 16:7 "refer explicitly and exclusively to the event of the parousia."[26]

Nor is it clear that the juxtaposition of the clause "just as he told you" involves a recollection of the prophecy of the eschatological return in Mk. 13:26. If Mk. 16:7 is compared with Mk. 14:28, as well as with Mk. 13:26, the advantage is altogether in favor of the view that a resurrection appearance is in prospect. Mark, it must be insisted, is completely silent in the concluding verses concerning a "coming in clouds with great power and glory" (Mk. 13:26; *cf.* 14:62), and this silence is left quite unaccounted for on the hypothesis that he had the parousia in mind.[27] Furthermore, Mark not only is silent about an appearance on the clouds, but specifically intimates that the appearance in prospect is an appearance *in Galilee where Jesus was to go before them*, implying continuity with the earthly career of Jesus rather than a heavenly manifestation of the Son of Man. The position of the word "there" connects the clause which it introduces so closely with the preceding clause that the whole might be paraphrased as follows:

---

[25] *Cf.* also I Jn. 3:2; Heb. 9:28; Rev. 1:7 and Testament of the Twelve Patriarchs, Zeb. 9:8.

[26] *Op. cit.*, p. 75.

[27] Lightfoot, *op. cit.*, pp. 39f. is quite inadequate in meeting this difficulty.

"In Galilee, where Jesus is going before you, ye shall see him, just as he told you." It would then appear that the clause "just as he told you" is not properly construed as having exclusive reference to the clause "there ye shall see him," and as recalling what Jesus had told them in Mk. 13:26. Since the word "there" subsumes the clause that precedes it, the clause "just as he told you" must be taken as applying to both preceding clauses, and therefore as having in view Mk. 14:28 rather than 13:26.[28] The language of Mk. 16:7 then, as well as the plan of the gospel as a whole, points to an awaited appearance of the resurrected Jesus.

Assuming that Mark brings his gospel to a close with the story of the empty tomb, and the angelic disclosure of an approaching appearance of Jesus in Galilee, there remains the difficulty, presented emphatically by the advocates of the supposition that the Marcan record is incomplete, that the gospel is silent concerning the fulfillment of the prophecy with which it ends. Since Mk. 14:28

---

[28] As a matter of fact Lightfoot, *op. cit.*, pp. 6of., 63f., following C. H. Turner, holds that the clause, "there ye shall see him", is parenthetical, and thus the words, "just as he told you," are understood as not pointing back more directly to Mk. 14:28 than to 13:26. He maintains, however, that Mk. 14:28 may have in view the parousia. But, as noted above, this is to fail to do justice to the sharp contrasts between the Galilean event and the parousia on the clouds of heaven.

Still another difficulty besetting this hypothesis is that when Mark wrote he and his readers still awaited the coming on the clouds with power and glory, but looked back some three decades to the appearances of the risen Jesus. The expected event in Galilee of which Mark speaks, which was to take place after both Jesus and the disciples had returned to Galilee, can hardly be regarded as still future at the time Mark wrote. If the event prophesied in Mk. 16:7 was the parousia, and the attitude of the women is due to the disclosure that it was to occur when once the disciples returned to Galilee, Mark could hardly fail to take some notice of the delay in its fulfillment.

and 16:7 point so definitely to a reunion in Galilee, can one successfully resist the conclusion that the gospel is incomplete? To a degree the charge of incompleteness and of abruptness may be admitted to be well taken. Nevertheless, in our judgment, if the characteristics of Mark are taken fully into account, the abruptness of the conclusion is not of such a nature as to require the hypothesis that originally there must have been more to this gospel than we now possess, or that at any rate Mark intended to write more.

The approach to Mark, and to the other gospels as well, has too long been under the spell of the Liberal point of view that the evangelists aimed to present biographies of Jesus Christ, or, if this be regarded as an overstatement, that they aimed to depict the historical career of Jesus of Nazareth. Any such view must find a stumblingblock in the "incompleteness" of Mark. The other extreme, to be sure, must also be avoided. In fleeing from the spell of Liberalism one stands in danger of falling into the embrace of radicalism. The radical criticism tends to shatter the gospels into a thousand isolated fragments and to isolate Jesus from the records, landing one in the morass of skepticism and agnosticism. The evidences of historical movement and progress in the life of Christ which the records present by no means need to be set aside by those who maintain that the aim of the evangelists, in presenting their witness to Christ, was something other than merely to supply a narrative of the origin, development and end of the life of a singular man.

The examination of the preface of Mark, as well as of the body of the gospel, has indicated with sufficient clearness that the evangelist is not attempting to provide his readers with anything like a complete account of the life of Christ. The preface is strikingly "abrupt" and "incomplete" in its introduction of Jesus to the readers, not clearly less so than the conclusion of the gospel in taking departure from him. In the preface there is nothing of the genealogy of Jesus or of his birth, no statement of the fact or nature of his incarnation, such as the other gospels provide. Jesus is simply there, and receives attestation as the Son of God through the testimony of a heavenly voice. In the conclusion likewise there are no elaborate accounts of the appearances of Jesus after the resurrection. The story of the resurrection is told tersely and even indirectly. The empty tomb implies it. The only direct witness is that which is provided by the heavenly messenger who explains what has happened and charges the women to remind the disciples of the word of Jesus spoken on the occasion of his imminent arrest and their consequent flight. If Mark can be satisfied to narrate so little concerning the beginnings of the life of Jesus, there is nothing to compel him to treat the conclusion at length. And, if the incarnation of the Son of God, stupendous as that fact must have been in Mark's thought, is not described nor placed in an historical setting but merely intimated, may not the awe-compelling event of the resurrection likewise be set forth indirectly and abruptly?

As a matter of fact, of course, strictly speaking Mark does not say farewell to Jesus. But even the other gospels, with the exception of Luke who had far broader literary aims, contain no parting scenes in spite of their more extensive treatment of the life of Christ after the resurrection. Matthew, who brings his narrative to a close in a great climax on a mount in Galilee, contains not a syllable to satisfy curiosity as to what happened to Jesus after the enunciation of the great commission. And John too, even if one finds its proper conclusion in chapter 20 rather than in chapter 21, stops in the midst of a scene where Jesus is busy talking to the disciples. And even Luke leaves the story of the ascension to the second part of his work, providing in anticipation only a brief reference to it at the end of his gospel (Lk. 24:51).[29] The publication of the glad tidings concerning Jesus Christ, as the evangelists conceived of it, did not therefore require an answer to all the questions that might be raised as to the end of the career of Jesus upon earth; they were concerned largely with the great events of the death and resurrection of Jesus and their significance for the salvation of men. This is true of Mark also, but he, more than the others, is absorbed with the story of the passion, and devotes less space to the resurrection. Nevertheless, in spite of the brevity of the account, the integral and meaningful place which the resurrection occupies in the glad tidings is no less clearly and emphatically set forth in Mark than in the other accounts.

---

[29] Even if with some editors, like Westcott and Hort, following the western text and Aleph, the clause, "and he ascended into heaven," is omitted, the ascension would still evidently be intimated by the words, "he was separated from them." On the shorter text, of course, it would be less obvious that Luke intended to indicate the end of the career of Jesus on earth. The longer text, it may be recalled, is defended, *e.g.*, by Streeter, *op. cit.*, pp. 142f., who in the main has been an exponent and defender of the theory of Westcott and Hort.

CHAPTER V

THE STRUCTURE OF THE EARLIER CHAPTERS OF MATTHEW

SYNOPSIS

Introduction.

Brief sketch of the state of critical opinion concerning Matthew; consequences for the treatment of Matthew.

I. *The Birth Narratives.*

Matthew's apparent interest in the origins of the historical life of Christ; yet the references to the time and place of the infancy show that the aim of the evangelist is not to deal with Christ's beginnings after the fashion of a secular historian; the examination of the data discloses positively that the evangelist's purpose is to depict Jesus as the messianic king whose history fulfills the Old Testament revelation and whose entrance into a land where a king of the Jews already reigned set up a crisis wherein through divine action the new-born king was preserved and came to dwell in Nazareth.

II. *The Baptism and Temptation.*

The relative indifference to locality and chronology.

III. *The Galilean Ministry.*

General characteristics: the Matthaean order of events most distinctive in this section; the marks of transition in Mt. 4:17 and 16:21; the stereotyped expressions at the end of the five great discourses.

1. The opening of the Galilean ministry: display of interest in the location, but this is dictated by Matthew's characteristic

appeal to prophecy; relative indifference to its chronological setting; indefiniteness in depicting the scene of the call of the disciples.

2. The initial phase (Mt. 4:23-9:34): its general disposition; setting of the sermon on the mount; detailed consideration of the narratives of healing activity: comparatively little interest in establishing the sequence of Jesus' acts within an itinerary is shown; the miraculous acts are viewed more as manifestations of messianic activity than as mere illustrations of a display of supernatural power.

3. A second phase (Mt. 9:35-16:12): its introduction in Mt. 9:35 compared with 4:23; few miracles, and only three healing acts, are recounted, but summary statements indicate that Matthew does not imply that such deeds were less characteristic of the later phase of his ministry; the emphasis upon Jesus' teaching; examination of the setting of the several incidents and discourses in this section; general conclusion as to the method of the evangelist; comparison between the two sections shows that, while the materials are not organized on the principle of development, his choice of materials is affected by his aim to disclose the growing intensity of hostility to Jesus as Jesus came nearer to the climax of his career.

THE Gospel according to Matthew is characteristically approached in our day in a fashion sharply at variance with the methods which we have observed to be in vogue with reference to Mark. The chief reason for this divergence is no doubt to be discovered in the fact that Matthew is not allowed any great measure of independence as a literary work, but is held to have been shaped in its main features by the sources which its author employed. Matthew is regarded as being essentially a revised edition of Mark. There is indeed one important qualification of this characterization, namely, that this evangelist, in his rôle of editor, also used another source, the (hypothetical) sayings-source, usually designated as "Q," from which most of his record of the teaching of Jesus is supposed to have been drawn.

The origin of Matthew, unlike that of Mark, is traced then to the editorial assimilation and revision of written sources rather than to an independent treatment of the career of Christ on the basis of firsthand knowledge of the tradition of the gospel. So long as the priority of Matthew to the other gospels was maintained, the approach to its interpretation was of a quite different sort. The Tübingen School, for example, treated Matthew in independent fashion, and concluded that it was written to express and vindicate the point of view of a Judaizing party within the early church. Since this approach is now regarded as outmoded, and the approach to all the gospels has come under the domination of the Marcan Hypothesis, Matthew is studied by way of a comparison with Mark, and the chief questions of interpretation have centered about the extent and character of the divergences of Matthew from Mark.

There has indeed not been complete agreement as to their divergences. In the thought of some the divergences apparently are so great that Matthew virtually becomes the representative of a distinctive theological school; in the opinion of others the differences affect the total product in a much less drastic fashion. The decision on this point is bound up with the varying judgments as to the place which its distinctive viewpoint occupies within the broad development of primitive Christianity, some critics connecting Matthew definitely with a Palestinian phase of the development, others insisting that this gospel clearly implies a situation in which Christianity had been transferred to Greek soil, while still others seek to mediate between these contrasting estimates, either by associating it with a manifestation of Christianity in the environment of Hellenistic Judaism or by the supposition that the completed gospel brings together in unreconciled fashion various divergent traditions and theological perspectives. Among the features which are often held to point to a development within a characteristically Jewish Christianity may be mentioned the presence of a vivid eschatological outlook and the emphasis upon the authority of the law and the prophets, while the universalism of the gospel, expressed conspicuously in the "great commission," together with the "ecclesiastical tone" of the gospel is regarded by many as marking an evolution to an advanced stage which is no longer controlled by the needs and interests of the earliest Christianity in Palestine.

On this perspective obviously we shall not expect to encounter any insistence upon the tradition of apostolic origin. The conclusions as to the extent of the divergence of Matthew from Mark are held to exclude that possibility. The only concession to tradition on this score is that there is an allowance on the part of some that this evangelist may have employed some apostolic, specifically Matthaean, source in addition to Mark, either the source "Q" (which some scholars think Papias had in view in his remarks about Matthew) or possibly a Matthaean document of a somewhat different character.[1] In any case Matthew as it has come down to us is viewed, where he diverges from Mark, as being in the main inferior to Mark as a witness to Christ, and as representing a more advanced stage of Christological reflection, a heightening of reverence for Jesus, which has

---

[1] K. and S. Lake, *Introduction*, p. 26, *e.g.*, think it probable that Papias has "Q" in mind when he speaks of the oracles of the Lord composed by Matthew. A conspicuous feature of the four-document hypothesis of Streeter is that the apostle Matthew was the probable author of the hypothetical source "M" but not of the completed gospel.

removed him further from the true humanity of the prophet of Nazareth.

In our study of Matthew we are not concerned therefore with any critical attempts to explain this gospel as offering a new and creative expression of Christianity, and our method of discussion will accordingly follow somewhat different lines from those pursued in the instance of Mark. The evidence of Matthew will disclose its character in a more positive fashion. On the other hand, we are of the opinion that greater progress will be made by taking cognizance of some of the leading features of the modern criticism of the details of Matthew than if we ignored them, and we shall therefore likewise compare Matthew's witness with that of Mark at many points. As in the study of Mark, the proper approach appears to be an initiation of our investigation with a survey of the framework of the gospel, for only on the background of an understanding of the evangelist's delineation of the historical career of Christ can one expect to come face to face with the ultimate issue of his distinctive witness to Christ. In this chapter we shall confine our survey largely to the birth narratives and the account of the Galilean ministry. A consideration in some detail seems to be demanded because the divergence from Mark is most conspicuous in this portion of Matthew, and its scrutiny should disclose quite readily the distinctive approach of this evangelist.

Whereas Mark introduces Christ, as it were, like Melchizedek, "without father, without mother, without genealogy, having neither beginning of days nor end of life," Matthew's portrayal seems concerned to accredit Christ by dwelling upon his illustrious ancestry and telling of the extraordinary origin of his life as the son of the virgin Mary. Moreover, in contrast to Mark's brief delineation of the career of the Baptist, and of the baptism of Jesus, and his meagre account of the temptation extending to merely thirty words, the Matthaean narrative is remarkably full. An inquirer as to the origins of the historical career of Jesus, whose knowledge was limited to what he read in Mark, would hardly begin to find satisfaction for his historical curiosity, but turning to Matthew's introduction of Jesus he would be grateful that he had encountered a writer who seemed to sense some of his questions and had endeavored to supply an answer.

Matthew undoubtedly approaches his subject from a broad historical perspective. As he proceeds, his purpose to present Jesus as standing squarely in the center of the historical movement of revelation and redemption becomes more and more conspicuous. At the very beginning he introduces him as "Son of David, son of Abraham" (Mt. 1:1; *cf.* 1:20). As Abraham's seed and as royal son of David's line Jesus is seen to be no isolated figure, no mere innovator, but one who can be adequately measured only in terms of what has gone before. Whether, however, Matthew really approached the life of Christ to satisfy curiosity about Christ and to present as fully as possible the course of his life is a question which can be disclosed only on the basis of a detailed examination of the chronological and topographical data.

Although Matthew begins, as a secular biographer might, with a genealogical table and the narration of the fact and circumstances of the birth of Jesus, it soon becomes obvious that his aim is not to place the beginnings of this life in a specific setting within the framework of secular history. Neither the genealogy nor the description of the birth states in any precise way where or when he was born. The structure of the genealogical table does indicate incidentally the relative time which had elapsed since the Babylonian captivity. Moreover, one learns from the birth narrative that follows that it took place before the death of king Herod, but that this Herod was Herod known as the Great, who reigned 40-4 B.C., is left to be inferred from the reference to his son Archelaus (Mt. 2:22). The account of the birth of Jesus in Mt. 1:18-25 likewise says nothing of its location. That it occurred in Bethlehem appears first in the story of the magi that follows, where it is introduced, not as a fact narrated for its own sake, but as an integral element of the story of the inquiry made by the magi concerning the precise place where the expected king should be born, the reply being derived from a prophecy of Micah (5:2). This narrative reaches its high point in their adoration of the child in Bethlehem, and ends with their departure for their own country, to the frustration of Herod's evil plan.

How, in spite of Herod's effort to make secure the tenure of the Herodians upon the Jewish royal throne by destroying him who had been hailed as the new-born King of the Jews, the life of the child was preserved is now set forth (Mt. 2:13-16). The flight into Egypt follows, not because Matthew is concerned with Jesus' travels as a significant feature of his early experience, but because this journey was undertaken by divine command and in accordance with divine prophecy. However much Herod might plot and scheme, the child remained secure under the special protection of him who had spoken in the Scriptures of the Old Testament concerning the coming of the Son of David into the world.

The full measure of Herod's hostility is next set forth in

the account of the massacre of the innocents, which is also described as the fulfillment of prophecy. The setting for this narrative, as demanded by the previous disclosures, is Bethlehem, but the time is not closely joined to what precedes. Nearly two years must have elapsed between the appearance of the star (2:7) and the slaying of the children (2:16). It is instructive to observe at this point the indefiniteness with which Matthew often uses the temporal adverb "then" (τότε), a word which he employs some ninety times, while Mark, *e.g.*, uses it only six times. In employing this word to introduce v. 16 he obviously does not have in view the precise time of the preceding verse, which refers to the death of Herod, nor of the flight into Egypt, which forms the main theme of the preceding section. The qualifying clause in Mt. 2:16, "when he saw that he was mocked of the magi," indicates that this verse is understood as standing in continuity with v. 12 which narrates the departure of the magi. Nevertheless, since some time must be allowed following their departure for Herod's discovery of what had taken place, the adverb "then" in this instance has no more precise significance than the English word "afterward."

The final episode relates the return from Egypt to "the land of Israel," and explains why, instead of settling in the region of his birth in Judea, he came to dwell in Nazareth of Galilee. That Jesus was a Galilean is of course not without great meaning for the understanding of the rest of the life and ministry of Christ. Here therefore there is clearly displayed an interest in geography as essential to the clarification of the future development. But even in this account there recurs the characteristic appeal to prophecy as determining in advance the course of his life. Moreover, there is no particular interest in fixing chronologically the early years of the life of Jesus. Incidentally the limits for the stay in Egypt are set by the notice of the death of Herod (4 B.C.) and of the end of the reign of Archelaus (6 A.D.), but these data are introduced apparently only to explain the course of his journey, and provide no information to satisfy one's curiosity as to the exact age of Jesus when he returned to Galilee.

The method of Matthew comes clearly into view therefore in the first two chapters. Although he dwells on the genealogy, birth and early life of Jesus, he by no means approaches his subject as a secular biographer. His purpose is to depict Jesus as the messianic king, the Son of David, whose history fulfills the revelation of the Old Testament. In accordance with this aim he selects his materials, each of the brief episodes pointing back to a particular prophecy of the Old Testament (*cf.* Mt. 1:23; 2:6, 15, 18, 23). Besides these frequent references to what had been spoken of old, however, the evangelist also explains the early movements of Christ by a consideration of the contemporary situation, selecting particularly the tradition of the manner in which the appearance of the new king affected Herod, the king of the Jews, and shows how in the face of Herod's unrelenting hostility it came about, under the divine protection, that Jesus escaped and came to live in Nazareth of Galilee. It is the tension set up by the entrance of the new Son of David into a land where a king of the Jews already ruled that forms the background of, and provides the continuity in, Matthew's birth narrative.

Matthew now leaps from the earliest years of the life of Christ to the time immediately preceding his public ministry when Jesus underwent baptism at the hands of John and was tempted by the devil (Mt. 3:1-4:11). In order to provide a setting for the understanding of John's relation to Jesus, Matthew prefaces the account of the baptism of Jesus with a summary of the Baptist's appearance and message. In spite of the long interval which separates Jesus' entrance into Nazareth after his return from Egypt and the ministry of John, Matthew nevertheless gives the impression of temporal continuity by the introductory phrase "in those days" (Mt. 3:1). The time in view is indeed the time of Jesus' life in Nazareth, which has been referred to as having begun after the close of his sojourn in Egypt. It appears however that the expression by no means is meant to be understood as a precise temporal phrase; it evidently must be construed as defining only in the most general terms the time when John began his activity. The equivalent expression is used similarly in the Old Testament (*cf.* Ex. 2:11, 23; Isa. 38:1).[2] Likewise, if one bears in mind the indefiniteness of the adverb "then" as employed in Mt. 2:16, which was noticed above, as well as the summary character of this section and the preceding context, it becomes probable that the use of "then" in Mt. 3:5 and 3:13, and as well perhaps in Mt. 4:1, is not intended to define the exact moment of the occurrence of the events described.

These events clearly took place in Judea (Mt. 3:1, 5; 4:12) and the Jordan River is specified as the scene of the baptisms of John (Mt. 3:6, 13). But for the rest the narrative is vague, indicating nothing as to the exact locale in Judea and at the Jordan where the incidents occurred. John appears in "the desert of Judea" (Mt. 3:1), in fulfillment of Isaiah's description of "a voice of one who cries in the desert." And after his baptism Jesus was led "into the desert" where he became hungry and the devil tempted

---

[2] *Cf.* Meyer *ad loc.;* Klostermann, *Matthäusevangelium*, p. 9.

him to change stones into loaves of bread (Mt. 4:1). There is no evidence that Matthew could not have been more precise in describing these scenes. In accordance with his purpose it was sufficient that the general locale be stated, the references to the desert being included because of the contribution which they made to an understanding of the events with which he was concerned.

We come now to a consideration of the broad features of the public ministry of Jesus as recorded in Matthew (Mt. 4:12ff.). Its broad disposition is remarkably in agreement with the Marcan outline. We shall observe, however, that far greater diversity appears in the account of the Galilean ministry than of the events following upon the confession of faith in Caesarea Philippi, and our survey of the ministry may accordingly be confined largely to the former.

The distinctiveness of Matthew also appears from the observation that he makes his readers more aware than Mark does of certain points of transition. This characteristic is disclosed most clearly in the manner in which Matthew marks new beginnings in 4:17 and 16:21:

"From that time began Jesus to preach and to say, Repent ye, for the kingdom of heaven is at hand."
"From that time began Jesus to show unto his disciples that he must go unto Jerusalem, and suffer many things of the elders and chief priests and scribes, and be killed, and the third day be raised up."

Now Mark uses similar language in 8:31, and indicates with sufficient clarity the beginning of the Galilean ministry in 1:14, but the two-fold division does not appear with the same explicitness as in Matthew. Matthew like Mark therefore divides the public ministry into two periods, the period before the confession of Peter and the period after it. Still the transition is not to be understood as marking an absolutely new phase of his activity, for the new instruction by no means presupposes that the older form of teaching ceased. In 4:17 Matthew sets forth in the broadest possible terms the message of the public ministry as the proclamation of the coming of the kingdom and the necessity of a radical adjustment on the part of his hearers if they are to participate in it. Jesus is nowhere again described as explicitly calling men to repentance, but he continues to be occupied with the coming of the kingdom (*cf. e.g.,* Mt. 18:1ff., 23; 19:12ff., 23ff.; 20:1ff.; 23:28ff., 33ff.; 22:2ff.; 23:13ff.; 24:14; 25:1ff.), and everywhere there is a continued insistence upon the disqualification of his hearers, in their present state, from entering the kingdom. The pronouncements concerning the passion and resurrection which begin with Mt. 16:21 must therefore be understood, not as a substitute for the proclamation of the kingdom, but as supplementary to it.

That Matthew is a gospel which shows clear signs of careful planning and arrangement of its contents, and that he uses stereotyped expressions to invite his readers' attention to its structure, appears even more conspicuously from a consideration of the manner in which he concludes the five great discourses which distinguish this gospel. The conclusions of the sermon on the mount (Mt. 5:3-7:27), of the address to the disciples (10:5-42), of the parabolic exposition of the kingdom (13:3-52), of the teaching on the meaning of discipleship (18:3-35), and of the eschatological discourse (24:4-25:46) are marked by the repetition of the same formula:

"And it came to pass, when Jesus had finished these words, the multitudes were astonished at his teaching, for he was teaching them as having authority, and not as their scribes" (7:28).
"And it came to pass, when Jesus had finished commanding his twelve disciples, he departed thence to teach and preach in their cities" (11:1).

"And it came to pass, when Jesus had finished these parables, he departed thence" (13:53).
"And it came to pass, when Jesus had finished these words, he departed from Galilee, and came into the borders of Judea beyond the Jordan" (19:1).
"And it came to pass, when Jesus had finished all these words, he said to his disciples, Ye know that after two days the passover cometh, and the Son of Man is delivered up to be crucified" (26:1).

Although the second, third and fourth of these expressions serve to introduce a new scene of activity, they evidently are not meant to conclude a definite stage of his ministry. The expression in Mt. 19:1 might indeed seem to conflict with the view which finds in Mt. 16:12 the proper end of the Galilean ministry, but in Matthew as in Mark the momentous events in Caesarea Philippi form unescapably the turning point in the gospel, and the references to Galilee which follow must be interpreted as incidental to the narration of the journey to Jerusalem.[3] Only the final reference (Mt. 26:1), which tells of the imminent approach of the passover, serves to introduce a new stage in the history of Christ, but even this is but a subordinate phase of the unfolding of the broad story of the passion. Consequently, while the particular setting of each of these great discourses requires to be noted within the larger structure of the gospel, these five expressions do not involve any significant modification of the divisions indicated by Mt. 4:17 and 16:21.[4]

On the background of our survey of the broad structure

---

[3] See above p. 27.

[4] The significance of these five discourses for Matthew's conception of the structure of his gospel is, we think, exaggerated by the view of Bacon, as set forth in *Studies in Matthew*, 1930, which conceives of Matthew as consisting of five books of the Commandments of Jesus, corresponding to the Law of the Old Testament. *Cf.* also Enslin, *Christian Beginnings*, pp. 389, 401f.

of Matthew we can now proceed to consider in greater detail the method of this evangelist in narrating the public ministry of Christ. In examining the treatment of the Galilean ministry, it is striking that Matthew marks the appearance in Galilee as dictated by a divine word of prophecy to Isaiah (Mt. 4:14ff.). It had been foretold that in Galilee of the Gentiles, to those who were sitting in darkness and in the region and shadow of death, there would appear a great light. That the center of this activity is Capernaum on the sea, in the land of Zebulun and Naphtali, rather than Nazareth, is also connected with the prophetic testimony. The prominence of Capernaum as a center of activity is also attested by Mark (Mk. 1:21), but only Matthew, because of his method of relating the history of Christ to the revelation of the Old Testament, speaks of its precise location.

While then it appears that Matthew manifests a special interest in the theatre of the public ministry of Jesus, a similar concern in its exact chronology is lacking. Whether the interval between the temptation in the desert of Judea and the ministry in Galilee was as brief as a few days or as long as several months is not indicated. The return to Galilee is fixed by the report of the arrest of the Baptist, which however itself is left undetermined chronologically (*cf.* Mt. 14:3ff.), and some time must be allowed after the return to Galilee for his entrance upon his work in Capernaum. Matthew therefore is relatively unconcerned about the chronological framework of the ministry. The facts do not justify the conclusion that the evangelist was clearly ignorant of the true course of events or dealt arbitrarily with the materials at his disposal. Because the Baptist was taken prisoner by Herod Antipas, whose realm included

Galilee, it does not follow that Matthew betrays ignorance of the true situation when he implies that Jesus entered Galilee following upon the report of John's arrest.[5] Matthew does not state why Jesus began his ministry in Galilee after John's arrest, but, in view of the knowledge which he displays in Mt. 14:3ff., it is altogether likely that he knew of the extent of the domain of Antipas. The place which Jesus ascribes to John as concluding the era of the law and the prophets, the period before the coming of the kingdom of God, suggests that Matthew has in mind the thought that the violent cessation of John's activity was the signal of the entrance of Jesus upon his proclamation of the kingdom in Galilee (*cf*. Mt. 11:11ff.).

After stating in summary fashion the proclamation of the kingdom which occurred in Capernaum of Galilee, Matthew relates the call of the first disciples along the shore of the Sea of Galilee (4:18-22). One may perhaps infer that the location of this event was somewhere near Capernaum, but no specific place is mentioned and there are no indications of the time when these fishermen left their secular occupations to follow Jesus.

Matthew's method is observed in unmistakable fashion from a consideration of the narration of an initial phase of the ministry described in Mt. 4:23-9:34. This ministry is first described briefly in terms of locale, kinds of activity and impact upon the people: he went about the whole of Galilee, bringing his message and healing the sick, with the

---

[5] This is Schmidt's charge, *op. cit.*, p. 35. Nor is his judgment well-taken when he accuses Matthew of a lack of realism in allowing Jesus to flee from the domain of Archelaus to that of another Herod. It is altogether possible that the particularly bad reputation of Archelaus was known and influenced the actions of Joseph and Mary long before he was deposed.

result that his reputation extended beyond the borders of Galilee, and great crowds, not only from Galilee but also from the regions to the east and south, followed him. Thereupon Matthew illustrates the activity of Jesus in detail, selecting the sermon on the mount as an example of his preaching (Mt. 5:3-7:27) and several works of healing as examples of the manifestations of his power and mercy (8:1-9:34). The latter for the most part find their parallel in Mark, but the discourse is quite unique, and therefore the manner in which it is introduced is highly meaningful for our understanding of Matthew's treatment of the public ministry.

It is widely maintained that the sermon on the mount is clearly Matthew's own composition based upon the collection and arrangement of materials which had come down in oral or written form. The discussion of that question belongs properly to the field of literary criticism, with which we are not immediately concerned, but it is worthwhile to stress the fact that Matthew himself presents it as a single discourse, spoken at a particular time and place (*cf.* Mt. 5:1; 8:1). The fact remains, however, that the particular setting of the sermon is not stated beyond the notice that it was spoken on "the mountain" (Mt. 5:1; 8:1). In view of the summary character of the preceding context it must be admitted that Matthew does not definitely localize the discourse. Perhaps his interest in specifying the place where Jesus sat was merely to indicate that Jesus occupied a conspicuous place where he could easily command the attention of the crowd (*cf.* Mt. 15:29). Now the fact that the exact place of the discourse is not mentioned, and it is represented as occasioned by no other fact than that crowds were present (Mt. 7:28; 5:1), centers attention upon its character as illustrative and typical of the teaching of Jesus on the subjects treated.[6]

If signs of a definite itinerary in Galilee are lacking in the record of the ministry as far as the end of chapter 7, the opposite impression seems to be created by the account of the incidents in the section which extends from Mt. 8:1 to 9:34. There are many references to time and place, some specific and others general. Nevertheless, when these data are carefully scrutinized, it remains doubtful that Matthew conceives of this section as a travel narrative.

The healing of the leper (Mt. 8:2-4) is not provided with a precise setting, although the fact that Mt. 8:1 opens a new chapter and is commonly printed as a part of the paragraph dealing with this incident may create the impression that Matthew intends to place the act of healing in the proximity of the foot of the mountain. This verse is of a summary character, however, and may quite aptly be grouped with Mt. 7:28, 29 as a part of the description of the impact which Jesus' message made upon the crowds. In any case Matthew does not say that the leper came to Jesus near the mountain, but that great crowds followed him after he came down from the mountain. Even if Mt. 8:1 were intended to provide the setting for the incident that follows, therefore, it would not do so more precisely than to intimate that the healing act occurred during a period when Jesus was being followed by crowds, some time after the delivery of the discourse on the mountain.[7]

---

[6] *Cf.* Mt. 7:28f. with Mk. 1:22 and Lk. 4:32. The latter associate the people's expression of astonishment at the authority of Jesus with his teaching in the synagogue in Capernaum, which is however not quoted.

[7] There is therefore not sufficient evidence for Schmidt's charge, *op. cit.*, p. 64, that Matthew, like Luke in 5:12 (*cf.* "one of their cities"), localizes the incident because of the lack of definiteness which was felt to be present in Mark 1:40-45.

It seems better, however, in keeping with what has previously been observed as to Matthew's method and plan, to regard the episode of the healing of the leper as intended simply as a single, powerful illustration of the miraculous activity of Jesus as he went about in Galilee.

The next story, the narrative of the faith of the centurion, is indeed localized (Mt. 8:5-13). It does not follow, however, that Matthew intends to fix the order of its occurrence. When it is recalled that Capernaum had become the center of his activity (Mt. 4:13), it is not at all plausible to suppose that Matthew means to imply that he entered Capernaum on only one occasion. Nor can one properly insist that this was the first visit to Capernaum after the sermon on the mount. The language of Mt. 8:5 may fairly be paraphrased as follows: "And once when he entered into Capernaum, a centurion came to him . . ." It was eminently fitting that in Capernaum, where Jesus' reputation as a mighty healer was well-known, and might well have reached the ears even of non-Jews, that a Gentile officer should have disclosed such implicit confidence in him and in his saving power.[8]

In similar fashion Matthew's account of the healing of Peter's mother-in-law contains nothing that demands or even suggests that it took place following the action which has just been reviewed. The entrance into the house of

---

[8] Schmidt, *op. cit.*, pp. 71ff., admits that Capernaum is mentioned as an integral element of the narrative, but argues on internal grounds, both from its implications as to previous miraculous activity (v. 10) and its universalism (vv. 11, 12), that there are serious chronological difficulties in its position here. Whatever one might judge as to the historicity of the universalism here attributed to Jesus, it is not proved that Matthew would have felt any difficulty. But the statement of v. 10 may well confirm the view that the evangelist does not intend to describe the miraculous activity of Jesus in strict chronological sequence.

Peter noted in Mt. 8:14, like the entrance in Capernaum in 8:5, is not offered as marking a stage in the course of Jesus' movements. The participle employed here qualifies the main verb which tells of what Jesus encountered when he entered the house. In the former instance attention is centered upon the fact that a centurion came to him when he entered into Capernaum, beseeching him on behalf of his child. And here, in relating a miracle of a less spectacular character, the evangelist states that Jesus saw, when he had entered into the house of Peter, the prostrate and ill condition of his wife's mother, and that through his healing touch she was able to minister to him in the home to which he had apparently retired for privacy and rest. That Jesus saw the need to be supplied in Peter's household at the time when he entered is an integral detail of the story which heightens the impression of Jesus' power to act miraculously. References like the entrance to Peter's house may not be fairly construed, therefore, as introduced in the interest of fitting the individual incidents into a chronological and topographical framework which the evangelist has found necessary to invent or which he has taken over with modifications from another.

To the story of the miracle in the house of Peter Matthew joins intimately, as do also the other synoptists, a summary of many other miracles of healing performed on the evening of the same day, perhaps while he was still at the house of Peter (8:16). The mention of "evening," it should be noted, is not clearly due to any concern on Matthew's part to observe the passing of time; he has not previously mentioned an earlier hour in a particular day, and has not been outlining the ministry in terms of days or even of longer periods of time. He must be understood as including this reference to the time of day because of the help it affords in making the account intelligible. The delay until evening was apparently dictated by the needs of those to whom Jesus ministered. That the crowds of sick and afflicted were not brought before evening was due, it may be supposed, to the inadvisability of their removal from places of rest during the heat of the day.

There now follows an account of a trip across the sea, and the various stages are clearly marked: there is first the expressed purpose to go to the other side (Mt. 8:18); the embarkation and voyage are described (vv. 23-28); the arrival in the land of the Gadarenes and what occurred there next come in view (vv. 28-34); and finally his return across the sea to his own city (9:1). Nevertheless, these data do not permit the conclusion that Matthew is concerned to present as full an account as possible of Jesus' travels. He is illustrating the miraculous activity of Jesus, as he had previously illustrated his teaching. Spectacular instances of Jesus' power in cleansing a leper and the son of the centurion, besides many exorcisms and other cures not particularly described, have been mentioned. Now, evidently, he wishes to join another instance of the amazing power of Christ, his power over a mighty tempest in the sea, and it is this purpose which determines the disposition of the entire section. To provide the setting for this miracle of the sea, which irresistibly focused attention upon the transcendent person with whom the disciples had to do, Matthew relates Jesus' plan to leave the crowds and sail away with his disciples, and after he has told of the safe arrival on the other side he introduces, as another instance

---

[9] *Cf.* Mt. 14:15 and 26:20 where the same participial phrase is employed to designate the time suitable for the evening meal, and Mt. 20:8 similarly for the time when the work of the laborers was completed.

of Jesus' healing activity, the story of the exorcism of the demon-possessed Gadarenes.

Matthew's distinctive introduction to the account of the stilling of the tempest is particularly illuminating for an understanding of his literary procedure. Verse 18 is not intended to mark continuity with the preceding narrative, for two distinct attitudes towards the crowds are in evidence. In the preceding account he mercifully heals their diseases; here the thronging of *a* crowd on a particular occasion awakens the desire to escape, at least for a time.[10] Matthew therefore, it appears again, cannot have in view strict chronological succession, but is supplying the background for the narrative of the miracle of the tempest. The import of his language then is as follows: "And on a certain occasion, when Jesus saw a crowd about him, he gave commandment to depart to the other side of the sea."

This view of the meaning of Mt. 8:18 receives confirmation from a consideration of Matthew's introduction in vv. 19-22 of Jesus' replies to individual followers. These verses seem to be abruptly introduced into a section that treats of Jesus' miraculous deeds. The previously recorded incidents, to be sure, have included significant teaching of Jesus (*cf.* 8:4, 10-12), but in these instances Jesus' words

---

[10] The reading "a crowd" is indeed not supported unanimously in Mt. 8:18. The reading "great crowds," found in A.V. and R.V. is supported by the Latin tradition and by the mass of the late mss., but otherwise is not strongly attested, and moreover may be explained from the reference in Mt. 8:1. Westcott and Hort and the Nestle edition, following Codex Vaticanus and the Sahidic Version, adopt the reading "a crowd." This reading best accounts for the origin of the reading "crowds" in Codex Sinaiticus and certain other testimonies, as for the reading "a great crowd" found in Codex Washington, the old Syriac, and several cursives. In any case, even "many crowds" is an indefinite expression, and stands in contrast with the preceding context.

constitute integral elements of the narratives of his mighty deeds, introduced in order to center attention upon the meaning of what had happened. Mt. 8:19-22, on the other hand, gives the impression of being an aside, which might have been omitted without detracting from the impact of the narrative as a whole. If however Mt. 8:18 is understood as providing the distinctive background of the miracle of the tempest, the introduction of vv. 19-22 may be explained as illuminating Jesus' desire to leave the crowd. There were many who crowded about him, and freely expressed loyalty to his cause, but who showed no sign of awareness of the cost of discipleship in terms of privation and self-denial. Consequently, there are joined in these two contexts quite diverse attitudes of Jesus: there was pity and mercy for them in their distress, but also a turning away from them, a not intrusting himself unto them, in the face of their superficial and insincere assertions of loyalty.

The conventional position of Mt. 9:1, at the opening of the chapter and paragraph which tell of the paralytic whose sins were forgiven, gives the impression that the evangelist means to place this story at a point following the stilling of the tempest and the exorcism of the Gadarene demoniacs, and thus places his record in contradiction with the order of Mark and Luke. The general insecurity of the topographical and chronological references would then be indicated. It is by no means clear, however, that this verse, like Mt. 8:1, is not more properly construed with the preceding context. Since the men of the city of the Gadarenes besought Jesus to leave their borders, the record of the journey back across the sea to his own city would serve to round off the sequence which began with Jesus' expressed desire to cross over the sea to the region beyond.[11] That Jesus should have returned to his own city, that is, to Capernaum, requires no further motivation, since it has constantly been in view as the center of his activity (Mt. 4:13).

In addition to the story of the healing of the paralytic, Matthew submits four other examples of Jesus' demonstration of power: the raising of the daughter of a ruler, the healing of a woman with an issue of blood, the restoration of sight to two blind men, and the exorcism of a deaf demoniac (9:18-34). These four acts are presented as following in close chronological succession, although the encounter with the blind men, introduced by the expression, "And as he passed by from thence," allows clearly for the possibility of other happenings after Jesus left the house of the ruler (cf. Mt. 9:20, 23, 27, 31). The references to location are less clear, the place of the home of the ruler and of the house where he privately touched the eyes of the blind not being specified. The question of the connection of these four events with the healing of the paralytic is complicated by the introduction in Mt. 9:9-17 of incidents of a different character: the call of Matthew, the answer of Jesus to the question of the Pharisees concerning his fellowship with publicans and sinners, and his reply to the inquiry

---

[11] That Mt. 9:2 begins with the expression "and behold" (καὶ ἰδού) does not constitute an objection to the conclusion that a new paragraph is being introduced, as its use in 19:16 indicates. New subject matter is often introduced by καί. Cf. Mt. 16:1; 19:3; 21:1, 12. Mt. 15:21, 22 might seem to support the view that 9:1 should be construed with 9:2 rather than with the preceding verse. However, the departure from the regions of Tyre and Sidon, described in 15:21, is explanatory of the narrative of the Canaanitish woman which follows, but would add nothing to the completeness of the preceding section, whereas the contents of 9:1 contribute nothing to the illumination of the story that follows but add a significant feature to the preceding statement.

concerning the failure of his disciples to fast. The call of Matthew is joined to the account of the healing of the paralytic by the somewhat flexible phrase, "And as Jesus passed from thence," used also in 9:27, which does not indicate where "the place of toll" was (Mt. 9:9). The account is silent moreover concerning the amount of time which elapsed between the call of the publican Matthew and the meal with publicans and sinners which provoked the attack of the Pharisees. And while the other synoptists imply or state that the feast was held in the house of the publican who had answered the call of Jesus, Matthew himself is content to say merely that it was "in the house" (9:10; *cf.* Mk. 2:15; Lk. 5:29). The inquiry concerning fasting is joined to this occasion by the adverb "then" which, as has been observed above, may mean merely "afterward" as well as "thereupon."

The disposition of the section which has been under review shows then that, while Matthew's main purpose was to illustrate the miraculous activity of Jesus, he was not content merely to list these acts as instances of the display of sheer supernatural power. In the larger context of Matthew's gospel these acts unavoidably receive their proper interpretation as messianic acts, but Matthew is also concerned to show that Jesus himself frequently attached such an interpretation to the performance of the miracles in order to reveal their true meaning. And it was the messianic interpretation of the events, more than the events themselves, which proved to be a stumblingblock to the Pharisees. If this characteristic of Jesus' activity is kept in view, the introduction of Mt. 9:9-17 in the midst of the section devoted largely to the narration of the mighty acts of Jesus will not appear strange. In the account of the healing of the paralytic the high point of the story is reached in the declaration that the Son of Man has authority on earth to forgive sins, thus interpreting and vindicating his approach to the paralytic (Mt. 9:6). Similarly the call of Matthew appears to be introduced not so much for its own sake as for its introduction of the portrayal of Jesus' association with publicans which becomes the occasion for his pronouncement: "For I did not come to call the righteous but sinners" (Mt. 9:13). The inquiry as to fasting also becomes the occasion for an exposition of the unique significance of his person and of the new order (Mt. 9:15-17). That these messianic intimations are not incidental, but basic to the purpose of the evangelist, appears also from the manner in which Matthew concludes this whole section. Just as he concluded the example of Jesus' teaching with a statement of the astonishment of the crowds that he spoke with singular authority (Mt. 7:28), he brings the whole series of illustrations of his mighty works to a close with the observation that the crowds in their wonder exclaimed: "Never has it been so seen in Israel" (Mt. 9:34; *cf.* 9:8). But he also significantly adds that there were enemies who, failing to recognize his claims to speak and act with divine authority and power, attributed his works to the prince of demons.

In our treatment of the following section, comprising Mt. 9:35-16:12, it will not be necessary to survey the data with the same fullness as in the preceding discussion. Only such an examination of the data is required as shall be sufficient to discover whether the previous observations as to the method of Matthew are confirmed or need to be modified. An additional question emerges in this connection, however, namely, the question as to how the evangelist conceives of the relation of Mt. 9:35-16:12 to Mt. 4:23-9:34.

That there is a parallelism in the construction of the two sections is obvious, but the particular problem that arises concerns their chronological sequence. If Matthew introduces the new section as treating of another, later period of the public ministry, does it necessarily follow that the new activity is viewed as *the second* stage of his Galilean ministry?

The new section begins, quite like the earlier one, with a general reference to his comprehensive itinerancy and with the characterization of his activity in terms of teaching, preaching and healing:

> "And Jesus went about all the cities and villages, teaching in their synagogues, and preaching the gospel of the kingdom, and healing all manner of disease and all manner of sickness" (Mt. 9:35).
> "And Jesus went about in Galilee, teaching in their synagogues, and preaching the gospel of the kingdom, and healing all manner of disease and all manner of sickness among the people" (Mt. 4:23).

The only material difference between these two summaries is that the later one does not specifically tell the geographical location of the cities and villages which he visited. The subsequent narrative nevertheless indicates that most, if not all, of the events presume a Galilean setting.

Both elements of Jesus' activity which are mentioned in Mt. 9:35, the elements of word and deed, are illustrated as before, but now a somewhat larger proportion of the space is assigned to a record of Jesus' teaching and preaching. This greater concern with the words of Jesus does not however reflect a judgment on the evangelist's part that the miraculous activity had now become less prominent than before. It is bound up rather with the consideration that Matthew for the most part is content to describe Jesus' deeds of healing and exorcism by way of summaries,

EARLIER CHAPTERS OF MATTHEW 145

such summaries being found in Mt. 12:15; 14:35f.; 15:30f.; *cf.* 13:54, 58; 14:2. There is record, moreover, of the endowment of the disciples with power and of their mission to perform similar acts (Mt. 10:1, 8). That these acts of mercy were not regarded merely as isolated philanthropic deeds, but were interpreted as a highly significant aspect of the disclosure of the meaning of his person and message appears from the manner in which, on various occasions, Jesus called attention to and interpreted his miracles: these acts and his message, when viewed in the perspective of prophecy, should have assured John the Baptist as to his identity (Mt. 11:2ff.); the cities of Galilee which had witnessed his mighty works should long ago have repented in sackcloth and ashes (11:20ff.); the Pharisees, who could not deny the reality of his mighty deeds, but referred their origin to demonic endowment, are told that his exorcism of demons by the power of the Spirit signifies the coming of the kingdom (12:24ff.).

Six miracles are specifically described in this section, but three of these are the extraordinary wonders of the feeding of the multitudes on two separate occasions and of the walking on the sea (Mt. 14:13-21; 15:32-39; 14:22-33). Only the other three, one a healing of a withered hand and the others cases of exorcism of demons, properly illustrate the activity described in Mt. 9:35 and in the other summary passages (Mt. 12:9-14; 22f.; 15:21-28). Moreover, the first two of these healing acts seem to be told not so much for their own sake as because they were the occasion of significant disclosures of Jesus in answer to accusations of the Pharisees (*cf.* 12:15-21, 25ff.), while the cure of the child of the Canaanitish woman is clearly significant, not simply as one more instance of a display of divine power, but as pointing to the flexibility of the rule that Jesus had been sent only to the lost sheep of the house of Israel (15:24, 28). The interweaving of fact and discourse in a single narrative is not distinctive of this section of Matthew, as we have seen, nor indeed of Matthew as over against the other evangelists, but it is remarkable that in this extended account of Jesus' activity in Galilee and its environs only three instances of his healing actions are described.

The emphasis which is placed upon the teaching function of Jesus in this section appears notably from the fact that two extended discourses, rather than one as in the preceding section, find their place here (10:5ff.; 13:3ff.). Although these two discourses together are somewhat shorter than the sermon on the mount, the double introduction of extensive discourses tends to convey an impression of the significance of the teaching ministry that a single, though longer, discourse could not do. And in addition to these two addresses, the Matthaean narrative contains large sections of discourse material, much of it being occasioned by attacks of the Pharisees, some by other events, and some being included which are not connected with any particular historical occasion. The whole of chapter 14 and half of chapter 15 are devoted to historical events, but all of the rest of this section (Mt. 9:35-16:12), except for very brief passages which provide the setting for Jesus' teaching or summarize his activity, is taken up with the recording of the message of Jesus.

Having noted the broad disposition of the materials in the record of a second phase of the Galilean ministry, we may profitably turn our attention to a consideration of the light that is cast upon the evangelist's method through his notices of location and temporal sequence in connection with the narration of the several episodes. The discourse to the twelve disciples in chapter 10, quite like the sermon on the mount, is introduced as spoken on a definite occasion at a particular place but without any specification of the time and place of its delivery (*cf*. Mt. 9:35-10:5; 11:1). The connection between the general summary in Mt. 9:35 and the particular occasion introduced by 9:36 is not indicated, but in view of what has previously been observed it seems best to regard the contents of 9:36ff. as intended to illustrate the teaching activity referred to in 9:35, or to indicate a particular aspect of it, rather than as a phase of activity which necessarily followed immediately upon the tour described in 9:35. On this understanding Mt. 11:1, which says that "when Jesus had finished commanding his twelve disciples, he departed thence to teach and preach in their cities," is more naturally viewed as subsumed under Mt. 9:35, as a part of the tour described there, than as belonging to an independent and subsequent period of activity. Although then the place of this discourse is not specified, one may fairly conclude from the disposition of the Matthaean narrative as a whole that it was somewhere in Galilee. On the other hand, it is significant that the directions to the twelve do not envisage a brief activity confined to the cities of Galilee: they are sent to the lost sheep of the house of Israel who live in the cities of Israel (Mt. 10:6, 23; *cf*. 2:20f.; 19:28). It becomes plain then that Matthew is not narrating the ministry of Christ in terms of several sharply separated periods of time or of precisely marked geographical divisions of Palestine. The broad scope of the mission of the twelve to Israel, which was contemporaneous with the historical mission of Christ, confirms the observation that the evangelist is far from intending to publish a complete chronicle of the beginnings of the Christian movement.

Further confirmation of this conclusion is derived from

observation of the references to time and place in chapters 11 and 12. When John made his inquiry, and where Jesus made his subsequent reply and discourse to the crowds concerning John, do not appear to concern the evangelist (11:2ff.). Only the indefinite "then" of Mt. 11:20 provides the connection between the upbraiding of the cities of Galilee for their failure to repent and the preceding discourse, and the even vaguer phrase "in that season" introduces the thanksgiving and invitation of Jesus which follow (11:25; *cf.* 12:1; 14:1). That Matthew does not have in mind a complete itinerary receives further corroboration from the fact that two of the three cities upon which Jesus pronounces woe, namely, Chorazin and Bethsaida, have not previously received mention in the gospel (11:21). Moreover, the ministry of Jesus which is characterized as having failed to produce repentance is evidently the entire previous activity of Jesus in these regions, not merely a particular segment of it, and therefore there is no support gained for the once-popular notion that the ministry of Jesus began with nearly universal success. Many indeed who at first followed him appear later on to have rejected him, but the extent of his outward success in the springtime of his Galilean ministry seems commonly to have been greatly exaggerated. The accounts in chapter 12 which tell of the controversies with the Pharisees concerning the sabbath likewise lack the data which might fix their place precisely within the historical framework of the life of Jesus. That the incidents which occasioned the attack upon Jesus occurred on the sabbath was of the essence of the narratives, but the location of the grainfields where the disciples were seen plucking and eating grain and of the synagogue where Jesus healed the withered hand are not recorded. The references to time are quite indefinite (*cf.*

12:1: "in that season"; 12:22, 38: "then"); likewise the indications of a change of scene (*cf.* "thence" in 12:9, 15). There is no intimation in Mt. 12:15 where Jesus went after perceiving the hostile intent of the Pharisees (12:15). Serious consideration must also be given to the possibility that Mt. 12:15b is intended to introduce a new context in which, on the background of a summary of healing action and his injunction to silence, the evangelist introduces in characteristic fashion an extensive quotation from the Old Testament as an explanation of Jesus' reserve.

The data in chapter 13 require careful scrutiny. The parabolic discourses of this chapter, like the discourses of chapters 5-7 and 10, are not connected with a specified locality. The scene indeed shifts back and forth between public and private places. In the first instance the public place is somewhere along the seaside, where Jesus speaks from a boat, and in the second instance it is left undetermined (13:1f., 24). Where the disciples conversed with Jesus privately concerning the purpose of his parables is not stated in the first case, and is described merely as "the house" in the second (13:10, 36). So far as the evidence in Matthew goes, there may have been a considerable lapse of time between the instruction of his disciples which ends with Mt. 13:23 and the resumption of the teaching of the crowds in 13:24. Accordingly, the statement in Mt. 13:53 that Jesus "departed thence" when he had finished "these parables" need not apply to all of the parables of this chapter. At this point the evangelist is clearly more concerned to group his materials according to subject matter than to fit them into a precise itinerary. But it does not follow, as a corollary of this judgment, that the references to time and place, in so far as they are distinctive of Matthew, are simply the creation of the evangelist in the interest of adding to the vividness of the narrative. If that were the case why does he not relate in more concrete terms where along the sea Jesus spoke, or at least where "the house" was in which Jesus interpreted the parable of the tares, and why does he leave us in complete uncertainty as to the time and place of other aspects of the instruction to the crowds and to the disciples (Mt. 13:10, 24)? The reference to "the house" in 13:36, it may be admitted, was introduced principally to indicate a change in scene from a public to a private place, and his purpose did not demand that he state exactly where the house was located. It may well have been the house in Capernaum which had been a center of activity.

Mt. 13:1 also quite abruptly introduces a reference to "the house" from which Jesus departed to sit by the seaside. This phrase is omitted by Codex Bezae, several mss. of the Old Latin Version and by the Sinaitic Syriac, but its omission is perhaps adequately accounted for by the difficulty of finding an antecedent. In order to account for the evangelist's failure to prepare for the mention of the house in 13:1, the suggestion is made, *e.g.*, by Allen (ICC) *ad. loc.*, that the phrase may be a reminiscence of Mk. 3:19b, "and he entereth into a house," which Matthew had omitted, but which still underlies Mt. 12:46. It is by no means obvious, however, that the adverb "outside" in Mt. 12:46 and Mk. 3:31 has reference to the house mentioned in Mk. 3:19. The employment of this adverb implies a contrast with an area which is "inside," but its use does not demand a specific mention of the latter in a preceding context; the immediate context may indicate expressly or by implication with sufficient clearness what the inside location is (*cf.* Mt. 5:13; Mk. 4:11). In Mk. 3:31f. Jesus was not immediately accessible to his mother and brethren because "a multitude was sitting about him" (*cf.* "the multitude" in Mk. 3:20). The view of Allen is at the disadvantage, moreover, of charging Matthew with an extremely clumsy treatment of his source material, and hence cannot be favored.

The use of the temporal phrase "in that day" in Mt. 13:1, on the other hand, appears to provide an intimate temporal connection with the preceding context. The use of this expression in Mt. 22:23 (*cf.* 22:46) is also noteworthy. Since Matthew, however, is not marking the progress of events in terms of days, and in view of the flexibility which the word "day" may have (*cf.* Thayer's *Lexicon, sub* 4), it may be that the evangelist has nothing more definite in mind than when he employs the expression "in that season," as *e.g.*, in Mt. 11:25; 12:1; 14:1.

No great advantage is to be gained, so far as the illumination of the distinctive method of the evangelist Matthew is concerned, by a detailed consideration of the section which follows the record of the parables and is followed by the narration of the great events in Caesarea Philippi (Mt. 13:54-16:12). Here the order of events and the presentation in general agree so closely with Mark 6:1-8:26 that very little new light is focused upon the peculiarities of Matthew. In any case references to locality and to chronological sequence are not more precise than before. In describing the rejection "in his own country" (13:54-58), for example, a comparison of Mt. 13:53 with 11:1 will show that there is no necessary connection between the entrance into Nazareth and what immediately precedes. It is significant also that Matthew like Mark identifies Nazareth simply as "his own country," as the composer of a travel narrative would hardly have done, although the expression serves sufficiently to clarify the course of the developments which results in Jesus' declaration that "a prophet is not without honor except in his own country and in his house." In the cycle of events that follows (Mt. 14:1ff.) there are of course several geographical references and some intimations of the passing of time, and it could not well be otherwise since now it is shown that prior to the journey to Jerusalem there was a period in which Jesus retired from the great centers of population along the western coast of the sea to more or less isolated regions. Since we plan to return, in connection with our treatment of Luke, to a discussion of certain problems raised by the records of this period, we shall not attempt any further consideration here, except to note that, along with various concrete geographical and temporal data, in this section incidents are also introduced without explicit connection with preceding developments (Mt. 16:1; *cf.* 16:13) or with only indefinite references to place and time (*cf.* Mt. 14:13; 15:21; 15:1).

The survey which has been presented shows that like Mark the evangelist Matthew is relatively unconcerned with the chronology and topography of the life and ministry of Jesus. Many references to time and place are indeed in evidence, and there is not sufficient reason to conclude that such references are introduced in an arbitrary manner. Still, the fact remains that his interest is clearly shown not to consist in publishing a complete itinerary of Jesus' travels, or one that is virtually complete, but rather in setting forth a witness to Jesus as the messianic Son of David, whose conception of his ministry and of the manner in which it was to be discharged proved a tragic stumbling-block to the leaders of the Jews. The fulfillment of this ministry, and the deepening conflict, unfold, however, on the specific historical scene of Palestine. The references to time and place serve the purpose therefore of centering attention upon the truly historical character of what is set forth concerning Jesus. The proclamation of the glad tidings of Jesus Christ did not require anything like an exhaustive account of his travels and activity, but only such an account of his history as would adequately display the meaning of his coming.

Since this history finds its climax in his death and resurrection, moreover, the evangelists could not remain indifferent to the progress and movement of his ministry towards its destined end. In order to mark such progress, however, it was not necessary to indicate in detail various sharply delineated stages of the ministry. Thus with respect to the section which has been under review in the immediately preceding pages (Mt. 9:35-16-12), it is our judgment that not enough data are provided to warrant the conclusion that Matthew clearly intended this section as a description of *the second* stage of Jesus' Galilean ministry. Nevertheless, the disposition of the material does disclose a sense of movement towards the goal of the entire account. The new note in this section is not found in any different emphasis in his words or works, but in the signs of growing tension between Jesus and the leaders of the Jews, particularly the Pharisees. From the time indeed that Jesus came forth with his call to repentance and demanded a righteousness beyond that of the scribes and Pharisees, and offended them by the authority with which he claimed to forgive sins, by his association with publicans and sinners and by his violation of their traditions, it seemed inevitable that they would remain unreconciled to Jesus' claims and would not rest satisfied until they had brought about his downfall (*cf.* Mt. 4:17; 5:20; 9:2ff., 14, 34). The extent to which the record of Jesus' teaching in the section following Mt. 9:35 is taken up with discourses occasioned by controversy with the Pharisees seems to show nevertheless that Matthew intends to indicate that as time went on the issue between Jesus and his opponents, rather than being resolved or moderated, became even more intense and pointed even more clearly to a catastrophic break in the future (*cf.* Mt. 10:17, 25; 11:25; 12:1ff., 9ff., 14, 24ff., 38ff.; 15:1ff.; 16:1ff., 12). The record of the failure of the Galilean cities to repent at his mighty works and of his own city to acknowledge him adds to the ominous outlook of this section (Mt. 11:20ff.; 13:54ff.). The disposition of the materials in the narrative which precedes the time when, in Caesarea Philippi, Jesus began to dwell on the necessity of his passion at Jerusalem, indicates that Matthew has an eye for the historical continuity between the early development of hostility towards him and its final issue in the condemnation to the cross. Yet, as the absence of precise chronological sequence and of other signs of transition indicates, Matthew is not, strictly speaking, organizing his materials on the principle of development. Matthew does not imply that incidents like those recorded in chapter 12, for example, could not have occurred and did not occur at a somewhat earlier point than the incidents which were narrated in the immediately preceding context. The total impact of the narrative is made principally by the choice of the materials; it is the accumulation of materials depicting the hostility of the Pharisees which serves to create the intended impression that the opposition of Jesus' enemies became more intense and relentless as Jesus more fully disclosed the meaning which he attached to his own person and mission.

CHAPTER VI

THE RESURRECTION NARRATIVE IN MATTHEW

SYNOPSIS

Introduction.

Comparison of the latter portion of Matthew with that of Mark.

I. *The Problem of the Order of the Events Immediately Following the Entry into Jerusalem.*

Mark's grouping of the events within three distinct days apparently discrepant with Matthew's references to two days; the flexibility and indefiniteness of the Matthaean account: the cleansing of the temple not precisely connected with the entry into Jerusalem; nor is exact time of cursing of the fig tree given; the disregard of sequence in telescoping the two phases of the latter story; the use of "immediately" in Mt. 21:19 and 20 does not preclude the possibility of some delay; remarks on harmonization in connection with the observation of the aims of the evangelists.

II. *The Resurrection Narrative.*

The appeal made to the narratives of Matthew and Mark in support of the Galilean Hypothesis; survey of the Matthaean narrative; preliminary observations of the aim and method of the evangelist: his selection of his materials; omissions and contractions in the narrative.

A. Consideration of the question whether Matthew clearly excludes the possibility of a reunion with the disciples prior to the reunion in Galilee.

1. The meaning of Mt. 26:32 (Mk. 14:28): the prediction

that the Shepherd would be smitten and the sheep dispersed would suggest, apart from a further word, that they would return to their Galilean homes while Jesus lay in a Judean grave; consequently Jesus' word that he would arrive in Galilee before they could return vividly conveys hope and assurance that the final issue will find them reunited.

2. Mt. 28:7 (Mk. 16:7) recalls this prophetic word and indicates that its fulfillment has been set in motion by the resurrection; the present tense of the verb "to go before"; the significance of the words "there ye shall see him"; the distinctive features of Mark.

3. Mt. 28:10 seems to contemplate the departure of disciples for Galilee at once, and so to exclude a reunion in Jerusalem; Matthew's usage of "brethren" and of "my brethren" makes it unnatural to restrict the reference here to the eleven, unless it appears that there were no other disciples in Jerusalem or its vicinity; Matthew's usage of "disciples" indicates that it comprehends many besides the twelve; and there is evidence that many disciples were present in Jerusalem at the time of the crucifixion; consequently scattered sheep would most naturally include broadly the entire fold of Christ's disciples, and the direction of Mt. 28:10 properly looks forward to a gathering of a considerable company of disciples.

4. Mt. 28:16-20 tells so little concerning the detailed circumstances of the reunion, evidently because of the concentration of the evangelist upon the message of Jesus which forms the climax of his record, that one may not insist that, if Matthew allowed for the presence of others besides the eleven, he would have been compelled to state it in explicit fashion; actually, however, the most natural interpretation of the phrase "but some doubted" in Mt. 28:17 implies incidentally the presence of others besides the eleven, and consequently that all along Matthew has had in view a reunion of Jesus with a large group of his followers in Galilee which was the occasion of the deliverance of "the great commission."

B. Consideration of the question of Matthew's absorption with an appearance in Galilee. The theory of Lohmeyer and Lightfoot that Matthew, closely following Mark, views Galilee as the "seat of revelation," and so as the proper place for the consummation of the career of Christ; Christ, according to Matthew, came to the whole land of Israel; his entrance into Jerusalem as King, no less than his appearance in Galilee, was in fulfillment of divine prophecy; the evangelist's record of Jesus' attitude of favor toward Jerusalem; his expressions of judgment upon Jerusalem for her unbelief are not more severe than upon the cities of Galilee that failed to repent and believe; other features of Matthew that associate revelation with areas outside of Galilee.

THE structure of the story of the passion of Christ according to Matthew—if we may so designate the entire portion of the gospel which begins with Peter's confession in Caesarea Philippi and concludes with the crucifixion and burial of Jesus—is so similar to that of Mark, both in the order of the events and in the details of their narration, that one can hardly expect to learn as much concerning Matthew's distinctive approach to the history of Christ as in earlier chapters where, as we have observed, the divergences between Mark and Matthew are frequent and conspicuous. In the latter portion indeed there are important differences. Matthew includes a few incidents which Mark lacks (Mt. 17:24-27; 27:62-66), and omits some which Mark includes (Mk. 9:38-41; 12:41-44). The most important difference is that Matthew characteristically devotes far greater space than Mark to the teaching of Jesus (*cf.* Mt. 18:12-35; 20:1-16; 21:28-32; 22:1-14; 23:14-36, 37-39; 24:45-51; 25:1-46 and Mt. 16:17-19). Perhaps for that reason, with a view to the limits of his space, this evangelist narrates many incidents more concisely, although, of course, the greater vividness and attention to detail in Mark may have their own explanation (*cf.* Mt. 17:14-20 and Mk. 9:14-29; Mt. 21:18-22 and Mk. 11:12-14, 20-24; Mt. 26:17-19 and Mk. 14:12-16; Mt. 27:57-61 and Mk. 15:42-47).

In spite of the remarkable agreement in the order of the events in Mark and Matthew, there are two points in the narratives where the divergences are conspicuous, and rather than attempt a detailed survey of the composition of the latter chapters we shall concern ourselves in this chapter with a discussion of the chief problems raised by these divergences as the most effective way of illuminating the broad question of the aims and methods of the evangelists. The most significant question concerns the problems raised by the extensive record which Matthew presents of an appearance of Jesus in Galilee after the resurrection, and we shall devote a large part of this chapter to their elucidation. There is an advantage in giving prior consideration to the other problem referred to, that, namely, which is raised by a comparison between the Matthaean and Marcan records of the events that followed upon the entry into Jerusalem (Mt. 21:1-22; Mk. 11:1-25). In this case we have to do with parallel accounts which are commonly held to be irreconcilable, and on the supposition of the priority of Mark the divergences of Matthew from the Marcan order are widely said to discredit Matthew as a completely trustworthy historian.

The Marcan narrative appears to set the entry into Jerusalem, the cursing of the fig tree, the cleansing of the temple, and the discovery of the withered state of the fig tree in a precise chronological framework. The events are definitely grouped within three distinct days. On the first day, the day of the entry, Mark states that Jesus entered into the temple, looked about, but in view of the lateness of the hour left directly for Bethany with the twelve (Mk. 11:11). On the second day, "on the morrow," he places two events: the cursing of the fig tree after they had left Bethany and at a time when Jesus was hungry (11:12-14) and the cleansing of the temple after they had come to Jerusalem (11:15-18). At this point Mark does not indicate the end of the second day by stating, as he had done in v. 11, that at eventide they returned to Bethany; instead he introduces a general statement as to Jesus' custom: "And whenever evening came he [or, "they"] went forth out of the city" (11:19). This general statement indicates that even Mark is not absorbed in providing a complete chronological framework. Nevertheless, even if one may not speak dogmatically of the occurrence of the discovery of the withered tree on *the* third day, it is unmistakable that Mark places this incident on *a* third day, definitely distinguished from the day when Jesus pronounced the curse, and further states that its withered condition was beheld "as they passed by in the morning" (11:20).

In contrast to Mark's distribution of these events on three distinct days, Matthew is said to contract the narrative to a period of only two days by his omission of the first evening's stay in Bethany and by telescoping into one continuous story the two separate stages of the incident of the fig tree.[1] The question arises whether Matthew quite unambiguously places these events within a period of two days, or whether his language is flexible enough to allow for a longer period. It must be conceded at once that there is nothing in Matthew that corresponds with the carefully marked sequence of days in Mark, nothing of the coming of evening or of what Jesus customarily did at evening (Mk. 11:11, 19), or again of what happened on "the next day" (Mk. 11:12). Instead of recounting, as Mark does, the vivid, concrete detail of Jesus' quick look into the temple before retiring to Bethany for the night, Matthew is content to conclude the reference to the entry into Jerusalem by noting the impact which the event made:

---

[1] *Cf. e.g.,* Schmidt, *op. cit.,* p. 283.

"All the city was stirred, saying, Who is this? And the multitude said, This is the prophet Jesus who is from Nazareth of Galilee" (Mt. 21:10f.; *cf*. Mk. 11:11).

This difference is typical of the two evangelists: Mark is concerned here with the precise details in the actual order of their occurrence; Matthew lets the various incidents be told in greater isolation as more distinctive witnesses to the person and mission of Christ.

That Matthew's method is more topical than that of Mark is confirmed by the indefinite manner in which he introduces the cleansing of the temple (Mt. 21:12). No precise connection with the entry into Jerusalem is indicated, for Matthew often introduces in similar fashion a new paragraph which has no clear temporal connection with the preceding context.[2] Only if one remains under the spell of the supposition that the evangelists aimed to publish a complete and continuous account of the life of Christ, and ignores the clear implications of the record as a whole, will one dare to maintain that Matthew positively does not allow for the possibility of an interval between the arrival in Jerusalem and the account of the cleansing of the temple. The narrative closes indeed with a reference to Jesus' departure from the city to lodge in Bethany, a reference which shows that he too was aware that Jesus did not remain continuously in the city where the tension between him and the Jewish leaders was mounting to fever pitch (Mt. 21:17). In similar fashion Matthew often rounds off his narrative of various incidents without implying that the following event took place immediately thereafter (*cf*. Mt. 2:23; 9:1; 11:1; 15:39; 19:1f.).

---

[2] *Cf*. Mt. 4:23; 9:35; 19:3; 20:29; 21:1; 21:23. See also 8:2, 14; 9:2, 9; 12:9, 15; 13:54; 15:22, 29; 16:1 and 19:3 in connection with the survey in the preceding pages.

If it be granted that Matthew does not fix the exact point after the entry when the temple was cleansed, one will be prepared to recognize that the position of the story of the cursing of the fig tree, following the cleansing of the temple, does not necessarily fix its order of occurrence. At first glance indeed the word translated "in the morning" (πρωΐ), which is the opening word of the new section (Mt. 21:18ff.), might appear to intimate that the evangelist is calling attention to the chronological sequence of this "morning" following the night in Bethany mentioned in the preceding verse. Such an interpretation, however, attributes a definiteness to this word which it does not possess. The Greek word πρωΐ means "early," "the early part of a day," and so also "in the morning," but it does not mean, without further specification, "in the morning of the day that has been in view" or "in the morning following the day previously mentioned" (cf. Mt. 16:3; 20:1, which are the only other instances in Matthew; Mk. 1:35; 11:20; 13:35). Even in Mk. 11:20, where the word appears in connection with the account of the journey on which the withered condition of the tree was discovered, the word cannot mean "in the morning which followed the night of the day when the temple was cleansed," for in the preceding verse, as was pointed out above, only a general reference to his customary practice is given. Mark evidently refers to the earliness of the hour when Jesus was on his way to Jerusalem again, not particularly to mark the beginning of a definite day, but to introduce a concrete situation. So in Mt. 21:18 the word supplies a detail which illuminates the story of the hunger of Jesus as he was on an early journey to the city.[3] Matthew may be understood as saying: "Now it was early one day, as he set out for the city, that he became hungry."

---

[3] Cf. also the remarks on the use of ὀψία above pp. 137f. and n. 10.

All of these considerations will not appear extraordinary to one who has examined the gospel with care. There remains, however, a distinct problem due to the fact that Matthew records as a single continuous narrative what Mark has clearly divided between two distinct days. Here one comes face to face once more with the question what the aim of the evangelist really was, whether it was to note carefully the sequence of the events which he reports, or whether it was to set forth the facts in such a manner as to furnish a true witness to the gospel. This witness, we hasten to add, would be unreliable if the disregard of chronological sequence introduced actual discrepancy into the account. But there is no definite evidence of that here. To one who follows the principle that the aim of the writer was to provide the reader with the exact succession of the details of Jesus' history, it would follow that Mt. 21:20 implies that the disciples saw the tree at the very instant that it became withered. Actually, however, he says nothing particularly as to the time when they saw the tree. But the objection may be offered that the use of the word "immediately" (παραχρῆμα) in both v. 19 and v. 20 precludes the possibility of any interval between the cursing of the tree and the disciples' perception of the actual result. The fact is, however, that this word does not exclude the possibility of some delay.[4] Moreover, the judgment which Jesus pronounced against the tree did not predict that it would wither without delay, but that it would bear fruit no longer, and the wonder of the disciples is noticed because the fulfillment of Jesus' word came to reality in such decisive and sudden fashion. In the narrative of Matthew, as in that of Mark, the main point is that there was no delay

---

[4] In Moulton and Milligan, *The Vocabulary of the Greek Testament*, an instance is given where a delay of a month is in view.

in the fulfillment of Jesus' prediction. The indication of the swift and conclusive execution of the curse, and not the exact temporal setting of the details, was evidently the aim of the evangelist Matthew.

Those who have been accustomed to cite the differences between Mt. 21 and Mk. 11 as proving discrepancy between them will perhaps be impatient with the "harmonistics" of the above. We confess that much that has been attempted in the interest of demonstrating the unity of the gospels has been extreme and far-fetched, not because of any positive proof of actual disunity, but because it has proceeded from a fundamentally false conception of the aim of the evangelists and the distinctive character of the gospels. To make this confession is, to be sure, not a late and regretful acknowledgment of the faults of all orthodox scholars in the past, for no less an exponent of the authority and unity of the Scriptures than John Calvin protested in his day against the faulty approach of Osiander.[5] If the evangelists aimed to compose a history or biography of Christ, as complete in detail as possible, with scrupulous attention to itinerary and chronological sequence, and to report the words of Jesus with stenographic accuracy, there would be very little in one gospel that could be regarded as finding its counterpart in any other. Since, however, none of these features is supported by the evidence, and since particularly none of the evangelists aims to supply a complete historical framework of the life of Christ, it follows that much of the disparagement of "harmonistics" is based upon radically erroneous conceptions of the character of the gospels. The defender of the truth and authority of the gospels does not face the necessity of fitting all the details of the records into a continuous framework. The evangelists

---

[5] *E.g.*, in his comment on Mt. 20:29.

do not provide sufficient data for such an effort, and did not intend to do so. Consequently, it is not scientific to shout "discrepancy" whenever it appears that details are not presented in the same order in various records, or it develops that one evangelist disregards the precise framework which another delineates in connection with the narration of a particular phase of the ministry of Christ.

The most distinctive feature of the latter portion of Matthew, at least when Matthew is compared with Mark, is the narrative of Jesus' appearance to his disciples on a mountain in Galilee. The divergence from Mark is in fact not as great on the assumption that the traditional ending is not an original part of this gospel as on the opposite view, for in place of the climax reached in Matthew through the portrayal of a reunion in Galilee the long conclusion of Mark presents a summary of appearances, none of which is localized, and ends with a reference to Christ's ascension and session at God's right hand, and to the successful prosecution of the apostolic mission. The abrupt conclusion of Mark, on the other hand, also clearly holds in prospect a reunion in Galilee. In spite of the not unimportant differences in the manner in which Mark and Matthew leave their readers, differences which recall the distinctive manner in which these evangelists introduce Christ to their readers, it is the agreement of Matthew and Mark which has been made the basis of the common critical theory, known as the Galilean Hypothesis, which maintains that the earliest Christian tradition concerning the origin of faith in the resurrection of Jesus knew nothing of a reunion of Jesus and the disciples in Jerusalem on the first day of the week following his crucifixion.[6] In view of

---

[6] In addition to this negative proposition, the Galilean Hypothesis

the crucial issues raised by this hypothesis, we may not treat it with only a passing reference. Moreover, our aim to consider the disposition of Matthew will by no means be submerged if we approach the study of the resurrection narrative from the point of view of the claim that it excludes the possibility of an initial meeting between Jesus and the disciples near the scene of his death and burial. It will be convenient, meanwhile, in connection with our examination of Matthew's more extensive narrative to treat the Marcan data which bear upon the Galilean Hypothesis as well as certain questions that are raised by a comparison of Mark's record with that of Matthew.

The Matthaean resurrection story closely parallels that of Mark to the point of the women's departure from the tomb. They coincide in reporting a preparatory reference to a future reunion in Galilee (Mt. 26:31f.; Mk. 14:28) and in telling of the angelic interpretation of the empty tomb and of the command to remind the disciples of the word that had been previously spoken (Mt. 28:1-7; Mk. 16:2-7). But from this point forward their ways part. Whereas Mark ends his narrative abruptly on the note of reverential awe, as he centers attention upon the impact made upon the women by the stupendous events and disclosures, Matthew completely overcomes this abruptness by describing the dispatch with which the women set out to obey the command of the angel (Mt. 28:8; Mk. 16:8). The women, ac-

---

includes, of course, many other features. On the supposition that the resurrection did not actually take place, and that consequently the belief that the tomb was empty originated as a late development, the hypothesis seeks to account for the origin of the belief in the resurrection of Jesus by positing an original experience of Peter, usually conceived of as an hallucination, wherein he became assured that Jesus was alive. It commonly maintains also that the disciples were not anywhere near Jerusalem on the Sunday following the crucifixion, having fled from the scene either after his arrest or after the crucifixion.

cording to Matthew, were indeed filled with fear, but this fear was mingled with joy as they ran to make the matter known to the disciples, who, as the angelic command implied, were still in the neighborhood.[7]

As the women were on the way to the disciples, Jesus appears to them. As a matter of fact, then, Matthew does not exclude the possibility of appearances in Jerusalem. The appearance which he relates is to certain women, and not to the disciples as a whole, but it is clear that the very thought of an initial manifestation of Jesus in Jerusalem or its environs was by no means irreconcilable with his conception of the course of events. After he tells of the obeisance and worship which the women offered, however, his interest in Galilee again comes to the fore, for Jesus concludes his association with them by repeating the command of the angel in the form that his brethren should go into Galilee where they would see him (Mt. 28:9-11).

The actual fulfillment of this charge to speak to the brethren is not reported, although, to be sure, it is clearly implied by the record of the reunion on a mountain in Galilee which closes the gospel. First, however, the evangelist introduces the announcement by the watch that the body of Jesus had been stolen by his disciples, an account previously prepared for by the description of the setting of the watch (Mt. 28:11-15; cf. 27:63-66; 28:4). This section seems to be included more or less parenthetically in the midst of the treatment of the events which reached their

---

[7] This feature is inconsistent with the judgment that the disciples had fled the scene many hours previously. The advocates of the Galilean Hypothesis are well aware of this inconsistency, but their answer is simply that the records as we have them, including Mark and Matthew, represent advanced stages in the transformation of tradition, and obscure the actual course of events to such an extent that only a few isolated details can be relied upon.

climax in the reunion in Galilee, although, in truth, it had independent value as an answer to Jewish calumnies. Moreover, the general context in which it is placed contributes the consideration, as evidence of the falsity of the charge against the disciples that they had stolen the body of Jesus, that in obedience to the command of Jesus and the angel the women had apprised them of the empty tomb, and that therefore they could have had no previous knowledge of what had happened.

What occurred after the women reached the disciples is not disclosed, but the evangelist does relate the journey of "the eleven disciples" into Galilee to fulfill a rendezvous with Jesus on a mountain (Mt. 28:16).[8] The appearance of Jesus there, like his manifestation to the women in or near Jerusalem, produced a worshipful response. The evangelist notes, however, that there were some present who doubted (28:17). He does not linger to describe any further

---

[8] The concluding clause of Mt. 28:16 is rendered in the standard versions, "where Jesus had appointed them," and it might appear to intend to recall the place where the apostles originally received appointment. If Matthew contained an account of their appointment on a mountain in Galilee, it would indeed be difficult to escape that conclusion. However, he evidently does not conceive of their appointment in any such fashion. B. Weiss understands the narrative as referring back to the mount where Jesus proclaimed the "Grundgesetze des Gottesreiches," but this is far-fetched. Cf. Klostermann ad loc. Moffatt renders the clause as follows: "where Jesus had arranged to meet them."

The reference to the previous arrangement of the place of meeting is wholly unprepared for in the preceding narrative, but is characteristic of the method of Matthew whose silences on many other developments have been noticed. The evangelist is not concerned to tell the whole story. Here is provided perhaps another confirmation of the view, developed more fully below, that Matthew allows for the supposition of a prior reunion with the eleven in Jerusalem, for he may well presuppose that the particular arrangements were made with the eleven at some time after the resurrection.

details of the scene, nor does he say how it concluded, whether by the departure of Jesus or of the disciples, but he brings the whole narrative to a climax by recording a brief but momentous disclosure of Jesus to them. He affirms his universal sovereignty, evidently as realized by his resurrection from the dead rather than as being merely in prospect; he charges the disciples to carry his demands for loyalty and obedience to all nations; and he promises them his presence without interruption until the consummation (28:18-20).

Before considering the critical questions in detail it is important to be clear as to certain preliminary considerations. It has become a widespread custom to advance the claim, when one of the writers of the New Testament is silent concerning a certain feature of the life of Jesus, that he therefore did not know anything about it. Thus Paul is often said not to have known anything of the empty tomb merely because his account of Christ's appearances in I Corinthians 15 limits itself to a summary of appearances of Jesus to individuals and to groups. Similarly, since Matthew does not report an appearance to the disciples in Jerusalem, it is sometimes claimed that he could have had no knowledge of such an event. Such apodictic judgments are altogether premature and unscientific. It is commonly admitted that the summary written by Paul must have been based upon Christian tradition that had been current in the Christian church for many years, as far back at least as the time of Paul's contact with the apostolic tradition. It would be a rash assumption therefore that the evangelist Matthew, since he tells of only a single appearance of Jesus to the members of the apostolic circle, could not have known of any others. Moreover, this gospel pervasively exhibits its author's consciousness that his narrative does not provide a complete account of the life of Christ upon earth; in fact, no more striking proof is offered than that which the conclusion affords. Matthew is completely silent as to the termination of the association of Jesus with his disciples; yet the abruptness with which he takes leave of Jesus presents an inexplicable riddle unless he is understood as assuming that the church generally was well-informed concerning the event which finally separated Jesus from the earthly scene. Since, then, Matthew must have known much more than he chooses to tell, the conclusion is at hand that he brought his gospel to a close by depicting the scene on the mountain in Galilee because it supplied a fitting climax to his entire work. The validity of this observation finds confirmation if notice is taken of the fact that the appearance of Jesus which is described is presented, not so much as a demonstration of the fact of the resurrection of Jesus, but as the occasion of a discourse which constitutes a most suitable conclusion to the Matthaean proclamation of the Christ who spoke with absolute authority.

Matthew, accordingly, selects his materials with a definite purpose in view, and he disposes them in such a fashion that nearly the whole of the resurrection narrative in chapter 28 is taken up with the preparations for the final scene. But even in narrating this event his characteristic method is displayed. He contracts the story and omits details, as such contractions and omissions suited his purpose. No attempt is made to clarify the reference to the doubt of some disciples; questions which arise as to their identity and whether their doubts were resolved by Jesus remain unanswered (Mt. 28:17). Nothing is told of the arrival of the women at the abode of the disciples. The departure of the eleven for Galilee is mentioned, but that the departure took place immediately upon the arrival of the women is by no means implied. And in spite of the fact that the reunion in Galilee has been in prospect for some time, we are altogether unprepared for the disclosure that the place of the rendezvous had been arranged in advance (28:16).

These considerations, it is freely admitted, do not dispose of the problems with which we are faced. Matthew does not aim to provide a complete record of the career after the resurrection, and he might well select an appearance which appropriately brought his gospel to an end. The fact remains, however, that the evangelist appears to look upon the scene in Galilee as *the* reunion or at least as *the first* reunion with them. The women indeed saw him in Jerusalem, but then there is reiterated the command that the disciples should go to Galilee in order to meet him. We shall perhaps be able to observe the perspective of Matthew's account most clearly if the pertinent data are set down in order.

"After I have been raised up I shall go before you into Galilee" (Mt. 26:32; Mk. 14:28).

"And go quickly and tell his disciples, He is risen from the dead; and behold he goeth before you into Galilee; there ye shall see him. Behold, I have told you" (Mt. 28:7; *cf.* Mk. 16:7).

"Go, tell my brethren that they depart into Galilee, and there they shall see me" (Mt. 28:10).

"And the eleven disciples went into Galilee, unto the mountain where Jesus had appointed them [to go], and when they saw him they worshipped; but some doubted" (Mt. 28:16).

While then the historian is clearly not in a position to deny that Matthew knew of other appearances of Jesus to his disciples, we must admit that the disposition of his narrative easily creates the impression that he did not contemplate the possibility of any reunion prior to the one in Galilee which he describes. Matthew and Mark therefore appear to be brought into sharp conflict with Luke; the first two gospels report directions to the disciples to go to Galilee, the third tells them to tarry at Jerusalem.⁹

We may well begin our examination of this problem by a consideration of the first of the passages quoted above. Since the reference to an appearance of Jesus in Galilee specifically recalls the prophetic word of Jesus spoken in Gethsemane, it is imperative that the meaning of this utterance be gauged in its original setting. In both Matthew and Mark Jesus supports his prediction, that all would find in him an occasion of stumbling, upon the word of the Lord in Zechariah 13:7: "I shall smite the shepherd, and the sheep will be scattered abroad." And to this reference to his imminent death there is joined, in a fashion characteristic of the gospel accounts, a word concerning his resurrection in the form: "But after I have been raised up I shall go into Galilee before you." ¹⁰ This utterance concerning his death

---

⁹ *Cf.* Lk. 24:49. This issue has perhaps never been stated more acutely than by Strauss, *Das Leben Jesu,* 1840, II, pp. 589f. (E. T., III, p. 328): "Here two questions inevitably arise: 1st, how can Jesus have directed the disciples to journey into Galilee, and yet at the same time have commanded them to remain in Jerusalem until Pentecost? and 2ndly, how could he refer them to a promised appearance in Galilee, when he had the intention of showing himself to them that very day in and near Jerusalem?"

We are not concerned here with all of the issues raised by these questions, and in particular not with the implications of the Lucan narrative. At this point we have to do mainly with the disposition of the Matthaean account, and with the special question whether the concentration of this narrative upon the previously arranged meeting in Galilee allows for the possibility of other encounters in Jerusalem or vicinity, which were not prepared for and even came at unexpected times.

¹⁰ For προάγειν in the sense "to go ahead," "to go beforehand," "to anticipate," cf. Mt. 14:22 (Mk. 6:45) and 21:31. It may also mean "to lead" (Mt. 2:9; 21:9; Mk. 10:32), and this meaning is supported by J. Weiss, *Das Urchristentum,* pp. 10f., in connection with his espousal of a "Jerusalem Hypothesis." His view presupposes considerable con-

and resurrection, unlike those which center attention upon the wickedness of the Jewish rulers and the ignominy which Jesus was to endure (*cf.* Mt. 16:21; 17:22; 20:18f.), relates these events to the experience of the disciples. Although his disciples should have denied themselves, taken up their cross and followed him (Mt. 16:24), actually they all, including the self-confident Peter, would desert him, but Jesus immediately adds the word of hope that he would precede them into Galilee after his resurrection. The employment of such language to express the reunion of the Shepherd and the sheep is certainly extraordinary. If Jesus were merely prophesying an appearance to the disciples in Galilee, he might simply have said: "Ye shall see me again, after I have been raised up, in Galilee." Actually the prophetic word says nothing directly about an appearance to them or a reunion with them, although the broad context implies as much. The use of the verb "to go before" in the sense of arriving beforehand must have been chosen because it served to express vividly and emphatically the opposite of what the prediction of their taking offense and being scattered might have seemed to hold in prospect. Apart from the hope of the resurrection, the disciples might have expected that, while Jesus remained in a Judean grave, they would return to their homeland in Galilee to seek safety and isolation from the scene of crushing tragedy. It was fitting therefore that the hope of restoration should be expressed in the form that, contrary to human expectations, Jesus would be in Galilee before they could return. The issue then is not what either Jesus or the disciples

---

fusion in the accounts as they are. While the second meaning is a possible rendering in Mt. 26:32 and 28:7, and is in some respects attractive, it cannot be harmonized with the representation of Mt. 28:16 that the eleven went to Galilee without the leadership of Jesus.

would do first of all after the resurrection in Jerusalem. The disciples do not depart for Galilee immediately any more than Jesus did, for both Matthew and Mark presuppose that they were in the vicinity of Jerusalem for some time. Since therefore the disciples did not at once leave Jerusalem, the word that Jesus would anticipate them in Galilee by no means excludes the possibility of prior appearances in Jerusalem.

Now the angelic command to the women after the discovery that the tomb was empty recalls this prophetic word of Jesus in connection with the explanation of the meaning of the empty grave: "And go quickly and say to his disciples, He is risen from the dead, and behold he goeth before you into Galilee; there ye shall see him" (Mt. 28:7; *cf.* Mk. 16:7). The stupendous event has occurred which sets in motion the fulfillment of the prophecy of Jesus: "After I have been raised up I shall go before you into Galilee." There are indeed two noteworthy differences between the prophecy and the command: (1) the tense of the verb "to go before" changes from the future to the present, and (2) there is added the words, "there ye shall see him," and these differences might seem to carry the implication that they would see him for the first time in Galilee. The present tense of the verb may not be pressed, however, to mean that even at that moment Jesus was on the journey into Galilee, for this would bring Mt. 28:7 into conflict with 28:10 which locates Jesus still in the vicinity of Jerusalem. Moreover, since, as has been observed, προάγειν means here "to go ahead," "to anticipate," if one were to understand v. 7 as implying that Jesus had already left Jerusalem for Galilee, it would also seem to presuppose that the disciples also were on the way to Galilee. Rather than being a progressive present, therefore, the form in question must be understood as a vivid future, which is essentially the equivalent of the future in Mt. 26:32.[11] With regard to the words "there ye shall see him," it should be observed that they are so closely connected with the reference to Galilee that they serve to make explicit what has been constantly implied in the prophetic word of Jesus, namely, that Jesus would be waiting for them in Galilee and would welcome them there. They do not represent an independent disclosure by the angel as to when the disciples would first see the risen Christ but, taken in connection with the preceding clause, they serve to recall the substance of Jesus' promise. Now that Jesus has risen from the dead, they may be assured that his declaration, that after his resurrection he would be in Galilee before they reached there, was about to be fulfilled. The time of its fulfillment is not specified, however, for the message to the disciples does not intimate when they were to start for Galilee.

This interpretation of Mt. 28:7, as recalling the extraordinary prophecy of Jesus, is confirmed by Mk. 16:7. The Marcan passage differs from the Matthaean in one "omission" and "two additions," lacking the words "He is risen from the dead" and including an explicit reference to Peter and the words, "as he said unto you." The mention of Peter is of no immediate significance, but the other differences concentrate one's attention most pointedly upon the fact that the prophecy of Jesus is being recalled. In connection with the discussion of this verse above (pp. 113ff.), it was argued that the words "as he said unto you" refer properly to both of the preceding clauses, and therefore recall Mk. 14:28 rather than any prophecy of an appearance on the clouds.

It may also be noticed that Mt. 28:8, although lacking the clause, "just as he said unto you" of Mk. 16:7, contains the words, "Behold I have told you." A few textual witnesses read εἶπεν, and Hort, *The N.T. in the Original Greek*, Appendix, p. 23, prefers this reading on the ground that a primitive corruption must have taken place. On this view, of course, Matthew would make the same point as Mark. The

---

[11] On the use of the present for the future *cf.* Burton, *Moods and Tenses*, Par. 15; Moulton, *Grammar*, I, 1906, p. 120; Robertson, *Grammar*, 1923, pp. 869f.; Chamberlain, *Exegetical Grammar*, 1941, p. 71.

evidence for the change is, however, hardly sufficient to justify this conclusion. *Cf.* also R. H. Lightfoot, *Locality and Doctrine*, p. 69, n. 1.

When one turns to Mt. 28:10 the problem becomes more involved. While neither the prophecy in Mt. 26:32 nor the command in 28:7 preclude the possibility of other appearances before the reunion in Galilee, the charge of Jesus in v. 10 seems to contemplate the immediate departure of the disciples for Galilee. But now a new aspect of the whole problem is thrust upon the investigator, the question as to the identity of "the brethren" of Jesus. Are "the brethren" of 28:10 the same as "the disciples" of 28:7? Are "the eleven disciples" who, according to 28:16, went to Galilee to the mountain where Jesus had commanded them to go, the only disciples who are in view in the earlier references to a reunion in Galilee? Matthew's use of these terms is illuminating.

By the term "my brethren," as used in Mt. 28:10, it is by no means clear that only the eleven disciples are meant. Apart from the instances where it is intended to describe a natural relationship, including the example in Mt. 12:46f. where "his mother and brethren" come to speak to him, the term "brother" or "brethren" is employed broadly to denote a spiritual relationship, in some cases more clearly than others referring directly to the fellowship of those who acknowledged Christ (Mt. 18:15; 23:8; *cf.* 5:22ff.; 7:3ff.; 18:21, 35). In only two instances besides Mt. 28:10 does Jesus use the expression "my brethren," and both clearly describe in the broadest possible way those who were attached to him. To those who reminded him that "his mother and brethren" were seeking him, Jesus intimated that these terms were more properly reserved for "his disciples," that is, for "whosoever doeth the will of my Father who is in heaven" (12:49f.). Here the expressions "his disciples" and "my brethren" are not restricted to the circle of the twelve (*cf.* Mk 3:34f.; Lk. 8:21). The other instance of the use of the phrase "my brethren" occurs in the discourse concerning the judgment, where the king pronounces blessing upon all who satisfied the needs of "one of these my brethren, even of the least" (Mt. 25:40). Here again it is clear that far more than the most intimate disciples are in mind. Accordingly the command of 28:10 that his brethren should depart for Galilee would most naturally be understood as including all persons attached to his cause who were then in the vicinity of Jerusalem. Only if it could be demonstrated that the twelve and the women comprised the whole company of Jesus' followers who were in Jerusalem and its environs at that time would it be plausible to limit the brethren to the eleven.

The narrow circle of disciples, who at first were twelve in number and later only eleven, appears indeed as a group that stands apart from all others as possessing special prerogatives and charged with unique responsibilities. And yet they are often seen to be a special group within a larger circle of disciples.[12] The distinction between the twelve and the larger group perhaps appears most clearly in connection with the record of the appointment of the apostles, for this select circle is ostensibly chosen from the entire company of his disciples (Mt. 9:37; 10:1; *cf.* Mk. 3:13ff.; 4:10, 34). It must be admitted that "the disciples" or "his disciples" does not at every point clearly include some in addition to the apostolic group. In the record of the transfiguration "the disciples" means only Peter, James and John

---

12 *Cf.* Mt. 10:1, 2, 5; 11:1; 19:28; 20:17; 26:14, 20, 47 and Mk. 3:13ff.; 4:10, 34; 6:7, 30; 9:35, 38; 10:32; 14:10, 13, 43. The disciples in turn are distinguished from "the crowds" and "the multitudes" who came into contact with Jesus but did not recognize his authority. Cf. Mt. 5:1; 7:28; 13:1, 10, 36; 23:1; 24:1, 3 and Mk. 3:7f., 32 and *passim.*

(Mt. 17:6, 10, 13), and in the account of the healing of the demoniac boy "thy disciples" perhaps includes none besides the other nine (17:16; *cf.* v. 19; Mk. 9:18, 28). Only the twelve participated in the last supper before his death, as well as in other intimate scenes of this period, but "the disciples" are definitely limited by the context to the twelve (Mt. 26:20 and 26:1, 8, 17f., 26, 35; *cf.* Mk. 14:17 and 14:12f.). It follows then that the words of Jesus concerning their being scattered and of the journey to Galilee were spoken to the twelve (Mt. 26:31f.). To conclude from this admission that the references in 28:7 and 10 were necessarily restricted in their application to the apostles would, however, be premature. Although Jesus called the twelve apart for private instruction, there were many others, including the women, who accompanied him into Jerusalem (Mt. 20:17; 21:8f., 15; 27:55; *cf.* 20:29; 21:46; 23:1; Mk. 10:32, 46; 11:8ff.; 15:40). There may have been, moreover, true disciples in addition to Joseph of Arimathea who lived in that region (*cf.* Mt. 19:13ff.; 27:57ff.; Mk. 10:13; 15:43ff.). Furthermore, although the prediction of the scattering of the sheep was spoken to the twelve, and their plight was the more shocking because of their previous intimacy and professions of loyalty, it would have included within its scope the whole company of disciples who were at the scene, not excepting even the women who beheld the crucifixion "from afar" (Mt. 27:55f.; Mk. 15:40f.). The "sheep of the flock" who were scattered comprehended more than the eleven; they must have included all of "the lost sheep of the house of Israel" who had been "found" by Christ. The application of the phrase "the sheep" at this point would require the exception only of disciples who were not in the same general vicinity (Mt. 26:31; 15:24; *cf.* 10:6, 16). Accordingly, the background of the resurrection narratives provided by Matthew and Mark suggests the definite possibility that the expression "my brethren" in Mt. 28:10, and as well perhaps also "the disciples" in 28:7 (Mk. 16:7), have in view a company of persons by no means restricted to the twelve.[13]

If the scattered sheep who, according to the Matthaean record, were to be reunited and welcomed by the smitten shepherd in Galilee comprise more than the eleven, it might well be expected that the final scene in Galilee, to which the narrative has been pointing forward, would provide some definite confirmation. Yet the details of the historical setting and developments are so meagre that such confirmation can hardly be more than incidental. Matthew is so absorbed with his purpose to center the reader's thought upon the momentous words of Jesus spoken on this occasion that little space is taken to picture the setting. Here too he is relatively unconcerned with geography and chronology. He has omitted any mention of the meeting of the women with "the disciples" or "the brethren." The question of the whereabouts of the women, whether they remained in Jerusalem or themselves returned to their Galilean homes, is left unanswered. The journey of the eleven to Galilee is introduced in an exceedingly abrupt manner. The particular place has been pre-arranged, we hear, but exactly when one does not discover. Nor is the scene of the rendezvous described more precisely than by the intimation that it was on "the mountain." All that we learn concerning the response of the eleven is that, when they saw him there, they worshipped. The paucity of historical details, and the concentration upon the message of Jesus, are however completely in accord with what has been

---

[13] *Cf.* also Lk. 24:9 which reports that the women told all these things "to the eleven and to all the rest."

observed previously as to the interest and method of the evangelist. No one dare insist therefore that Matthew would have been compelled to call attention explicitly to the presence of others besides the eleven if he so conceived of the situation. It may not be overlooked in particular that even in Matthew's earlier references to the reunion in Galilee the mention of the persons whom Jesus would await in Galilee is quite incidental to the main consideration, namely, the assurance that "the shepherd" would reach Galilee ahead of "the sheep" who at his death would be scattered abroad, and that he would appear to them there.

So far no account has been taken of the cryptic statement in Mt. 28:17, "but some doubted." May not this disturbing detail presuppose the presence of a larger company than the eleven? The evangelist's principal interest is in the apostles who here receive "the great commission." The eleven, he relates, met Jesus according to plan upon the mount, and when Jesus appeared to them to deliver his momentous message they worshipped. The word "worship" as used by Matthew may not always involve a full comprehension of deity. That it refers to an act of obeisance implying confidence and submission on the part of the worshipper rather than doubt or hesitation cannot, however, be questioned. It is employed, for example, to indicate the response of the women when Jesus hailed them after they had left the tomb (Mt. 28:9; *cf.* 2:2, 8, 11; 4:9f.; 8:2; 9:18; 14:33; 15:25; 18:26; 20:20). Two distinct attitudes towards Jesus seem clearly to be in view, an attitude of faith and obeisance and one of doubt or hesitation. The word "doubt" is of course not the equivalent of stark unbelief. In the only other instance of the use of this verb in the New Testament, in Mt. 14:31, it expresses Peter's lack of an adequate faith when he started to meet Jesus upon the water. Nevertheless in this narrative Peter's "little faith" and "doubt" stand in sharp antithesis to the later attitude of the disciples who, after the wind suddenly ceased, "worshipped" and said, "Truly thou art God's Son" (14:33). If then Matthew has in mind two distinct attitudes in reporting worship and doubt in 28:17, he must also have in view two distinct groups of persons; and since the eleven are described as worshipping, the doubt must be predicated of certain others. In a wholly incidental fashion, therefore, Matthew indicates the presence of others besides the apostles on this occasion. In the face of the early Christian tradition, reported by Paul in I Cor. 15:6, that Jesus appeared to "above five hundred brethren at once," the implication of Matthew's account that a considerable company of persons may have been present upon the mount in Galilee may not be summarily dismissed.

The view that the clause "but some doubted" implies the presence of others besides the eleven is supported, with more or less positiveness, by Alford, Plummer, Allen (p. 303), McNeile, Wellhausen and Klostermann. J. Weiss, in SNT, argues that the clause is so "stimmungswidrig" that it is best to regard it as an early textual gloss. Among those who understand Matthew as referring to "some" of the eleven are Meyer (E. T.), Bruce (ExGT), H. J. Holtzmann (HC) Zahn and Grosheide. See also Goguel, *La Foi a la Resurrection de Jesus*, 1933, pp. 278ff. and R. H. Lightfoot, *Locality and Doctrine*, p. 71, n. 2. The chief arguments advanced by the latter group of commentators are (1) that otherwise one would expect οἱ μέν in the first clause to contrast with οἱ δέ in the second, and (2) that the parallel constructions in Mt. 26:67 and Lk. 9:19 indicate that a distinct group is not in view.

Recognizing that the "worship" and the "doubt" described represent two irreconcilable attitudes, Meyer and Holtzmann understand Matthew as implying that a *majority* of the eleven, and not the entire company of apostles, "worshipped" while the rest "doubted." Since however Matthew states that the eleven worshipped, most advocates of the position that Matthew has in mind only the eleven as constituting the company present relieve the contrast between worship and doubt, by reducing the former to mere physical prostration in the presence of a supernatural manifestation (Zahn, Goguel) or the latter to a degree of hesitation (Grosheide, R. H. Lightfoot). It is doubtful, however, whether Matthew's use of these terms allows such obliterations of the contrast. Even the lowest possible connotation of προσκυνεῖν, a connotation which is highly inappropriate in the climax of Matthew's account, is hardly congruous with hesitation and doubt. And if the high sense of worship is retained, it becomes necessary to suppose that Matthew intends us to understand that not all of the eleven at once attained to the high level of adoration (Lightfoot) or that the doubt was only partial, being concerned not with the fact of the resurrection as such but with the identity of the person who now appeared, or the manner in which he was to be honored (Grosheide). These interpretations seem too subtle to be commended by the evangelist's language.

It may be admitted that the contrast between two groups might have been expressed more precisely if μέν had been inserted after οἱ in the former clause, or if ἄλλοι had been substituted for the article in the second. That the contrast could have been borne out only in some such fashion is, however, too bold an assumption. The appeal by Holtzmann to Lk. 9:19 is not to the point, since the construction there is not a parallel one. Mt. 26:67 does indeed provide a case in point, for the "some" who smote Jesus with the palms of their hands evidently comprise a group within the larger circle who have been described as having spit in his face and buffeted him. This passage does not, however, offer even formal support for the view of Meyer and Holtzmann, since the "some" here are clearly not a minority whose action is set in contrast with that of the majority. This passage offers a formal parallelism only for the view that some of the eleven hesitated or doubted even while they were worshipping or prostrating themselves before Christ. In our judgment the formal parallelism of this passage is not of sufficient weight to overcome the contrast that is set up by προσκυνεῖν and διστάζειν.

The appeal which has been made to the resurrection narrative of Matthew to support the Galilean Hypothesis has not taken due cognizance of the evangelist's aims and methods as disclosed both by what he actually says and what he passes over in silence. Quite apart from the evidence of Luke and John, and judging Matthew's testimony in the light of the structure of his resurrection narrative as a whole, as well as of the character of his gospel, the conclusion that he definitely excludes the possibility of a prior reunion with the eleven in Jerusalem seems to us not to be well established. Nothing is more obvious than that the evangelist does not aim to tell a complete story of what happened after the resurrection. Although his narrative does not appear to end as abruptly as Mark, it also would have to be regarded as incomplete if it were judged according to the standards of secular biography. His aim is not to tell the whole story, nor even to list as many evidences of the truth of the resurrection as possible. That his principal design is not to prove the reality of the resurrection by such testimony appears even from the exceedingly brief and incidental fashion in which the two appearances which he mentions are described: the appearance to the women near Jerusalem and to a company of disciples in Galilee (Mt. 28:9, 16ff.). Nevertheless, one may not fairly conclude from this negative consideration, namely, the consideration that he is not busy marshalling as much evidence as possible as proof of the resurrection, that he is indifferent to the physical reality of that event. For his account, even more emphatically than Mark's, dwells upon this fact by recounting not only the witness of the angel and of the women but also the testimony of the watch (Mt. 28:11ff.; *cf.* 27:63ff.; 28:4) to the empty tomb. His chief purpose, however, appears to be, not so much to recount appearances as isolated testimonies to an historical fact which was basic to the faith of the Christian church, as to trace the developments which were indispensable for an understanding of the occasion and meaning of the momentous disclosure of Jesus which he had chosen as the capstone of his gospel.

The question remains as to the reason for Matthew's absorption at the end of his narrative with the Galilean scene.[14] While Mark's record of the history of Christ ends, strictly speaking, with the story of the empty tomb, and merely intimates the imminent fulfillment of Jesus' word concerning a reunion in Galilee, Matthew actually finds the climax of his gospel in the revelation made on that occasion.

The answer commonly given by those who deny the historicity of the physical resurrection takes the form, as we have seen, of the Galilean Hypothesis. On this theory the faith in the resurrected Christ emerged in Galilee, far removed from the scene of the crucifixion, as the result of subjective experiences there of one or more of the disciples. Matthew and Mark, it is held, while admittedly not describing any such experience, contain a kernel of historical truth because of their common testimony to a reunion there. The record of prior appearances in Jerusalem, or its vicinity, as found in Luke and John and, it should be added, in Matthew, represent then a thoroughly dogmatic construction.[15]

This entire question has recently been placed in an entirely new perspective, as we have noticed above in connection with our study of Mark, by the theories of Lohmeyer

---

[14] See also the discussion of the Galilean interest of Mark above, pp. 38ff.

[15] In so far as this theory appeals to the evidence in Matthew and Mark, it has received adequate treatment above. The broader aspects of the theory, since they involve decisive presuppositions with respect to the historical credibility of the physical resurrection of Christ and a conjectural reconstruction of the history of the origin of the Christian faith, is not properly before us in this discussion.

On some of the broader questions see especially W. P. Armstrong, "The Resurrection of Jesus and Historical Criticism" in PThR, VIII (1910), pp. 247ff. Other significant articles on the resurrection of Jesus by the same author were published in PThR, V (1907), pp. 1ff. and XII (1914), pp. 586ff., in addition to the article in BTS previously cited.

and R. H. Lightfoot. On the background of a broad study of the topographical data these scholars conclude that the place which Galilee and Jerusalem occupy in the various gospels is dictated by, or at least strongly colored by, dogmatic conceptions. Mark's treatment of the life of Christ, it will be recalled, is dominated by the concept that Galilee was the "seat of revelation," the land of eschatological fulfillment, while Jerusalem was the "city of destruction and death." Matthew, it is maintained, differs from Mark only slightly: the contrast between Galilee and Jerusalem has been toned down at various points, and yet there is fundamentally the same regard for Galilee as the most truly holy land and birthplace of the Christian church.[16]

Does the Matthaean record actually display an adverse attitude toward Jerusalem which may explain the omission of a reunion with the disciples in that city? Galilee was indeed the place where, according to the divine will, he began his public ministry, and where he carried it on with the minimum of interference from the Jewish leaders. And Jerusalem was the appointed place of judgment and death. But the ministry of Jesus plainly was not directed only to Galilee, nor only to its environs, but to the whole of Israel (cf. Mt. 10:6, 23; 15:24). The fiercest opposition came from the Jewish leaders who had their residence in Jerusalem, and this city was the scene of his death, but these facts are far from implying that Jerusalem could not be intrusted with any disclosure of the glad tidings. If

---

[16] Cf. R. H. Lightfoot, *Locality and Doctrine*, pp. 66ff., 128ff.; Lohmeyer, *Galiläa und Jerusalem*, pp. 15f., 36ff. In view of the broad discussion of this theory in connection with the review of the Marcan data, no extensive treatment of its appeal to Matthew need be undertaken here. The main criticisms advanced there apply also at this point.

THE RESURRECTION NARRATIVE 185

Matthew does characterize the entrance of Christ into Galilee as the shining of light in a dark place, in accordance with the divine prophecy in Isaiah, he likewise, appealing to Zechariah, acclaims his entrance into Jerusalem as the coming of the king (Mt. 4:14ff.; 21:4f.). While the evangelist's record of the last days at Jerusalem reports extensively the judgment of Jesus upon the leaders and upon the city, there is also nevertheless the expression of his frequent desire to gather her children together (23:37). There too he was hailed as "blessed" (23:39). The fact that Jerusalem did not accept him does not alter the fact that Jesus offered himself graciously to her, and this consideration alone is of sufficient weight to demonstrate the untenability of the theory that Galilee alone was conceived of as the scene of revelation. Moreover, if the issue is viewed from the side of the people's response, it does not appear that the unbelief of Jerusalem is judged more blameworthy than the unbelief of the cities of Galilee, including even his own cities Nazareth and Capernaum (Mt. 11:20ff.; 13:54ff.). It is meaningful also that Jerusalem is still called "the holy city" (4:5; 27:53).

The force of this characterization of Jerusalem is by no means overcome by the observation that this was the traditional name of the city, and that it has reference to its age-long significance, not to its present state (so Lightfoot, *Locality and Doctrine*, p. 71, n. 1; pp. 127ff.; *cf.* also Lohmeyer, *Galiläa u. Jerusalem*, pp. 37, 91). Matthew can hardly have in mind a contrast between its traditional significance and its present rôle, for he specifically characterizes Jerusalem as owning the age-long record of having killed the prophets, thus stressing the continuity of its present attitude with the past (23:37). And if this gospel were dominated by the dogma that Jerusalem was the scene only of destruction and death, as opposed to revelation, the dogma could hardly fail to affect his characterizations of the city.

Most of the data mentioned above as impinging upon the theory of Lohmeyer and Lightfoot are actually mentioned by them, and are taken as evidence that Matthew moderated the point of view of Mark to a degree, or did not carry through the scheme with the same consistency. In our judgment such considerations do not allow due weight to the evidence.

There are other conspicuous features of Matthew that also fail to support this theory. Bethlehem of Judea, in accordance with divine prophecy, was the scene of the miraculous birth with its attendant disclosures. As in Mark the divine revelation at the baptism finds its setting outside of Galilee. Moreover, the universalism expressed in Mt. 8:11 and 28:19 militates against the dogma that excludes a particular area from the scope of the manifestations of blessings brought by Christ. Finally, it may not be overlooked that Jerusalem was the scene of the resurrection of Christ and of its accompanying revelation, as well as of an appearance of Jesus to the women. It may be argued indeed that the entire resurrection narrative in Matthew points forward so insistently to the scene in Galilee that all that precedes must be judged as merely preparatory and as of secondary significance. Such a judgment must be corrected, however, in the light of the extensive and weighty testimony to the empty tomb, but even if its preparatory and secondary character were admitted, the fact would remain that the scene *is* Jerusalem and the contents are revelatory in nature. If Matthew was obsessed with a dogma which restricted revelation to Galilee, it does not appear how he could have allowed such prominence to be given to the divine action in Jerusalem.

The evangelists select their materials in accordance with their distinctive aims. Mark is content to intimate the imminent fulfillment of the extraordinary prophecy of Jesus and closes his gospel on the note of the reverent awe of the women who had seen and heard the divine work and word at the empty tomb. Matthew closely follows Mark but adds an account of the fulfillment of the word of Jesus, which discloses that the full significance of this reunion was to be found, not so much in the fact that Jesus confirmed their faith in him, as that it was the occasion of a stupendous revelation, a revelation of the divine investiture of the risen Christ with universal sovereignty, of the consequent commission of the disciples, and of his continuous presence with them until the consummation. A proclamation of the glad tidings of Jesus Christ could most appropriately conclude on this high note of Christ's presence with his servants; a secular history of Christ would have needed to relate the end of his earthly career. But Matthew is not writing as a secular historian or chronicler of the life of Jesus, or of the origin of the Christian church, when he ends his narrative with the description of the scene in Galilee. The whole of his resurrection narrative is suspended between the two poles of the extraordinary prophecy of Christ on the mount of Olives concerning the reunion in Galilee and the stupendous revelation on the mount in Galilee concerning the world-wide mission. The interest of the evangelist in Galilee therefore is quite incidental to his interest in the revelations of Christ. In so far as there is an absorption with Galilee it may be explained as due to his concern to establish the fulfillment of the word of Jesus.

CHAPTER VII

THE AUTHORITY OF THE OLD TESTAMENT AND THE AUTHORITY OF CHRIST

SYNOPSIS

I. *Jesus and the Old Testament.*

A. Matthew's appeal to prophecy: establishes the divine character of the history of Christ; involves a philosophy of the history of revelation; the question whether this philosophy coincides with that of Jesus depends on the historicity of the messianic consciousness and of Jesus' use of the Old Testament to interpret this consciousness.

B. The pervasive evidence in Matthew of Jesus' affirmation of the Scriptures of the Old Testament: (1) Jesus' appeal to the Old Testament in controversy; (2) Mt. 5:17-19 implies validity of the Old Testament, but also the dawn of a new era of divine action and speech; (3) The antitheses in Mt. 5 stress the absoluteness of Jesus' authority, but not at the expense of the authority of the Old Testament:

a. Shown especially in teaching concerning anger, fleshly desire, and hate, where Jesus affirms the law but also utters a polemic against an externalistic interpretation of the law, but

b. Also true of the other antitheses, as shown particularly by the teaching concerning divorce, in which Jesus demands that a legal provision directed to a particular occasion be seen in the perspective of the basic teaching of the law.

II. *The Authority of the Son of God.*

A. The authority with which Jesus speaks alongside of the Old Testament is grounded in his personal qualification as Son of God: the fundamental character of Mt. 11:27, intimating that the Son is both subject and object of sovereign divine disclosure; Mt. 14:33 and 16:16 as two extraordinary instances of apprehension of the divine revelation concerning Jesus; the latter, recording Peter's confession, expresses an estimate of Jesus implicit in Mark's account; Mt. 16:17 does not imply that a new epochal disclosure was made at this juncture, nor does it intimate that Peter experiences a completely new subjective apprehension, but contrasts the apprehension of those who had eyes to see with the purely human estimates of others; Mt. 14:33 then is not anachronistic; its harmony with Mk. 6:51f.

B. The question whether Matthew tones down the human side of Christ: the emotional life of Jesus is not completely absent, although not as prominent as in Mark; not the result of theological dogmatizing but to be traced to the personal qualities of the evangelist and especially to his distinctive aim; the latter clearly includes the purpose to set forth the history of Jesus in the perspective of the history of revelation, and this would call for less occupation with the subjective aspects of his life; that Jesus had a truly human life is everywhere presupposed; the Son of David as well as the Son of God.

IN PURSUANCE of our effort to discover the distinctiveness of the testimony of Matthew, our attention has been directed to certain features which come to conspicuous disclosure through a comparison of the disposition of this gospel with that of Mark. The occupation with details of the life of Jesus before his public ministry and after the resurrection and the extensive report of the message of Jesus obviously comprise two of these distinguishing features. Yet neither serves effectively to set Matthew off from the other gospels. The former feature he shares with Luke and, in part, with John; the latter likewise is characteristic of Luke and John, and, in any case, in view of the space which Mark devotes to the teaching of Jesus, is of relative importance. There is, however, a third feature of Matthew's narrative which apparently provides a cue for the understanding of this evangelist's individual approach to his subject, namely, that afforded by his interpretation of the history of Christ by reference to Old Testament prophecy. This trait is in truth not completely absent from the other gospels, but it is so prominent in Matthew that few readers can have failed to notice it. Only as he depicts the life and ministry of Jesus as the fulfillment of the revelation of the Old Testament does the evangelist, as it were, write in the first person singular; otherwise his personality remains completely hidden behind the proclamation of the gospel. Accordingly the ultimate question of the authority of Jesus Christ must be approached by way of the consideration of the affirmation of the authority of the Scriptures of the Old Testament.

Matthew's appeal to the Old Testament, we have had occasion to observe in Chapter V, is displayed prominently in his record of the birth and infancy of Jesus (Mt. 1:22f.; (2:5f.); 2:15, 17f., 23). As a matter of fact there are nearly as many appeals to prophetic testimony in this brief section as in the whole of the rest of the gospel, this concentration receiving its most adequate explanation perhaps from the fact that, when Jesus began his public ministry, his own deeds and words served to indicate the divine nature of his person and mission. Nevertheless, the Matthaean portrayal of the public ministry is distinguished from the Marcan record which it parallels by several indications that the ministry of Jesus had followed a divine plan which had been intimated to the prophets long beforehand. The initiation of his work in Galilee and the entrance into

Jerusalem just before his death, the two focal points of Jesus' mission, fulfill declarations made through the prophet Isaiah and Zechariah (Mt. 4:14ff.; 21:4f.). Specific aspects of the healing and teaching ministry, moreover, are represented as being performed in order to fulfill prophetic testimony. From the Isaianic discourses concerning the Suffering Servant, Matthew derives both the active and passive aspects of the healing ministry of Jesus, both the mercy which he constantly demonstrated toward the afflicted and humble and the quiet reserve which commanded that he should not be made manifest (Mt. 8:17; 12:17ff.). A passage from the Psalter is fulfilled in Jesus' parabolic discourses concerning the kingdom of heaven (Mt. 13:35). In the passion narrative of Matthew, as in that of Mark, the fulfillment of the divine will is fully disclosed by Jesus' own references to the Scriptures, but Matthew also observes that certain details of the unfolding of the events, the reward which Judas received for his iniquity and its final disposition, as well as the manner of Jesus' entrance upon the scene of his death, has been intimated in the Scriptures (Mt. 27:9f.; 21:4f.).

An impressive confirmation of the evangelist's faith in the divine character of the Old Testament revelation is provided by these concrete quotations. But his affirmation of the Old Testament is not introduced for its own sake, for it is clearly incidental to an affirmation of the divine character of the history of Christ. The evangelist is not developing an argument for the divinity of the prophetic record by reference to the fulfillment of specific predictions, but, presupposing with his readers the inspiration of the Old Testament, he is concerned to establish or confirm the belief that the history of Jesus, in its origin, purpose, unfolding and consummation, was to be understood as the action of God in fulfilling his own word to the prophets. Here there is involved therefore a philosophy of revelation, an understanding of the history of revelation, which is of the most profound significance for the illumination of the whole of Matthew's gospel.

The interpretation of the history of revelation in terms of prophecy and fulfillment, it may be observed, involves a doctrine of the progressive character of revelation. In recognizing the revelation as progressive, however, we must take note that, while it as such is antithetical to a mechanical conception of revelation, it also must be qualitatively distinguished from an evolutionary interpretation of religion. The disclosures of the divine purpose and action in the history of Christ are not isolated blocks of revelation which are to be joined to blocks which have been previously placed in position, nor are they related to what had come before simply as the full flowering of a bud. Both the divine prophecy and the divine fulfillment require to be comprehended in their distinctiveness and in their unity, neither one being stressed at the expense of the other. There is a unity guaranteed by the single divine actor and expressed in a single message of righteousness and salvation, but there is also a qualitative difference between prophecy and fulfillment which excludes the supposition that the latter follows from the former as a matter of course. In Matthew's appeal to the Old Testament, in other words, there is implicit the doctrine of the covenants, the old and the new, each representing a separate manifestation of the divine action and speech.

Among the questions which have risen in our times with reference to Matthew's use of the Old Testament, none is more pressing than that which raises the issue of the historical validity of his interpretation of the career of

Jesus in terms of divine prophecy. Is Matthew himself, or one of the early Christian communities, responsible for this feature as an aspect of the primitive defense of the truth of Christianity? Or does this interpretation of the history of Jesus rest ultimately upon Jesus' own interpretation of the meaning of his life?

The final decision between these two main positions is bound up with the decision reached as to the credibility of the witness of Matthew, and of the other gospels, to the messianic consciousness of Jesus. For, by common consent, the position of Matthew, shared with the other records, is that Jesus was controlled by the conviction that he was the promised Messiah of the Old Testament. While Matthew himself appears to be responsible for the several separate instances of appeal to prophetic testimony which have been mentioned, he clearly was not the originator of the belief that Jesus viewed his own history as the fulfillment of messianic prophecy. To establish that proposition would require nothing less than the demonstration that all of the other records derived their messianic estimate of Jesus from him.

The most explicit evidence of Jesus' messianic self-appraisal is found in the record of the discourses delivered during the last days in Jerusalem. Direct appeal is made to the Old Testament to substantiate the judgment that, though rejected of "the builders," he was made "the head of the corner" in the new structure of God's building (Mt. 21:42ff.; Ps. 118:22f.; *cf*. Mk. 12:10f.; Lk. 20:17). In a controversy with the Pharisees, wherein indeed he does not make direct claim of messiahship, he proves from an inspired word of David that the Messiah's sovereignty extends even to David himself, and that therefore the title Son of David does not express the full transcendence and authority of the Messiah (Mt. 22:43ff.; Ps. 110:1; *cf.* Mk. 12:35ff.; Lk. 20:41ff.). Similarly the divine instrumentality in his death is expressed by use of Zechariah's description of the Shepherd whom the Lord would smite (Mt. 26:31; Zech. 13:7; *cf.* Mk. 14:27). The frequency of such appeals to Old Testament prophecy in the climactic situations at the end of his career may not, however, be construed as proof that this characteristic emerged as a late development in the process of his self-appraisal. Only slightly less clearly does Jesus reflect upon his person and mission in his employment of Isaianic prophecy to answer the inquiry of the Baptist and in his quotation from Malachi to interpret the preparatory significance of the forerunner (Mt. 11:4ff., 10; Isa. 35:5f.; 61:1; Mal. 3:1; *cf.* Lk. 7:22f., 27). Moreover, it is now admitted on all sides that the gospels represent Jesus as being completely sure of his mission at least as early as the beginning of his public ministry.

In order to appreciate Jesus' regard for the Old Testament prophetic teaching concerning himself, and on its background to evaluate Matthew's distinctive appeal to prophecy, it is necessary to divest one's self of the notion that the correspondence discovered between isolated utterances of the prophets and isolated details of Jesus' history involves a mechanistic or atomistic understanding of the revelation of Scripture. The isolated utterances are not thought of as so many individual disclosures as to the future, but as integral parts of an organism. As an organism, for all of its diversity and growth, it constitutes in its entirety a revelation of the will of God. Since the Messiah as the Anointed of the Lord is invested with divine authority and appointed to accomplish the divine will, his appearance and activity on the scene of history must at every point give evidence of correspondence and compliance with the revealed will of God. Religion for Jesus was not mysticism; it was rather the conscious response of the individual to the revelation of God in history. The evidences of agreement with the Old Testament supplied by Matthew's comments and by Jesus' quotations alike have meaning only on this high view of the Old Testament.[1]

The evidence that Jesus' appeal to messianic prophecy involved an affirmation of the whole of the revelation of the Old Testament Scriptures, and not merely of a few isolated prophetic utterances, is supplied by Matthew in abundant measure. Critics who are busy with efforts to reconstruct the "historical" life of Jesus commonly seek to dissociate Jesus from the Matthaean portrayal of his attitude toward the Old Testament, but there is little readiness to deny that the Jesus of Matthew's testimony accepted the Old Testament as inspired Scripture. In his replies to Satan's temptations in the wilderness, the decisive word is constantly the authoritative commands of Scripture: it is sufficient to say simply, "It is written" (Mt. 4:4, 6, 10; *cf.* Lk. 4:4, 8, 12). Likewise the final court of appeal in his controversies with the Jewish leaders, Pharisees and Sadducees alike, is the Scriptures. His reply to the Sadduceean

---

[1] *Cf.* Vos, *The Teaching of Jesus Concerning the Kingdom of God and the Church*, pp. 12f.: "No array of explicit statements in which he acknowledges his acceptance of the Old Testament Scriptures as the word of God can equal in force this implied subordination of himself and of his work to the one great scheme of which the ancient revelation given to Israel formed the preparatory stage. Indeed, in appropriating for himself the function of bringing the kingdom, in laying claim to the Messianic dignity, Jesus seized upon that in the Old Testament which enabled him at one stroke to make its whole historic movement converge in himself. There is in this a unique combination of the most sublime self-consciousness and the most humble submission to the revelation of God in former ages. Jesus knew himself at once as the goal of history and the servant of history."

attack upon the doctrine of the resurrection took the form of the simple query whether they had not read what God had spoken in Exodus 3:6 (Mt. 22:23ff.; *cf*. Mk. 12:18-27; Lk. 20:27-38). While Jesus shared the Sadduceean affirmation of the authority of the Pentateuch, his position had greater formal agreement with that of the Pharisees who accepted the rest of the Old Testament as well. In spite of his agreement with the Pharisees on the extent of the Scriptures, however, he regarded their position as in reality impinging upon the divine authority of the Scriptures. Jesus charged the Pharisees with transgressing and making void the commandment and word of God since they accorded their traditions a place alongside of and in effect above the law of God, thus obscuring the qualitative distinction between the word of God and the commandments of men, and actually abrogating the divine law (Mt. 15:1ff.; *cf*. Mk. 7:1).[2]

---

[2] *Cf*. also Mt. 19:3ff.; 21:42; 22:41ff. for other instances of Jesus' appeal to the Scriptures to silence his opponents.

Mt. 23:2f., which places the scribes and Pharisees on Moses' seat, and enjoins obedience to their injunctions, apparently contradicts the qualitative distinction between the law of God and the tradition of the elders. "Here," says Streeter, *The Four Gospels*, p. 257, "we have attributed to our Lord an emphatic commandment to obey, not only the Law, but the scribal interpretation of it. That is to say, He is represented as inculcating scrupulous obedience to that very 'tradition of the elders' which He specifically denounces in Mk. vii:13." And Streeter adds that the point of view is to be explained as due to the derivation of this discourse in large part from a special source of the evangelist.

In spite of the *prima facie* impression that, in affirming the validity of the Law of Moses, these verses go to the extreme of acknowledging the authority of the teaching of the scribes and Pharisees, this interpretation must be set aside, for it involves a contradiction with the rest of the discourse. In the very next verse (Mt. 23:4) Jesus speaks evidently without approval of their imposition of "heavy burdens" upon men. In Mt. 23:16ff. he condemns them as "blind guides" because of their

And in addition to the impressive weight of the testimony borne by Jesus' use of Scripture, we learn from Matthew of his express didactic teaching of the binding force of the law and the prophets:

> "Think not that I came to destroy the law or the prophets; I came not to destroy, but to fulfill. For verily I say unto you, until heaven and earth pass away, one jot or one tittle shall in no wise pass from the law until all things be accomplished. Whosoever therefore shall break one of these least commandments, and shall teach men so, shall be called least in the kingdom of heaven, but whosoever shall do and teach them, he shall be called great in the kingdom of heaven" (Mt. 5:17-19).

The fulfillment and accomplishment of the law and the prophets, as opposed to their destruction and mutilation, which Jesus expresses here as the purpose of his mission, involves inescapably the conviction that the entire Old Testament possesses permanent validity as the Word of God.

To observe that this teaching of Jesus involves his affirmation of the divine character of the Old Testament does not, however, exhaust its implications. The fulfillment of the law, like the fulfillment of the prophets, while presupposing and reaffirming its divine truth and authority, predicates the dawn of a new era. The law and the prophets do not produce their own fulfillment. It is the presence

---

casuistic deliverances regarding swearing, and in 23:23f. he condemns them for leaving undone "the weightier matters of the law, justice and mercy and faith." The polemic against the scribes and Pharisees in this chapter is therefore by no means confined to their sins of omission; it also is directed against their traditions. In so far then as Jesus approves their teaching because they "sit on Moses' seat," he cannot be understood as countenancing interpretations of Moses which added to Moses, or in effect set him aside. In the light of the whole discourse therefore, the teaching of Jesus in Mt. 23:2f. is to the effect that the scribes and Pharisees were to be honored in their affirmation of the law of Moses, but decidedly not to be imitated in their non-observance of it.

of Christ alone which accomplished this end, and this fact, in the light of Matthew's total witness to Christ, clearly involves new divine action and speech. The fulfillment of the law and the prophets represents not a mere repetition or reiteration of the old revelation, but the announcement of the appearance of the age to which the old revelation looked forward. Accordingly, Matthew's witness to Christ finds its distinctiveness, or at least a highly important aspect of it, in its portrayal of the history of Jesus Christ in the perspective of the history of revelation. And this means far more than that he was the Messiah of the Old Testament Scriptures. The profound affirmation of Matthew is that *the coming of the Messiah of promise signifies the coming of one whose life and teaching were themselves a new epochal revelation that was the consummation of the old.*

That Jesus' fulfillment of the Old Testament law involved far more than an affirmation of the validity of the law appears unmistakably in the illustrations of his interpretation of the law provided by the antitheses of the sermon on the mount. The accent on the authoritative new utterances of Christ in truth is so powerful that in certain instances an apparent impingement upon the abiding authority of the law is disclosed. Six times Jesus, completely on his own authority, and without any attempt to vindicate his categorical declarations, seems to set his own pronouncements in antithesis to "that which had been spoken," the latter deliverances consisting of, or at least including, in every instance a quotation from the law of Moses (Mt. 5:21ff., 27ff., 31f., 33ff., 38ff., 43ff.). It was the absoluteness with which Jesus spoke, as possessing authority in his own right, and not deriving the authority of his utterances from Scripture or revered traditions like the scribes, that caused the crowds to express amazement at this teaching (Mt. 7:28). There had appeared on the scene a new self-confident voice, the voice of one who assumed an authority which was in no sense inferior to that of the commandments of God given through Moses.

The sovereignty with which Jesus speaks is so absolute and unequivocal that his fulfillment of the law seems to carry with it the invalidation of the law of Moses. In the light of Jesus' categorical affirmation of the validity of the law and the prophets which immediately precedes the antithesis, and of his decisive use of the authority of the Scriptures in controversy, however, it would be rash to conclude, without the most careful scrutiny of Jesus' words, that he actually meant to abrogate the authority of the law.

In three of the antitheses it is perfectly clear that Jesus' pronouncements presuppose the authority of the Old Testament commands, and that his own teaching represents a proclamation of the full implications of these commandments in opposition to the casuistic and legalistic interpretations of the scribes. What Jesus says about the sins of anger against one's brother, of fleshly desire, and of hate against one's enemies (Mt. 5:21ff., 27ff., 43f.), cannot plausibly be construed as impinging in the least upon the validity of the sixth and seventh commandments of the Decalogue and of the injunction to love one's neighbor. No hint is given of a relaxing of the authority of the law; on the contrary he indicates that the demands of God are more comprehensive and more exacting than men had supposed. Most pointedly his utterances are directed against the current interpretations of the law. It is perhaps in the sixth of the antitheses that this implication appears most clearly:

> "Ye have heard that it was said, Thou shalt love thy neighbor, and thou shalt hate thine enemy. But I say unto you, Love your enemies, and pray for those who persecute you" (Mt. 5:43f.).

Only the words, "Thou shalt love thy neighbor," comprise a divine injunction (Lev. 19:18); the conclusion, "Thou shalt hate thine enemy," is an inference which could be drawn only on the basis of an externalistic and atomistic approach to the law of God.[3]

That the approach of Jesus to the Scriptures was far from being externalistic and atomistic is confirmed at many points. Not all of the commands stood on the same level as isolated precepts, but all were unified and controlled by the commandments to love God himself with heart, soul, mind and strength, and one's neighbor as one's self (Mt. 22:37ff.; *cf.* Mk. 12:29ff.; Lk. 10:27ff.). Similarly he comprehends the demands of the law and the prophets under the injunction, "All things therefore whatsoever ye would that men should do unto you, even so do ye also to them" (Mt. 7:12). The same repudiation of a shallow externalism appears in Jesus' teaching concerning the fourth command. Without implying for a moment that the command was no longer valid, he condemns the application of the Pharisees on the ground that they failed to comprehend it in the light of the preeminent requirement of mercy (Mt. 12:7; *cf.* 9:13; 23:23f.).[4]

---

[3] According to Billerbeck, S-BK, I, p. 353, the injunction, "Thou shalt hate thine enemy," cannot be traced to any particular source, and he conjectures that it probably was a popular maxim of the day. In reviewing the rabbinic teaching, pp. 264ff., he indicates that in general hate was condemned, but in certain instances it was permitted and in others even commanded.

[4] *Cf.* Vos, *op. cit.*, p. 109: "He once more made the voice of the Law the voice of the living God, who is present in every commandment, so absolute in his demands, so personally interested in man's conduct, so all-observant, that the thought of yielding to him less than the

It follows from these observations that the formulae employed to introduce the first member of the several antitheses, whether in the form, "Ye have heard that it was said unto them of old time" (Mt. 5:21, 33),[5] or, "Ye have heard that it was said" (5:27, 38, 43), or simply, "It was said" (5:31), are not intended to correspond to "It is written," which Jesus often employs in appealing to the final authority of Scripture. In every other instance where the form "it was said," or its equivalent, is used in connection with a passage of Scripture, it is specifically stated that the speaker is the Lord himself or one of his prophets (cf., e.g., Mt. 1:22; 2:17; 22:31; 24:15). Here, on the contrary, the non-designation of the speaker and the ostensible reference to instruction which had been *heard* by the people from their teachers rather than read directly from the Scriptures, taken in connection with the polemic which Jesus is directing against the Pharisees in his teaching concerning righteousness, (cf., e.g., Mt. 5:20), indicates that the quotations of Scripture are introduced as illustrations of scribal interpretations rather than as Jesus' own evaluations of the meaning of the commandments.

---

whole inner life, the heart, the soul, the mind, the strength, can no longer be tolerated. Thus quickened by the spirit of God's personality, the law becomes in our Lord's hands a living organism, in which soul and body, spirit and letter, the greater and smaller commandments are to be distinguished, and which admits of being reduced to great comprehensive principles in whose light the weight and purport of all single precepts are to be intelligently appreciated."

[5] The A.V. renders τοῖς ἀρχαίοις "by them of old time," and this construction finds some modern support, e.g., by Grosheide, *Mattheus*, KNT, *ad loc*. The contrast is then between "the ancients" and Jesus (ἐγώ). In support of the position that the dative is an indirect object, in contrast to ὑμῖν, see the comments of Alexander, Zahn (note 90), McNeile, Klostermann. This view is grammatically easier and is intrinsically strong, whether "the ancients" are understood as the men of Moses' time or more broadly as referring to earlier generations.

With respect to the other three antitheses, which concern divorce, oaths and *ius talionis*, there appears at first blush to be an abrogation on Jesus' part of that which had been written in the law of Moses. He seems to set aside Mosaic provisions which allowed for separation from a wife, for swearing and for retribution, and to have substituted for them absolute prohibitions. Since these utterances are commonly regarded as evidences of a radical break with the objective authority of the law, and as requiring that Matthew 5:17-19 be interpreted either as allowing for such a relaxation of the law, or as originating from Matthew rather than from Christ (involving then the presence in the early church of a legalism from which Christ himself was free), it is obligatory to consider these passages with care. In our judgment, no escape from the plain implications of Mt. 5:17-19 is possible by way of exegesis. The explicit and emphatic affirmation of the authority of the law and the prophets excludes the interpretation of "fulfillment" and "accomplishment" as euphemisms for "relaxation" or "invalidation" or "spiritualization." The real issue is therefore whether Matthew introduces a contradiction into the record of Jesus' teaching by making him affirm most emphatically the validity of the law and then equally emphatically its annulment.[6]

---

[6] For the position that understands Mt. 5:17-19 as implying a Judaistic legalism, see Bultmann, *Jesus*, 1926, pp. 60f. (E.T., *Jesus and the Word*, 1934, pp. 62f.); *Geschichte d. syn. Trad.*, 1931, pp. 146f. Dibelius similarly speaks of legalistic and secular influences: *The Message of Jesus Christ*, 1939, pp. 160f.; cf. *Jesus*, 1939, p. 100. See also Streeter, *op. cit.*, pp. 256f. The merit of this position is that it plainly recognizes that these verses imply the objective validity of the law and the prophets.

As an example of the point of view which seeks to resolve the problem by an exegesis which in effect denies that Jesus meant to affirm the objective authority of the Old Testament, I may cite Robinson's

Does Jesus' teaching on divorce involve a weakening of the authority of the law of Moses? Several considerations bear upon the determination of the answer to this question. So far as the quotation from Deut. 24:1 is concerned, it may not be overlooked that it is not introduced into the discussion by Jesus, introduced, that is, only in order to contradict it, but as a passage which the Pharisees were wont to cite in order to substantiate a lax attitude towards divorce. This appears not only from the repetition of the formula, "It was said," which in this context points to Pharisaic interpretations, but also from the contexts in which the reference appears here and in Matthew 19:3ff. (*cf.* Mk. 10:2ff.). In the latter context the passage is explicitly quoted by the Pharisees in order to ground a liberal policy, and in Mt. 5:32 the implication of Jesus' words is to the same effect. The meaning of Mt. 5:31 is therefore somewhat as follows: "Ye have heard of the appeal of Jewish teachers to Deut. 24:1 in the interest of substantiating a policy which permits husbands, freely at their own pleasure, to divorce their wives simply by providing them with a duly attested document of the transaction."

The Deuteronomic passage definitely implies then a reck-

---

estimate of the meaning of Jesus (MNT): "He did not come to destroy, but to fulfil, to make complete, to perfect, to emend, to give the temporary thing, with its numerous occasional details, an eternal validity. The Law had been an interim expedient, the best that could be devised until the fulness of time, for the securing of certain ends. But under the regime of Jesus these ends can be still better secured, and the Law, though superseded as the final authority, will be fulfilled, completed, absorbed into a higher rule of life." On our part, of course, we are far from disregarding the progressive character of divine revelation, including especially the radical implications of the new revelation in Christ, but these implications are set forth in the teaching of Jesus with an insistence upon continuity with respect to truth and authority between the revelation of the Old Testament and that of the new dispensation.

oning with the practice of divorce when the husband found "something unseemly" in his wife, and makes provision for the issuance of a certification of the divorce. There was a dispute among the rabbis as to what might be included under "something unseemly," the school of Shammai maintaining that it referred to something distinctly shameful while the school of Hillel allowed that it might even include the provocation caused by the burning of his food.[7] It is clear then that the passage was appealed to currently to substantiate a much more liberal attitude toward divorce than Jesus was willing to countenance. However, whatever grounds for divorce the Mosaic enactment may have had in view, the thrust of the passage in its original setting is not to establish grounds for divorce, but, presupposing the practice of divorce on various grounds, to provide some protection for the woman from the harshness of her husband. The aim of the legislation is not to condone divorce as such, but to mitigate its evil consequences. Although then the use made of this passage in order to substantiate laxness was illegitimate, the fact remains that the Mosaic provision for the protection of the woman assumes that divorce was permissible. Christ condemns what Moses accepted as part of the *status quo*.

Does it follow, however, that Jesus actually implies that he is setting aside the objective authority of the law of Moses? Before anyone presumes to answer this question in the affirmative, he must take account of certain weighty considerations on the other side. In this very context where Jesus disputes with the Pharisees concerning the legitimacy of divorce, he assumes the validity of the law! For he appeals to the record of the creation and of the creation ordinance of marriage in Genesis to substantiate his teach-

---

[7] See Billerbeck, S-BK, I, pp. 312ff.

ing that the marriage union is indissoluble (Mt. 19:4ff.; Gen. 1:27; 5:2; 2:24). Moreover, in condemning divorce as adultery, he condemns it as a violation of the seventh commandment. If therefore Jesus were setting aside the law he would have to be acknowledged as doing so by way of affirming the binding authority of the same law. There is then no impingement of the authority of the law as such, but there is an insistence that a certain isolated provision be placed in its proper perspective within the context of the entire law. As we have observed above, the affirmation of the authority of law on Jesus' part did not carry with it the implication that its provisions were to be understood mechanically and atomistically. The lesser commands are to be subordinated to the greater commands of the law; the details must be regarded as elements in a comprehensive unity.

The particular place which the Deuteronomic provision occupied within the revelation of the entire law is intimated by Jesus himself in his observations in Matthew (19:8f.; *cf.* Mk. 10:5). He states that the commandment with reference to a bill of divorce was enacted "with regard to the hardness of their heart." It was not a commandment dictated by the nature of God and his righteousness in relation to his creatures, as was true of the creation ordinance of marriage, but by the subjective state of sinful men. The commandment was contingent, not absolute; it was temporary and positive rather than permanent as an expression of God's moral will.[8] This distinction between the permanent and

---

[8] Whether the reference to the hardness of men's hearts as the occasion of the enactment respecting a bill of divorce has in view the harshness of the husband which was to be mitigated, a thought entirely in keeping with the context in Deuteronomy, or envisages the generally low spiritual state of the children of the Exodus, is difficult to decide. In either case the occasion is a concrete historical situation

temporary in God's law does qualify one's understanding of it and its application to a concrete situation, but in no wise diminishes the objective authority of the law and the prophets.

Jesus indeed is so far from substituting his own authority for that of the law in his teaching concerning divorce that, as a matter of fact, the sovereignty of his own utterance, introduced by the formula, "But I say unto you," does not receive quite the same accent as in the antitheses previously reviewed. There is not even the semblance of the enunciation of new principles, but rather the authoritative interpretation of the revealed will of God as, from the beginning, involving the inference which he explicitly pronounces, namely, that "he who divorces his wife, saving for the cause of fornication, maketh her an adulteress" (Mt. 5:32).

We turn now to a consideration of the questions raised by the fourth of the antitheses which concerns the utterance of oaths (Mt. 5:33ff.). The teaching of Jesus that the disciples should not swear at all appears to set up an antithesis between his doctrine and the Old Testament provisions with respect to oaths. And the authority with which Jesus speaks on this subject seems to be asserted at the expense of the authority of the Old Testament. If one looks beneath the surface, however, appearance and reality will be seen again not to coincide. The words quoted as spoken to "them of old time" are accurate enough as a summary of Old Testament teaching, although not a precise quotation (Ex. 20:7; Lev. 19:12; Num. 30:2; Deut. 23:21). Evidently, this formulation, considered as a summary of the divine requirements concerning swearing, was

---

in the life of the theocracy, and the legislation bears more of a civil than a moral character. See Alexander on Mark 10:5.

represented as implying that if only swearing were not to a false proposition and did not profane the name of God, there was no need to take oaths seriously. Once again a fundamentally false approach to the divine law is in view and is being condemned, an approach which through externalistic and casuistic interpretation of isolated passages resulted in the justification of frivolous oaths, oaths by heaven and earth, by Jerusalem, by one's head, or the like.[9] Jesus condemns such vain efforts to avoid a reckoning with God in all of one's asseverations, whether in the form of oaths or not, by the declaration that they were not to swear at all. Although no qualification of this statement is mentioned, it clearly is qualified by the context so as to demand its confinement to the relationship between brethren. The righteousness of the kingdom, Jesus teaches, involves such a regard for the truth that simple affirmations and denials should suffice. That the declaration of Jesus cannot be meant to apply to oaths as required in civil relationships, for example, is confirmed by the fact that Jesus himself, when adjured by the high priest to say whether he was the Christ, the Son of God, gave his assent (Mt. 26:63). To discover in Jesus' teaching in Mt. 5:34ff. an absolute prohibition of oaths under all circumstances, and to conclude that Jesus took issue with the requirements of the Mosaic law concerning false or profane swearing, is to apply to these words the same externalistic approach which Jesus condemned in the Pharisees. The fulfillment of the law in this instance likewise, therefore, does not relax the authority of the law but sets forth its radical and ultimate meaning. It remains significant, nevertheless, that it is

---

[9] *Cf.* Mt. 5:34-36; 23:16-22. See Billerbeck, S-BK, I, pp. 332ff. for illustrations from rabbinic teaching.

Jesus who, setting aside current misinterpretation, pronounces with sovereign self-assurance what God truly requires.

Brief consideration must also be given to the fifth antithesis (Mt. 5:38ff.). If Jesus' teaching concerning retaliation is viewed in the light of the principles which have emerged from a study of the other antitheses, the harmony of his pronouncement of his own authority with the recognition of the objective authority of the Old Testament cannot be denied. Jesus' quotation of *ius talionis*, as recorded in Ex. 21:24 and other passages, was evidently not intended to express his own judgment as to what the Old Testament taught on the subject of personal rights, but as a recollection of the teaching which had been appealed to in order to justify personal revenge. The purpose of Jesus is not to annul the law of retribution as applying to civil life, but to set forth the ethical principles which are demanded by the righteousness of God and which must come to expression in the kingdom of God. Hence he teaches in characteristically paradoxical and figurative form that, rather than resort to vindictiveness, one should readily allow one's self to suffer loss.[10]

---

[10] *Cf.* Mt. 5:29f. See Alexander *ad loc.* and Ridderbos, *De Strekking der Bergrede naar Mattheus*, 1936, Par. 36. It is interesting that Zeitlin, *Who Crucified Jesus?* 1942, pp. 119ff., while admitting that the Pharisees set aside the *lex talionis* by a legal fiction, holds that Jesus affirmed the validity of this law. The difference between Jesus and the Pharisees on this point, he says, was that instead of following the pharisaic process of "interpretation," Jesus "appealed to the conscience of the plaintiff not to demand an eye for an eye and not to resist evil by repaying evil" (p. 121). Actually Jesus went far beyond appealing to men not to use their rights, for the heart of his instruction is that personal vindictiveness is to be condemned as contrary to God's will. See the writer's discussion in WThJ, V (May, 1943), pp. 156ff. The quotation from *Who Crucified Jesus?* is by permission of the publishers, Harper & Brothers.

Understood as illustrations of Jesus' fulfillment of the law, the antitheses then provide no support of the thesis that they involve an abrogation of the objective authority of the law. In the single instance where an enactment through Moses is set aside as provisional, namely, in the instance of the provision for a bill of divorcement, Jesus appeals decisively to the teaching of the law which is not circumscribed by reference to a temporary state of affairs. In the five other cases the design of Jesus is to show that current interpretations are inadequate as abiding by the externals or are in error as to the actual requirements of the law. As we have intimated, however, the significance of the utterances of Jesus in these contexts is by no means exhausted in the evidence they provide of his affirmation of the binding force of the revelation of the old covenant. For alongside of the affirmations of the law there is found constantly an emphatic note of authority, independent of the authority of the law itself, which fulfills it by declaring the radical demands of the righteousness of God. Ultimately, the thought of two independent authorities, both coming with absolute binding force, is to be sure intolerable and inconceivable. And it was such for Jesus. The only absolute authority which he recognized was the authority of the living God. But standing where he did, and conscious of his messianic authority, he called attention inevitably to the structure of the history of revelation, and, without setting aside the old covenant, proclaimed the arrival of a new authority which had to be obeyed because it, too, was divine.

The independent authority of Christ, so conspicuously displayed on the background of the maintenance of the authority of the Old Testament Scriptures, finds further emphasis in Matthew in the frequency of the use of the first person singular of the verb "to say." This form occurs far more often in Matthew than in the other gospels in the record of Jesus' utterances: some fifty-five times as compared with some forty-three in Luke, thirty-four in John, and only eighteen in Mark. Although the emphatic personal pronoun of the first person is found outside of the antitheses in only a single saying (Mt. 16:18), "I say" often gains solemnity from the conjunction of "verily." Of the fifty-five instances mentioned above, Matthew reports thirty-one in the form, "Verily, I say unto you." Even John has only twenty-six cases of "Verily, verily, I say unto you," while Mark contains only thirteen and Luke six passages like Matthew's, although in four other cases the latter uses other similar expressions (Lk. 4:25; 9:27; 12:44; 21:3). Matthew's distinctive use of this solemn expression is concentrated in the five long sections of discourse material. Of the eighteen times that it is used in these discourses, only one or two can be paralleled from the other gospels, while some six of the other thirteen instances in Matthew find parallels in Mark or Luke or both.

In a pervasive fashion, therefore, Matthew presents Christ as constituting a new authority alongside that of the Old Testament. While he affirms the revelation of the law and the prophets, and is even subservient to it, yet paradoxically his own authority is not derived from the revelation that had gone before, and even completes and transcends it. As not derived from the Old Testament or from any other extraneous source, his authority is seen to inhere in his own person, that is, in his sheer right, simply because of who and what he is, to speak as he spoke. Consequently, one may not isolate his teaching from his person. The former cannot be affirmed without the latter. Consequently, not his words only but his person and life also come as a new revelation. The revelatory meaning of Jesus himself, implying that to fail to comprehend him as constituting a divine disclosure is to fail utterly to understand him at all, is taught in all the gospels, but it is preëminently the testimony of Matthew. It is Matthew who is chiefly concerned to show the place of the history of Christ and of his disclosures within the whole structure of God's word to men. In a word this is done by demonstrating that Jesus came for the very purpose of fulfilling the law and the prophets.

That the authority with which Jesus spoke was bound up with his estimate of his own person needs now to be set forth in some detail. An important part of the evidence for this proposition is implicit in the exalted titles which Jesus used in speaking of himself and which were employed by others in addressing him. As the Son of Man, for example, he claimed to possess authority of a most exalted and comprehensive kind. Reserving the discussion of the use of that title for the following chapter, where it may more appropriately be considered in connection with the study of the message of the coming of the kingdom, we shall here limit ourselves chiefly to the revelatory significance associated with the use of the name Son of God.

In Mark, too, Christ is conspicuously disclosed as the Son of God, whose words and deeds are clothed with divine authority, and who may with all propriety be regarded as the object of worship. In view of the sheer transcendence and supernaturalness of the person of Christ in Mark, we are not much impressed with many attempts to cite Matthew as the representative of a higher Christology. It is true indeed that Matthew records the use of the name Son of God at a number of points where Mark is silent as, for example, in Mt. 14:33 and 16:16. Moreover, he alone reports the discourse after the resurrection in which "the

Son" is spoken of as a person in the divine trinity (Mt. 28:19). And like Luke, in characterizing the Son's exclusive knowledge of the Father (Mt. 11:27; Lk. 10:22), he implies the equality of the Son and the Father. While then Matthew's witness of Christ contains several highly significant instances of the name Son of God which are lacking in Mark, these data, in our judgment, serve not so much to display a Christological emphasis as to confirm the observation that Matthew is chiefly occupied with the exhibition of the place held by Jesus Christ, the Son of God, in the history of divine revelation.

The conjunction of divine sonship and divine revelation is most perspicuous in Mt. 11:25-27:

> "At that season Jesus answered and said, I thank thee, O Father, Lord of heaven and earth, that thou didst hide these things from the wise and understanding, and didst reveal them unto babes; yea, Father, for thus it was well-pleasing in thy sight. All things have been delivered unto me of my Father, and no one knoweth the Son save the Father; neither doth any know the Father save the Son, and he to whomsoever the Son willeth to reveal him."

Here Jesus claims such an exclusive knowledge of the Father, and a consequent exclusive right to reveal the Father (both corresponding with the Father's exclusive knowledge and revelation of the Son), that nothing less than an absolutely unique self-consciousness, on an equality with that of the Father, is involved. To summarize Zahn's comment on this passage, the Son is not only the organ of revelation but is himself a mystery to be revealed; the knowledge of the Father and the knowledge of the Son are two sides of the same mystery, which is now revealed, and so the Father and the Son in fellowship with one another are both subject and object of revelation.[11] What Jesus is speaking about is

---

[11] Zahn, *Evangelium des Matthäus* p. 442. See also the discussion of this passage by Vos, *The Self-Disclosure of Jesus*, pp. 142-160. On the

THE AUTHORITY OF CHRIST   213

no mere mystical perception of God, for even if a mystic would dare to claim to know God as God knows him, he would not so easily forget his devotion to the mystic ideal as to conceive of his mission in terms of revelation to others.[12] What is strikingly distinctive in this passage, as compared with Mark's total witness, is not the estimate of the person

---

textual questions, see also Creed, *Luke*, pp. 149f. The absence of the "Father . . . Son" clause in a single Latin ms. of Luke, the variations between the present and past tenses of the verb "know" in certain patristic quotations, and instances of the inversion of the clauses in a few testimonies, plainly provide an altogether inadequate basis for the transformation of this passage into a declaration of ethico-religious sonship or mystical human experience. One particular point may be noticed here. Justin, the earliest father to quote the passage, in one instance (Dial. c. Trypho, 100:1) uses the present form γινώσκει, but in two other passages (Apol. 63:3, 13) the aorist ἔγνω. However, it is illuminating that in the latter passages, in both cases, the saying of Jesus is immediately preceded by quotations of Isa. 1:3 which twice in the LXX uses ἔγνω with reference to the knowledge of God. The reversal of the clauses may be simple inadvertence, but may be due here, as in other patristic quotations, to the fact that the subject in the foreground of thought is the knowledge of God rather than specifically the knowledge of the Son.

[12] The attempt of Norden, *Agnostos Theos*, 1913, pp. 277ff., followed closely by Dibelius, *From Tradition to Gospel*, pp. 279ff., to interpret the saying as expressing oriental mysticism, cannot be regarded as successful, nor are the supposed parallels from Hellenistic mysticism really pertinent. It is also significant that both writers adopt some modification of the text. Norden, for example, even on his assumption that the verb "know" was originally an aorist, is far from doing justice to the implications of the passage when he interprets it as meaning that "Das Erkennen Gottes von seiten des Menschen setzt also voraus, dass der Mensch seinerseits von Gott zuvor erkannt wurde" (p. 287)! On the basis of the patristic citations which reverse the clauses of Mt. 11:27, Dibelius (p. 280, note 2) is ready to conclude that "The theme is thus the knowledge of the Father, and that may be the original because Jesus the revealer from whom men should learn is not really the unknown . . ."! To assume that Jesus is not really the unknown is to beg the question at issue. It appears that the high Christology of the passage can be eradicated on through radical excisions from the text.

of Christ but the specific place given to his revelatory character as both subject and object of sovereign divine disclosure. After his resurrection the same Christ speaks of the new commission which has been given unto him who is the transcendent Son, the establishment of the fellowship of those who in all the world acknowledged him and obeyed his commands, and his perpetual activity on their behalf (Mt. 28:18-20), but even during his ministry on earth he possessed, in virtue of his sonship, an exclusive knowledge of the Father, and a commission to make him known to whomsoever he would. Here then is to be found the explanation of the amazing words, heard so often throughout the gospel: "I say unto you." Matthew 11:27 accordingly does not introduce a foreign note into the gospel. It cannot be set aside as a "Johannine logion." Rather it makes explicit what is expressed or is implicit at many points in the total witness of Matthew to Jesus. It brings the whole of Christ's ministry under the head of revelation. Jesus, who reveals the Father, himself becomes known through the Father's disclosure of the Son. Since the Father's revelation of the Son is inextricably bound up with the Son's revelation of the Father, since, that is to say, one cannot know God as the Father of Christ without knowing Christ as the Son of the Father, ultimately the two mysteries coincide and the action of revelation is conceived of as a single action. This action of the Father in fellowship with the Son is carried out in the historical life of Christ, and hence that life is both history and revelation, in short a revelation in history. Nevertheless, the revelation is apprehended only by "babes" according to the Father's good-pleasure (11:25; *cf.* v. 27).

Matthew 14:33 and 16:16 accordingly are two extraordinary instances of apprehension on the part of the disciples of the revelation which the Father has chosen to make concerning the Son, and wherein the Father is himself necessarily made known. The latter passage, relating the confession voiced by Peter in Caesarea Philippi, is highly meaningful for the understanding of Matthew for at least two outstanding reasons. The first reason is that Matthew reports the confession in the form, "Thou art the Christ, the Son of the living God," whereas Mark merely has, "Thou art the Christ." In Mark Peter might seem to recognize merely the messiahship of Jesus whereas Matthew reports the acknowledgment of his divine nature. Yet, as our study of Mark has shown, in the context of that gospel as a whole, and in the light of the previous disclosures of his divine messiahship, Mark must be understood as implying as much as Matthew records. It is inconceivable that he means to imply that Peter acknowledged Jesus as Messiah in some inferior and inadequate sense. Rather the Messiah, who is about to go to the cross, is acknowledged at his true worth, only Peter finds it intolerable that the one whose proper dignity and glory he has just confessed should insist upon the necessity of his passion and death (Mk. 8:29ff.). While then there is no basis for the judgment that Matthew and Mark contain two diverse evaluations of Jesus, the form of the confession as reported by Matthew serves to underscore the implication of this episode that Peter expresses an acknowledgment of Jesus which corresponds with his own self-estimate.

The second reason why Matthew's report of Peter's confession is noteworthy is that he alone records the declaration of Jesus that Peter's apprehension of the true nature of Christ was the result of the revelation of the Father (Mt. 16:17). In discussing the Marcan portrayal of the events connected with Caesarea Philippi the position was taken that the epochal character of this episode is not to be construed as constituted by a fresh disclosure of the Messiahship of Jesus. None is recorded or implied. What is new is the instruction concerning the passion of Christ which Jesus prepared for by eliciting an open avowal of his messianic dignity.[13] It is necessary to insist here that the situation is not otherwise in Matthew, in spite of the conspicuous reference to the divine revelation. If Mt. 16:17 is viewed in the perspective which Mt. 11:27 provides, as well as in the light of the entire previous record of the activity of Christ, it will appear that no new objective revelation of the moment can be in mind. Rather, the entire history of Christ has been in the nature of a divine revelation which the disciples, with greater or lesser clarity, and with admixture of doubt and bewilderment, have come to comprehend. In Peter's confession we are invited to observe then, not a new objective revelation, but genuine subjective apprehension. And even this apprehension is not clearly intimated to be a completely new apprehension. The fundamental contrast of the narrative is not between the disciples' previous lack of apprehension and their suddenly bestowed understanding, but between the inadequate and erroneous estimates of men, who held that he was at best one of the prophets, and the evaluation of his disciples who belonged to the inner circle and who had eyes to see and ears to hear. (Mt. 16:13ff.; *cf.* 13:11-17).[14]

---

[13] See above, pp. 66ff.

[14] It is not overlooked in the discussion above that the verb "reveal" as used in Mt. 11:25, 27 and 16:17 evidently includes the idea of the subjective perception of what is objectively disclosed. But this would not warrant the inference that the disclosure which comes through Jesus and of which he is the object is conceived of by Matthew as wholly subjective. His historical life, including his deeds and his words, are viewed as an objectively valid disclosure of the divine will, and

From this perspective no difficulty is presented by the acknowledgment of Jesus as God's Son which appears in Mt. 14:33. If the confession of Peter in Mt. 16:16 represented a turningpoint in the attitude of the disciples, grounded in a completely new revelation of the person of Jesus to them, the acknowledgment of Jesus' sonship which Matthew records in the narrative of the walking upon the sea might appear to introduce confusion and inconsistency into Matthew's delineation of the historical developments. Since, however, the whole of the ministry of Jesus is viewed as constituting a divine revelation, the apprehension of the revelation expressed in the words, "Of a truth thou art God's Son," does not imply that Matthew is reading back

---

men are judged by their response to his historical manifestation. Mt. 13:16, 17 happily combine the objective and subjective in characterizing the true followers of Jesus as having the gift of hearing and seeing, that is, of understanding and faith, along with the privilege of beholding and hearing the things which many prophets and righteous men desired to see and hear. The recognition of the essential place given to the divinely granted apprehension of the divine disclosure does not, therefore, require a modification of the conclusions (1) that the confession of Peter is not grounded in a new epochal disclosure of the messiahship at this juncture, and (2) that it is not represented as a sudden new apprehension of Christ on his part.

The fact, moreover, that Matthew, in addition to the disclosure concerning the passion (16:21), includes also the highly meaningful declaration concerning the church (16:17f.), does not affect the main issue. The point of Jesus' evaluation of Simon is not that it indicates a completely new estimate of Peter's significance, but that it constitutes a divinely authoritative evaluation, occasioned indeed by Peter's divinely granted response as well perhaps as other historical circumstances. Whereas, on the one hand, Peter expresses the divine evaluation of Jesus as the Christ, the Son of the living God, an evaluation completely at variance with ordinary human estimates of Jesus, Jesus, on the other hand, declares the significance which the person known to men as Simon obtains in the establishment of the church. There is then, as the introductory words of Mt. 16:18 confirm, a striking parallelism between the two affirmations, "Thou art the Christ" and "Thou art Peter."

into an earlier stage of the disciples' experience an estimate of Christ's person which actually emerged at a later juncture. In fact, the confession in Mt. 14:33 is fully as intelligible as that in 16:16 since in the context the response is called forth by the miraculous action of Jesus in walking upon the water, rescuing Peter from the deep, and apparently also quieting the wind, besides Jesus' words of challenge to faith and of rebuke for doubt (Mt. 14:24-32).

Although then the acknowledgment of Jesus as God's Son in Mt. 14:33 is completely consistent with the implications of Mt. 16:16, there emerges an acute problem of a different sort when this passage is compared with the same story as recorded in Mark. Even if neither evangelist is controlled by a concept of development which would exclude such apprehension at this stage of the ministry, the two narratives seem to leave two mutually exclusive impressions:

"And they that were in the boat worshipped him, saying, Of a truth thou art God's Son" (Mt. 14:33).
"And they were exceedingly astonished in themselves; for they understood not concerning the loaves, but their heart was hardened" (Mk. 6:51b, 52).

The claim has been frequently advanced that Matthew has altered Mark in the interest of a more favorable view of the disciples.[15] Appearances to the contrary notwithstanding we believe that the two evangelists intimate essentially the same reaction. The amazement and lack of understanding are not of one piece, as has been pointed out before. The latter is introduced as an explanation of the former, indicating why there had not been an immediate apprehension of Christ as he came walking on the sea. On the background of their first reaction of fright, their dawning apprehension

---

[15] Recently, *e.g.*, by Enslin, *Christian Beginnings*, p. 395.

took the form of amazement. And it must not be overlooked that Mark uses the term "astonishment" to describe a normal attitude of a disciple in the presence of the supernatural working of God's power.[16] Now it is important to observe that only the astonishment expressed in Mk. 6:51, and not the lack of understanding in 6:52, is properly parallel to Mt. 14:33, and thus the words which Matthew attributes to the disciples are completely consonant with the astonishment described by Mark. One who is filled with astonishment because of a sudden apprehension of the action of God through Christ might appropriately exclaim: "Of a truth thou art God's Son." Matthew as well as Mark dwells on the original fear of the disciples, but includes in addition a picture of Peter's lack of faith (Mt. 14:26, 28ff.). Mark differs therefore only in that he explains their previous lack of apprehension, intimating that it had been due to the consideration that they had been passing through a period during which their hearts had been hardened.

For Matthew then as for Mark Jesus is the Son of God. In keeping with the larger compass of Matthew, and his purpose to set forth the revelatory and eschatological significance of Christ on the background of the disclosures of the law and the prophets, however, some matters that are merely intimated in Mark come to sharper and fuller expression in Matthew. Before leaving the subject of Matthew's delineation of Jesus as the Son of God, nevertheless, some consideration must be given to the charge that Matthew demonstrates its secondary and inferior character by its omission of details that reflect the human nature of Christ's life.[17] On the whole, in truth, it may be admitted

---

[16] See above pp. 71, 106.

[17] See above pp. 82f., and for certain literature bearing on this point p. 82, note 21.

that Matthew devotes little space to the portrayal of the emotional life of our Lord, and it is profitable to consider the reason for this lack. First, however, we do well to observe that such elements are not completely lacking. If Matthew may be charged with dehumanizing Jesus because the reference to the compassion of Christ in Mk. 1:41 is not paralleled in Mt. 8:3, what is to explain his readiness to mention it in the two other instances where Mark reports it, and besides to mention it in Mt. 9:36 and 20:34? We doubt therefore that the lack of emphasis upon such details in the gospel as a whole may be explained as due to theological dogmatizing. If we seek the reason for Matthew's relative silence concerning the subjective side of the life of Jesus in the personal qualities of the evangelist and in his distinctive aims, we shall be on more solid ground. So far as the personality of the evangelist is concerned, we must admit that nothing positive can be affirmed. It may be that this evangelist lacked the capacity for strong emotional reactions which characterized Peter, and which seems to have left its impress upon Mark's gospel. We are on surer ground when we explore the significance of the distinctive aims of Matthew for the understanding of the manner in which the human life of Jesus is intimated in his gospel.

Whereas Mark portrays Christ as the Son of God whose appearance and actions come with startling abruptness, and provoke powerful emotional reactions among those who are confronted with his display of power and authority, Matthew is concerned less with subjective action and interaction than with the external developments. As has been frequently observed, Matthew is much more concise in his record of many incidents of the public ministry.[18] Vivid details found in Mark are often lacking. He often seems

---

[18] Cf. e.g., Hawkins, *Horae Synopticae*, pp. 158ff.

content to present to the reader a summary and contracted narration of what had happened. A partial explanation for such brevity may be the limitation of space dictated by the length of a papyrus roll together with his particular interest to report in considerable detail the teaching of Jesus.[19] In observing the greater conciseness of Matthew, however, care must be taken to avoid the impression that this is due to any lack of interest in the external events themselves. Apart from a positive interest in the historical career of Christ there can be no explanation of the evangelist's extensive report of the life of Christ which preceded the public ministry. In contrast to Mark's almost cryptic narration of the appearance of the Baptist, the coming of Jesus for baptism, and the temptation, Matthew finds room for a record of genealogy, an account of Christ's birth and infancy, as well as for a much more detailed record of the events which introduced the public ministry. As we have seen, however, Matthew does not treat the external course of Christ's life as a biographer. Rather his treatment of the years before the appearance in Galilee is explicable only if there is a perception of his purpose to set forth the meaning of the history of Christ as a part, in truth nothing less than the most significant part, of the history of revelation. His narration of subsequent events likewise discloses this motive, as well through the concentration upon the outward aspects of the divine action as through the specific indications of the fulfillment of divine prophecy.

This central motif of Matthew also illuminates the issue raised by the relative silence concerning the subjective, emotional side of the life of Jesus. Revelation by its very nature represents an action that proceeds from God to man; it is

---

[19] On the length of payrus rolls, see Kenyon, *Our Bible and the Ancient Manuscripts*, 1940, p. 10.

not human experience, nor even merely fellowship with the divine, but an objective disclosure from God to men. Hence the subjective reactions of Christ to human sin and weakness—his anger at their hardness of heart, his wonder at their unbelief, his sighing at their obtuseness—would not require mention as indispensable for the understanding of the place which the history of Christ occupied within the total structure of the history of revelation.

It remains to point out that in Matthew's record of the external events of the life of Christ an important place is given to its truly human character. If Matthew's account were the result of a process of dogmatizing dictated by an increasing reverence for Christ, it would be inexplicable that he preserves so full a record of the birth, temptation, and suffering of Jesus. The virgin birth, for example, while certainly not at variance with the affirmation of the deity of Jesus, does not establish his divine sonship in the highest sense. It presupposes a supernatural act of God in the origin of the human life of Jesus, but it also establishes the truth of his human life. Mark, it will be recalled, does not take time to tell of his birth as a man. Hence, the sinlessness of Jesus, presupposed by the Matthaean account of the baptism, does not introduce a heightening of Jesus' character. What Matthew makes explicit is surely implied in Mark of the one who appears, meteor-like, on the historical scene as the Son of God and the Son of Man.[20] But even the denial of Jesus' subjective need for baptism, as recorded by Matthew, goes hand in hand with the recognition that it

---

[20] For a discussion of the allegation that Mk. 10:18 constitutes a confession of sin on the part of Jesus, see the article by B. B. Warfield in PThR, XII, 1914, pp. 177-228, and reprinted in *Christology and Criticism*, 1929, pp. 97ff.

was necessary to humble himself in order to fulfill the divine will for his life (Mt. 3:14f.).

Perhaps the most characteristic evidence of Matthew's recognition of the humanity of Jesus is found in the record of the use of the title Son of David. Only in a single context in Mark and Luke is Jesus acknowledged as the Son of David (Mk. 10:47f.; Lk. 18:38f.; *cf.* Mt. 20:30).[21] In Matthew the name appears in several additional instances. He reports two additional cases of its use by those who sought Christ's aid (Mt. 9:27; 15:22) and a somewhat hesitant use by the crowds (Mt. 12:23). Of greater significance perhaps is his report of the employment of this title in the acclamation which Jesus received as he entered Jerusalem, which may be compared with the records of the other synoptists:

---

21 In Mt. 22:45ff. (Mk. 12:35ff.; Lk. 20:41ff.) Jesus himself, without specific reference to his own person, demonstrates to the Pharisees on the basis of Ps. 110:1 that the messianic Son of David is David's sovereign Lord. It has often been said that this passage represents a polemic against the Son of David concept on the part of the church which had come to acknowledge Jesus as Lord. *Cf. e.g.,* Bousset, *Kyrios Christos*, 1913, pp. 5, 51; Bultmann, *Geschichte d. syn. Tradition*, pp. 70, 144ff. This position is strong exegetically in so far as it recognizes the plain implications of transcendent messiahship and even preexistence in Jesus' declaration. It breaks down historically, however, in the face of the pervasive recognition of Jesus as Son of David in the Christian records. Bultmann virtually admits this when he conjectures that the point of view represented by this passage represents, not that of the Christian church as a whole, but only that of a narrow circle.

It may be added that reflection on the Davidic origin of Jesus is prominent in Luke's introductory sections. *Cf.* Lk. 1:27, 32, 69; 2:4, 11; 3:31. In John the only allusion is found in 7:42 where some who doubted Jesus' messiahship offer as their reason the Scriptural attestation of the Christ's Davidic origin in Bethlehem, contradicted as it was supposed by his origin in Galilee.

"Hosanna to the Son of David! Blessed is he that cometh in the name of the Lord. Hosanna in the highest" (Mt. 21:9, 15).

"Hosanna! Blessed is he that cometh in the name of the Lord. Blessed is the kingdom that cometh, the kingdom of our Father David. Hosanna in the highest" (Mk. 11:9f.).

"Blessed is the king that cometh in the name of the Lord; peace in heaven and glory in the highest" (Lk. 19:38).

In all three reports there is the same expectation of the messianic kingdom and of the coming king, and Mark as well as Matthew recalls the promise made to David, but only Matthew's quotation centers attention explicitly on Christ as Son of David. Most forcibly of all, however, Matthew's witness to Jesus as the Son of David is exhibited by the conspicuous place accorded this designation at the beginning of the gospel, where both the genealogy and the birth narrative proclaim him as the promised Son of David (Mt. 1:1, 20).

The name Son of David, we freely recognize, is a messianic title, and as such is used to express his royal prerogatives and mission rather than merely the fact of his physical descent from David; nevertheless, the opening sections of Matthew stress the conviction, evidently shared by Jesus' Jewish contemporaries, that Davidic descent was an indispensable qualification of the messianic king. Accordingly, in conspicuous fashion Matthew recognizes the true humanity of Jesus, certainly not less conspicuously than Mark, but he does so in a manner that conforms to his total witness to Christ as the one who fulfills the law and the prophets, and himself establishes, through the divine word and deed, the new order of God's rule. The survey of the use of this name has inevitably taken us beyond the specific theme of this chapter, in which we have been principally concerned with the witness of Matthew to the authority of Jesus Christ, the Son of God, to the testimony which it offers to Jesus as the messianic king who proclaimed and brought to realization the kingdom of God. To the consideration of this theme we shall turn in the following chapter.

CHAPTER VIII

THE SON OF MAN AND THE COMING OF THE KINGDOM

SYNOPSIS

I. *The Message of the Kingdom.*

The kingdom as gospel; occupation of Matthew with the coming of the kingdom.

A. The kingdom as present before the coming of Christ: Mt. 21:43 and 8:11f.

B. The kingdom of consummation viewed as a future reality, but also as coming beforehand, especially through the resurrection, in the establishment of the church (Mt. 16:18f.; 28:18ff.); confirmation from the place given to the resurrection in the pronouncements concerning the passion, intimating that the glory of the Son of Man was to be manifested, not only upon the clouds, but also through the resurrection, which thus signifies the entrance of Jesus upon the full exercise of his sovereignty in the establishment of his rule; confirmation from the parables of the tares and dragnet; the interpretation of Mt. 10:23; 16:28; and 26:64 in this perspective; the teaching concerning the kingdom manifests reflection upon the structure of the history of redemption.

C. The kingdom as a reality within the historical career of Christ: Mt. 12:28 teaches that the kingdom is present through the divine action in Jesus; confirmation from Mt. 11:11f., which speaks of the kingdom as manifesting its presence through a display of power, and of an energetic entrance into it; the breaking through of the kingdom before the resurrection is explained from the messianic character of Jesus' entire life.

II. *The Kingdom and the Son of Man.*

   A. The various stages of the coming of the kingdom correspond to separate aspects of the manifestation of the authority and power of the Son of Man. The Son of Man in Dan. 7:13f.: the prophet describes a messianic figure who shares in the glory and sovereignty of God but is not viewed as a man; the "coming" of this person is a coming to the Ancient of Days, not a coming to earth; in Matthew and the other gospels there is added the affirmation of the coming of this heavenly being to earth, of his exaltation to God's right hand, and of his coming on the clouds with great power and glory.
   B. The Son of Man as Lord exercises his sovereignty in comprehensive fashion.
   Some final questions.

CHRISTIANITY, according to Matthew, is far more than a new law.[1] In spite of the conspicuous place given to the proclamation of the law of Christ, alongside the affirmation of the old law, this is not even the most distinctive feature of Matthew's portrayal of Christ's message. The demand for true righteousness is plainly subordinated to the proclamation of glad tidings, the good news of the coming of the kingdom. From the very beginning the message of Jesus announced the nearness of the kingdom (Mt. 4:17). It could be summed up simply as "the gospel of the kingdom" (Mt. 4:23; 9:35; *cf.* 24:14). That it also demanded repentance followed from the very nature of the kingdom as a kingdom of righteousness; and the call to repentance, therefore, was subordinate to the main theme of coming of the kingdom. A righteousness excelling the righteousness of the scribes and Pharisees is required with a view to the happy prospect of entrance into the kingdom (Mt. 5:20;

---

[1] This is essentially the position, for example, of Bacon and Enslin. See the references p. 131, note 4.

cf. 7:21; 18:3; 21:31). Although the sermon on the mount is largely occupied with the exposition of the nature of the righteousness demanded by Christ, the beatitudes which open the sermon are of the nature of gospel rather than law, for they tell of the blessedness of the children of God which is to be found in their sharing in the kingdom of heaven (*cf.* esp. Mt. 5:3, 10).

No one supposes of course that the concentration upon the message of the coming of the kingdom is peculiar to Matthew. It is conspicuous in the tradition common to all three synoptic evangelists; it also is prominent in the tradition which Matthew shares alone with Mark and in that which he shares alone with Luke. Nevertheless, the references to the kingdom are far more frequent in Matthew than in Luke and Mark, and to use one of its phrases in a different sense, Matthew might be characterized as "the gospel of the kingdom." Matthew contains at least fifty instances of the term "the kingdom," in the form "the kingdom of heaven," "the kingdom of God," "the kingdom of their Father," "the kingdom of my Father," "thy kingdom" (referring to Christ), or simply "the kingdom." Luke has 39, Mark 15 and John only 5 instances, all three together, accordingly, containing only a few more than Matthew. The real disparity between the Matthaean and Lucan usage appears, however, only when it is noticed that approximately two-thirds of the instances in Matthew have no parallel in Mark or Luke while approximately one-half of Luke's are distinctive.

A few of the distinctive passages in Matthew are distinctive only in the use of the word "kingdom." Thus Matthew has "thy kingdom" in Mt. 20:21 while Mark has "thy glory" in Mk. 10:37. And while Mark has only "the gospel" in 13:10, Matthew has "the gospel of the kingdom" in 24:14.

To offset such cases, however, there are instances where Mark or Luke alone has the word "kingdom" and closely parallel passages in the other gospels use other language.[2] The interchange with "kingdom" of terms like "glory," "life," "the gospel" and "the king" in these passages shows that in Matthew, as in the other gospels, the term "kingdom" had not become a rigidly technical and closely circumscribed word. The distinctiveness of Matthew in this regard lies accordingly not in such an absorption with the concept as results in the introduction of the term into all kinds of new contexts, but in the far richer tradition of the teaching of Jesus concerning such subjects as the nature of the kingdom, and the requirements of entrance into the kingdom, these materials being found mainly in chapters 5, 13, 21 and 25.

Matthew's occupation with the gospel of the kingdom may be traced to the same motive which appeared in the discussion of the place given to the law and the prophets in Matthew's portrayal of Christ. For the subject of the kingdom also treats of Christ's place in the structure of the history of God's dealings with his people. Although the emphasis falls upon consummation and fulfillment, upon the emergence of something new, yet the kingdom is also viewed as something present before the coming of Christ.

The period of the Old Testament dispensation, viewed as a period of preparatory revelation, presupposed the reign of God and a community of people who constituted his own kingdom and received his gifts and his laws. The continuity between the kingdom which God would establish, Christ being the head of the corner, and the theocracy of

---

[2] *Cf.* Mk. 9:47 and Mt. 18:9; Mk. 11:10 and Mt. 21:9, Lk. 19:38; Mk. 15:43, Lk. 23:51 and Mt. 27:57; Lk. 18:29 and Mt. 19:29; Mk. 10:29; Lk. 21:31 and Mt. 24:33, Mk. 13:29.

Israel comes to its most conspicuous expression in the supplement to the parable of the wicked husbandmen, which Matthew alone provides. Matthew alone reports that, after the quotation from Psalm 118 concerning the stone set at nought of the builders and become the head of the corner, Jesus said:

> "On this account I say unto you that the kingdom of God shall be taken from you and given to a nation that bringeth forth its fruits" (21:43).

In all three accounts indeed there is the implication that "the wicked husbandmen" are the rulers of the Jewish people, who were responsible to God for their stewardship in his realm, but who, through selfish exploitation of and ruthless attack upon those who were sent to call them to account, failed miserably to discharge their responsibility. The limit of their defection was exhibited when they plotted to kill "his son," but the entire history of their previous actions is viewed as gross insubordination in a realm in which they had been appointed overseers. While therefore Matthew cannot be charged with having introduced an incongruous notion into the context of this parable, it remains significant that his gospel alone includes the specific application that the kingdom of God, whose coming Christ proclaimed, is not completely new, but a new phase of the kingdom which was present under the old dispensation.

This recognition of the continuity of the coming kingdom of God with the divine rule under the old covenant is perhaps also found in Matthew's account of the healing of the centurion's servant in Capernaum (Mt. 8:5-13; *cf.* Lk. 7:1-10). This evangelist alone reports the following words of Christ:

"And I say unto you that many shall come from the east and the west, and shall sit down with Abraham, and Isaac, and Jacob, in the kingdom of heaven, but the sons of the kingdom shall be cast forth into the outer darkness; there shall be the weeping and the gnashing of teeth" (Mt. 8:11, 12).

In another connection Luke reports a similar utterance of Jesus concerning the casting out of many members of the Jewish nation while Abraham, Isaac, Jacob and the prophets together with many from the four corners of the earth shall enjoy the rest of the kingdom of God (Lk. 13:26-30). The kingdom of God in view in both accounts is clearly the kingdom of the consummation, and the exclusion of many Jews is associated with the end of time; nevertheless, the extraordinary character of these disclosures lies in the fact that Gentiles are to join the patriarchs and prophets in the bliss of the coming kingdom while the members of the theocratic family are expelled. It may be that the verb "cast forth" is to be understood figuratively, since these persons are not conceived of as having actually gained admittance to the future kingdom. Still the choice of this verb points to the historic position of the Jews as children of Abraham.

A crucial point at issue here is the implication of the phrase "the sons of the kingdom." This phrase is often understood as referring to the Jews as having a prior right to the kingdom in view of the promises of God, and so as the equivalent of "heirs" of the coming kingdom, or its *potential* subjects.[3] In the only other instance of the use of this phrase in the New Testament, however, there is no suggestion of a potentiality which may not become an actuality: "the sons of the kingdom," in contrast to "the sons of the evil one," are those who positively belong to the

---

[3] *Cf., e.g.*, Meyer (E.T.) and H. J. Holtzmann (HC) *ad loc.* and Vos, *Teaching of Jesus*, etc., pp. 15f.

kingdom (Mt. 13:38). "The sons of the bridechamber" in Mk. 2:19 are those who belong to the special circle of the bridegroom. Such phrases are evidently illustrations of a Semitic idiom which expresses relations of membership, dependence, and the like, but never seems to allow for the possibility of a merely subjective judgment which does not correspond with reality. Even the rabbinic phrase "son of the world to come," which might seem to be an exact parallel to "sons of the kingdom," describes one with regard to whom there is a sure expectation of participation in the future world.[4] As used by Jesus the phrase "sons of the kingdom" then does not naturally signify those Jews who mistakenly supposed that they would participate in the coming kingdom, but those who, in Jesus' own judgment, were properly characterized in this fashion. Since, however, the context excludes their actual participation in, or appointment unto, the final manifestation of the rule of God, it must be their participation in the theocratic kingdom that is in view. The folly of these sons of the kingdom was in supposing that their membership in the theocratic kingdom guaranteed their participation in the kingdom of the Messiah. It could appropriately be said of them, therefore, as Jesus said of the Jewish leaders according to Mt. 21:43, that the kingdom would be taken from them and given to a nation bringing forth its fruits.

In spite of these reflections upon the kingdom of God which was manifested under the old covenant, the full weight of Jesus' teaching concerning the kingdom falls upon

---

[4] *Cf.* Billerbeck, S-BK, I, pp. 476ff. This scholar summarizes the rabbinic usage as expressing the relations of "Zugehörigkeit, der Abhängigkeit, der Wesens gemeinschaft, des Verpflichtetseins u. ähl.," and concludes with reference to the phrase in Mt. 8:12 that it describes the Israelites as sons "weil sie dem Reiche Gottes angehören oder für es bestimmt sein."

its proclamation as a future reality. Although the limits of this study do not permit an exhaustive discussion of the teaching of Jesus concerning the kingdom, in view of the large place which this teaching occupies in Matthew some attention must be given to its main features. In the interest of clarifying Matthew's portrayal of Christ, it will be imperative to observe also the relationship between Christ's history and the emergence of the kingdom of God.

Of all the instances where Matthew refers to the kingdom, only a few demand an exclusive reference to the coming of the kingdom at the consummation of the age. Remarkably few passages specifically connect the manifestation of the kingdom with the end of the world, or with the coming of Christ on the clouds of heaven. The description of the kingdom in which Abraham and the other patriarchs have a place, and from which the Jews are cast forth into the outer darkness, marks the kingdom as subsequent to the resurrection of the dead and the final judgment (Mt. 8:11, 12). The manifestation of the kingdom following upon the coming of the Son of Man in his glory is set forth perhaps most clearly of all in the discourse concerning the great judgment scene in Matthew 25:

> "When the Son of Man cometh in his glory, and all the angels with him, then he shall sit upon the throne of his glory; and before him shall be gathered all the nations. . . . Then shall the king say to them on his right hand, Come, ye blessed of my Father, inherit the kingdom prepared for you from the foundation of the world" (25:31f., 34).

Matthew 24 refers to the coming kingdom only in v. 14, which tells of the necessity of the proclamation of the glad tidings of the kingdom in the whole inhabited world before "the end." However, the constitution of the kingdom must be in view in Mt. 24:30f., for these verses tell of the gathering of Christ's elect through the instrumentality of his angels, after the coming of the Son of Man upon the clouds of heaven with great power and glory (*cf.* also Mt. 16:27; 19:28; 20:21, 23).

Perhaps many other references to the kingdom in the teaching of Jesus as reported by Matthew have in view the consummation of the kingdom which is associated with the coming of the Son of Man on the clouds of heaven with great power and glory. The prayer which Jesus taught his disciples, "Thy kingdom come," finds its complete answer only in the consummation of the age. The "nearness" of the kingdom which Jesus proclaimed may also have been seen in the same perspective in which the return of Christ was viewed as near (4:17; 10:7; *cf.* Rev. 1:3; 22:10). Notwithstanding these qualifications, it is plain that the coming of the kingdom was not conceived of, at the time when Matthew published his gospel, as exclusively future. This evangelist wrote at a time when "the last things," in the strict sense of that phrase, had not been realized; yet, there can be no doubt that when he wrote in the second half of the first Christian century, he was aware that, in a most significant sense, the kingdom had come. In common with the other spokesmen of the Christian church Matthew evidently shared, along with the hope of a future glorious manifestation of the kingdom, the faith that the eschatological hope of the people of God under the old covenant had been partially realized—had, indeed, been so wonderfully realized that one could speak of the arrival of "the last days" and of the "ends of the ages" having come upon them (*cf.* Acts 2:16f.; I Cor. 10:11). The evidence for this conclusion with reference to Matthew is found most conspicuously in the place which this evangelist gives to Jesus' teaching concerning the church.

The intimate connection between the building of Christ's

church and the manifestation of the kingdom is apparent in the word spoken to Peter:

> "And I also say unto thee that thou art Peter, and upon this rock I will build my church, and the gates of Hades shall not prevail against it, and whatsoever thou shalt bind upon the earth shall be bound in heaven; and whatsoever thou shalt loose on the earth shall be loosed in heaven" (Mt. 16:18, 19).

The church of Christ and the manifestation of the kingdom were indeed future at the time of this utterance of Jesus, but at the time when Matthew wrote they were as clearly realized. While Christ *foretold* his establishment of his church and Peter's significance for and activity in the church, Matthew could look back upon this as history. That he refrained from recording its fulfillment was due simply to the limited scope of his literary aim, which was to set forth the glad tidings concerning Christ as disclosed in his history, and not to tell of the historical establishment of the Christian church. Although then the church and kingdom are spoken of in the future tense, the implication is inescapable that, in the establishment of the church, there was to be a manifestation of the kingdom or rule of God. Even if it could be plausibly argued that Peter's relation to the church, described in v. 18, is distinct from his relation to the kingdom, described in v. 19—the first being realized in the origin of the Christian church and the second in an eschatological event, or in the super-earthly sphere—,it is unmistakable that Peter is described as exercising *on the earth* the power of the keys of the kingdom. The words of Christ describe an administration of the kingdom of heaven which is exercised on earth, an administration that receives the stamp of divine approval, and the only place where such an external administration of the kingdom could conceivably take place is in the Christian church. Peter's function in the kingdom on earth is therefore in view of his connection with the church.[5]

While Peter's prerogatives in the church, as a manifestation of the kingdom of heaven, necessarily received considerable prominence in these words of Christ, the church does not thereby appear to be any less supernatural in its origin, constitution and preservation than the eschatological kingdom which is to be consummated by the return of the Son of Man on the clouds. The church does not belong to any man but to Christ; it is his by virtue of his constitution of it; and his continuous solicitude for it is shown in the provision which he makes for its government. There can hardly be any doubt that Matthew's reference to that great future act whereby Christ would establish his church has in view an act of the exalted Lord. This is borne out emphatically by the record which Matthew alone preserves of the discourse on the Galilean mount, which has been discussed above in the perspective of the resurrection narrative (Mt. 28:18-20). Although no specific mention of the church is made in that context, no one will question its pertinence to the establishment of the church rather than to the manifestation of the eschatological kingdom. The commands with reference to the making of disciples, baptizing them, and committing to them the teachings of Christ, plainly relate to the constitution and administration of the Christian church. The promise of Christ's presence is still more eloquent on this point, since it tells of Christ's action during the whole time until the consummation of the age. Now these commands and this promise flow from a new commission that has been given to Christ, a comprehensive authority in heaven and upon the earth (Mt. 28:18). The setting of this momentous declaration intimates that

---

[5] *Cf.* Vos, *op. cit.*, pp. 146ff.

this commission dated from the exaltation of Christ through the resurrection. It is the stupendous supernatural event of the resurrection which served to introduce Christ to a new position of Lordship and to a new exercise of kingly sovereignty from which his church came into being.

Although the passages in Matthew 16 and 28 which have been passed in review are distinctive of Matthew, he shares with others the thought that the cross would be followed by a vindication of the Son of Man through the resurrection. The tradition of the pronouncements of the approaching passion and resurrection of the Son of Man is found in all the synoptics.[6] Although, as we have seen in the case of Mark, these pronouncements form an integral part of the passion story, and along with other sayings concerning the death of the Son of Man, such as Mt. 17:12; 20:28; 26:2, 24, 45, and parallel or similar passages in the other synoptic gospels, center one's thought chiefly upon the submission of the Son of Man to the divine plan which required that he take the road to the cross, it remains true that the full significance of these utterances is not perceived apart from a recognition of the fact that *the resurrection* is an integral and highly significant element in these pronouncements. At the transfiguration mount, too, where the divine voice intimates that the divine favor continues to rest upon the Son as he goes to the cross, Jesus himself speaks of the new era which is in prospect through the approaching resurrection of the Son of Man (Mt. 17:9; *cf.* Mk. 9:9). The glory which belongs to the Son of Man will not wait to appear until his return on the clouds of heaven; it will be manifested likewise through another stupendous supernatural event, the resurrection of the crucified one from the dead. It is

---

[6] Mt. 16:21, Mk. 8:31; Lk. 9:22; Mt. 17:22f., Mk. 9:31, Lk. 9:44; Mt. 20:18f., Mk. 10:33f.

through this exaltation of the Son of Man that he will first enter upon a full exercise of his sovereignty in the establishment of his rule and realm.

That the kingdom which Christ proclaimed was to come to realization in an era preceding the consummation comes to expression, moreover, in the teaching concerning the kingdom in Matthew 13. The parables of the tares and of the drag net teach that, before the consummation of the age, the kingdom of heaven contains both "the sons of the kingdom" and the "sons of the evil one," the "wicked" and the "righteous" (Mt. 13:24-30, 36-43, 47-50). The explanation of the parable of the tares is especially illuminating since it appears that the Son of Man, who has been responsible for the sowing of good seed, shall at the end of the world, "send forth his angels, and they shall gather *out of his kingdom* all things that cause stumbling, and them that do iniquity, and shall cast them into the furnace of fire: there shall be the weeping and the gnashing of teeth" (*cf.* Mt. 13:37, 41f.).

On the background of these observations as to Jesus' teaching concerning the establishment of the church and the coming of the kingdom, a perspective is gained for the understanding of some of the most difficult utterances recorded in this gospel, namely, Matthew 10:23; 16:28 and 26:64:

"Verily I say unto you, ye shall by no means complete the cities of Israel till the Son of Man come."

"Verily I say unto you, There are some of them that stand here who shall in no wise taste of death until they see the Son of Man coming in his kingdom."

"Nevertheless, I say unto you, Henceforth ye shall see the Son of Man sitting at the right hand of power, and coming on the clouds of heaven."

All three passages stress the imminence of the coming of the Son of Man, an impression which is heightened by a comparison of the last two passages with corresponding passages in Mark and Luke:

> "Verily I say unto you, There are some of them that stand here who shall in no wise taste of death until they see *the kingdom of God come with power*" (Mk. 9:1).
>
> "But I tell you of a truth, There are some of them that stand here who shall in no wise taste of death until they see *the kingdom of God*" (Lk. 9:27).
>
> "And ye shall see the Son of Man sitting at the right hand of Power, and coming with the clouds of heaven" (Mk. 14:62).
>
> "But from now on shall the Son of Man be seated at the right hand of the Power of God" (Luke 22:69).

Matthew alone has the passage in 10:23; he alone, in the second context, speaks of the coming of the Son of Man; and in the third context, as opposed to Mark, though in common with Luke, he reports that Jesus associates the session at God's right hand with the immediate future. While all the gospels are recognized as reporting an eschatological message, and all are thought to intimate the presence in the early church of a hope of the parousia of Christ, it is commonly maintained that Matthew represents this hope in an extreme form as compared with the other gospels. It is held by some that he reflects the eschatological faith of the section of the church in which his gospel was produced.[7] Others maintain that he reports a genuine tradition of the primitive Christian eschatological faith, which was retained in spite of its intrinsic difficulties and its evident conflict with his own universalism.[8] These theories raise broad historical questions which cannot be discussed here. Suffice it to say that they rest upon an inadequately grounded interpretation of the data, an interpretation which has gone astray apparently because of its one-sidedly eschatological reconstruction of the message of Jesus.

---

[7] *Cf., e.g.,* Streeter, *The Four Gospels,* pp. 520ff.
[8] *Cf., e.g.,* J. Weiss *ad* Mt. 10:23 in SNT.

The assumption is gratuitous that the coming of the Son of Man referred to by Matthew in 10:23 and 16:28 is identical with the coming on the clouds of heaven with great power and glory, described in Mt. 24:30 and 25:31. The absence from the former passages of all references to the clouds of heaven, the presence of angels, and the like, is significant. And since, as we have observed, Matthew clearly regards the exaltation of the Son of Man through the resurrection as inaugurating a new era, which was to be momentous both for Christ and for those who were his disciples, it is altogether congruous to regard the expression "the Son of Man coming in his kingdom" in Mt. 16:28 as referring to the supernatural activity of the risen Lord in establishing his church. The expression in the parallel passages in Mark and Luke are not really less eschatological than Matthew's; the distinctiveness of Matthew's record is that it is more Christological, rather than more eschatological, than the others, for he explicitly connects the coming event with the person of the Son of Man. If Mt. 10:23 is understood according to the analogy of 16:28, it is not necessary to assume that Jesus was mistaken with reference to his parousia.[9]

The third of these passages, containing Jesus' reply to the high priest presents distinctive problems. Here there is, in Matthew and Mark, an explicit reference to the coming of the Son of Man with the clouds in contrast to the utterances in 10:23 and 16:28. The reason that Mt. 26:64 and Lk.

---

[9] Moreover, the problem of the relation of the particularistic and universalistic elements in Matthew is not clarified on the view which overlooks the temporary character of the ministry of the disciples to Israel alone, described in Mt. 10, in contrast to the coming emergence of a universalistic kingdom, comprehending Gentiles as well as Jews, expressed in Mt. 8:11f. (*cf.* 21:43; 28:19f.).

22:69 are grouped with the other two passages is that they seem, by the qualification "henceforth," to envisage the immediate fulfillment of Jesus' words. Although the Jewish rulers are now his judges, and he himself is facing execution on the cross, Jesus promises that forthwith there will be a reversal of their position. The true transcendence of his person and sovereignty is about to appear. If then Jesus here speaks of an immediate coming of the Son of Man on the clouds of heaven, there might seem to be insufficient reason for understanding the references to the coming of the Son of Man in Mt. 10:23 and 16:28 in a different sense.

The fact is, however, that Matthew does not speak, in contrast to Mark, of an immediate coming on the clouds of heaven. The contrast with Mark is more apparent than real, for, in spite of the absence in Mark of the temporal qualification "henceforth," the implication of the statement of Jesus, as Mark reports it, is that his exaltation as the Messiah will appear to the Jewish leaders without delay. Since, moreover, according to Mark as well as Matthew, as we have seen, the exaltation of the Son of Man dates from the resurrection on the third day, it would be far-fetched to claim that Mark signifies a more remote fulfillment of Jesus' promise that they would see a complete overturn of their respective positions.

Does this imply however, that Jesus, according to this saying expected his coming on the clouds of heaven at once? This would follow only if the "sitting at the right hand of power" is construed as identical or coincidental with the "coming with the clouds." Most modern commentators appear simply to coalesce the first participial clause with the second, and thus virtually reduce Jesus' utterance to the promise that they would recognize him as the Messiah when they beheld the Son of Man coming on the clouds. Allen, for example, in commenting on the Matthaean form, paraphrases the passage as follows:

> "I am the Messiah, but the Messiah of the future, not of the present; you will understand when you shall see the Son of Man coming on the clouds of heaven."

The comment of Swete, in our judgment, represents sounder exegesis, inasmuch as it involves closer attention to the exact language employed. The significance of the allusion to Daniel 7:13 is not obscured, but the allusion to Psalm 110:1 also receives its proper recognition. Noting the distinctive feature of the Matthaean and Lucan form, he says:

> "The vision of the Son of Man sitting on the Right Hand of the Power of God . . . began from the year of the Crucifixion (*cf.* Acts ii:33f., vii:55, Rom. viii:34, Heb. i:3f., I Pet. iii:22, Apoc. ii:21, xii:5, 'Mc.' xvi:19), and is to be followed in due course by the vision which all must see of His Return (Apoc. i:7). The Jewish leaders by their rejection of His Messiahship secured His exaltation (Phil. ii:9) and their own ultimate confusion."

The session at God's right hand, that is, the exaltation to messianic glory, is preliminary to the advent with the clouds of heaven, but this implies that it describes a separate stage of exaltation (*cf.* Mt. 22:43f.). The effects of the exaltation cannot be restricted to his coming back with great power and glory. The reply to the high priest and his associates, accordingly, is to the effect that they themselves would witness, and that without delay, their own undoing, because Christ himself was about to enter upon a state of heavenly glory and power. These two stages of Christ's exaltation are not specifically connected with the manifestation of the kingdom in this context, but, in view of the data previously reviewed, it is not a bold assumption that the new order, soon to bring chagrin and judgment to the Jewish leaders, would include not only the glorious effects of the return of Christ but also the blessings of his rule at God's right hand.

This division of the messianic age into two stages, which find their initiation respectively through the resurrection and the advent of the Son of Man, along with the limited recognition of the presence of the rule of God under the old dispensation, shows that Matthew's record of Jesus' teaching is distinguished by its attention to the structure of the history of God's gracious action on behalf of his people. The absorption with the history of revelation which has been observed in the preceding chapter finds its counterpart in the absorption in the history of redemption as displayed in the divine establishment of his kingdom. In both instances, in the reflection upon both the history of revelation and the history of redemption, the divine sanction of the old covenant is indicated as the background for the stupendous affirmation of the coming of the new order through the word and work of the messianic Son of Man. Although the historical manifestation of the rule of God does not reach its ideal and absolute form until the consummation of the age, the transition from the old to the new takes place properly speaking at the exaltation of Christ to the full exercise of his Lordship through the resurrection. The accent placed upon the resurrection of Christ in the proclamation of the gospel of salvation, accordingly, is of a piece with the occupation with the kingdom manifested on earth through the constitution of the church.

But even the evidence for the conjunction between Christ's resurrection and the coming of the kingdom does not exhaust the place which Matthew gives to the doctrine that the kingdom, while awaiting a future consummation, became a reality through the history of Jesus Christ. For there is also a preliminary manifestation of the messianic kingdom through the presence and activity of Jesus before the resurrection.

The most explicit evidence of this conception of the kingdom is to be found in Mt. 12:28, a passage closely paralleled in Lk. 11:20. In reply to the accusation of the Pharisees that his exorcism of demons was accomplished through Beelzebub the prince of demons, Jesus declares that such a charge is absurd, since in that event Satan would be bringing desolation into his own kingdom, and he positively affirms that his action, constituting a binding of "the strong man," signifies a manifestation of the kingdom of God:

"If I by the Spirit of God cast out demons, then is the kingdom of God come upon you."

Representatives of the "consistent" eschatological interpretation of Jesus' message have sought indeed to fit this saying into the eschatological mold by interpreting the verb to express the imminence of the kingdom rather than its actual arrival. Dibelius, for example, renders the verb ἔφθασεν as meaning "reached as far as you," which he seeks to contrast with an actual coming of the kingdom, and interprets it as signifying little more than that the deeds of Jesus proclaim the nearness of the kingdom.[10] Even if the verb required

---

[10] Cf. *Jesus*, pp. 65f.; *The Message of Jesus Christ*, p. 75 and the author's article "Martin Dibelius and the Relation of History and Faith" in WThJ, II, 2 (May, 1940), pp. 116f. For other "eschatological" interpretations cf. J. Weiss in SNT; Bultmann, *Geschichte d. syn. Tradition*, p. 12; K. W. Clark, "Realized Eschatology" in JBL, LIX (1940), pp. 367ff. On the other side, see Dodd, *The Parables of the Kingdom*, 1935, pp. 43ff.; Otto, *The Kingdom of God and the Son of Man*, pp. 90, 97, 101ff.

some such translation as "has reached unto you," or "is at the door," rather than simply "has come," it would hardly serve to express the idea of futurity or even of imminence. Something that has reached you, or is at your door, surely is regarded as something that has arrived. Moreover, the separation between Christ's miraculous action and the divine establishment of the kingdom, which this view presupposes, is not borne out by the context. Jesus describes his action as God's action, through his Spirit, which not merely augurs but actually accomplishes the destruction of the kingdom of Satan, and this is surely the equivalent of announcing that God's rule is being substituted for Satan's through his present activity.

In Jesus' discourse concerning John the Baptist, as found in Mt. 11:7ff. and Lk. 7:24ff.; 16:16, there also appears the clear implication that, while John himself belonged to the old order, the new has now dawned. John brings to a conclusion the revelatory epoch of the law and the prophets, according to Jesus, and John himself, while not belonging properly to the coming kingdom, is the Elijah of Malachi 3:1 and 4:5f., who performs the preparatory and restorative work which ushers in the eschatological age (*cf.* Mt. 17:11ff.; Mk. 9:11ff.).

In this same context, in v. 12, Matthew reports a saying which has been understood in sharply varied senses. No thorough discussion of all of the features of its interpretation can be attempted here, but its pertinence to the subject of the nature of the kingdom demands that it be briefly considered. The diversity of exegesis may be illustrated by a comparison of the rendering of the Authorized Version and the recent translation of Rudolph Otto:

> "And from the days of John the Baptist until now, the kingdom of heaven suffereth violence, and the violent take it by force."

"From the days of John until now, the kingdom of heaven exercises its force (biazetai), and those who exercise force capture it."[11]

A rendering approximately in the form of the Authorized Version, which construes the verb of the first clause as in the passive voice, and appears to interpret it and the cognate subject of the second clause in a derogatory sense, is adopted by those who seek to fit this saying into an exclusively eschatological view of the kingdom. Johannes Weiss, for example, understands "the violent," who are referred to, as the Zealots of Jesus' day, who through revolutionary efforts sought to introduce the kingdom by force on the theory that, if they did their part, God would establish it miraculously; and Jesus is said to imply that, as opposed to such enthusiastic and violent efforts, he was content to wait for God himself to manifest the kingdom.[12]

To find such a polemic against the Zealots as J. Weiss does, is to read a good deal into this utterance of Jesus. The Zealots might indeed be characterized as βιασταί (violent men), but neither affirmation of this passage agrees with their activity. It can hardly be said that the kingdom of heaven, which Jesus proclaimed, actually suffered violence through their revolutionary activity, and much less that they seized or pressed into the kingdom of heaven. Moreover, in view of the parables of the hidden treasure and of the pearl of great price (Mt. 13:44ff.), it is far-fetched to understand this saying as a polemic against putting forth energetic efforts to possess the kingdom. The least impressive

---

[11] *Op. cit.*, p. 108. The Greek text of Mt. 11:12 is as follows: ἀπὸ δὲ τῶν ἡμερῶν Ἰωάνου τοῦ βαπτιστοῦ ἕως ἄρτι ἡ βασιλεία τῶν οὐρανῶν βιάζεται, καὶ βιασταὶ ἁρπάζουσιν αὐτήν. Lk. 16:16 reports a similar saying in a different context: ὁ νόμος καὶ οἱ προφῆται μέχρι Ἰωάνου. ἀπὸ τότε ἡ βασιλεία τοῦ θεοῦ εὐαγγελίζεται καὶ πᾶς εἰς αὐτὴν βιάζεται.

[12] SNT *ad* Mt. 11:12. *Cf.* also Robinson (MNT) and Klostermann (HB), and *ad* Lk. 16:16 Creed.

feature of this interpretation, however, is that which implies, in spite of the context and specific references to the present time of Jesus' activity, that Jesus was talking about a future appearance of the kingdom. According to Jesus, as we have seen, John signified the end of an epoch which "prophesied"; "from the days of John until now" there has been fulfillment in the kingdom of heaven. The present tense of the two verbs employed proves conclusively that the kingdom is regarded as a present reality since the days of John, the days of his prophetic ministry.

Other views of the meaning of the passage, likewise assuming the passive sense of the verb and unfavorable connotation of the cognate terms, are those of Allen (ICC), who understands it as referring to the violent treatment which the kingdom suffered in the person of its messengers and heralds, John the Baptist and later Christian preachers, and of Dibelius (noted by Klostermann and Creed), who interprets it as describing the violent opposition of evil spirits. These two views, so far as their exegesis of the first clause is concerned, possess a degree of plausibility that the view of J. Weiss does not have, but they break down completely in the treatment of the second clause, for it is impossible to suppose that Jesus could have meant to say that either the civil powers or that Satan actually "seized" or "captured" the kingdom of heaven. But even if these views were commended intrinsically, they would offer no support for the view that, in Jesus' teaching, the kingdom of heaven is always a future reality.

The view of this passage linked above with the name of Otto has far more to commend it.[13] The use of the verb βιάζεται as a middle form is illustrated in Lk. 16:16 and,

---

[13] *Op. cit.*, pp. 108ff. *Cf.* also Zahn and Grosheide (KNT) *ad loc.*, Harnack in SBA, 1907, pp. 947ff., and Dodd, *op. cit.*, p. 48.

furthermore, was widely current in Hellenistic Greek.[14] Moreover, the explicit connection of this verse with verse 13, through the conjunction "for," shows that a comparison is being made between the epoch just brought to a close, and the new epoch that has arrived: until John the characteristic activity was prophecy; from the days of John until now the kingdom of God reveals its presence, and this activity is described strikingly as *a display of power*. The kingdom made known its presence through the conspicuous and abrupt manifestations of the divine action. Perhaps the miraculous activity of Jesus, after the analogy of Mt. 12:28, is in view. That Jesus goes on to speak of a forceful apprehension of the kingdom is not to contradict this view of the first clause: that would follow only if the second clauses were tautological. If the second clause is viewed on the background of Mt. 12:11a, and not as its repetition, it expresses the further truth that, corresponding with the forceful nature of the revelation of the kingdom, those who laid hold on it were characterized by energy and enthusiasm.[15]

Our survey of the coming of the kingdom results in a three-fold distinction: the manifestation of the kingdom through (1) the presence of the promised king, (2) the exaltation of the Messiah to God's right hand, and (3) the action of the returning Son of Man. In view of the very close continuity between the first and second phases, how-

---

14 Cf. Zahn, *Evangelium des Matthäus*, p. 427, note 20 and Moulton and Milligan, *Vocabulary of the Greek N.T.*

15 Another view of this passage worthy of consideration finds expression in Alexander and Plummer *ad* Mt. 11:12. This interpretation also construes βιάζεται as a passive, but interprets it, and the second clause likewise, as describing a thronging into, or pressing into, the kingdom by the crowds who followed Jesus. While not introducing the most objectionable features of the other views which have been criticized, this position also makes the second clause tautological, and fails adequately to integrate this verse with its context.

ever, a somewhat more felicitous understanding of the data will result if these two are closely joined as aspects of the realization of the messianic kingdom through the action of Christ in the realm of history. If only one recognizes that the whole of Christ's incarnate life, including his activity before the resurrection as well as his action at the right hand of God, is pervasively messianic, the evidence of the anticipation of the messianic kingdom within his lifetime will not appear incongruous. In spite of his passivity and submission to the will of God, he was necessarily actively revealing his messianic power and authority. And wherever his messianic authority and power were exercised, and wherever men submitted to them and trusted in them, there the rule of God came to realization. Even before the resurrection, therefore, there was a breaking through, not a mere prophecy but an actual historical realization, of the messianic kingdom. The transition from the old order to the new may not too rigidly be fixed at the cross and resurrection. Just as the old order was judged and found its end in the cross, and yet lived on for a time, so the new order inaugurated by the authority of the risen Lord manifested its life beforehand. Christ even in his humiliation was acknowledged as Lord, and even in his exaltation was anathematized by "the sons of the kingdom." While the life of Christ was lived under the old order, that life, because of its intrinsic meaning as the fulfillment of the messianic hope, signified the dawn of the messianic age.

We approach now the consideration of the place occupied by Jesus himself within the message of the coming of the kingdom. Our discussion has shown that the history of Christ and the coming of the kingdom are indissolubly joined. The kingdom in all of its absoluteness and glory will appear when the Son of Man comes on the clouds of heaven with great power and glory. There is also a coming of the Son of Man in his kingdom which was still future when Jesus taught, an external manifestation of the kingdom upon earth, to be constituted through the exaltation of the Son of Man at the resurrection, to be administered by those who rightly hold the keys of the kingdom, and finally to be separated from all that cause stumbling and do iniquity through the action of the Son of Man himself. But in spite of his passivity and submission during his public ministry, there also broke forth through his deeds such a manifestation of divine power against the kingdom of Satan that the rule of God came to incipient realization already in the days of his flesh. In the community of his faithful disciples there came into being the society of the true sons of the kingdom which was soon to be constituted and organized as the church of Jesus Christ. All of the teaching of the kingdom is, therefore, persuasively messianic, or Christological.

The modern prevalence of an exclusively eschatological view of the kingdom which Jesus proclaimed has gone hand in hand with an inadequate appraisal of the teaching of Jesus concerning his own person. The recognition of the historicity of the message concerning an apocalyptic kingdom and the coming of an apocalyptic Son of Man has led unfortunately to a one-sided, and essentially false, conception of the message of Jesus, because it has not recognized the comprehensive significance both of the title Son of Man and of the kingdom associated with his coming. This criticism of the "eschatologists" might be put in the form that the message concerning the Son of Man and the kingdom is not nearly so one-sidedly apocalyptic as men have supposed. A happier formulation would be, however, that this message is indeed pervasively apocalyptic, or eschatological, but that most modern interpreters have not given the apocalyptic, or eschatological, character of this message its comprehensive scope. There is in Jesus' teaching only the single coming kingdom, and this kingdom is the eschatological fulfillment of the history of redemption, but this kingdom comes to realization in various stages, each stage corresponding with a separate stage in the manifestation of the authority and power of the Son of Man. All authority in heaven and earth are committed to him through the resurrection, and the full manifestation of this might and glory will wait to be revealed at the consummation of the age, but even in the days of his flesh he appears as the Son of Man who has power and authority on earth.[16] Hence it may be said that the whole of Christ's appearance was eschatological and apocalyptic, fulfilling the disclosed plan of the coming divine rule and constituting a revelation of the divine glory and power. This perspective is not confined to Matthew by any means, but it comes to its most conspicuous expression in this gospel because of its occupation with the proclamation of the kingdom.

For some fifty years there has been a remarkable consensus of opinion supporting the judgment that the message concerning the Son of Man, and to a slightly lesser extent the kingdom associated with his coming, is derived from, or finds its ultimate Biblical background, in the Book of Daniel. Although the title as such does not occur there, Daniel's description of the concrete figure "like unto a son of man" and associated with "the clouds of heaven," who is given "dominion, glory and a kingdom" unmistakably is presupposed in Jesus' use of the title Son of Man (7:13, 14). This concrete figure is too transcendent and too intimately

---

[16] See Mt. 9:6 and 12:8 *Cf.* also Mt. 8:20, 11:19; 12:40; 16:13; 17:12, 22; 20:18, 28; 26:2, 24f. On Mark, see above pp. 111f.

associated with the "Ancient of Days" to allow that it is merely symbolical of the kingdom itself or of "the saints of the kingdom" (Dan. 7:18, 27); and, for the same reason, in spite of the absence of the term "Messiah," he cannot be regarded simply as an angelic being. On the other hand, the phrase "like unto a son of man" is not intended to describe the person as a human being, for it is clearly not intended as didactic language. As "the four great beasts" symbolize four kings, and the four kingdoms, of the world (Dan. 7:17) so the one "like unto a son of man" symbolically identifies the king, whose kingdom will not be destroyed. No human traits appear in this description, nor is there in evidence any veiling of his glory; he shares in the dignity, glory and sovereignty of God.[17]

Any appearance of such a heavenly figure would in the nature of the case be an apocalypse or revelation, and it is clear that Jesus seized upon it to describe the coming of the Son of Man upon the clouds of heaven. What is commonly overlooked however is the fact that Daniel does not describe explicitly the event which Jesus describes, for example, in Mt. 24:30. Daniel does not as such prophesy the second advent, nor indeed the first advent. The "coming with the clouds of heaven" which Daniel narrates is a coming into the presence of the "Ancient of Days," not a coming to earth. It is for this very reason however that there is greater agreement between Daniel's description of this heavenly figure, and Jesus' use of the title "the Son of Man" than is commonly supposed. As we have seen from the evidence in Mark and Matthew, Jesus frequently uses this title when

---

[17] For a survey of the linguistic, historical and exegetical questions see especially Vos, *The Self-Disclosure of Jesus*, 42ff., 228ff. *Cf.* also the present writer's criticism of Otto's views in WThJ, I, 2 (May, 1939), pp. 113ff.

he is describing his activity before the resurrection and the second advent, and it is exactly because Daniel does not specify the time or manner of the visible constitution of the kingdom through an appearance of one "like unto a son of man" that it provides comprehensively the background for Jesus' use of the title. The difference between Daniel and Matthew is this: Daniel describes a heavenly scene, an apocalypse in heaven of the one to whom was given "dominion, glory and a kingdom"; Matthew portrays one who, out of the exalted self-consciousness that he is the one of whom Daniel spoke, tells of his coming glory and of the glorious kingdom, but also on earth manifests the kingdom through his sovereign words and deeds.

The singleness of Matthew's perspective is hereby confirmed. On the basis of the place which Matthew gives to the history of revelation the conclusion was drawn that, according to Matthew the coming of the Messiah who had been promised signifies the coming of the one whose life and teaching are themselves a new revelation that is the consummation of the old (p. 198 above). The survey of the coming of the Son of Man and of the kingdom confirms and deepens this insight, for the appearance of the Son of Man is regarded as an apocalypse from heaven, whether in his ministry upon earth, from the right hand of God, or his coming again; and the kingdom, while not without a manifestation under the old covenant, comes as a new and consummate manifestation of God's sovereignty through the presence and activity of the Messiah: his presence on earth in the days of his flesh, his presence with the church "all the days even unto the consummation," and the parousia, or presence, with great power and glory, at the consummation.

The acknowledgment of Jesus as Lord is in complete

harmony with the witness to him as the Son of Man. As the Son of Man, who shares in the divine glory and authority, his lordship must become known. The flexibility of the Greek word "Lord" must indeed be recognized: not every instance of its use implies a consciousness of divine authority. Not everyone who addressed Jesus as Lord clearly chose this name as the equivalent of deity; it could as a polite form of address mean little more than our "sir." At the same time the recognition of the flexibility of the designation does not warrant the conclusion that every instance of its use during the life of Christ must have been merely a polite form of address. Something more is surely implied when supernatural aid is sought, and in Jesus' own teaching too the name is frequently found in a context which requires us to understand it as implying divine prerogatives.[18] Such implications are perhaps most inescapable in contexts which relate to the place occupied by Christ in the events of the consummation. The expectation of the coming of "the Lord" is not completely absent from Mark, but it is especially Matthew, and to a somewhat lesser extent Luke, who report this prospect. It is Christ who "in that day" will be addressed as "Lord" and who will pronounce the dread words: "I never knew you; depart from me, ye that work iniquity" (Mt. 7:21ff.). Speaking of the parousia of the Son of Man Jesus warns the disciples: "Watch therefore because ye know not in what day your Lord cometh" (Mt. 24:39, 42; *cf.* Mk. 13:35; Lk. 12:40). This warning serves to introduce the parable of the faithful and unfaithful servants whose Lord will come to reward and to punish, and, though the language is not strictly didactic, the pertinence of the reference

---

[18] On these questions see especially, Dalman, *The Words of Jesus*, 1902, pp. 324ff.; Vos. *op. cit.*, pp. 117ff.; von Dobschütz, "Kyrios Iesous," in ZNW, XXX, 1931, Heft 2.

of the name Lord to the coming Son of Man is unmistakable (Mt. 24:45ff.; *cf.* 25:14ff.; Lk. 12:40ff.; 13:25ff.).

The lordship of the Son of Man does not begin, however, with his coming on the clouds of heaven. Even in the eschatological parables there is the plain implication that the authority of the Lord over his servants was exercised before his departure, and continued in effect during the whole time of his absence. It is remarkable indeed, in view of the acknowledgment by the Christian church of the lordship of Jesus, that even Matthew, the most "ecclesiastical" of the evangelists, does not specifically use this terminology in his characterization of the risen Son of Man, although of course the concept of his active exercise of his sovereignty after the resurrection is present in contexts like Mt. 16:18ff. and 28:18ff.[19] Nevertheless, Matthew in common with Mark and Luke does specifically report the claim of the Son of Man to be Lord of the sabbath, and consequently to set forth its true meaning and demands (Mt. 12:8; Mk. 2:28; Lk. 6:5). Moreover, the place of authority which Jesus had come to have within the circle of his followers is reflected in the instantaneous obedience which he expected the mere expression of the will of "the Lord" would find, and which it actually did find, as he prepared to enter Jerusalem (Mt. 21:3; Mk. 11:3; Lk. 19:31).

It must be recognized, nevertheless, that, however high the connotation demanded by these contexts, none of them requires the implication of an eternal or pre-existent lordship. The kind of lordship ascribed to him when, for example, he is described as possessing lordship over the sabbath, or as acting as judge at the last day, is indeed of a kind

---

[19] "The Lord" in Mt. 28:6 does not enjoy adequate textual support, and, in any case, it would appear to presuppose an earlier use rather than a new estimate. *Cf.* also Lk. 24:34.

that is hardly conceivable of one who is a mere man; yet these prerogatives appear as received by divine appointment, in virtue of his messianic office, rather than strictly as belonging to him by virtue of his personal nature. In the nature of the case the name Lord, as distinguished from Son of God, calls to mind a manward rather than a Godward relation, and since the gospel history has largely to do with the activity of Christ, it would be extraordinary to find a use of this name to designate any pre-historical relations. There is however one such extraordinary instance of the name "Lord," which is used, in dependence upon Ps. 110, to characterize the Messiah as "Lord of David" (Mt. 24:43f.; Mk. 12:36f.; Lk. 20:42f.). The fact that Jesus does not explicitly claim for himself Lordship over David at this point does not affect the issue, for in the larger contexts of the gospels the implication is inescapable that Jesus himself here interprets his messianic claims in this exalted sense. Radical scholars, while denying the historicity of this saying, support the exegesis that nothing less than the preexistence and comprehensive lordship of the Messiah is implied.[20]

On the background of Matthew's record of the coming of Christ and of the kingdom, it is possible to evaluate the criticism that Matthew is the most ecclesiastical of the gospels. This charge is commonly meant in the sense that the place given to the church in Matthew 16:18f. and 18:17, as well as the disposition of the message as a whole, reflects the origin of the gospel in the midst of the developing Christian church, disclosing an effort to satisfy the needs of the church by reshaping the tradition of Christ's life, and even by creating new tradition. According to this viewpoint, doctrines and practices which had emerged in the life of the

---

[20] *Cf.* J. Weiss, *ad* Mk. 12:36 in SNT; Bousset, *Kyrios Christos*, 1913 pp. 5, 51; Bultmann, *op. cit.*, pp. 70, 144f.

church were clothed with Christ's sanction. It has appeared from our discussion, as a matter of fact, that Matthew's gospel most explicitly represents Christ as looking to the establishment of the church. Moreover, it as well as the other gospels in an important sense reflects the faith of the church and was suited to meet the needs of the church. Matthew does not write as a historian whose own personal attitude towards the events was a matter of no moment; he writes as a believer in Christ, and so as one who holds to the truth of the stupendous affirmations he sets forth. And since he is not concerned merely to satisfy idle curiosity about the course of the life of Jesus of Nazareth, but to proclaim the glad tidings concerning Christ, first of all for a Christian audience, his handling of his materials was dictated by his aim to suit the needs of the church. But the recognition of these facts, which a study of his gospel requires us to do, by no means warrants the conclusion that he, and the Christian church of his time, had lost the ability to distinguish between the history of Christ and the history of the Christian church; in fact the obliteration of this distinction would have undermined the very foundation of the Christian faith and make the evangelist a herald of falsehood. Nor is this appraisal to be scorned as a modern, dogmatic claim, fashioned by a vision that is obscured through centuries of the use of cloudy lenses, for the record of Matthew simply will not allow for any other judgment than that what he wrote he held to be true, and to constitute the very foundation of the Christian faith. Matthew can have the church in view, because he believed that Christ had the church in view, and his occupation with the unfolding history of God's action in the new epoch introduced by Christ's coming accounts for his perspective.[21]

---

[21] On the historical questions see especially Linton, *Das Problem der Urkirche in der neueren Forschung*, 1932, pp. 157ff.

Did the Christian church to which Matthew was first sent consist of Christians of Jewish origin? And, viewed as a missionary document, did it have in view the Jews of that day? The witness of Matthew lends considerable plausibility to the position which affirms these questions. This is not to say that the gospel is a party-document, representing a Judaizing tendency, as the Tübingen school held. The large place given to the universalism of the gospel excludes this view. Furthermore, the recognition of the Jewish background of the Christian movement and the restriction of the activity of Christ himself, as well as the original activity of his disciples, to Israel, is simply due to the sound historical sense of the writer. Nor is it clear that the teaching of Jesus, as reported by Matthew, has suffered from a legalizing tendency, for there is no solid evidence to substantiate the claim that Christ did not uphold the objective authority of the revealed law of God. It is true, however, that Matthew was most remarkably suited to proclaim the message of Christ to the Jew, whether he was a Christian or not, because of its broad historical perspective. It served to answer the questions concerning Christ which would have been uppermost in the minds of those who had been nurtured upon the Old Testament revelation. Nevertheless, these facts do not require the conclusion that the contents are in any sense unsuited to the needs of Gentiles. The other New Testament writings, as well as other early Christian documents, clearly show that the presentation of Christianity to the Gentiles included an affirmation of the authority of the Old Testament, and made free use of its contents as the background for the interpretation of the meaning of the new events. Moreover, the great popularity of Matthew in subsequent centuries of church history should warn against any narrow notion of the audience which the evangelist had in mind.

INDEXES

I. Names and Subjects

Alford, H., 180
Allen, W. C., 8, 82, 180, 241f., 247
Armstrong, W. P., 31, 100, 183

Bacon, B. W., 8, 79, 131, 227
Billerbeck, P., 200, 204, 207, 232
Bousset, W., 100, 223, 256
Branscomb, B. H., 8, 17, 97, 100
Briggs, C. A., 19
Bruce, A. B., 180
Brun, L., 100
Bultmann, R., 18, 36, 53, 75, 100, 202, 223, 244, 256
Burgon, J. W., 88, 92, 95
Burkitt, F. C., 25, 79, 97f.
Burton, E. DeW., 174

Cadbury, H. J., 102
Calvin, J., 163
Chamberlain, W. D., 174
Clarke, K. W., 244
Creed, J. M., 100, 103, 213, 246

Dalman, G., 28, 254
Dausch, P., 88
Demons, see Exorcism of
Dibelius, M., 36, 53, 75, 202, 213, 244, 247
Divorce, Jesus' teaching on, 202ff.
Dobschütz, E. von, 254
Dodd, C. H., 30, 244, 247

Enslin, M. S., 82, 97, 100, 102, 131, 218, 227
Eusebius, 79, 89
Exorcism of demons, 55ff.

Filson, F. V., 37, 98
Form-criticism, 26, 35ff.
Friedrich, G., 10, 12

Galilean Hypothesis, 39, 164ff., 183ff.
Glad tidings, see Gospel of Jesus Christ
Goguel, M., 100, 180f.
Goodspeed, E. J., 97f., 102
Gospel of Jesus Christ, the, 10f., 13, 27, 37, 49, 51f., 54, 83, 118, 162, 187
Gospels, the: ultimate issue concerning, 4; harmony of, 163f.; methods employed in, 152f., 157f., 168
Gould, E. P., 8
Gressmann, H., 20
Grosheide, F. W., 8, 180f., 201, 247

Hall, R. O., 81
Harnack, A. von, 11, 100, 247
Hawkins, J. C., 82, 220
Hippolytus, 89
History and the gospel, 4, 37, 49, 52, 54, 82, 123, 221, 257

Holtzmann, H. J., 8, 13, 25, 180f., 231
Hort, F. J. A., 13, 87, 88, 97, 118, 139, 174
Humanity of Jesus, the, 82ff., 219ff.

Irenaeus, 89

Jesus Christ, the career of: birth, 20f., 124ff., 222; baptism, 6, 14ff., 127f., 222; temptation, 21, 128f.; public ministry, 26ff., 129ff.; events in Caesarea Philippi, 66ff., 215f.; transfiguration, 40, 68f., 78, 102, 107, 237; passion, 37, 46f., 67f., 80f., 84, 112f.; resurrection, 47, 77, 85, 104ff., 108ff., 155ff., 164ff., 237, 243; return, 109ff., 233ff., 249f. See also Humanity, Opposition, Teaching, Works, Lord, Messiah, Son of David, Son of God, Son of Man
John, Gospel according to, 3, 117f., 189f., 228
John the Baptist, 6, 8f., 14ff., 40f., 127f., 132f., 245ff.
Jülicher, A., 100
Justin Martyr, 89, 102, 213

Kenyon, F., 93, 221
Kingdom of God, Jesus' teaching concerning the, 130, 226ff., 248ff.
Klostermann, E., 8, 10, 14, 128, 167, 180, 201, 246
Kraeling, C. H., 102

Lake, K., 98, 100, 122
Lake, S., 98, 122
Leeuwen, J. A. C. van, 8, 88, 95f.
Lenski, R. C. H., 88, 95
Lightfoot, R. H., 14, 16, 33, 38ff., 53ff., 100f., 103, 107, 109ff., 180f., 183ff.
Linton, O., 257
Lohmeyer, E., 8, 9, 10, 13, 33, 38ff., 53, 100f., 103, 109ff., 183ff.
Lord, the, 253ff.
Luke, the Gospel according to, 117f., 189f., 228

MacLean, A. S., 98
Manson, W., 17
Mark, the Gospel according to: I. *contents of*—preface of, 1ff., 24, 40f., 87, 96, 116f., 124; Galilean ministry in, 26ff., 41ff., 48f., 70ff.; "Way of the Cross" in, 34f., 44f., 76f., 157; Jerusalem ministry in, 35, 45, 46, 158ff.; passion narrative in, 35f., 46f., 76f., 80, 118; resurrection narrative in, 47f., 77, 85, 104ff., 108ff., 117, 164ff.; return of Christ in, 109ff., 233ff., 249f.; conclusion of, 47f., 86ff., 164ff., 186; II. *characteristics of*—aim and method of, 51f., 83f., 157, 160; absence of development in, 84; concern with chronology and topography in, 28ff., 36f., 38ff.; critical views of, 2ff., 25f., 30, 38ff., 51f., 53ff., 109ff., 116; delineation of the preaching of Jesus, 43ff., of Jesus' exorcism of demons, 55ff., of other works of Jesus, 59ff., of the disciples of Jesus, 44, 64ff.; disposition of, 4f.; eschatological outlook of, 109ff., lack of biographical interest in, 30f., 51f.; silences of, 6f., 15, 20, 24, 228
Matthew, the Gospel according to: I. *contents of*—birth narratives in, 124ff.; public ministry in, 129ff.; Galilean ministry

in, 143ff.; passion narrative in, 157; last week in Jerusalem, 158ff.; resurrection narrative in, 164ff., 182; return of Christ in, 233ff., 250f.; II. *characteristics of*—aim and method of, 123f., 127, 130f., 157, 160, 168f., 181, 189f., 198, 221, 257; concern with chronology and topography in, 124f., 128f., 132ff., 146ff., 152ff., 156ff., 162, 183ff.; critical views of, 120ff., 183f., 219f., 239ff., 250f., 256, 258; delineation of the teaching of Jesus in, 130f., 134f., 146ff., 149, 157, 227f., of his miracles, 141ff., 144ff.; interest in history of revelation in, 124, 127, 186f., 188ff., 197, 209f., 221, 229, 243, 253; question of development in, 152f.; readers of, 258

McNeile, A. H., 104, 180, 201
Menzies, A., 8
Messiah, the, 11ff., 17ff., 21, 34, 50ff., 57ff., 61ff., 84, 210ff., 249ff. See also Lord, Son of David, Son of God, Son of Man
Messianic secret, theory of the, 53ff.
Meyer, E., 100, 103
Meyer, H. A. W., 128, 190f., 231
Miller, E., 88, 92
Milligan, G., 162, 248
Milne, H. J. M., 93f.
Moffatt, J., 82, 167
Moulton, J. H., 162, 174, 248

Nestle, E., 13, 139
Norden, E., 213

Ogg, G., 31f.
Old Testament, the: Jesus' view of, 193ff., 200ff., 209; the messianic hope in, 12, 193ff.; Matthew and, 190ff.; prophecy in, 132, 190ff.
Opposition to Jesus, 152f., 184f.
Ottley, R. R., 101
Otto, R., 37, 244, 245, 252

Parables of Jesus, the, 74ff.
Papias, 79, 94, 122
Peter: and Mark, 3, 77ff., 95f.; confession of, 66ff., 79, 179f., 215f.; and the church, 235f.
Plato, 102
Plummer, A., 19, 180, 248

Rawlinson, A. E. J., 8, 10, 13, 33, 72, 88, 97, 104
Renan, E., 38
Revelation, biblical, 192, 194. See also Gospel, History and the Gospel, and Matthew, interest in history of revelation
Ridderbos, H. N., 208
Robertson, A. T., 174
Robinson, J. A., 98
Robinson, T. H., 202f., 246

Satan, 21, 56f., 59, 245, 250
Schmidt, K. L., 26, 30, 31, 32, 33, 34, 35, 36, 133, 135, 136, 159
Schlatter, A., 62
Scott, E. F., 97f.
Schweitzer, A., 68
Sermon on Mount, the, 134f., 197ff., 227f.
Skeat, T. C., 93f.
Son of David, the, 124, 127, 223f.
Son of God, the, 6, 12f., 16ff., 21, 43, 57, 82, 117, 211ff., 219
Son of Man, the, 60, 100, 110ff., 211, 227, 237ff., 249f., 251ff.
Strauss, D. F., 171
Streeter, B. H., 88, 90, 97, 98, 100, 118, 196, 202, 239

Swete, B. H., 8, 28, 73, 88, 104, 242

Tatian, 89
Taylor, V., 36
Teaching of Jesus, the: authority in, 209ff.; concerning the church, 235ff., 256ff.; divorce, 202ff., the kingdom of God, 130, 226ff., 248ff.; oaths, 206ff.; the Old Testament, 193ff., 209; retaliation, 208. See also Parables and Sermon on the Mount
Textual criticism, 88
Thayer, J. H., 150
Tischendorf, C., 82f.
Transfiguration of Jesus, the, 40, 68f., 78, 102, 107, 237
Turner, C. H., 31, 60, 115

Vos, G., 19, 62, 77, 195, 200, 212, 231, 236, 252, 254

Warfield, B. B., 20, 82, 222
Weiss, B., 167
Weiss, J., 8, 14, 16, 19, 20, 171, 180, 239, 244, 246f., 256
Wellhausen, J., 3, 8, 17f., 26, 100, 103, 180
Westcott, B. F., 13, 87, 118, 139
Windisch, H., 32
Works of Jesus, the, 43, 46, 55ff., 59ff., 142f., 145f., 248
Wrede, W., 3, 26, 53ff.

Zahn, T., 8, 11, 19, 88, 93, 95, 99, 180f., 201, 212, 247, 248
Zeitlin, S., 208

II. SCRIPTURE REFERENCES

GENESIS
18:15 102

EXODUS
2:11 128
2:23 128
3:6 196
20:7 206
21:24 208

LEVITICUS
19:12 206
19:18 200

NUMBERS
30:2 206

DEUTERONOMY
23:21 206
24:1 ....203f.

II KINGS
1:8 15

PSALMS
110:1 ..194, 223, 242, 256
118:22f. 193, 230

ISAIAH
35:5f. 194
38:1 128
40:9 12
52:7 12
61:1 ....12, 194
61:3 213

DANIEL
7:13f. 251
7:13 242
7:17 252
7:18 252
7:27 252

MICAH
5:2 125

ZECHARIAH
13:7 ....171, 194

MALACHI
3:1 ....194, 245
4:5f. 245
4:5 15

MATTHEW
1:1 ....124, 224
1:18-25 125
1:20 .....124, 201, 224
1:22f. 190
1:22 201
1:23 127
2:2 179
2:5f. 190
2:6 127
2:8 179
2:9 171
2:11 179
2:13-16 125
2:15 ....127, 190

2:16 126	5:38 200	9:27 . . . . 141, 142, 143
2:17f. 190	5:43ff. . . . . 198ff.	9:31 141
2:17 200	5:43 200	9:34 . . . . 134, 153
2:18 127	7:3ff. 175	9:35-16:12 . . 143ff., 146, 153
2:20f. 147	7:12 200	9:35-10:5 147
2:22 125	7:21ff. 254	9:35 . . 145, 153, 160, 227
2:23 . . . . . 127, 160, 190	7:21 228	9:36ff. 147
3:1-4:11 127	7:28f. 135	9:36 220
3:1 . . . . 127, 128	7:28 . . 130, 134f., 143, 176, 199	9:37 176
3:5 128	8:1-9:34 . . . . 134, 135ff.	10:1 . . . . 145, 176
3:6 128	8:1 . . . . 134, 140	10:2 176
3:13 128	8:2-4 135	10:5-42 130
3:17 19	8:2 . . . . 166, 179	10:5f. 146
4:1 . . . . 128, 129	8:3 220	10:5 176
4:5 185	8:4 139	10:6 . . . . . 147, 177, 184
4:9f. 179	8:5-13 . . . . 136, 230	10:7 234
4:12ff. . . . . 129ff.	8:10-12 139	10:8 145
4:12 128	8:11, 12 . . . . . . 232, 240	10:16 177
4:13 . . . . 136, 141	8:11 186	10:17 153
4:14ff. . . 132, 185, 191, 223	8:14 . . . . . 137, 160, 231	10:23 . . 147, 184, 238ff.
4:17 . . 129, 131, 153, 227, 234	8:16 137	10:25 153
4:18-22 133	8:17 191	10:28 107
4:23-9:34 . . . 133ff., 143	8:18 . . . . . 138, 139, 140	11:1 . . 130, 147, 151, 160, 176
4:23 . . . . . 144, 160, 227	8:19-22 . . . . . . 139, 140	11:2ff. 145, 148
5:1 . . . . 134, 176	8:20 251	11:4ff. 194
5:3-7:27 . . . . . . 130, 134	8:23-28 138	11:7ff. 245
5:3 228	8:28-34 138	11:10 194
5:10 228	9:1 . . 138, 140, 141, 160	11:11ff. 133
5:13 150	9:2ff. 153	11:12 . . . . 245ff.
5:17-19 . . . . 197ff., 202	9:2 . . . . 141, 160	11:19 251
5:20 . . . . . 153, 201, 227	9:6 . . . . 143, 251	11:20ff. . . 145, 153, 185
5:21ff. . . . . 198f.	9:8 . . . . 106, 143	11:20 148
5:21 201	9:9-17 . . . . 141, 142	11:21 148
5:22ff. 175	9:9 . . . . 142, 160	11:25-27 . . . . 17, 212ff.
5:27ff. . . . . 198f.	9:10 142	11:25 . . . . 148, 151, 153
5:27 200	9:13 . . . . 143, 200	12:1ff. 153
5:29f. 208	9:14 153	12:1 . . . . . 148, 149, 151
5:31f. . . . . . . 198, 203ff.	9:15-17 143	12:7 200
5:31 200	9:18-34 141	12:8 . . . . 251, 255
5:33ff. . . . . . 198, 206ff.	9:18 179	12:9-14 145
5:33 201	9:20 141	12:9ff. 153
5:38ff. 198, 208	9:23 141	
	9:25 78	

12:9 ....149, 160	14:1ff. 151	16:27 234
12:11 248	14:1 ....148, 151	16:28 ....238ff.
12:14 153	14:2 145	16:31 129
12:15-21 145	14:3ff. ....132f.	17:6 177
12:15 ....145, 149, 160	14:13-21 145	17:9 237
12:17ff. 191	14:13 152	17:10 177
12:22f. ...145, 148, 153	14:15 138	17:11ff. 245
12:23 ....106, 223	14:22-33 145	17:12 ....237, 251
12:24ff. 145	14:22 171	17:13 177
12:25ff. 145	14:24-32 218	17:14-20 157
12:28 ....244, 248	14:26 219	17:14 78
12:38ff. 153	14:28-31 ......80, 219	17:16 177
12:38 149	14:31 179	17:19 177
12:40 251	14:33 ....179, 180, 211,	17:22f. 237
12:46f. 175	214f., 217f.	17:22 ....172, 251
12:46 150	14:35f. 145	17:24-27 157
12:49f. 175	15:1ff. ...146, 153, 196	18:1ff. 130
13 ....149ff.	15:1 152	18:3-35 130
13:1f. 149	15:21-28 145	18:3 228
13:1 176	15:21f. 141	18:9 227
13:3-52 130	15:21 152	18:12-35 157
13:3ff. 146	15:22 ....160, 223	18:15 175
13:10 ....149, 150, 176	15:24 ....146, 177, 184	18:17 256
13:11-17 216	15:25 179	18:21 175
13:16, 17 217	15:28 146	18:23 130
13:17f. 217	15:29 ....134, 160	18:26 179
13:21 217	15:30f. 145	18:35 175
13:23 149	15:32-39 145	19:1f. 160
13:24-30 .....150, 238	15:39 160	19:1 131
13:24 149	16:1ff. 153	19:3ff. 196, 203
13:35 191	16:1 ....141, 152, 160	19:3 ....141, 160
13:36-43 238	16:3 161	19:8f. 205
13:36 ....149, 150, 176	16:12 ....131, 153	19:12ff. 130
13:37 238	16:13ff. 216	19:13ff. 177
13:38 232	16:13 ....152, 251	19:16 141
13:41f. 238	16:16 ..211, 214f., 217	19:23ff. 130
13:47-50 238	16:17-19 ......80, 157	19:28 ....147, 176, 234
13:53 ....131, 149, 151	16:17 215	19:29 229
13:54-16:12 .....151f.	16:18ff. 255	20:1-16 157
13:54-58 151	16:18f. 235ff., 256	20:1ff. 130
13:54ff. 153, 185	16:18 210	20:1 161
13:54 ....145, 160	16:21 ...66, 130, 131,	20:17 ....176, 177
13:58 145	172, 237	20:18f. 172, 237
14 146	16:24 172	20:18 251

INDEXES

20:20 179	23:37-39 157	27:53 195
20:21 ....228, 234	23:37 ....185f.	27:55ff. 177
20:23 234	23:39 185	27:57-61 157
20:28 ....237, 251	24:1 176	27:57 229
20:29 ....160, 163, 177	24:3 176	27:59ff. 177
20:30 223	24:4 130	27:62-66 157
20:34 220	24:14 ...130, 227, 228,	27:63-66 166
21:1-22 ....158ff.	233	27:63ff. 182
21:1 ....141, 160	24:15 201	28:1-7 165
21:3 255	24:30f. 233	28:1 89
21:4f. 185, 191	24:30 ....240, 252	28:4 ....166, 182
21:8f. 177	24:33 229	28:6 255
21:9 ....171, 224, 229	24:39 254	28:7 ..91, 170ff., 173ff., 177
21:12 141	24:42 254	28:8 ..104, 107, 138, 165, 174
21:15 ....177, 224	24:43ff. 256	
21:18-22 157	24:45-51 157	28:9-11 166
21:23 160	24:57ff. 255	28:9 ....179, 181
21:26 106	25:1-46 157	28:10 ......170, 175ff.
21:28-32 157	25:1ff. 130	28:11-15 166
21:31 ....171, 228	25:14ff. 255	28:11ff. 182
21:42ff. 193	25:31f. 233	28:16ff. 91, 182
21:42 196	25:31 240	28:17 ...167, 169, 170, 172, 175
21:43 ....230, 232, 240	25:34 233	
21:46 ....106, 177	25:40 176	28:18-20 ..168ff., 236, 255
22:1-14 157	25:46 130	
22:2ff. 130	26:1 ....131, 176	28:19f. 240
22:23ff. 196	26:2 ....237, 251	28:19 186
22:23 150	26:8 176	
22:31 201	26:14 176	**Mark**
22:37ff. 200	26:17-19 157	
22:41ff. 196	26:17f. 176	1:1-16:8 ....90f.
22:43ff. 194, 242	26:20 ....138, 176, 177	1:1-13 ....5ff., 96
22:45ff. 223	26:24f. 251	1:1 ....7ff., 97, 99
22:46 150	26:24 237	1:2f. 8f., 15
23:1 ....176, 177	26:26 176	1:4 44
23:2f. ....196f.	26:31f. ...165, 177, 194	1:7 44
23:4 196	26:32 ..91, 170ff., 172, 175	1:9 ....26, 29
23:8 175		1:11 ....13, 16ff.
23:13ff. 130	26:35 176	1:12f. ....21f.
23:14-36 157	26:47 176	1:14-9:52 27
23:16ff. 196, 207	26:63 207	1:14-8:26 ....27ff.
23:23ff. 197, 200	26:64 ......238, 240f.	1:14-4:34 28
23:28ff. 130	26:67 ....180f.	1:14f. 29
23:33ff. 130	27:9f. 191	

INDEXES

1:14 ..10, 11, 14, 26, 43, 48, 129	3:7 29	5:34 44
1:15 10	3:10 59	5:35-43 .....60, 62ff.
1:16-20 70	3:11f. 56, 57	5:35-41 49
1:16 ....29, 103	3:11 13	5:36 103
1:20f. 30	3:13ff. 70, 176	5:37 70
1:21 ....29, 132	3:13 29	5:40-42 78
1:22 135	3:14 ....43, 44	5:42 ....44, 106
1:23-37 56	3:15 56	5:43 60
1:24 56	3:16 78	6:1-8:26 151
1:25 57	3:19 150	6:1 ....29, 64
1:27 105	3:20 150	6:5, 6 63
1:28 42	3:21 103	6:6 82
1:29-31 59	3:22-30 56	6:7ff. 70
1:29 ....30, 78	3:23 56	6:7 ....56, 176
1:31 44	3:27 56	6:12ff. 70
1:32ff. 59	3:31f. 150	6:12 43
1:32 ....30, 56	3:32 176	6:13 56
1:34 ....56, 57	3:34f. 176	6:30 ....70, 176
1:35 ......29, 30, 161	4:1 29	6:31f. 29
1:38f. 30, 43	4:10-20 ....74ff.	6:32-44 59
1:39 ....29, 56	4:10-12 75	6:35 29
1:40-45 ......60, 135	4:10 176	6:39 ....32f.
1:41 ....82, 220	4:11ff. 108	6:45ff. ....28, 70, 71ff.
1:42f. 60	4:11 150	6:45 171
1:43 82	4:13 75	6:46 29
1:45 ....29, 43, 62	4:14ff. 70	6:47-52 59
2:1-3:6 60	4:33f. 70	6:50 .....80, 103, 106
2:1 31	4:34 176	6:51f. ......71ff., 218f.
2:2-12 59	4:35 28	6:51 106
2:10 ....60, 111	4:36ff. 70	6:53-7:23 28
2:12 ....44, 71, 106	4:40f. ....70f.	6:54-56 59
2:13 29	4:40 65	7:1ff. 70
2:14 70	4:41 106	7:1 196
2:15 142	5:1-20 ....28, 56	7:13 196
2:18f. 70	5:7 ....13, 56, 58	7:18 75
2:19 232	5:15 103	7:24-30 28
2:23-28 ....31f.	5:18 58	7:24 56
2:23ff. 70	5:19 58	7:25-30 56
2:28 ......60, 111, 255	5:20 ....43, 58	7:31-8:9 28
3:1-6 ....59, 60	5:21-6:44 28	7:31 29
3:5f. 44	5:21 29	7:32-37 60
3:5 ....71, 82	5:22-24 60	7:36 ......43, 60, 62
3:7f. 42, 176	5:25-34 59	7:37 57
	5:33 ....103, 106, 107	8:1-9 60

8:1ff. 70	9:38 . . . . . . 56, 77, 176	11:20-24 157
8:4 . . . . 29, 72	9:47 229	11:20ff. 46, 60
8:10-12 28	10:1 34	11:27-35 45
8:12 82	10:2-12 45	12:1-35 45
8:13 28	10:2ff. 203	12:10f. 193
8:17-21 72	10:2 34	12:18-27 196
8:17ff. 75	10:5 . . . . 205, 206	12:29ff. 200
8:17 65	10:13f. 77	12:35-44 . . . . . . 45, 223
8:19f. 72	10:13 . . . . 34, 177	12:35ff. 194
8:22-26 60	10:14 82	12:35 11
8:26 60	10:17 34	12:36f. 256
8:27-10:52 27	10:18 222	12:38 45
8:27-9:30 . .34, 45, 66ff.	10:22 103	12:41-44 157
8:27ff. 27	10:23 34	13 111
8:29ff. . . . . . 80, 215ff.	10:24 . . . . 77, 105	13:5-8 113
8:29 . . . . 11, 67, 79	10:26 77	13:10 . . . . . 10, 113, 228
8:30 . . . . 66, 67	10:28 79	13:14 113
8:31 . . 47, 48, 66, 110, 112, 129, 237	10:29 . . . . 10, 229	13:21-23 113
8:32f. 79	10:32 . . . 34, 77, 103, 105, 171, 176, 177	13:24 113
8:33 . . . . 47, 67	10:33f. 48, 237	13:26 . . .111, 113, 114, 115
8:34-38 68	10:33 . . . . 110, 112	13:29 229
8:35 16	10:35-45 77	13:32 113
8:38 . . . . 111, 113	10:35 34	13:35 . . . .113, 161, 254
9:1 239	10:37 228	14:3 33
9:6 . . . . . . 69, 102, 107	10:45 . . . . 47, 112	14:8f. 77
9:7 . . . . . 13, 18, 19, 68	10:46-52 . . . . 44, 46, 59	14:9 . . . . 10, 11
9:9 . . .68, 108, 112, 237	10:46 . . . . 35, 177	14:10 . . . . 77, 176
9:10 69	10:47ff. 223	14:12-16 157
9:11ff. 15, 245	10:52 27	14:12ff. 33
9:14-29 157	11:1-16:8 27	14:12f. 177
9:14 78	11:1-25 . . . . 158ff.	14:13 176
9:15-29 56	11:1 35	14:17f. 77
9:15 105	11:2 33	14:17 177
9:18 . . . . 56, 177	11:3 255	14:21 112
9:24 66	11:5f. 33	14:27 194
9:28 177	11:8ff. 177	14:28 . .27, 39, 77, 91, 108, 114, 115, 165, 170ff.
9:30ff. 34	11:9f. 224	
9:30 27	11:10 229	
9:31 . .48, 110, 112, 237	11:12-19 35	14:29 79
9:32 77	11:12-14 . . .46, 60, 157	14:33 105
9:33-50 . . . . 27, 34	11:15-18 45	14:37 70
9:35 176	11:18 106	14:41 112
9:38-41 157	11:20-13:37 35	14:43 176

14:49 33	4:25 210	24:34 ....114, 255
14:54 93	4:32 135	24:39 114
14:61 11	5:12 135	24:49 171
14:62 ...13, 111, 113, 114, 239	5:25f. 71	24:51 118
14:66-72 79	5:26 106	
14:72 81	5:29 142	JOHN
15:32 11	6:5 255	
15:39 13	7:1-10 230	6:4ff. 32
15:40f. 177	7:22f. 194	7:42 223
15:41 27	7:24ff. 245	20:18ff. 114
15:42-47 157	7:27 194	21 223
15:43ff. 177	8:21 176	
15:43 ....33, 229	8:47 108	ACTS
16:1-8 ....109ff.	8:53ff. 78	
16:2-7 165	8:56 108	1:1 8
16:4 103	9:19 ....180f.	1:21f. 8
16:5f. 105	9:22 237	2:7 106
16:5 ....104, 105	9:27 ....210, 239	2:12 106
16:6 109	9:37 78	2:16f. 234
16:7 ..27, 39, 47, 77, 81, 91, 96, 103, 105, 108, 109, 111, 113ff., 170f., 173ff.	9:44 237	2:33f. 242
	10:21, 22 17	3:10 106
	10:27ff. 200	7:55 242
	11:20 244	8:9 106
	12:40ff. ....254ff.	8:11 106
16:8 ..89, 92, 101, 102, 104, 105, 106, 107, 165	12:44 210	8:13 106
	13:25ff. 255	10:10 106
	13:26-30 231	10:37f. 8
16:9-20 ....88ff.	16:16 ....245ff.	10:45 106
16:12 91	18:2 107	11:15 106
16:14 91	18:29 229	12:16 106
16:19 242	18:38f. 223	13:21 114
	19:31 255	13:24f. 8
LUKE	19:38 ....224, 229	22:17 106
	20:17 193	26:16 114
1:1-56 94	20:27-38 196	
1:27 223	20:41ff. 223	ROMANS
1:32 223	20:41 194	
1:50 107	20:42f. 256	8:34 242
1:69 223	21:3 210	9-11 75
2:4 223	21:31 229	11:20 107
2:11 223	22:69 ....239, 241	
2:47 106	23:40 107	I CORINTHIANS
3:31 223	23:51 229	
4:4ff. 195	24:22 106	9:1 114

10:11 234	**COLOSSIANS**	**I JOHN**
15:5-8 114	3:22 107	3:2 114
15:6 180	**HEBREWS**	**REVELATION**
EPHESIANS	1:3f. 242	1:3 234
2:17 11	2:3 8	1:7 ....114, 242
	9:28 114	2:21 242
PHILIPPIANS	**I PETER**	12:5 242
2:9 242	3:22 242	22:10 234

The Witness of Luke to Christ

PREFACE

THIS volume contains, in considerably expanded form, the special lectures which the author had the honour of delivering under the auspices of the Free Church College in Edinburgh during the last week of April, 1949. The public lectures were largely confined to materials presented in Chapters II, III, IV, VI and VII. The opportunity of lecturing on and discussing 'The Gospel at Nazareth' (the substance of Chapter IV) in Sheffield University on 3 May 1949, at the invitation of the Department of Biblical Studies, is also gratefully recalled as having contributed to the final result. Previously I had spoken somewhat less formally on the general theme of the book at the Annual Summer Conference conducted by Hope College and Western Theological Seminary in Holland, Michigan, in August, 1947. It is a pleasure to give expression here to my gratitude for these invitations and my continued appreciation of the exceptional kindness shown me by members of the faculties of these institutions when I was their guest.

The studies themselves were initiated as far back as the year 1941 when I enjoyed a leave of absence from my regular duties at Westminster and undertook an investigation of the distinctive testimony of the canonical Gospels. The publication of *The Witness of Matthew and Mark to Christ* in 1944 was a direct result, and the present volume may be viewed as a sequel to the treatment of the first two Gospels.

The title of the book is intended to suggest that the basic concern has been exegesis of the sacred text and that therefore the chapters that follow are presented as studies in the interpretation of the Third Gospel. The importance of turning back again and again to the Bible itself to discover what it actually says can hardly be exaggerated. Contemporaneous study of the New Testament abounds with modernizations of Jesus and the Gospels which betray a tragic lack of exegetical fidelity. Conservatives may and ought to do better, because they generally approach the exegetical problems with a sympathy rooted in their commitment to the Christian presuppositions of the authors of

Scripture. But conservatives are prone to a traditionalism which is uncritical of the past and is not sufficiently alert to the distinction between what is written and what may have been erroneously inferred from the biblical text. In particular it has seemed to me that Christians who are assured as to the unity of the witness of the Gospels should take greater pains to do justice to the diversity of expression of that witness. It is a thrilling experience to observe this unity, to be overwhelmed at the contemplation of the *one* Christ proclaimed by the four evangelists. But that experience is far richer and more satisfying if one has been absorbed and captured by each portrait in turn and has conscientiously been concerned with the minutest differentiating details as well as with the total impact of the evangelical witness.

As occupied with Christ, and therefore with Christianity, this work deals with a profound and broad theme. Yet there are self-imposed limitations which I trust will be kept in view by the reader. The book is basically concerned with exegesis, as I have stressed, but it does not make the pretence of dealing with all the major exegetical problems which have emerged in the study of Luke. There is also present a subordinate apologetic interest. Exposition of the truth indeed can hardly fail to be a defence of it. But it is beyond the scope of this book to discuss the broad subject of Christian presuppositions or to set forth a comprehensive argument for the truth of biblical Christianity. My own goal has been the more modest one of dealing with the witness of Luke to Christ in the context of certain modern interpretations of Christ and the Gospel.

My hearty thanks are expressed to Professor John H. Skilton, my co-worker in the New Testament Department in Westminster, who graciously read the manuscript and gave me the benefit of his observations and to Miss Margaret S. Robinson who kindly assisted in the preparation of the typescript. I am also deeply grateful to my wife for encouragement and help from the initiation of the work to its completion.

N. B. S.

CONTENTS

		PAGE
	PREFACE	5
I.	INTRODUCTION	9
II.	CHRISTIANITY ACCORDING TO THE PROLOGUE	24
III.	THE GOSPEL AND THE HISTORICAL BEGINNINGS	46
IV.	PREACHING AND CONFLICT AT NAZARETH	68
V.	THE GALILEAN MINISTRY AS A WHOLE	93
VI.	FROM GALILEE TO JERUSALEM	110
VII.	DEATH AND RESURRECTION	128
VIII.	THE KINGDOM AND THE MESSIAH	152
	INDEXES	178

ABBREVIATIONS

AV	Authorized Version
ARV	American Revised Version (1901)
BTS	Biblical and Theological Studies: Princeton
DB	Dictionary of the Bible (Hastings)
DCG	Dictionary of Christ and the Gospels (Hastings)
EQ	The Evangelical Quarterly
ERV	English Revised Version (1881)
ExGT	Expositor's Greek Testament
GThT	Gereformeerd Theologisch Tijdschrift
HB	Handbuch zum Neuen Testament (Lietzmann)
HC	Hand-Commentar zum Neuen Testament (Holtzmann)
ICC	International Critical Commentary
ISBE	International Standard Bible Encyclopedia
JBL	Journal of Biblical Literature
JThS	Journal of Theological Studies
KNT	Kommentaar op het Nieuwe Testament (Grosheide and Greijdanus)
KV	Korte Verklaring der Heilige Schrift
MM	Vocabulary of the Greek New Testament (Moulton and Milligan)
MNT	Moffatt New Testament Commentary
PThR	Princeton Theological Review
SBK	Kommentar zum Neuen Testament aus Talmud und Midrasch (Strack and Billerbeck)
SNT	Schriften des Neuen Testaments (J. Weiss)
TWNT	Theologisches Wörterbuch zum Neuen Testament (Kittel)
RSV	Revised Standard Version of the New Testament
WC	Westminster Commentaries (Lock) (1946)
WMMC	The Witness of Matthew and Mark to Christ
WThJ	Westminster Theological Journal
ZNW	Zeitschrift für die Neutestamentliche Wissenschaft

Biblical quotations are taken for the most part from the English Revised Version

THE WITNESS OF LUKE TO CHRIST

CHAPTER I

INTRODUCTION

THE witness of Luke to Christ has always possessed a high degree of fascination. Although its author intimates that he was not a member of the circle of disciples who were associates and confidants of Jesus in the days of his flesh, the work has won universal acclaim because of its distinctive message and its literary beauty and charm. While perhaps never attaining the popularity of Matthew, it has likewise by no means shared the relative obscurity of Mark.

Renan called the Gospel according to Luke 'the most beautiful book in the world.'[1] Certainly its literary qualities have been universally recognized as of a very high order. Harnack, who was occupied more fully than any other scholar in this century with the linguistic character of the Lucan writings, declares that Luke 'was a master of language'. And after observing how the author with masterful artistry 'accommodated his style in different portions of his work to the scene of action and the dignity of his subject matter,' he concludes that 'in respect of its style this work can be compared with the best literary productions of the Hellenico-Roman period.'[2] His skill as a narrator, moreover, is such as to charm every one, the humble reader as well as the specialist in linguistics and literature.

The fascination of this book is, however, more than that of a superficial beauty which tends to vanish as one lives with it and hears what it is concerned to say. Its contents also grip the reader. This is no doubt true because it tells so delightfully the incomparable story of Jesus the Christ. But it is also bound up with the consideration that Luke reports much that is not to be learned

---

[1] *Les Évangiles*, 1877, p. 283: 'C'est le plus beau livre qu'il y ait.'
[2] *The Acts of the Apostles*, 1909, pp. xxxvii f.

from the other records. It is not inconsequential in this connection to observe that Luke is the most voluminous contributor to the New Testament, the two parts of his great work constituting more than one-fourth of the volume. His Gospel is the longest book in the New Testament. In the Text of Nestle Mark takes only about fifty-seven pages, John about seventy, and Matthew eighty-seven, while Luke takes nearly ninety-five pages. The autograph of Luke, assuming that it was written on a papyrus roll, must have run to more than thirty feet, which apparently is longer than was ordinarily considered practicable.[1] It should not be rashly supposed that the length of Luke is due to a tendency towards verbosity. Actually Luke is far more concise than Mark at many points. The length of Luke was determined by his judgment as to the materials which he was required to present in order to accomplish his purpose.

The greater extent of Luke is accounted for partially by the distinctiveness of the birth and resurrection narratives which are more than twice as long as those in Matthew. But the most decisive factor is the singularness of his treatment of the public ministry of Jesus. While Luke devotes somewhat less space than Mark, and considerably less than Matthew, to the narration of the Galilean ministry and of the events which occurred in Jerusalem until the death of our Lord, it takes approximately three times as much space to set forth the story of the approach from the borders of Galilee to the arrival in Jerusalem. One must look, accordingly, especially to the great middle section of Luke, as well as to the birth and resurrection narratives, for distinctive features of the Gospel, although, to be sure, the sections where Luke more closely parallels the other Gospels also provide most pertinent insights for the understanding of his witness to Christ.

LUKE AND ACTS

Since in this study we are specifically dealing with the Gospel according to Luke, and have in view the evaluation of the distinctive place which it occupies in the Gospel canon, it might appear that little or no attention would have to be paid to The Acts. But the student of Luke would certainly fail to take due advantage of his exegetical assets if the single authorship and other relations

[1] See F. Kenyon, *Our Bible and the Ancient Manuscripts*, 1940, p. 10.

of the two writings were not kept constantly in mind. The Acts brings before us, anonymously and somewhat abruptly, but none the less definitely, the figure of a companion of Paul who is indisputably most significantly connected with the origin of the Acts, and is regarded by most scholars as unmistakably the real author of Luke-Acts. In addition to this testimony as to the origin of the Lucan writings, the Acts provides specific testimony as to the scope and disposition of the Gospel. In the opening sentence, the 'former treatise' is characterized as having to do with 'all that Jesus began both to do and teach until the day he was taken up.' Besides such pertinent information regarding the origin and contents of Luke, the Acts offers a treasury of data concerning Lucan vocabulary and usage which are of incalculable benefit for the interpreter of this Gospel.

No doubt these considerations are commonly recognized and utilized by students of Luke. But not less significant is the consideration, not so widely recognized, that Luke and Acts constitute a single work rather than two independently conceived writings.[1] This conclusion is based chiefly upon a study of the prefaces of Luke and Acts in comparison with prefaces in literary works of that era. Within a single literary work consisting of a number of divisions, writers were wont to utilize the device of prefaces of various sorts to indicate the scope and progress of their undertakings. Josephus, for example, in his work *Against Apion* begins with an extensive preface in which he reviews the ground covered in his monumental historical work, the *Antiquities*, and then intimates the purpose in view in his special treatise written as an answer to charges made against the Jewish people:

'I suppose that, by my book concerned with our antiquity, most excellent Epaphroditus, I have made it sufficiently evident to those who peruse them that our Jewish nation is of very great antiquity, and had a distinct subsistence of its own originally; and how we came to inhabit this country in which we now live. Those *Antiquities* contain the history of five thousand years, and are composed by me in Greek on the basis of our sacred books. However, since I observe a considerable number

---

[1] Cf. Zahn, *Einleitung in das N.T.*, 1907, II, Par. 60, note 10; Cadbury, *The Beginnings of Christianity*, Part I, Vol. II, pp. 489 f.; the same, *The Making of Luke-Acts*, 1927, pp. 194 ff.; Creed, *The Gospel according to St. Luke*, 1930, ad loc.

of people giving ear to the reproaches that are laid against us by those who bear ill-will to us, and do not believe what I have written concerning the antiquity of our nation, while they take it for a plain sign that our nation is of a later date, because it was not counted worthy of a bare mention by the most famous historiographers among the Grecians, I therefore have thought myself under an obligation to write somewhat briefly about all these subjects in order to refute the spite and voluntary falsehood of those that reproach us, and to correct the ignorance of others, and withal to instruct all those who are desirous of knowing the truth concerning our antiquity . . .'

At the beginning of Book II, Josephus introduces his discussion with a preface of much more restricted character, which is offered to apprise his readers of the progress he has made and the scope of that which is to come:

'In the former book, most honoured Epaphroditus, I have demonstrated our antiquity, and confirmed the truth of what I have said from the writings of the Phoenicians, and Chaldeans, and Egyptians. I have moreover produced many of the Grecian writers as witnesses thereto . . . I shall now therefore begin a refutation of the remaining authors who have written anything against us . . .'[1]

That the prefaces of Luke and the Acts, similarly, are essentially different from each other, and that the latter appropriately is subordinate to the more comprehensive preface at the commencement of the Gospel becomes clear. If Luke conceived of the Acts as a quite independent undertaking, and if, as would necessarily follow, Lk. i. 1-4 were intended as a preface merely to the Gospel, one would expect a somewhat similar preface at the beginning of the Acts. Since, however, a resumé of the first work is formulated and then the scope of the second portion is intimated, it cannot be doubted that the author intends to associate the Acts in a most intimate fashion with his earlier composition, and even to indicate that the Acts forms a second portion of a single undertaking in view at the very beginning.

To this line of argument it has been objected that the Acts does not set forth the scope of the second volume in specific terms, and

[1] The translations are largely from Whiston.

that therefore Luke could not have designed the opening words of the Acts, in imitation of literary practice, as a subordinate preface. The scope of the second volume is indeed not stated precisely and this argument is therefore not without weight. Nevertheless, it is intimated with sufficient clearness that the Acts has to do with the activity of the ascended Christ through the Holy Spirit, whom He was to pour out upon those who were to bear witness beginning from Jerusalem. At any rate a decisive consideration is found in the manner in which the writer takes stock of the ground covered in the previous volume before he proceeds with his narration of the unfolding of the new epoch with which the Acts is concerned.

If, however, the view that Luke and Acts constitute a single work is to be established on the basis of a true evaluation of the prefatory material, the Lucan preface in the four opening verses of the Gospel must be shown to possess the comprehensive character which, as has been intimated, commonly obtains in the case of prefaces at the beginning of a work of more than one volume. While perhaps the view that Luke and Acts are parts of a single work does not depend solely for support on the evidence that Lk. i. 1-4 applies to the whole work, and not merely to the Gospel, yet the demonstration of the pertinency of the Lucan prologue to the whole would go far in the direction of establishing it. This can be shown only on the basis of a careful examination of the prologue, and we shall turn to that task in the following chapter. But here we may anticipate the conclusion that, in our judgment, positive confirmation is forthcoming, and that, therefore, we cannot escape the fact that there must be constant reckoning with the Acts in our study of Luke.

It will appear that the conjunction with the Acts places this Gospel in the perspective of the history of Christianity. Whether, in common with the other evangelists, Luke is dealing with the historical career of Jesus Christ, or whether he is concentrating on his work as historian of the founding of the Christian Church, he is treating a single theme. His theme is Jesus Christ. More particularly he aims to deal with the action of Jesus Christ, both in word and deed, as He once for all laid the foundations of Christianity. The living Lord of the Church is the same as the person who lived as a man among men. The Jesus who is portrayed as being Himself led of the Holy Spirit is the One whose effusion of the Holy Spirit from on high brought the Church into existence and who through His bestowal of the Spirit continued to manifest His gracious rule of and on behalf of the Church.

But Luke is not so much under the spell of the unity of his theme that he obscures the diversity of its manifestation. The ascension of Christ draws a firm line between the two segments of that history, and so the career on earth stands apart in sharp contrast with the heavenly ministry of the ascended Lord. Though the Gospel was not written as bare history, isolated from the faith of the writer and of the Christian Church, yet it was set down as that which actually occurred. The contrasts between the Acts and the Gospel demonstrate that Luke had a strong historical sense. He was far from supposing that the story which he narrated in the Gospel had been transformed by the developing faith of the early Christians.

LUKE THE AUTHOR

The question of the identity of the author of the Third Gospel is not of basic importance in these studies since the first and last concern is with meaning rather than origins. Nevertheless, since Luke is, strictly speaking, not an anonymous work, and the original readers, at least, must have been influenced in their evaluation of its message by their thoughts concerning the qualifications of the author, brief treatment of this question will be advantageous.

That all the church fathers who have left us testimony on this point agree in ascribing both the Gospel and Acts to Luke, who is frequently identified as a companion of Paul, is clearly of the utmost significance. The testimony of the fathers is indeed not particularly early, for Irenaeus (c. A.D. 185) offers apparently the first extant witness. However, the evidence represented by the superscription in the Gospel manuscripts reflects the recognition of Lucan authorship several decades earlier.[1] Since a very large part of Luke's claim to distinction rests upon the association of his name with Luke-Acts, the tradition gives a *prima facie* impression of owing its origin to accurate information.

[1] Cf. J. H. Ropes, *The Synoptic Gospels*, 1934, pp. 102 f., where it is argued that the Gospel titles must date from about A.D. 125. The testimony of the Lucan Anti-Marcionite Prologue (probably A.D. 160–180) is also significant.

Owing to the undisputed unity of authorship of Luke and Acts, this Gospel has the advantage of a broader base of internal testimony than the others. The 'we'-sections in Acts, as Irenaeus himself argued, show that Luke was inseparable from Paul and present at all the occurrences narrated therein.[1] It is generally admitted today that the author of the 'we'-sections was a companion of Paul. And most if not all who deny the Lucan authorship of Luke-Acts are sufficiently impressed by the historical tradition to allow that that companion must have been Luke. But in modern times there has been widespread doubt as to the correctness of identifying the author of the complete work with the author, or 'diarist,' of the sections which employ the first person plural.[2]

Harnack, who had shared this negative position, created a minor sensation when he became a vigorous advocate of the traditional view. He argued effectively that there is an accumulation of Lucan linguistic characteristics in these sections, which is understandable when one considers that the author of Luke-Acts would here be his own reporter, and thus not influenced by the linguistic peculiarities of sources.[3]

Though the arguments of Harnack and various allies have convinced many scholars, there have been others who have remained unpersuaded. Windisch, for example, has vigorously presented 'The Case Against The Tradition'[4] and Cadbury has argued that the tradition may be merely an inference from certain data in Luke-Acts (such as the prefaces and the 'we' references) and from such a statement as 2 Tim. iv. 11 ('Only Luke is with me').[5]

The decision necessarily turns largely about the evaluation of the 'we'-sections. Windisch does not of course base his negative judgment upon the supposition that the use of 'we' is the literary

---

[1] *Adv. Haer.* III, xiv. 1.

[2] The sections are Acts xvi. 10-17 (or 18); xx. 5-xxi. 26 (cf. verse 18); xxvii. 1-xxviii. 16. In addition, the western text of Acts xi. 28 contains the phrase 'when we were gathered together', and thus places the anonymous companion at Antioch.

[3] Cf. *Luke the Physician*, 1906 (Eng. Trans. 1907); *The Acts of the Apostles*, 1908 (Eng. Trans. 1909); *The Date of the Acts and of the Synoptic Gospels*, 1911. J. C. Hawkins, *Horae Synopticae*, 2nd edit., 1909, pp. 182 ff. is also important.

[4] In *The Beginnings of Christianity*, Part I, Vol. II, pp. 304 ff., 343 f.

[5] *Making of Luke-Acts*, pp. 353 ff.

fiction of a writer who, though far from the historic scene, sought to give the impression that he was writing his treatise with the qualifications of an eye-witness. For if he were trying to convey such an impression, he would have used the device far more pervasively than he has done. One would indeed have a problem on one's hands if it were necessary to account for the restraint in which virtual claims of eye-witnessship are made if they are pure inventions. Windisch's argument rather takes the line that the author of Acts used a diary which originally came from Luke. That the author and the diarist are not to be identified follows especially, he maintains, from the consideration that we should otherwise expect him to explain his sudden appearances and disappearances. Cadbury similarly is impressed with the 'abrupt and unexplained "we" ' and considers the problem posed by these literary phenomena 'an insoluble riddle.'

Are the appearances and disappearances as abrupt and sudden, however, as is supposed? And can we rightly demand that the author-diarist ought to have informed his readers more particularly as to his own movements? Clearly the diary was used intelligently, with due regard to situation and sequence. The anonymous companion does not turn up in surprising places: he first appears as Paul is about to go to Philippi; he remains behind in that city when Paul leaves; he joins Paul at the apostle's next visit to Philippi and accompanies him to Jerusalem; for a time he evidently goes his own way, but is again found in Paul's company on the journey from Palestine to Rome. And though he takes account of his own presence at certain phases of Paul's career, he quite deliberately, and in accordance with the inconspicuous character of his own role, keeps himself in the background. To have dwelt upon the reasons why he stayed behind in Philippi the first time, and why he accompanied Paul the second time, and did not remain with Paul during his entire stay in Jerusalem would have shifted the centre of interest, at least to some extent, from Paul to himself. One can understand that a modest companion of the great apostle would have been determined to avoid distracting the attention of his readers from Paul to himself. In short, the unobtrusive way in which the first person plural is utilized contributes to the total effect without allowing the work to become autobiographical.

If the supposedly unknown author of Luke-Acts decided to make use of a diary of Luke, one might claim that this is simply another instance of the use of sources which were available to him. But why then did the author not employ this source as he does other sources? Why did he clumsily retain the 'we' of his source? It is in attempting to answer this question that Windisch most openly displays the basic weakness of his own position. His answer, in a word, is that it can be accounted for by the literary methods of antiquity, and that 'the same naïveté which impels the author of Acts to leave the "we" of another's diary which he incorporates into his own history appears elsewhere, when he attributes speeches which he himself invented or elaborated to Peter, Gamaliel, Stephen, or Paul.'[1] However, even if it were granted that the speeches were composed by the author of Acts,[2] Windisch's point with regard to the 'we'-phenomena would not be well taken. As Windisch himself says, the former would today be regarded as 'deception.' But the retention of 'we' in no sense involves an ethical question; it is a purely literary matter, and would warrant the charge of extreme clumsiness. And it is exactly this charge that would be virtually indefensible in the light of the accumulation of evidence of the extraordinary literary skill of the author of Luke-Acts. This is pointedly true in the present instance because, on the assumption that author and diarist are not identical, it would have to be admitted that the very author who had clumsily retained 'we' had for the rest conformed the 'we' sections linguistically to his own language and style.[3]

It appears actually that those scholars who still today reject the tradition of Lucan authorship are far more basically influenced by doctrinal and historical judgments than by literary considerations. Windisch specifically states that 'the so-called "lower criticism" is never able . . . to maintain itself against "higher criticism",' and his case against the tradition is seen to consist largely of arguments to the effect that 'the Lucan Paul is not consistent with

[1] Op. cit., p. 343.

[2] On the authenticity of the speeches, cf. F. F. Bruce, *The Speeches in the Acts*, Tyndale Press, London, 1942.

[3] Cf. Creed, op. cit., p. xiv, note 1. Cadbury states the difficulty (*Making*, etc., p. 358), but does not overcome it.

the Paul of the authentic Epistles.'[1] Cadbury agrees that a main issue is 'whether the treatment of Paul's visits to Jerusalem, especially that of Acts xv with its decrees, is too unhistorical to have emanated from one who later was Paul's associate,' but concludes that we are here carried 'into realms where our information is quite insufficient for secure judgment.'[2] Creed analyses the situation similarly, and finds certain 'historical improbabilities' in Acts, but evidently judges that there is nothing that disproves Lucan authorship.[3] It is fortunate that on these basic matters one may appeal to the thorough and satisfying treatment given by Machen.[4]

The exceedingly weighty evidence of the 'we' sections does not indeed establish the Lucan authorship of Luke-Acts. Its corroboration of the tradition does not go beyond proving that the author was a companion of Paul. However, the significance of this conclusion should not be underestimated. There is, for example, nothing in Matthew or Mark comparable to this internal testimony. And in the modern discussion of the origins of the Gospels the central question is not precisely that of authorship so much as that of the nearness of the authors to the events which they narrate. If the diarist was the author of Luke-Acts, he was a person who not only knew Paul intimately but also had abundant opportunities for establishing intimate contact with other leading figures of the Christian Church including James (Acts xxi. 18) and Philip (Acts xxi. 8-12). Not merely the tradition of Lucan authorship, therefore, but also the testimony of Luke-Acts itself supports the judgment that the work owes its origin, not to one who was out of touch with the persons and events he describes, but to one who himself visited Jerusalem within three decades of the death of our Lord, and had splendid opportunities of becoming intimately acquainted with many of the earliest and best-informed Christians.

There are other considerations, moreover, which, though not positively identifying the author as Luke, are highly congruous

---

[1] Op. cit., p. 344; p. 317; pp. 321 ff.
[2] *Making*, p. 357.
[3] Op. cit. pp. xv f.
[4] In *The Origin of Paul's Religion*, 1921, pp. 37 ff. 43 ff., 71 ff. The answer of B. H. Streeter, *The Four Gospels*, 1930, pp. 543 ff., 548 f., note 1, is also of special interest.

with the tradition, and possess a certain cumulative force in substantiation of it.[1] The author of this work has chosen to introduce himself only as an anonymous companion of Paul on certain sections of his missionary journeys, and therefore such companions as Timothy, Silas and Aristarchus, who are mentioned in Acts, may not be regarded as candidates for the honour. On the other hand, Luke, though otherwise evidently well-known, remains unmentioned. The same might be said of Titus, but Luke has every advantage over him since Titus does not appear in those Epistles of Paul evidently written in the period introduced by the conclusion of Acts. Luke, however, is present as an intimate fellow-worker of Paul (Phm. 24; Col. iv. 14; cf. 2 Tim. iv. 11). This fact is important, not only because, if Luke is the author, Acts and Paul would agree in placing Luke in Rome in Paul's company, but also because the several concluding chapters of Acts suggest that their author was a person who was in intimate touch with Paul and was especially concerned with the critical events leading to his arrest. It is also of interest that Luke is not mentioned in the Thessalonian Epistles nor in the Corinthian and Roman Epistles, and this is exactly what one would expect if the diarist was Luke. For the former were written on the second missionary journey after Paul had left him behind in Macedonia; and the latter evidently on the third journey before he joined Paul at Acts xx. 4 for the trip to Jerusalem.

There are a few other facts concerning Luke which accord well with the tradition. Luke's acquaintance with Mark is intimated by Paul (Col. iv. 10, 14; Phm. 24), and the author was obviously remarkably well-informed concerning Mark's life, even to the point of knowing the name of the maid in his mother's home in Jerusalem (cf. Acts xii. 12, 25, xiii. 13, xv. 37 ff.). Luke was a Greek (cf. Col. iv. 14 and iv. 10 f.), and the language is best understood on the supposition that the author was a Greek of considerable literary skill. Of still greater interest is Paul's designation of Luke as 'the beloved physician' (Col. iv. 14). Following the monumental study of Hobart, such students of Luke as Plummer, Zahn and Harnack have acknowledged that Luke-Acts displays various medical traits and interests that confirm the tradition that

[1] Windisch, op. cit., pp. 315 f., admits that such considerations as follow are 'strong arguments in favour of the correctness of the tradition.'

its author was a physician.[1] This contention has been subjected to a very severe criticism by Cadbury, who supports the charge that the whole argument is 'an immense fallacy.'[2] More recently, however, Creed has observed that, though the argument as originally stated was exaggerated, there has, on the other hand, been an undue depreciation of the force of the medical parallels. He also presents the timely reminder that the final question is not whether the medical language establishes the conclusion that the author was a physician, but whether it contributes corroboration of the tradition.[3]

These several considerations taken singly would perhaps be of relatively little weight, but together they possess cumulative force of a high order when one takes due account of the strength of the early Christian tradition of Lucan authorship. If such considerations as these pointed much more definitely to Luke as the author than they actually do, the argument might lose much of its weight. For then one might perhaps argue with some plausibility that the tradition was an inference from these data. The true situation is, however, that early Christian tradition unanimously and confidently assigns the work to Luke, who otherwise was not remembered as an influential member of the Christian community, and that in a very incidental and unobtrusive fashion the New Testament exhibits the congruity and tenability of the tradition. As the prefaces of Luke and Acts show with particular clarity, Luke-Acts is not strictly speaking an anonymous work. And the first readers would surely have been apprised of the identity of the author. Hence there would have been from very early times a Christian tradition as to the author. If this person was some one other than Luke, his name and connection with the work must have disappeared completely from view at a very early time, and were replaced by the allegedly fictitious tradition of Lucan authorship.

[1] Cf. W. K. Hobart, *The Medical Language of St. Luke*, 1882; A. Plummer, *The Gospel according to St. Luke* (ICC), 1896, pp. lxiii ff.; Zahn, op. cit., Par. 62 and note 5 (pp. 433 f.; 442 f.); Harnack, *Luke the Physician*, pp. 175 ff.

[2] Cf. *Beginnings*, etc., pp. 346 ff.; *Making*, etc., p. 219, p. 358; and especially *The Style and Literary Method of Luke*, 1920, pp. 39 ff.

[3] Op. cit., pp. xviii ff.

CRITICAL PERSPECTIVES

On the whole the tendencies of modern criticism have not enhanced the reputation of the third evangelist as an accurate and trustworthy narrator. For some the writings of Luke have never fully recovered from the attack of the Tübingen School. In spite of the almost universal rejection of its radical, Hegel-inspired, reconstruction of history, and of many of its judgments on detailed points, certain basic perspectives of this School remain influential. The conjecture of Baur that Luke was really a revision of Marcion's Gospel, and was first published as late as about the middle of the second century, did not hold the field for any considerable length of time. But his low view of Acts, based largely on alleged discrepancies with Paul's Epistles, has continued to be an important factor in recent criticism of the Lucan writings.[1]

The development of the Marcan Hypothesis, while itself representing a sharp divergence from the position of Baur, involved a depreciation of the right of Luke to be heard on its own merits. For the very act of elevating Mark to a position of priority and superiority to the other Gospels assigned Luke, along with Matthew, to a secondary rank. Nor has the incisive criticism of the Marcan Hypothesis associated with the names of Wrede and Wellhausen, and which forms a background for the development of Form-criticism, served substantially to increase respect for Luke. For this radical attack upon the historical worth of Mark has also presupposed the priority of Mark, and, except perhaps for certain aspects of the message of Jesus, the relative superiority of Mark to the other Gospels. The illuminating commentary of J. M. Creed, published in 1930, is typical of this tendency. While allowing that Luke may have had access to some literary sources and some historical tradition, he interprets Luke as in the main a consummate literary artist who freely adapted his sources to suit his ends and in all probability was himself responsible for the literary creation of a considerable part of his distinctive material.[2]

---

[1] Windisch's approach is rather typical of the modern revised and moderated form of the Tübingen approach. But Baur's thesis that Marcion's Canon largely influenced the formation of Luke-Acts has been sympathetically re-examined and restated by J. Knox, *Marcion and the New Testament*, 1942. See my review in WTJ, Nov. 1943, pp. 86 ff., 95 ff.

[2] Creed maintains, for example, that the preaching at Nazareth, the com-

A somewhat more conservative tendency is represented by the development of the four-document theory, which has gained considerable vogue as the result of the original work of Streeter and the support given by Taylor, Easton and W. Manson among others.[1] This approach is more conservative particularly in that most of the distinctively Lucan materials are regarded as having been in written form considerably before the evangelist published his Gospel, and as having a right accordingly to be weighed on their own merits as a source or sources independent of Mark. Although it is not an essential feature of this literary hypothesis that Luke was the author of Proto-Luke as well as of the finished Gospel, Streeter does maintain this position. Indeed, he concludes that Luke himself was active in collecting information and making copious notes during the last two years that he was in Caesarea in the company of Paul, and that he later combined these materials with 'Q' to form Proto-Luke. It is beyond the scope of our present undertaking to evaluate this hypothesis. And in calling attention to its 'conservative' character, my intention is not to imply that it offers a necessarily more satisfactory theory of Gospel origins than the two-document theory. Its multiplication of literary sources of a hypothetical nature, for example, does not commend it. And in continuing to approach the synoptic problem almost exclusively in terms of documents, it does not do justice to the factor of the oral proclamation of the Gospel. But there is a gratifying amount of historical realism in its evaluation of the situation in which Luke and the other Gospels came into existence. To a far greater extent than the prevalent forms of the two-document theory, it allows for the viewpoint that the distinctive testimony of Luke constitutes authentic tradition.

Mention must also be made here of the highly significant work of Cadbury. His approach is rather independent and therefore also somewhat difficult of classification. His major work on Luke, *The Making of Luke-Acts*, appeared in 1927, three years after the first edition of Streeter's *The Four Gospels*, and he

mission of the risen Lord, the Ascension, and Pentecost constitute free creations of the author's historical imagination, p. xviii. But Luke is also said to be conservative in his treatment of sources, pp. lxii, lxxi.

[1] Streeter, op. cit., V. Taylor, *Behind the Third Gospel*, 1926; B. S. Easton, *The Gospel according to St. Luke*, 1926; W. Manson, *The Gospel of Luke*, 1930.

expresses himself on Streeter's position, chiefly in footnotes, with reserve but somewhat favourably. In the main, however, his views seem to correspond more closely with the position which Creed was to set forth in his Commentary of 1930, although he places more emphasis upon the factor of Luke's environment—the materials which were available and the methods and standards of the time—and less upon the creative imagination of the author, than is true of Creed. But, as has been noted, Cadbury exceeds most modern students in the general agnosticism of his approach to the question of origins. And, in keeping with his emphasis upon the historical environment which he finds reflected in Luke-Acts, rather than upon the decisive influence of historic personalities, one gains the impression that this work is regarded as being a first-class witness only for the time and situation in which it came into existence. But as we shall see in our examination of the Prologue, and many other features of the Gospel, the modern student has been placed greatly in his debt both because of the learning and acuteness of many of his observations and because of the stimulus to fresh study which results from an evaluation of his theories.

It will be recognized that the foregoing review of opinion does not aim at comprehensiveness. Like the other materials in this introductory chapter, it will have accomplished the end in view if the summary and selective treatment has succeeded in indicating perspectives which may profitably be kept in mind as one examines the witness of the Gospel. These perspectives are of immediate moment as one reflects upon the testimony of the prologue.

CHAPTER II

CHRISTIANITY ACCORDING TO THE PROLOGUE

EASILY the most specific testimony which Luke provides for the understanding of his own evaluation of his work is afforded by the stately and meaningful sentence with which he begins his Gospel. Although he takes only one sentence to enunciate what he is undertaking to do, this sentence of more than forty words is so weighty in its declarations and implications that it commands minute and painstaking examination. Here at the very beginning, determined to leave no doubt as to his qualifications, methods and goal, the author makes a personal bow to his readers. Except for this statement the Gospel might be regarded as an anonymous work. We should take care, indeed, not to base our conclusions as to Luke's claims exclusively upon the prologue, for that would be as foolhardy as to judge an architect's design solely from the blueprints after the completed building has been opened to inspection. The Gospel as it lies before us, and the Acts as well, must be allowed to tell all that they have to testify concerning what Luke evidently intended to accomplish. Nevertheless, it would be difficult to exaggerate the distinctive contribution which is made to our knowledge of the origin of Luke-Acts by the opening words.

The prologue is of special significance today from a different point of view. Although its chief interest lies in what the author tells in advance concerning himself and his undertaking, the fact remains that this information is set forth against a background of activity by certain predecessors. And what Luke says concerning these predecessors provides us with a most valuable testimony concerning a crucial, but not too well known, period of Christian history. This is the period between the ascension of Christ and the commencement of the documentation of Christianity, the period of close on twenty years before the earliest Epistles were written, of perhaps thirty years or more before the earliest Gospel was published. These writings of the New Testament supply us with all our certain historical information concerning the career of Christ. They also directly and indirectly light up the earliest days of the

Christian church. It may not be overlooked, however, that the gospel of Jesus Christ was handed down *orally*, at least for the most part, during the first decades. And one may quite legitimately be concerned with that earliest phase of the proclamation of the gospel which forms the background for its commitment to writing.

The method of Form-criticism, which has come to the fore since the close of the first World War, has centred attention upon this period and has sought to explain the origins of the Gospels in terms of the developing faith and life of the early Christian communities. Its historical presuppositions and critical methods are open to weighty objections, and it is radically astray in its central evaluation of Christianity and its writings as being more fundamentally the product of social forces than the realization of the purposes of Jesus Christ. But it has the merit of centring attention upon the significance of this period for our understanding of Christianity and acknowledging oral tradition as a basic factor in the formation of the Gospels.[1] Luke's prologue, to be sure, is not oriented to the modern critical situation, but he does have some significant things to say concerning developments in this period. He deserves to be considered more fully and earnestly by those who are dealing with the subject of the formation of the gospel tradition.

LUKE'S PREDECESSORS

Luke's characterization of the work of his predecessors may conveniently be discussed under the following heads: (1) the facts with which they were concerned; (2) the transmission of these facts; and (3) the beginnings of the composition of documents.

The subject matter with which Luke's predecessors dealt is described in an arresting phrase, translated in the Revised Version with apparent matter-of-factness as 'those matters which have been fulfilled among us', but with somewhat greater force in the margin by those matters which have been 'fully established' among us. More religiously colourful is the familiar language of the Authorized Version, 'those things which are most surely believed among us,' but this quality does not justify the translation.

---

[1] For analysis and criticism of *Formgeschichte*, see articles and reviews in WTJ, 1938-39, pp. 13 ff.; 1939-40, pp. 110 ff., 135 ff.; 1943-44, pp. 200 ff.

The verb may, indeed, mean to *convince* or *persuade*; it is thus used several times by Paul in the passive voice, as for example in Rom. xiv. 5: 'Let each man be fully persuaded in his own mind.' But this meaning can hardly stand here for, though persons may be persuaded, things cannot.[1]

The meaning of the verb: *to fulfil, establish,* or *accomplish* (cf. 2 Tim. iv. 5, 17), on the other hand, completely satisfies the Greek construction. Renderings in the direction of the Revision of 1881, therefore, are definitely more acceptable than the translation of the Authorized Version of 1611. It should not be lost sight of, however, that the verb used here is not the word ordinarily translated by 'fulfil,' as for example in Lk. iv. 21, where our Lord says, 'Today hath this Scripture been fulfilled in your ears.' Perhaps the rarer Greek word has been chosen for merely formal reasons because of the literary interest of Luke. Blass, who has helpfully dealt with the language and style of the prologue, and speaks of it as 'a very remarkable specimen of fine and well-balanced structure, and at the same time of well-chosen vocabulary,' explains this and other terms as being selected because they are 'grander and sonorous.'[2] Although, accordingly, the word chosen does not necessarily connote more than the more common, simpler verb 'fulfil' in various contexts where divine or human plans are spoken of as being accomplished, yet the use of this unusual word does centre attention upon the Lucan philosophy of history. According to Luke's understanding the matters accomplished were of such a character that they did not somehow accomplish themselves in the onrush of the stream of history. For in Acts i. 1 he sums up the Gospel as being concerned with what *Jesus* began to do and teach, and in the total perspective of Luke-Acts Jesus is viewed as the divine Lord who through His

---

[1] Eusebius (*H.E.* III, xxiv. 15) also seems to have been influenced by this meaning of the verb, for he declares that Luke explains that many others had somewhat rashly undertaken to compose a narrative of the things of which 'he himself had acquired full assurance' or, 'he himself had been brought to conviction' (αὐτὸς πεπληροφόρητο λόγων). But no special weight should be attached to Eusebius' interpretation since evidently it is based upon his imperfect memory of the prologue rather than upon a careful consideration of what Luke actually said. Luke is clearly speaking of his predecessors rather than of himself at this point.

[2] *The Philology of the Gospels*, 1898, pp. 7, 12. See also Cadbury, *Beginnings of Christianity*, I, ii. 1922, p. 496: 'a longer and more sonorous word'.

presence upon earth and through the agency of the Holy Spirit after His ascension accomplished the divine plan.[1]

The events fulfilled 'among us,' that is, in the midst of the Christian community in Palestine, were accordingly thought of as being far from ordinary. They were in short a series of events, intimately associated with respect to time and place, having taken place within a brief epoch in Palestine; events of a public or semi-public nature, having occurred in the midst of the life of men ('among us'), and of epochal meaning for the life of the Christian church. As the Gospel makes clear, these events are the facts of foundational significance for the Church, including especially the birth, the death and the resurrection of Jesus Christ. Though these events are viewed as belonging to the past, the choice of the perfect tense confirms the impression that they are thought of as being of abiding significance.

We proceed now to examine what Luke has to say on the timely question of the transmission of knowledge concerning the foundational facts to the point of documentation in the writings of his predecessors. This period of transmission obviously cannot be marked off sharply as a precisely delineated interval between the occurrence of the events and the preparation of written records. For significant events took place after the transmission of a knowledge of other events had begun and probably even after the earliest composition of documents. Nevertheless, the great events of the Gospel belonged to the past when their communication to the church began.

Of primary interest is the question as to the persons who, according to Luke, were responsible for the transmission of this knowledge of what had taken place. Luke describes them as those 'who from the beginning were eyewitnesses and ministers of the word.'[2] The task of identifying the eyewitnesses and ministers is advanced considerably when one observes that Luke evidently has only one group of persons in view rather than two. Perhaps the most conclusive proof that Luke is not distinguishing eyewitnesses from ministers of the word is the use of the single

[1] Cf. also Cadbury, *Making*, pp. 303 f. and O. Piper, 'The Purpose of Luke', in *Union Seminary Review*, Nov. 1945 (LVII), pp. 15 ff.
[2] So rendered in RV; similarly in AV and RSV.

predicate 'handed down' (παρέδοσαν) with the compound subject, which alone explains why Luke introduces his reference to this company of persons here; it is their activity in transmitting a knowledge of certain events which is the connecting link between the occurrence of the events and the literary activity of Luke's predecessors. Two different groups of persons could indeed be engaged in this single activity, but, whereas ministers of the word would as such necessarily *transmit* information, eyewitnesses would as such only *receive* it. Hence, Luke includes the term eyewitnesses, not to designate a separate group, but in order to call attention to the historical qualification of these ministers of the word to transmit the facts. The conclusion that Luke has only one group of persons in mind receives confirmation, moreover, from the participial construction which, employing a single article, serves to join together the persons designated by the nouns into one close-knit group. Finally, there are sound reasons for construing the phrase 'from the beginning' with the participle, rather than merely with the noun 'eyewitnesses,' and this provides another indication that Luke is referring to the *original* company of qualified persons, the eyewitness-ministers, who were responsible for the transmission of 'the things fulfilled among us.'[1]

If, therefore, the group responsible for the transmission of the facts is the original company of qualified persons, the earliest eyewitnesses and first preachers, who can Luke have specifically in mind but the apostles and perhaps a few of their associates? In my judgment all possible remaining doubt that Luke has the apostolic circle pointedly in view is removed when account is taken of the clear distinction drawn between this group and Luke's predecessors. If these predecessors, and evidently Luke himself as a later associate (at least so far as the Gospel facts are concerned), are viewed as dependent upon the eyewitness-ministers, Luke cannot be thinking of this group as loosely comprehending a

[1] Acts xxvi. 4, illustrates the propriety of construing the prepositional phrase with the participle. 'From the beginning' has appropriate reference to 'eyewitnesses,' indicating their qualification to witness to things fulfilled from the beginning (cf. Acts i. 21 f., x. 37), but this is not a reason for restricting its reference to 'eyewitnesses.' See also Cadbury, *Beginnings*, I, ii, p. 498.

The aorist tense of the participle points to the qualification possessed by the original company of eyewitness-ministers to transmit knowledge to Luke's predecessors; it does not imply that they were no longer active when the prologue was written.

broad circle of disciples of the apostles or younger contemporaries.[1]

This conclusion is of far-reaching significance for the evaluation of the subject of the origins of the Gospels. In the present century, as has been noted, criticism has tended to view the gospel as basically a social product and the Gospels as theological creations of the Christian community. The Gospels were indeed written by believing members of the Christian church and were written to meet actual needs which existed at the time of their composition. But they can be regarded as social products only if the distinctive place occupied by Jesus Christ, and that filled by His immediate disciples, is radically discounted and obscured. Certainly, if Luke's testimony is taken at all seriously, such views must be set aside. According to the testimony of the prologue, the community is not even viewed as the principal agent for the transmission of the tradition, much less as responsible for its origin and formulation. Rather Luke intimates that there was a small well-defined group of persons who had been in immediate touch with the events and who had special authority and responsibility for their earliest proclamation. That Luke actually attached unique significance to the apostolic preaching is abundantly confirmed by the place assigned to the apostles' testimony in the early chapters of Acts. It was the apostles who 'went in and went out among us, beginning from the baptism of John unto the day that he was received up from us,' and thus were qualified to preach the message which found its climax in the resurrection of Jesus.[2]

Concerning the form in which Luke's predecessors received their information we learn nothing definite from the prologue. Since the verb 'handed down' could be used of transmission through written documents (as in Acts vi. 14 where reference is made to 'the customs which Moses delivered to us'), we cannot exclude the possibility that some of the tradition to which Luke refers may have been in written form. Nevertheless, there can be little doubt that oral tradition is chiefly, if not exclusively, in view. Luke appears to draw a contrast between those who like himself (the 'many') were concerned to compose a narrative in

[1] Cadbury's distinctive view is considered below.
[2] Cf. Acts i. 22, ii. 42, vi. 4, and the record of the apostolic preaching which is a conspicuous feature of the Acts.

written form and the company of persons who, by their oral proclamation of the things which they had seen and heard, provided the materials for such literary works.[1]

The only other information Luke provides concerning these early documents is found in his intimation that 'many' had been engaged in such literary efforts. The general tendency of modern interpreters is to discount this detail as being a conventional feature of a largely conventional preface. This is the position, for example, of Cadbury and Dibelius. And Streeter thinks that Mark must have been mainly in view but that the 'vague and general' mention of 'many' was employed in order that readers brought up on Mark could not have their feelings hurt.[2] In my judgment, however, there is nothing improbable in the view that by the sixth decade of the first century several attempts had been made in the various churches to provide written accounts of the apostolic preaching and teaching. The need which Mark and Luke supplied, for example, may well have been felt previously in many churches. To suppose, however, that several such compositions came into existence prior to Luke's literary activity does not imply that they were generally as comprehensive as our canonical Gospels or that they were ever regarded as possessing the authority and competence of our Gospels. Even quite provisional and fairly brief written formulations of the apostolic

---

[1] Blass, op. cit., pp. 15 ff. appeals to the use of the verb in Plutarch and Irenaeus to substantiate the rendering 'to restore from memory,' and concludes that Luke has in mind the restoration of oral tradition from living memory. However, the data appear to be too meagre to warrant a dogmatic conclusion. Moreover, in the use of this verb by Irenaeus (*Adv. Haer.* III xxi. 2) it is well to observe that, though Ezra is described as having 'reconstructed from memory' what the ancient writer had composed, and therefore as having depended on his memory of tradition, the fact remains that the tradition in view is regarded as having existed originally in written form before it was lost. So even if Blass's rendering could be insisted upon, this fact would not be decisive for the determination of the original form of the tradition. See also Creed, ad loc.

[2] Cadbury, *Beginnings*, I. ii, pp. 492 f.; Dibelius, *Gospel Criticism and Christology*, 1935, pp. 30 f.; Streeter, *The Four Gospels*, p. 559. On the other hand, Harnack, *Date of the Acts*, p. 125 n., in connection with his support of the early dating of Luke, declares that 'with our complete ignorance of the circumstances it is quite inadmissible for us any longer so to tie ourselves down to one decade as to say that a decade later there were "many" that could have written, while a decade earlier there could not have been many.' F. W. Grosheide, 'The Synoptic Problem' in EQ, January 1931, takes the reference to 'many' quite literally, but supposes that oral Gospels are in view.

preaching would have qualified under the terms Luke applies to the works of his predecessors.

DOES LUKE DISPARAGE HIS PREDECESSORS?

If Luke's direct testimony as to his qualifications, methods and goal is to be placed in its correct perspective, it will be essential to gauge his evaluation of the work of his predecessors in relation to his own. One question at issue here is whether he had a favourable or an unfavourable view of their efforts. Eusebius definitely took the latter view, for he states that Luke explains that 'since many others had *rather rashly attempted* to compose a narrative of the things of which he himself had acquired full assurance, and feeling the necessity of freeing us from *the doubtful opinions of the others*, he delivered in his own Gospel the accurate account of the things of which he had firmly apprehended the truth ... being aided by his association and contact with Paul and his conversation with the remaining apostles.'[1] But the antiquity of this interpretation is about all that can be said in its favour, for it varies at several points from what Luke actually says. Evidently Eusebius is depending on his memory rather than upon actual examination of the text of Luke, and hence gives a very free paraphrase rather than an accurate exegesis.

If careful account is taken of what Luke actually says, it will appear that there is no real support for the view that he is depreciating the work of his predecessors. On the contrary, his general characterizations of their qualifications and actions create at least a presumption in favour of the view that he means to acknowledge their positive worth. In fact, when the language of the opening two verses (the protasis) is compared with that of the final two (the apodosis), it appears that the parallelism is so pervasive that virtually all that he says about them he might as well have said concerning himself.

One should observe, first of all, that the use of the verb 'undertaken' in describing their efforts by no means implies disparagement. If it is translated 'attempted,' it might indeed imply that Luke intended to do what others had tried but failed to carry out satisfactorily. But such a derogatory connotation

[1] H.E., III, xxiv. 15. Cf. note [1], p. 26, above.

finds no positive basis in the use of this verb. As Moulton and Milligan indicate on the background of their examination of various instances of the use of this verb in non-literary Hellenistic Greek, 'any idea of failure, though often suggested by the context, does not lie in the verb itself.'

And in the context Luke makes clear that he mentions them, not to discount or disparage them, but to indicate that he is not engaged in a novel enterprise. He says, 'it seemed good *to me also to write . . .*' He thereby associates himself in the most intimate manner with those who had undertaken to draw up a narrative.

In harmony with this approach Luke implies that he occupies essentially the same ground as his predecessors with regard to subject matter, the transmission of information, and literary aim. The subject matter is quite the same. When he says that they dealt with 'the things fulfilled among us,' he clearly has in view the events which were of immediate concern to, and one might say also the common property of, the entire Christian church, including Luke just as much as the 'many.' Moreover, he regards them as possessing the same happy relation to the facts as he. This is borne out by what he has to say in verse 2 concerning the agents of the transmission of the facts and their actual interest in a faithful transmission of them. The many have undertaken to compose an account of the things fulfilled among us 'just as those who from the beginning were eyewitnesses and ministers of the word delivered them unto us.' Accordingly, they as well as he were dependent upon the original company of eyewitness-ministers, not upon persons whose connection with the history was more tenuous. And they, too, were concerned to see that their accounts constituted a fair representation of the matter that was handed down. In view of Luke's intimate and respectful association of himself with his predecessors, it follows that the testimony concerning them bears very pointedly upon the question of his estimation of his own work.

LUKE'S SELF-TESTIMONY

We turn now to an evaluation of Luke's own direct characterization of his work as set forth in the final two verses of the prologue. We shall note what he has to say concerning (1) the subject matter of his undertaking, (2) his own relation to the facts, and (3) the orderliness and goal of his composition.

One is impressed at once with the comprehensiveness of Luke's investigation, for he states that he was concerned with 'all things.' The scope of his own endeavour is, accordingly, hardly more restricted than that of his predecessors who had been occupied with 'the things fulfilled among us.' Luke states somewhat more precisely what his subject matter is when he formulates his goal as that of providing Theophilus with certainty concerning the things wherein he was instructed. Regardless of the decisions reached on other matters relating to Theophilus, such as the question whether or not he was a Christian (a problem which will be considered below), we may affirm without hesitation that the information conveyed to him had to do with the origin and progress of Christianity.

These data bear significantly upon the question whether the prologue comprehends in its perspective the book of Acts as well as the Gospel. Even the general description of Luke's subject matter found in the prologue hardly permits of restriction to the events prior to the ascension of Christ. Theophilus could hardly have remained totally uninformed, even on the earliest plausible dating of Luke's writings, concerning those momentous happenings after the departure of Christ, such as the outpouring of the Spirit at Pentecost, which were of decisive significance for the spread of Christianity.

Luke is most personal when he informs us of his special qualifications to write. It seemed good to him to write, he says, 'having followed all things accurately from the first.' The participle translated 'having followed' is rendered more impressively in the Revised Version as 'having traced the course of' all things. Although the basic meaning of the verb 'follow' is not to be lost sight of, neither should the rich significance of Luke's claims remain unappreciated. Modernization must be avoided; Luke did not operate as a modern scholar carrying on historical research. Nevertheless, the verb 'follow' in this context, concerned as it is with the pursuit of knowledge of historical facts, and being directed to the examination of sources of information, means essentially 'to acquire familiarity with' all things. Accordingly, investigation is definitely implied in the use of the verb 'follow,' even though it may not have been conducted precisely like that of a twentieth-century scholar.[1]

We observe, therefore, that Luke's comprehensive inquiry into the history of Christianity is carried out with an eye for explicit and accurate knowledge. It appears that his own participation in the broad course of events with which he is concerned was so limited that he might well fail to mention it in his compact preface, and refer specifically only to his own dependence upon the apostolic tradition which was at the foundation of Luke and of a considerable portion of Acts. On this view Luke emphasizes both his dependence and his independence. He is dependent upon tradition, the most competent tradition. But he is not a mere reviser of the efforts of his predecessors. His language is flexible enough, indeed, to allow for a use of the writings of his predecessors, including the Gospel according to Mark, whenever such use might prove helpful. But the principal claim which he makes, and that with considerable force, is that, rather than having been necessarily dependent upon his predecessors, he was in the fortunate position of having been able to undertake a comprehensive and accurate inquiry into the course of Christian history as that had been disclosed to the church by the original witnesses.

In view of the extraordinary importance of these conclusions as to Luke's meaning we shall not dismiss this point without examining a quite different evaluation. Henry J. Cadbury, whose considerations of the meaning of the prologue are among the most learned and stimulating of modern studies devoted to it, maintains that Luke is here claiming that he was actually present at and participated in the events as a member of the group of eye-witness-ministers. To this judgment, moreover, is joined the radical charge that the claim to belong to the category of eye-witnesses must be understood as largely rhetorical and conventional.[2] Appealing to prefaces in historical writings of that era,

---

[1] See Creed's comments. It is of interest that Cadbury appears to allow for this interpretation in *Beginnings*, I, ii, p. 501 (2), although, as will be observed below, his own viewpoint is quite different.

[2] *Making of Luke-Acts*, pp. 346 f.: 'Thus παρηκολουθηκότι claims something better than research, namely, first-hand or contemporary knowledge and ἄνωθεν carries back, not from the ministry of John to Luke's birth stories, but from the time of writing back over a considerable period of the author's

and concluding that Luke's preface is typical, Cadbury infers that the claim of intimate association with the facts must be largely discounted. On this view Luke is made to claim to be an eye-witness in a very comprehensive way—although he has usually been thought to distinguish carefully between himself and the eye-witnesses. And he is thought to be giving convincing proof that his claims are largely formal—although most readers have gained the impression that he was in dead earnest in establishing his qualifications to provide *certainty* regarding the matters in which Theophilus, and doubtless countless others, had been instructed. Cadbury's interpretation is accordingly nothing short of revolutionary. But nothing is achieved by dismissing the revolutionary with a shrug of the shoulders. In view of the far-reaching implications and standing of this interpretation, we shall do well to give it serious consideration.

First of all, we must examine the interpretation of the language which Cadbury translates 'since I have been now for a long time back in immediate touch with everything circumstantially.'[1] Though Cadbury has a point in protesting against certain modernizing interpretations which apparently conceive of Luke as engaging in research after a modern manner, we cannot agree that he does justice to what Luke actually says.

At least three exegetical considerations militate against Cadbury's interpretation. The first of these is that Luke too sharply distinguishes himself from the group of eyewitness-ministers and too clearly allies himself with the many predecessors, to allow for this interpretation. This appears pointedly in Luke's declaration that 'it seemed good *to me also* to write.'[2]

---

own association with the movement he is describing.' In *Beginnings*, I, ii, pp. 501 ff., he allows for various other possibilities. He seems, moreover, to acknowledge the difficulty, on his own interpretation of 'follow' as signifying actual presence at the events, of construing the adverb ἀκριβῶς with the participle. He judges that this difficulty may be overcome by taking the adverb with the infinitive 'to write' (p. 504). J. H. Ropes, *The Synoptic Gospels*, p. 62, agrees with the view preferred by Cadbury, and translates: 'since I have been closely and competently associated with everything for a long time back.'

[1] *Making*, p. 347. The RSV rendering, 'having followed all things closely (mg. accurately) for some time past,' apparently reflects this exegesis.

[2] Cadbury himself virtually supports this argument when he says that 'the καί in κἀμοί classes the "me," referring to the author, with the πολλοί who had made attempts to construct a narrative, not with the givers of the tradition'

Sceondly, this construction apparently requires the weakening of ἄνωθεν—'from the beginning'—to 'for a long time back.' On this view, Luke does not have in mind the familiarity which he had acquired with all things from the beginning, including the birth narratives and the baptism of Jesus, but is speaking only generally of his own association with the movement he is describing from the time of his writing *back over a considerable period*. The 'we'-sections of Acts indicate, in truth, that Luke was actually present when some of the events he records took place, but these sections comprehend only small, and rather late, portions of his narrative. And even if one might stretch his personal contact to embrace a somewhat broader period, he would still have to be denied any personal contact with the momentous developments recorded in Luke and in the beginnings of the Acts. Since Luke's purpose is to provide Theophilus with certainty as to the things concerning which he has been informed, and to write broadly concerning 'the things fulfilled among us,' he can hardly be supposed to be content to indicate as his qualification for this comprehensive task the fact that, for hardly more than the last quarter of the period covered, he himself had been in touch with the course of events. Theophilus could not be expected to be assured to any great extent on the basis of such a meagre claim. If Luke is to be understood as engaging in more than mere formalities, he must be commending to his readers his entire work, including especially his account of the earlier events which were not so easily capable of confirmation to persons remote from the time and place of their occurrence as the later happenings.

Finally, the adverb 'accurately' receives scant emphasis on this view, or none at all. In his earlier study Cadbury construes the adverb with the infinitive 'to write' rather than with the participle 'having followed,' and thereby cuts the Gordian knot of the difficulty. In the later study, however, while not indicating his grounds for making the change, he definitely takes the adverb as a qualification of the participle. It seems clear that the rhythm and balance of the sentence are decisive for the latter view which

(p. 510), but he apparently fails to take this into account in his final estimate of Luke's meaning, at least not as formulated in his later treatise, *The Making of Luke-Acts*.

takes the adverb with 'having followed.'[1] But how can the adverb be construed with 'having followed' if the latter means merely 'having been in immediate touch through my presence and participation in the events?' Cadbury seeks to meet this difficulty by translating the adverb 'circumstantially.'[2] However, such an adverb would not so much qualify his association with the course of events as his qualification to write because of his contacts. Cadbury, in commenting on the meaning of the adverb, insists that it refers to 'explicitness of information.'[3] He fails, however, to observe that explicitness of information could be only *the result* of participation in certain events, and that it could hardly characterize participation in them. In other words, if due weight is given to this adverb, it transports us from the sphere of mere association in certain events to that of evaluation and critical judgment with regard to them.

Lest the impression be given that Cadbury bases his view of the thrust of the prologue solely on his exegesis of the participial clause which has been under consideration, we shall give some attention here to another exegetical argument. This argument relates to the reference in the second verse, which has been considered above, to 'those who from the beginning were eyewitnesses and ministers of the word.' On the basis of his examination of its diction and grammar, Cadbury is prepared to indicate his basic agreement with this rendering.[4] His own particular interpretation, however, finds more precise expression in the translation, 'those who had been at the start witnesses and helpers in the mission.'[5] The rendering 'helpers in the mission,' as a substitute for the more familiar 'ministers of the word,' reflects one of the chief reasons advanced in support of Cadbury's thesis. This rendering is based upon the observation that the Greek word ὑπηρέτης translated as 'ministers' or 'helpers' is employed in Acts xiii. 5 with reference to Mark as one who accompanied Barnabas and Paul on their missionary journey. Since the activity of the two leaders is described as proclamation of *the*

---

[1] Creed, ad loc. Cf. Blass, op. cit., p. 10.
[2] Or 'minutely,' 'particularly,' 'carefully' (*Making*, p. 347; *Beginnings*, I, ii, p. 504. Ropes, op. cit., p. 62, translates it by 'competently.'
[3] *Making*, p. 346.
[4] *Beginnings*, I, ii, p. 498.
[5] *Making*, p. 347.

word (Acts xiii. 5, cf. xv. 36), it is thought that Mark's service must be in that sphere, that Mark is virtually spoken of as a minister of the word (ὑπηρέτης) in Acts xiii. 5, and hence that this reference to Mark recalls the very term used more broadly in the prologue. If, therefore, Mark is specifically in view as one of the 'ministers of the word' or 'helpers in the mission,' Luke himself would similarly qualify, and he would be claiming activity as an eyewitness at this point as well as when he speaks of 'having followed all things from the beginning.'

The appeal of Cadbury to the usage of Acts xiii. 5 as establishing the meaning of Luke in Lk. i. 2 has a degree of plausibility. But a closer examination of the language in the different contexts will disclose that the meaning in Acts xiii. 5 is by no means to be identified with that in Lk. i. 2. The statement in Acts does not describe Mark as a 'minister of the word' but only as a 'helper,' or 'assistant' or 'servant' of Barnabas and Paul. His role was clearly a subordinate one, and the exact service which Mark rendered is not indicated. In the prologue, however, no such subordination is in view, and the translation required in Acts xiii. 5 is not appropriate; the persons referred to are evidently those pre-eminent persons who were the original eyewitnesses and first preachers. A much closer parallel to the usage in the prologue is accordingly found in Acts xxvi. 16 where Paul is referred to as appointed 'a minister and witness both of the things wherein thou hast seen me, and of the things wherein I will appear unto thee.'[1]

Cadbury mentions a third consideration as supporting his conclusion that Luke intends to include himself among the eyewitnesses. His argument is that the 'us' in the phrase 'fulfilled among us' (i. 1) 'cannot possibly exclude eyewitnesses and so we cannot insist upon such an exclusion' in the second use of 'us' in verse 2 where Luke is thought to be referring to his predecessors and himself. With regard to this argument it is sufficient to remark: (1) The word 'us' in verse 1, and perhaps even in verse 2, may have in view the Christian community in general[2] and thus

---

[1] One may also compare 1 Cor. iv. 1: 'let a man so account of us as of ministers of Christ' (ὑπηρέται Χριστοῦ), although of course 'the word' in Luke i. 2 does not have in mind Christ as the Logos, but the message as in Acts vi. 4.

[2] So Blass, op. cit., p. 14.

would not necessarily include Luke. (2) Even though Luke implies the presence of eyewitnesses among whom the events took place, it is a quite different matter to infer that Luke means to make a direct claim that he is an eyewitness and especially to maintain that such a claim constitutes the main thrust of the prologue.

We conclude, therefore, that the arguments of Professor Cadbury in support of his view that Luke is claiming in the prologue to be an eyewitness who has participated in the events for a long time back are not of sufficient weight to set aside the solid considerations which have been presented to show that Luke carefully distinguishes himself and his predecessors from the company of original eyewitnesses and ministers of the word.

There remains, however, the radical judgment that the claim of Luke to qualify as an eyewitness is shown, by comparison with claims made by other ancient historians, to be merely or largely conventional. Thus it is to be regarded as more rhetorical than factual. This charge has been subjected to a painstaking analysis by F. H. Colson in an article published twenty-five years ago which remains to be answered.[1] After indicating that Cadbury's evidence for the conclusion that the claim to be an eyewitness had become a rhetorical commonplace among historians is not adequately established, and disputing the propriety of speaking of such a practice in general as conventional, as a 'rhetorical commonplace' or 'a literary artifice,' even in those cases where the claims to be an eyewitness and to special knowledge can be shown to be fallacious, Colson declares:

> 'But I fail to see what purpose a "conventional" claim to eyewitnessship in what purports to be sober history can serve. If it ceases to insure credence, it has no *raison d'être*. If I am told that it had no purpose—that writer after writer inserted it because it was the fashion, as we begin letters by "Dear"—then I think it is an unsupported libel on both the seriousness and the literary ability of the age.
>
> 'The utmost then that we can say is that a training in

---

[1] 'Notes on St. Luke's Preface' in JThS, XXIV, 1923, pp. 300-09. Cf. Creed, p. 4, who says that 'an ancient writer would no more claim the authority of eyewitness without expecting his statement to be believed than a modern.'

rhetoric and a study and observation of historical practice may have contributed to move Luke to put in the forefront of his narrative a statement as to his sources of knowledge, and his claim must be judged on its merits. If that claim is that he himself was an eyewitness of the events in the Gospel, it is manifestly false and he has bungled to boot. For he has managed to give the vast majority of his readers the impression that he does *not* assert eyewitnessship. If the claim is, as we have generally understood, that he had been in touch with the *autoptai* (eyewitnesses) and had carefully observed what they said, then it must be judged by what we conclude otherwise as to his date, accuracy and sincerity. And it is not a whit affected for *better* or worse by the *fact* that he lived in a "rhetorical" age, an age, that is, in which the "ars bene dicendi" was the staple of education, and was more highly valued by the general public than it has been in subsequent times.'[1]

Finally, consideration must be given to Luke's characterization of his own literary activity. The emphasis falls upon the climactic purpose clause which informs us concerning his goal, and we shall be mainly occupied with that subject. The fact may not be overlooked, however, that he mentions as a distinguishing quality of his writing that it was 'in order.'[2]

It has been insisted upon rather widely that Luke must have *chronological* order in mind, and on this understanding he is often thought to be advancing the claim that he is improving upon the chronological order in which the others, including Mark, had presented their materials.[3] That Luke is referring to chronological sequence, is, however, by no means established. As Cadbury points out, this adverb 'does not imply concordance between the order of events and the order of their narration. It means rather a

[1] Pp. 308 f. Cf. Dibelius, op. cit., p. 31.
[2] One should not exaggerate the significance of this characterization as if it were intended by Luke to mark the most distinctive feature of his work, for obviously all that he has to say concerning its contents, his regard for his sources of information, his ability to undertake an inquiry that is both comprehensive and accurate, and his goal in writing—all these affect the decision as to the distinctiveness of Luke's production.
[3] Cf. Meyer (Eng. Trans.), Easton and Creed ad loc.; K. L. Schmidt, *Der Rahmen der Geschichte Jesu*, 1919, p. 317; Jülicher, *Einleitung in das N.T.*, 7th edit., p. 313.

narrative orderly and continuous in itself.'[1] The question of Luke's interest in chronological order, or lack of it, is therefore not determined in advance in his preface. It will have to be decided by evaluation of the data of the narratives which themselves elucidate this point. If I may anticipate here conclusions reached in my study of the Gospel as a whole, the judgment on the present issue may be clarified by the observation that Luke decidedly does not, as compared, for example, with Mark, manifest a special interest in the exact chronological sequence of the separate events. His narratives contain some precise chronological data, and display, of course, a consciousness of the general sequence of events in Luke and Acts, but quite different is the supposition that he aimed to set the several incidents in a precise chronological framework.

The use of the adverb 'in order' ($\kappa\alpha\theta\epsilon\xi\tilde{\eta}s$) is probably, therefore, to be explained as due to Luke's interest in a connected narrative. As distinguished from the narratives of his predecessors, which perhaps were confined to certain phases of the public ministry of Christ, and which for the most part probably were rather abrupt and piece-meal in character, Luke apparently wishes to construct a connected and orderly narrative. Taken with the reference to his interest in 'all things,' he suggests that he wishes to produce a continuous and comprehensive account. That he fulfilled this aim is borne out fully by his achievement in the composition of Luke-Acts which excels in orderliness as in comprehensiveness.

The goal which Luke sets before him is of far-reaching significance for our understanding of his work. Addressing his treatise to 'most excellent Theophilus,' he states as his aim 'that thou mightest know the certainty concerning the matters wherein thou wast instructed.' Nothing more is known concerning him than appears in Luke's allusions here and at the beginning of Acts, but that Theophilus was a real individual, rather than merely a symbolic name for the Christian readers, as 'lovers of God,' is admitted on all sides today. Confirmation of this conclusion is

---

[1] *Making*, p. 345. Cf. *Beginnings*, I, ii, pp. 504 f., where he suggests 'successively' and 'continuously,' and adds, 'It need not therefore imply accordance with some fixed order, either chronological, geographical, or literary.' See also Klostermann, HB, ad loc., who says that it refers less to chronological accuracy than to 'wohldurchdachte Anordnung'; Blass, p. 18; Greijdanus ad loc.

found especially in the use of the honorific adjective, which Luke later also uses with reference to the procurators Felix and Festus (Acts xxiii. 26, xxiv. 3, xxvi. 25). The epithet is roughly the equivalent of 'your excellency,' and is thus so flexible that one cannot derive from it exact information regarding the rank of Theophilus. That he was a person of some eminence, however, can hardly be doubted.[1]

The question whether or not Theophilus was a Christian when Luke addressed him is of more practical consequence. Since Luke seems clearly to use the designation as a recognition of official rank, we may dismiss the view that Luke would certainly have addressed him as a 'brother' if he had been a Christian at the time.[2] For the same reason we cannot agree with Zahn that the absence of the epithet in Acts i. 1, is evidence that Theophilus had become converted in the interval before Luke undertook the second volume. The issue whether Theophilus was a Christian will have to be determined by other considerations.

Cadbury is the leading advocate of the view that Theophilus was not a Christian but an influential non-Christian, and that, accordingly, the preface contains the implication that Luke-Acts was conceived of as an *apologia* for Christianity. He says, 'We cannot be sure that Theophilus would be more interested in "all that Jesus began both to do and teach" than the second-century emperors were in the works dedicated to them on the Greek word accent (twenty volumes by Herodian), on military strategy (by Aelian and Polyaenus) . . . and many defences of Christianity by the apologists . . .'[3] We may well agree that the address to Theophilus does not carry with it the implication that the work was not intended ultimately for a wide-reading public. Still, the issue remains whether the preface, when studied in relation to the contents of Luke-Acts, allows for the isolation from the Christian movement presupposed by Cadbury's construction. Does it not imply that Theophilus had come into intimate contact with the Christian movement, and had even received

---

[1] Streeter's speculation that Theophilus may have been a prudential pseudonym for some Roman of position, perhaps Flavius Clemens, cousin of Domitian, is of interest in this connection. Op. cit., pp. 534 ff.

[2] This view is taken by Zahn, *Einleitung*, p. 365; J. Weiss, SNT, I, p. 395; W. Manson, MNT, pp. 2 f.

[3] *Making*, pp. 203 f.

instruction, if not as a confessing Christian or a catechumen, then clearly at least as an inquirer?

The chief exegetical argument relied upon by Cadbury to support his view is drawn from his judgment as to the meaning of the words which have been translated, 'that thou mightest know the certainty concerning the matter wherein thou wast instructed.' If Theophilus received 'instruction' concerning Christianity, that would seem to settle the matter against Cadbury. It must be admitted, however, that the verb translated 'thou wast instructed' does not necessarily presuppose a docile attitude on the part of the person addressed. As the usage in Acts xxi. 21 and 24 indicates, the verb could also be employed where hostile reports are concerned. The verb itself does not determine the issue; it might be used, depending on the context, of the impartation of reports which were either hostile or favourable or quite neutral. Now Cadbury himself does not argue from the use of this verb as such, as is intimated by his suggested rendering: 'that you may gather the correctness as regards the accounts that you have been given to understand.'[1] Although then Cadbury allows a neutral interpretation of the clause in question to stand, he nevertheless argues that the work was nominally 'dedicated or addressed with the intention of meeting incriminating reports or impressions by the presentation of exonerating facts.' The basis for this far-reaching conclusion is formulated in the statement that 'similar passages in Acts deal with the accusation of Christians due to misrepresentations or ignorance, and make it likely that here also they have an apologetic connotation.'[2] The passages in view here are Acts xxi. 34, xxii. 30, and xxv. 26, where there is mention of inquiries as to 'the certainty' ($\tau\grave{o}$ $\dot{a}\sigma\phi a\lambda\acute{e}s$) in connection with certain charges. Do the passages in Acts, however, present true parallels to the statement in Lk. i. 4? In our judgment the pertinent contexts indicate that the parallelism, such as it is, does not affect the substance of the matter.[3]

The situations in Acts have in mind inquiries as to what could be relied upon as to the *nature* of certain charges, not what could be relied upon in the determination of the *truth* of these charges.

---

[1] *Making*, p. 347; cf. *Beginnings*, I, ii, pp. 509 f.
[2] *Beginnings*, p. 510.
[3] For what follows cf. especially Colson, op. cit., pp 300 ff.

The chief captain who held Paul in chains could not know the certainty as to 'who he was and what he had done,' the reason being that there was an 'uproar' (xxi. 33 f.); there is nothing to suggest that a point had been reached where *the truth* of the charges was to be determined. Later the chief captain made another effort, again apparently without much success, 'to know the certainty whereof he was accused of the Jews' (xxii. 30, cf. xxiii. 1 ff.). Likewise, Festus, possessing 'no certain thing to write' to the emperor, decided upon a hearing in order that 'the charges' against Paul might be signified (xxv. 26 f.).

There is nothing parallel to these situations in Lk. i. 4. The evangelist is clearly not writing to inform Theophilus as to what could be relied upon as to certain charges made against Christianity. Luke intimates nothing as to charges made. He is completely silent concerning incriminating reports. But how could he remain silent on this point if the inquiries in the latter chapters of Acts form genuine parallels to his thought in the prologue? And the apologetic motif of Luke-Acts is not explicit enough to colour Luke's language at this point. What he claims as his goal is to provide Theophilus, who is already an *informed* person, with *certainty* as to the origins of Christianity. Neither the language of the preface nor the disposition of the Lucan narrative, therefore, afford any positive support of the conclusion that the writer has distinctly in view certain incriminating reports which have reached the non-Christian world and that his book has been written to answer these reports. The emphasis upon *thorough* (ἐπιγνῶς) knowledge, and especially upon *certain* knowledge accords rather with the view that Luke had in mind an audience which was favourably informed concerning Christianity, howbeit perhaps in fragmentary and unsystematic fashion, and that what was required was a completely trustworthy record of all things from the beginning in order that faith might be further informed and might receive confirmation.

What, then, is the main impact made by the prologue? It gives explicit expression to the conviction, which obviously all the writers of the New Testament share, that Christianity is true and is capable of confirmation by appeal to what had happened. Christianity according to Luke was no mere ideology, nor a pragmatic or positivist philosophy of life or ethic. For him it stood or fell with the objective reality of certain happenings, which took place in the full light of day, in the midst of a considerable company who made up the membership of the Christian church, were reported by competent witnesses, and had become widely known.

For himself Luke claims the competence to provide a completely trustworthy account of what had happened, so that he could satisfy the need of any who lacked assurance. He does not make any explicit claim to be an organ of divine inspiration. He does not say that 'it seemed good to the Holy Spirit and to me to write.'[1] Nevertheless, the confidence with which Luke assures his readers of the truth of his record is profoundly congruous, to say the least, with the fact of divine inspiration. The consideration that the council at Jerusalem invoked the authority of the Holy Spirit in its formal decree would not require on Luke's part an express avowal of inspiration as the basis of his completely trustworthy narrative. Only if divine inspiration had to operate in a mechanical fashion, quite apart from historical inquiry and with indifference to personal qualities, would there be a contradiction between Luke's claims and the implications of canonicity.[2] Luke says nothing directly about inspiration but the fact remains that his claim that he is publishing a completely reliable narrative poses a most serious problem for those who deny his trustworthiness. To some students of Luke he must indeed appear exceedingly presumptuous or self-deceived. But to others his claims are received as uttered in all soberness and his work continues to be read with a view to the attainment of certainty regarding the things that Jesus did and taught among men.

[1] Cf. Jülicher, op. cit., p. 459, and Acts xv. 28. Note, however, that Klostermann says that the expression 'it seems to me' does not as such exclude inspiration, although in certain MSS. of the Old Latin it is joined by the phrase 'et spiritu sancto.'

[2] Inspiration may be a fact even where there is no specific claim, for in receiving the Old Testament as divine Scripture the Lord acknowledged as canonical several books which make no direct claims of inspiration. In the case of the apostolic decree, Luke felt no incongruity in accepting the decree as given by the Holy Spirit and the fact that it was formulated on the background of discussion at the council.

CHAPTER III

THE GOSPEL AND THE HISTORICAL BEGINNINGS

AMONG the things 'fulfilled among us,' concerning which Luke writes with the purpose of establishing and confirming Christian faith, first place is given to the beginnings of the life of Jesus Christ. In this respect his approach to the publication of the gospel is at one with Matthew's. Whereas Mark is content to intimate the presence in the world of the Son of God, and John rather abruptly affirms that the eternal Logos 'became flesh and dwelt among us,' Matthew and Luke report at length concerning the circumstances of His birth. The very agreement with Matthew, however, serves to centre attention upon the distinctiveness of the Lucan account. If Luke's narrative merely supplemented at some length what Matthew had set forth with comparative brevity, our problem would be relatively simple. But the fact is that the considerably greater extent of Luke's account is not its most basic difference. Indeed, Luke's narrative appears hardly to coincide with Matthew's at all. Little wonder that the diversity of the two reports of the birth of Jesus should have led in modern times to questions as to the historicity of one or the other. Our concern here is not with questions of historicity, but rather with interpretation. But the diversity of Luke and Matthew do challenge the interpreter to gauge aright the disposition of Luke in relation to that of Matthew, and to take some account of the problems raised by their divergences.

Matthew confines his narrative basically to a brief description of the virgin birth of Jesus Christ. In addition he shows how Joseph came to wed Mary in spite of his discovery of her condition, and explains, by reference to prophecy, how God safeguarded the life of the newborn son of David in the face of the violent efforts of the reigning king of the Jews to destroy Him. Since this account tells of private experiences which Joseph or Mary alone could have reported, the tradition apparently goes back to them. Nevertheless, only so much of the private life of the family is told as explains the course of events which were more or less of a public nature, namely, the marriage of Joseph and Mary and the flight into Egypt.

In contrast Luke sets forth many minute details of the life of the family into which Jesus was born. The intimate disclosures that Mary would have given only to her closest confidants are set down. As one follows Mary through various stages of her extraordinary experience, her very soul seems to be laid bare. It is this intimate, revealing nature of Luke's narration, together with features like the glowing prophetic poetry of Mary and Zacharias, which accounts chiefly for the irresistible charm of these chapters.

Another distinguishing feature of the Lucan narrative is the place given to the birth of John the Baptist. His birth is solemnly announced (Lk. i. 5-25) and later its occurrence and the extraordinary attendant circumstances are related at length (Lk. i. 57-80). The parallelism of these sections with those which tell of the announcement of the birth of Jesus and of his birth itself (Lk. i. 25-38, ii. 1-7) gives added prominence to the history of the Baptist.

One might judge from these features of the Lucan narrative that the writing is distinguished from Matthew's because of the biographical interest of its author. Thus the intimate details of the life of the family of Jesus, including the psychological observations concerning Mary, might be explained. The attention given to the Baptist might also be accounted for as due to a biographer's or historian's interest to satisfy curiosity as to the origins of the leading personalities in the Christian movement. Such conclusions appear, however, not to be well founded in fact, as I shall show at length in the discussion in this chapter.

REVELATION AND HISTORY

The actual disposition of Luke is recognized only when it is observed that the intimate details concerning Mary and the Baptist and the other secondary figures of the story are set forth only because they illumine the significance of the birth of Christ, and so contribute to the proclamation of the gospel. In particular these historical details provide the occasions for a long series of inspired disclosures which cast a brilliant light upon the Child who was born in Bethlehem. There is, therefore, no disparagement of history. Luke clearly intends to provide a record of a series of actual happenings. His narrative is a record of events, and especially of one great event. That momentous event, around which everything else turns and to which everything else points, is the fact that Jesus was born of the virgin Mary in the town of Bethlehem.[1] That event is set forth as a divine act. But if no further explanation were offered, it would be quite unintelligible. The cluster of divine revelation, which both precedes and follows the account of the birth of Jesus, serves, however, to expound the true significance of the divine action.

Matthew also views the birth of Christ in terms of divine revelation. But he sees the history of Christ mainly as the fulfilment of the prophecy of the Old Testament, a fulfilment that comes to realization only because of the divine government of events as God guides and protects the course of events to their appointed end. This element is not completely lacking in Luke. He tells of the annunciation of the Son of David who fulfils the promise that He should reign over the house of Jacob for ever, and recalls the assurance that of His kingdom there should be no end (Lk. i. 32 f., cf. v. 69). But in the main the revelational message reported by Luke is a *contemporary* prophetic message, which, though breathing the atmosphere of Old Testament prophecy, points to the imminent manifestation of the divine presence and power through the birth of the son of Mary. This contemporary annunciation of the coming One is itself a preaching of glad tidings (Lk. i. 19, ii. 10),[2] and thus, in spite of its prophetic mould, it is a constituent element of the gospel of Jesus Christ to which Luke bears witness. The gospel, according to Luke, is therefore divine not merely as a word of prophecy spoken through the prophets; nor again merely because that prophecy has been fulfilled by divine action, but also because the present divine action is accompanied by inspired utterances. As this conclusion is supported in detail, it will appear how far removed Luke is from approaching his subject as a modern

[1] It should not be overlooked that, in spite of the diversity of the birth narratives of Matthew and Luke, Matthew also sets forth this central fact (cf. Mt. ii. 1). He also reports that after some time Mary and Joseph took up residence in Nazareth (Mt. ii. 1, 23; cf. Lk. ii. 1 ff., 39, iv. 16).

[2] εὐαγγελίζομαι is used both in the announcement of Gabriel to Zacharias and in the message of the angel to the shepherds.

THE GOSPEL AND THE HISTORICAL BEGINNINGS 49

biographer. He writes as a publisher of the glad tidings of Jesus Christ.

The extent to which Luke is occupied with contemporaneous revelation will appear most graphically from the following outline of the narrative of events and the accompanying disclosures:

1. Announcement of the birth of John (Lk. i. 5-25).
   - (*a*) Disclosure of the Angel of the Lord concerning John's mission to go before the Lord in the spirit and power of Elijah (i. 7, cf. i. 13-17, 19-20).
2. Announcement of the birth of Jesus (i. 26-38).
   - (*b*) Communications of the Angel Gabriel to Mary: she shall conceive a son through the overshadowing of the power of the Most High, a son who shall be called the Son of God and who shall reign over the house of Jacob forever (i. 28, 30-33, 35).
3. Visit of Mary to Elizabeth (i. 39-56).
   - (*c*) Elizabeth, 'full of the Holy Spirit,' addresses Mary as 'the mother of my Lord' (i. 43, cf. verses 42-45).
   - (*d*) Mary's response: she magnifies the Lord for His mercy in fulfilment of His covenant (i. 46-55).
4. The birth of John (i. 57-79; cf. verse 80).
   - (*e*) Zacharias prophesies, blessing the God of Israel because He had visited and wrought redemption for His people, and declaring that John should be called the prophet of the Most High, who would go before the face of the Lord to make ready His ways.
5. The birth of Jesus (ii. 1-7).
6. Visit of the shepherds (ii. 8-20).
   - (*f*) Proclamation of the angel of the good tidings of a Saviour, who is Christ the Lord (ii. 10-12).
   - (*g*) Song of the heavenly hosts ascribing glory to God and proclaiming the message of peace to those who are the objects of the divine good-pleasure (ii. 14).
7. Circumcision of Jesus and giving of name Jesus in accordance with angelic disclosure (ii. 21).
8. Presentation at Jerusalem (ii. 22-38).
   - (*h*) Oracle to Simeon by the Holy Spirit that he would not die before he should see the Lord's Christ (ii. 26).

(i) Simeon's prophecy concerning the manifestation of salvation, a salvation for Gentiles as well as Israel, and his word to Mary that the coming of her Son will result in the fall as well as the rising of many in Israel (ii. 29, 34, 35).
(j) Anna, a prophetess, spoke of Him to all them that were looking for the redemption of Jerusalem (ii. 38).
9. Return to Nazareth (ii. 39, 40).
10. Visit of the boy Jesus to Jerusalem (ii. 41-52).
(k) Jesus's declaration that He must be about His Father's concerns (ii. 49).

These eleven disclosures, accordingly, are not merely incidental to the story of the birth of Jesus. They are not presented simply to dress up the narrative in a poetic manner. Rather they are of the very warp and woof of Luke's message concerning Jesus. Through angelic annunciations and prophetic communications, and finally (in a somewhat detached manner), through the intimation of Jesus Himself, we observe the true significance of the event upon which Luke concentrates our attention. The disclosures, like the birth of Jesus itself, are distinctly supernatural, and both the nature of His birth and the revelations accompanying it point to the supernatural person presented to men in the gospel.

The witness of the birth narratives to the person of Christ is remarkable for the manner in which various strands of the Biblical revelation converge within it to bring before the reader a most illuminating and even overwhelming portrayal of the divine Messiah. The one who is born is named Jesus (i. 31, ii. 21), who is the Christ, the Lord's Anointed (ii. 26). As Messiah He is the Son of David, who will occupy eternally the throne of His father David and reign over the house of Jacob for ever (i. 32 f.). As the One who is begotten through the coming of the Holy Spirit and the overshadowing of the Most High, He is appropriately called Son of God (i. 35). But His coming is also viewed as being nothing less than the long-awaited coming of the Lord Himself (i. 17, 76; cf. i. 43, ii. 11), so that we are confronted with the staggering paradox that He who is the Lord's Anointed (*Christos Kyriou*) is in truth the Lord Himself (*Christos Kyrios*). His place and mission in the history of revelation and redemption

THE GOSPEL AND THE HISTORICAL BEGINNINGS 51

receive further clarification when His coming is viewed as accomplishing the fulfilment of the covenant established with Abraham (i. 54 f., 72 f.) and as effecting the redemption and salvation of Israel (i. 68, ii. 38, i. 69, 77, ii. 11,30; cf. i. 47).

THE ROLE OF SIMEON

These summary observations as to the disposition of the Lucan birth narrative may be set in sharper relief when the details of certain episodes are subjected to closer scrutiny. The record of Simeon's utterances concerning Christ affords a particularly illuminating example of Luke's perspective. And the consideration of Simeon's role will prove especially instructive when compared with the place occupied by the career and testimony of the Baptist.

As compared with the Baptist, Simeon played a distinctly secondary part. He did not attract the notice of his contemporaries; he was merely 'a man in Jerusalem' (ii. 25). His significance is seen to be exhausted in his appraisal of Christ. But that appraisal is noteworthy because of Simeon's personal and historical qualifications as a pious Israelite, a prophet to whom was disclosed the nearness of the coming of the Messiah, and a witness of the fulfilment of that revelation.

In the first place, he was 'righteous and devout,' a man distinguished for godliness of life and by godly fear in a time of lawlessness and apostasy. And his piety is seen to be no mere mysticism, but to be rooted in the Biblical historical revelation in that he was 'looking for the consolation of Israel.' The consolation of Israel was nothing other than the messianic hope of which the prophets had spoken. Isaiah especially characterized the coming age as one of consolation or comfort for the people of God:

> 'Comfort ye, comfort ye my people, saith your God.
> Speak ye comfortably to Jerusalem,
> And cry unto her, that her warfare is accomplished,
> That her iniquity is pardoned.'
>
> (Is. xl. 1, 2; cf. xlix. 13; li. 3)

Among the duties of the Anointed of the Lord, as described in Is. lxi, there is the charge

> 'To comfort all that mourn;
> To appoint unto them that mourn in Zion,
> To give unto them a garland for ashes,
> The oil of joy for mourning,
> The garment of praise for the spirit of heaviness;
> That they may be called trees of righteousness,
> The planting of the Lord, that He might be glorified.'
>
> (lxi. 2, 3.)

Laden with iniquity, afflicted and oppressed, the people of God is offered the happy prospect of a new day when the grace and power of the Lord of Hosts will have accomplished her salvation. Simeon as a true child of God enjoyed the God-centred faith which rested in the divine promise and found its expectation in God. His religion, the revealed and enjoined religion of the Scriptures, was accordingly eschatological.

But Simeon was more than a pious man; he was a prophet. As one who was called to speak on God's behalf to men he was granted a direct and special revelation of the divine purpose. A solemn oracular utterance came to him through the Holy Spirit, and the extraordinary content of this disclosure was that before he should die he would see the Lord's Christ (ii. 26)! The consolation of Israel was to be accomplished through the coming of the Anointed of the Lord, the Messiah commissioned and endowed by the living, covenant God. So much was what the prophets had repeatedly declared. But the new ingredient was that the fulfilment of the messianic expectation was so near at hand that the waiting was virtually over. The ends of the ages have come. The greatest event in history is about to be unfolded, and Simeon is immediately at hand.

The divine word of prophecy is now fulfilled through Simeon's encounter with the child Jesus (ii. 27 f.). Mary and Joseph, having come to Jerusalem to fulfil the law regarding purification in the case of the birth of a firstborn son, actually prepared the way for the fulfilment of messianic prophecy in general and particularly the contemporaneous prophecy to Simeon. What many prophets and righteous men had desired to see, but did not, Simeon was now given the privilege of seeing (cf. Mt. xiii. 17). But not content with merely beholding the Messiah, he embraced

Him, thus expressing his fervour and enthusiasm at what had overtaken him. All centred then in the great fact of the coming of Christ, an event for which the divine prophecy had been preparing men in order that, when it took place, it might be understood at its true worth. The presence of this babe in Simeon's arms, seemingly quite like countless other instances of tender regard shown to infants in the history of the race, was thus viewed as an absolutely unique historical phenomenon. The Lord Himself is present in His Anointed One to accomplish the redemption of His people.

There now follow the moving words of Simeon's Song, the *Nunc Dimittis*, filling out the preparatory revelation with further reflection upon the historic significance of what had taken place. 'Now, O Sovereign Master, Thou art releasing Thy slave in peace for mine eyes have seen Thy salvation' (ii. 29, 30). Salvation has come in the person of this child; the consolation of Israel is realized. This is the gospel of salvation in the one name given under heaven among men by which we must be saved (cf. iii. 6, i. 69, 71, 79; Acts iv. 12, xxviii. 28). The peculiar personal reaction of Simeon serves only to make more vivid the sense of the decisiveness of what has taken place. The language employed serves to describe the release from service of a servant, or more probably the manumission of a slave, with death regarded as the liberating agent which is used by the sovereign master. In the context it appears, moreover, that the special task of the slave is that of a watchman. Accordingly, Simeon's words give powerful expression to the thought that Simeon, having beheld Christ in fulfilment of the divine word concerning his life, has fully performed his service. His watch is concluded with the arrival of the One for whom he was waiting. The watchman may now retire; the slave may in truth now be emancipated. There is nothing more to do, there is nothing more to live for. And therefore in confidence Simeon addresses his Lord with the words, 'And now, O Sovereign Master, Thou are releasing Thy slave in peace for mine eyes have seen Thy salvation.'

Here, then, we are confronted with the recognition of an event of history as constituting divine action and thus, as also, being an objectively valid revelation. This is not mere historism, not the attaching of religious or revelational value to merely human history. It is not a religion rooted in nothing higher historically than the impression made by the personality of Jesus upon men. It is not an attachment to his message as a timeless idealism which has significance and is valid quite apart from one's thought concerning the truth of the history of Jesus Christ. The very presence in the world of this babe of Bethlehem, well before his public ministry could be discharged in terms of deeds and words, was acknowledged as the manifestation of the divine action of salvation. Bound up as it was with the person of Christ and his appearance in the world, it possessed a finality and exclusiveness, a decisive once-for-all character, that gave the religion based upon it a character of its own, far removed from mystic idealism or similar expressions of religiosity which think to preserve the interests of religion by divorcing it from what are regarded as the contingencies of history.

But in addition to the accent upon *historical* salvation, we encounter certain other evaluations of the significance of the coming of Christ which enlarge our view of Simeon's witness to Christ. That the salvation now in view is *universal* is conspicuously brought to mind. The salvation proclaimed and being realized is that which God 'prepared before the face of all peoples, a light for revelation to the Gentiles and glory for thy people Israel' (Lk. ii. 31 f.). The universality of Christianity, while it awaited historical developments to be grasped in its fuller implications and realized in practice, is thus rooted in the revelation contemporaneous with the birth of Christ. But this revelation in turn is but a reiteration of an arresting feature of the earlier prophetic testimony, in fact the very words employed here echo the language of Isaiah:

> 'The Lord hath made bare His holy arm
> In the eyes of all the nations;
> And all the ends of the earth shall see
> The salvation of our God.'
>
> (Is. lii. 10.)

> 'And the glory of the Lord shall be revealed,
> And all flesh shall see it together:
> For the mouth of the Lord hath spoken it.'
>
> (Is. xl. 5.)

The particularization of this salvation into light for revelation to the Gentiles and glory for Israel also, partially at least, reflects the language of Isaiah concerning the mission of the Servant:

'It is too light a thing that Thou shouldest be my servant
To raise up the tribes of Jacob,
And to restore the preserved of Israel:
I will also give Thee for a light to the Gentiles
That Thou mayest be My salvation unto the end of the earth.'
(xlix. 6; cf. xlii. 6.)

It is not insignificant that Luke, who was to show how the universalism of Christianity came to be realized in the early history of Christianity, underscores here at the beginning the universality of the gospel as a note of the revelation contemporaneous with Christ's birth. But Simeon's prophecy is characterized by the same restraint that marks the prophetic testimonies of these chapters generally. In declaring that the salvation to be realized through the new-born Messiah was to be 'a light for revelation and glory for thy people Israel,' Simeon hardly becomes more specific than the prophets of earlier centuries. Only the historical note that the fulfilment of such prophecy was now in process of actual realization is new.

A somewhat different accent appears in the closing words of Simeon. In the midst of the joyous song of universal salvation a most sombre chord is heard. Though the glory of Israel was about to be realized through her Messiah, the fact had to be recorded that 'this Child is set for the falling . . . of many in Israel; and for a sign which is spoken against' (ii. 34). There comes to expression at this point a thought which was to be expounded profoundly by the apostle Paul in Romans ix-xi, where he declares that according to the divine purpose 'they are not all Israel who are of Israel' (Rom. ix. 6). Jesus Himself, as the passion narratives disclose with special clearness, anticipated His rejection on the part of Israel and also taught that He had come to bring division (Mt. x. 34 ff.). But this feature, as introduced by Simeon in the birth narratives of Luke, is not a novelty. For like the theme of the universality of the gospel it also appears in the prophets. Just as behind the historical universalism of the New Testament there is a deeper particularism bound up with the sovereign operations of God's grace and with the rejection of the gospel on the part of sinful men, so there was already behind the rather pervasive historical particularism of the Old Testament a more basic particularism which constantly stands in judgment upon the presumption of any race or any individual to appear in the presence of Him who alone is holy, apart from the divine redemption and apart from genuine conversion. Among the many expressions of this motif mention may be made here only of the doctrine of the remnant. Again and again the warning is given that only a remnant shall be saved, and that this in itself is a wonder of grace (cf., e.g., Is. i. 9, x. 22 f.). And Isaiah declared also that the Lord Himself would be 'a stone of stumbling and rock of offence to both the houses of Israel' (viii. 14), and that the Servant of the Lord, who would justify many and bear their iniquities, was despised and rejected of man (liii. 3, 11).

Only when Simeon speaks, particularly concerning Mary's own personal experience, of a sword which would pierce through her own soul (ii. 35), does he pass from the rather general prophetic witness to a concrete prediction concerning what was about to take place. But once the fact is recognized that the universality of the promised salvation is bound up with its divisive particularism, the prophecy of Mary's anguish will be seen to be of a piece with Simeon's acknowledgment of the presence of the divine salvation in the person of Jesus. The historical realization of the divine salvation was perceived as being so imminent that the rejection of the Child as the sign appointed by God would spell the sharpest smart for His mother. Here the cross is indeed virtually in view, and Mary is standing before it, sorrowing at what would befall her son. Nevertheless the utmost restraint is employed in tracing beforehand the course of the ministry of the Lord's Anointed who was 'set for the falling and rising of many in Israel.' His manifestation would disclose 'the thoughts of many hearts' as men either embraced Him, as Simeon did, or repudiated the divine revelation which He embodied.

THE MISSION OF THE BAPTIST

While, then, Simeon is introduced and is significant only for the sake of his inspired testimony to Christ, John the Baptist emerges as a figure of considerable historical proportions and importance.

His birth and career are set forth so fully and conspicuously that it might appear that he is presented for his own sake, as a figure alongside of Jesus who contributed substantially to the origins of the Christian movement. While all the Gospels give prominence to John, Luke contains a number of distinctive features which place the role of John in even sharper focus and seem to attest a large measure of independence.

Reference has already been made to the striking parallelism of presentation of the birth of John and that of Jesus: a parallelism commencing with angelic annunciations of their births and extending to the records of their occurrence as fulfilments of the supernatural announcements. Moreover, the birth of John, as well as that of Jesus, is followed by solemn disclosures which provide further authoritative interpretations of what had happened. In the case of John, his father Zacharias, filled with the Holy Spirit, describes his son prophetically as 'prophet of the Most High' (i. 76). That the parallelism extends to other material features as well as to the formal aspects is seen, moreover, from the occupation of the narrative with the extraordinary character of John's birth. Although only the origin of Jesus is set forth as distinctly miraculous, in virtue of the conception by the Holy Spirit and birth of the Virgin, John's birth is shown to have been no ordinary event. Emphasis is laid upon the facts that Elizabeth was barren and that both she and Zacharias were advanced in years, and there are definite intimations that the child was conceived only as the result of an intervention of divine favour. The father was punished with dumbness for a time because of his failure to believe the divine promise communicated by the angel Gabriel, but Elizabeth rejoices in the promise and work of the Lord (i. 17, 18, 20, 25, 45, 58). She acknowledges, 'Thus hath the Lord done unto me in the days wherein He looked upon me, to take away my reproach among men' (i. 25).

Luke's testimony concerning the career of the Baptist also emphasizes the significance of John's ministry. His message is reported more fully than in the other synoptic Gospels. There is also a summary statement of John's 'many other exhortations,' in which his preaching is distinctively characterized as a proclamation of 'good tidings,' as the angelic proclamation had been described previously (iii. 10-14, 18; cf. i. 19, ii. 10). Except for

Matthew's use in xi. 15, Luke alone of the evangelists employs this verb εὐαγγελίζεσθαι to characterize the preaching of Jesus.[1] This is a further example of the way in which the agreement of John's message with that of Jesus is emphasized.

More arresting is the manner in which the public career of the Baptist is introduced. One of the most impressive features of the early chapters of the Gospel is the elaborate synchronism with which Luke marks the beginning of the ministry of John:

> 'Now in the fifteenth year of the reign of Tiberius Caesar, Pontius Pilate being governor of Judæa, and Herod being tetrarch of Galilee, and his brother Philip tetrarch of the region of Ituraea and Trachonitis, and Lysanias tetrarch of Abilene, in the high-priesthood of Annas and Caiaphas, the word of God came unto John the son of Zacharias in the wilderness' (iii. 1, 2).

Some of these secular and religious rulers may have been introduced here because of their participation in the ensuing development. However, as the reference to the fifteenth year of Tiberius particularly shows, foremost in the evangelist's mind must have been the desire to indicate precisely when the movement began in which John was to play a conspicuous part.

Still, even this single indication of time is not completely without ambiguity. Since Augustus, the predecessor of Tiberius, died on the 19th of August A.D. 14, it might appear that the time when 'the word of God came unto John' fell within the year beginning on the 19th of August A.D. 28. Two important considerations, however, affect the decision. In the first place, the common mode of reckoning apparently followed the calendar year rather than the dynastic year, and in all likelihood the Jewish year would have been in Luke's mind. It is therefore more satisfactory in the context of Luke to suppose that the reckoning is from the first of Nisan rather than from the 19th of August. John may then have begun his ministry within the year beginning 1st Nisan A.D. 28, and concluding on the same date A.D. 29.[2]

---

[1] Cf. Lk. iv. 18, 43, vii. 22, viii. 1, ix. 16, xvi. 16, xx. 1. It is also used fifteen times in Acts of the Christian proclamation of the gospel. On the meaning of 'gospel' see WMMC, pp. 10 ff.

[2] Cf. especially G. Ogg, *The Chronology of the Public Ministry of Jesus*, 1940, pp. 184 ff., and my review in WTJ IV. 1 (Nov. 1941), pp. 38 ff., 42 f.

In the second place, it is quite possible that Luke has in view a time two or three years earlier than A.D. 28, reckoning from the time when Tiberius began to be associated with Augustus. Otherwise Luke's own reference to the approximate age of Jesus at the time of the commencement of his public ministry (iii. 23: 'about thirty years of age') would require us to place the birth of Jesus considerably later than the death of Herod (4 B.C.). This difficulty is removed if the baptism of Jesus occurred considerably before 28 or 29.[1] In spite of difficulties of this character, however, the interest of Luke to indicate the historical setting of the beginnings of the Christian movement in its public phase is plain.

This synchronism, together with a number of somewhat less elaborate historical and chronological data in Luke, have strongly contributed to the judgment that Luke is 'the historian' among the evangelists. He reflects indeed the consciousness that the events he narrates concern a movement which found expression, not in some remote corner of the world, but in the midst of the Roman empire in the full light of day. In his grandly conceived work Luke tells how this movement had its beginnings in the vassal kingdom of Herod, in Judæa (i. 5), in the province of Syria, while Caesar Augustus was emperor (ii. 1 f.). He reflects further how Christianity became a public movement during the reign of Tiberius Caesar, when sons of Herod, as tetrarchs rather than as kings, ruled over the northern regions of Palestine while in Judæa proper a Roman procurator had stepped in the place of another son who had been deposed (iii. 1 f.). And he proceeds to tell how, after the ascension of Christ, His message and church made their way under other Herods and many governors from Jerusalem to Rome, in a world which everywhere recognized the sovereignty of Roman emperors. For Luke, therefore, Christianity was a movement specifically within the framework of world history.

Now the fact that it is John's ministry, rather than Christ's, which Luke introduces with this elaborate and formal synchronism seems to some to offer proof that Luke is controlled by the approach of the secular historian rather than by a pervasively

---

[1] See W. P. Armstrong, 'Chronology of the New Testament,' in ISBE, I, p. 647; C. H. Turner, 'Chronology of the NT,' in HDB, I, pp. 405 f.; my review of Ogg, WTJ, IV. 1, p. 43.

theological or christological interest as a publisher of the gospel of Jesus Christ. There is something approaching the disconcerting in the special attention bestowed upon John, and it is not surprising that the history of the exegesis of this passage has yielded interpretations to the effect that Luke, as an historian of Christ's life, must have in view some event in the life of our Lord rather than in the life of the Baptist.[1] It is true, indeed, that this formal and elaborate description of the beginning of John's ministry attaches great importance to his role within the foundational history of Christianity. However, this narration of the commencement of John's public mission is not the reader's introduction to John nor does it stand in isolation from what has gone before. Its integration with the testimony to John within the birth narratives appears in sharpest focus from Lk. i. 80, where we read that John 'grew, and waxed strong in spirit, and was in the deserts *till the day of his showing to Israel.*' The reader has been prepared to expect the dawn of a great day when John would come forth from his obscurity to herald the coming of the Christ. Commenting on Lk. i. 80, J. Gresham Machen has said:

'Does that verse not lead the reader to look for the great day that is there held in prospect, the day when John would emerge from his obscurity and appear publicly as the forerunner of the messianic salvation? Whenever that day should come, surely it would be heralded by the writer who included i. 80 in his book, with all the solemnity that he could command. And just exactly that is done in Lk. iii. 1 f. The period of obscurity and waiting in which the reader was left in the former passage is over; the forerunner emerges from the deserts and the day of the messianic salvation has dawned. What wonder that the concomitant political conditions are marked with all the precision that the writer can command; what wonder that rulers and high priests are marshalled to do honour to the great event that signalized their reign?'[2]

[1] Cf. Ogg, op. cit., p. 192, for a survey of such opinions: Caspari refers it to the baptism of Christ; Wieseler to the Galilean ministry; Loisy and Goguel to the crucifixion.

Note also that some have argued on the basis of the opening words of Luke iii that they must have constituted the original beginning of the gospel, and that the birth narratives are to be regarded as of later origin. On this subject see J. Gresham Machen, *The Virgin Birth of Christ*, 2nd edit., pp. 47 ff.

[2] Op. cit., p. 57. Permission to quote this passage has been kindly granted by the publishers, Harper & Brothers.

THE GOSPEL AND THE HISTORICAL BEGINNINGS 61

The prominence assigned to the Baptist is therefore not gained at the expense of Jesus; on the contrary, the greater the significance attached to John's mission, the greater the glory of the One whom he was sent to herald. And Luke's very readiness to allow the spotlight to rest upon John at the beginning of his ministry is another proof that Luke was not writing a secular biography with Jesus as his hero. Rather he is occupied here with his task of publishing the gospel of Jesus Christ which came to public expression in history with John's witness to, and baptism of, Jesus.[1]

This conclusion regarding the relation of the Baptist to the Christ within the gospel is confirmed by other significant Lucan testimony. Both the angelic annunciation of John's birth and the prophetic testimony of Zacharias after the event stress John's mission to prepare the way of 'the Lord.' He is 'to make ready for the Lord a people prepared for Him' (i. 17), and as 'the prophet of Most High' he is to 'go before the face of the Lord to make ready His ways' (i. 76). Even if the coming of the Lord referred to in these utterances should be regarded as an echo of Old Testament prophecies of the coming of the great day of God, rather than precisely and narrowly of the coming of the Messiah, the preparatory and subordinate character of John's mission would still be emphasized. Moreover, there can be no question that these two lines of prophecy converge in the New Testament: the coming of the Lord God and the coming of the messianic salvation are one. Not John but Jesus is the divine Messiah who accomplishes the redemption of Israel.

And in view of the prominence given to the Lordship of Jesus by Luke, both within the birth narratives and afterward, one cannot dismiss the thought that Luke actually has the Lord Jesus Himself in mind when he reports the declarations of the angel and of John's father concerning John's mission to make ready for the coming of the Lord. At any rate, Luke himself offers the most vivid and striking testimony of the fact that the Lord's Christ is Christ the Lord (cf. ii. 26 and ii. 11). And not only an angel of the Lord but Elizabeth, the mother of John, is a witness to the Lordship of Jesus. And John is represented as having prepared the

[1] Acts underscores the significant place occupied by the Baptist's ministry within the apostolic preaching. Cf. i. 22, x, 37, xiii. 24.

way for his mother's confession. This occurs in the account of the visit of Mary to Elizabeth about three months before the birth of John, a visit apparently occasioned by the declaration of the angel Gabriel, assuring Mary 'that no word of God shall be void of power,' that Elizabeth had conceived a son in her old age (i. 36 f.). Mary, who previously had asked, 'how shall this be, seeing I know not a man?' (i. 34), receives new assurance when she calls upon Elizabeth, for Elizabeth becomes the vehicle of the Holy Spirit in revealing the true relationship between their yet unborn sons:

> 'Blessed art thou among women
> And blessed is the fruit of thy womb.
> And whence is this to me,
> That the mother of my Lord should come unto me.
> For behold,
> When the voice of thy salutation came into mine ears,
> The babe leaped in my womb for joy.
> And blessed is she that believed;
> For there shall be a fulfilment of the things
> Which have been spoken to her from the Lord.'
> (i. 42-45.)

Thus John, before his birth, is represented as sensing that a momentous event was about to occur, and he shares in the joy which it was to spell to men. And his mother, responding to that impetus, in greeting Mary acknowledges her greater Son as her own Lord. The interweaving of the intimate histories of Mary and Elizabeth (cf. i. 24, 26, 36, 56), and their coming together for a visit of three months, are not told, therefore, to colour the narrative with charming details, or to satisfy curiosity as to the character of their mothers, or to hold the women up before us as examples of piety, or, and this least of all, to exalt Mary as 'the mother of God.' Mary and Elizabeth and John are present only because of the light that is focused by their actions and words upon Him who is acknowledged as having the right to bear the incomparably exalted name of Lord, which in the Greek Old Testament was used far and away most frequently as the name of God, the great Jehovah.

Other indications are not wanting that Luke, in spite of the prominence given to the Baptist, assigns him the role of servant in the house of the Lord. If Luke were really intending to ascribe to the Baptist a place of relative independence in relation to Christ, or even to dwell upon his significance as a secondary character in the origin and early development of Christian history, his silence with regard to certain aspects of John's career would be inscrutable. Most remarkable in this connection is the abruptness of his treatment of the baptism of Jesus:

> 'Now it came to pass, when all the people were baptized, that, Jesus also having been baptized, and praying, the heaven was opened, and the Holy Spirit descended in a bodily form, as a dove, upon Him, and a voice came out of heaven, Thou art my beloved Son; in Thee I am well pleased' (iii. 21, 22).

While both Matthew and Mark report the journey of Jesus from Galilee to the Jordan river for the baptism, Luke does not say anything concerning it. Jesus is simply there at the place of baptism. And His baptism is recorded in two words—by means of a genitive absolute participial construction, the reference to the baptism being incidental to the record of the descent of the Spirit and the acclamation of the heavenly voice. Since John's ministry as a preacher of the necessity of baptism and as an administrator of baptism has been prominently brought before the reader (iii. 3 ff., 16), it may be taken for granted that Luke thinks of him as the baptizer of Jesus. But it is extraordinary that exactly at the baptism of Jesus, where one might expect John at least to share some of the limelight with Jesus, he is not mentioned at all.[1]

That Luke is not characterized by a stronger biographical motif than the other evangelists appears also from his treatment of the close of John's career. He briefly concludes his record of the history of John by introducing, immediately before the reference to the baptism of Jesus, a notice of Herod's imprisonment of John (iii. 19, 20). This the other synoptics do not describe until much later in their accounts, at the point where they tell of

[1] In Acts the perspective remains basically the same. 'The baptism of John' in i. 22, might indeed refer to John's baptism of Jesus, but more probably it points broadly to the ministry of John. Acts x. 37, and xiii. 24, speak of the *preaching* of baptism, and x. 38, significantly states that 'God anointed him with the Holy Spirit and with power.'

John's execution (Mt. xiv. 1-12; Mk. vi. 14-29; but cf. Mt. iv. 12; Mk. i. 14). Since Jesus had not yet been baptized, Luke is evidently anticipating a later event. Luke also presupposes that John lived for some time after the beginnings of the ministry of Jesus (vii. 18 ff.). But Luke alone of the synoptists fails to tell the story of the death of John. This silence, like that concerning John's baptism of Jesus, provides eloquent testimony that John is not introduced for his own sake.[1]

We see, therefore, that John the Baptist, than whom there was no greater born among women (vii. 28), as well as the obscure Simeon, owes his place in the early chapters of Luke to the light that his testimony casts upon the significance of Jesus Christ. The contacts of these two men with the origin and early history of Jesus provide occasions for disclosures which interpret authoritatively the meaning of the stupendous event represented by the birth of Christ and His presence in the world.

Although, as previously stated, Luke views Christianity as a movement within the framework of world history, the secular interest of Luke must not be exaggerated. One may not, without careful qualifications, suppose that he self-consciously writes as 'the historian' of Christianity. As the selective character of Acts shows, he is not endeavouring to publish a history of the apostolic church. And the Gospel likewise provides many evidences of a choice of materials with a view to the publication of a distinctive testimony to Christ. His interest in the chronological setting of the commencement of the public phase of the gospel history, as demonstrated in the opening words of the third chapter, is by no means characteristic of his writing as a whole.

THE INTRODUCTION OF JESUS

These conclusions regarding the disposition and theme of the chapters Luke devotes to the historical beginnings of Christianity may be tested further as we finally consider briefly the manner in which Jesus Himself is introduced within the temporal framework of world history. Although chronological data of considerable

---

[1] In Lk. ix. 9, indeed, Luke reports Herod as saying: 'John I beheaded, but who is this about whom I hear such things?' However, the very incidental character of this reference to the death of the Baptist confirms our conclusion as to Luke's method.

interest occur, it is doubtful that they are presented because of secular or biographical interests.

The priestly activity of Zacharias is declared to have taken place 'in the days of Herod, king of Judæa' (i. 5). From the use of this phrase at the very beginning of the closely linked and integrated narration of the origins of John and Jesus, one is perhaps meant to infer that the birth of Christ also took place during the reign of Herod, as Matthew explicitly reports. But the fact remains that Luke does not provide explicit confirmation of Matthew's statement.

When Luke comes to the narration of the birth of Christ, he introduces a more precise secular reference, the reference to an enrolment made while Quirinius was governor over the province of Syria as a consequence of a decree of Caesar Augustus (ii. 1 f.). Still the interest in the mention of this event is not barely chronological. Luke's reason for referring to the enrolment is to indicate the historical occasion of the journey of Joseph and Mary from their home in northern Palestine to the town of Bethlehem where the Christ was to be born. And it is entirely in keeping with his literary method and style to describe that enrolment in concrete and precise terms. Whatever chronological knowledge one may glean from these references is gained quite incidentally. Since Caesar Augustus reigned for some forty years, from 27 B.C. to A.D. 14, not much specific knowledge is gained from the intimation that the enrolment followed a decree of this emperor. And the summary manner in which Luke speaks of the enrolment under Quirinius as a 'first enrolment,' without clarifying whatever other enrolment or enrolments may have been in view, furnishes the reader, at least the modern one, with precious little exact information as to the time when this enrolment, and consequently when the birth of Christ, took place.[1]

There remains the fascinating temporal reference in Lk. iii. 23 to the commencement of the public ministry of Jesus in connection with which Luke states that Jesus was approximately thirty years of age. There are difficulties in the translation of this statement due largely to the fact that the participle 'beginning' is

---

[1] On the exegetical and historical questions connected with Lk. ii. 2, cf. especially Armstrong, 'Chronology of the N.T.', in ISBE, I, pp. 404 f.; Machen, op. cit., pp. 239 ff.

unqualified, but the most natural rendering is that in which the participle is understood as referring to the inauguration of the public ministry of Christ: 'Jesus Himself, when He began, was about thirty years of age.' As the day when 'the word of God came to John,' the day of 'his showing to Israel' (iii. 1 f., i. 80), marked the dawn of a new epoch, so the day when Christ entered upon His work could be designated, in a more absolute sense, as *the beginning*. In spite of the more formal introduction of the beginning of John's ministry in contrast to the rather bare and somewhat abrupt reference to Jesus' 'beginning,' Luke unmistakably marks the latter as of incomparably greater moment. It is the moment when He who has been acclaimed by a heavenly voice as the beloved Son of God (iii. 22) is about to undertake the fulfilment of His mission.[1]

Although, then, the intimation that Jesus was about thirty years of age at the commencement of His public ministry is a chronological datum of the utmost interest it can hardly be regarded as presented with a view to giving us a precise framework of the course of His life. Otherwise Luke could hardly have failed to state later on the age of Jesus at His death.[2] Perhaps Luke had in mind only the fact that at the time He entered upon His public work He had reached mature manhood; but this remains uncertain.[3]

Our general conclusion with regard to the approach of the early chapters of Luke is, accordingly, that biographical and

[1] On the interpretation of v. 23, cf. Plummer, ad loc.; Machen, op. cit., p. 53. See also Acts i. 22, and x. 37, where the beginning of Jesus' action is also intimately associated with John's career. The rendering of the AV: 'And Jesus Himself began to be about thirty years of age . . .' is to be rejected as reading into the Greek more than it says, and as not being wholly intelligible. The RV furnishes a more natural construction: 'And Jesus himself, when he began *to teach*, was about thirty years of age . . .' However, there is no good reason for restricting the ministry to teaching activity. The RSV paraphrases the view taken here: 'Jesus, when he began his ministry, was about thirty years of age. . . .'

[2] An implication of some importance for the chronology of the life of Jesus is that His ministry must have lasted considerably over a year. If Luke supposed that Jesus had completed His ministry when He was still about thirty years of age, he would hardly have expressed himself as he does. Cf. Zahn, *Einleitung*, II, p. 443 (E.T., III, p. 168); *Kommentar* (1913), pp. 204 f.; Schmidt, *Rahmen*, pp. 30 f. Ogg, op. cit., pp. 13 ff. argues against the conclusiveness of this reasoning, but not very impressively.

[3] Turner, op. cit., p. 405, opposed the notion that the maturity of Jesus at the commencement of His public ministry is in view.

secular interests are wholly or almost completely absent, and that Luke is everywhere an evangelist. He is demonstrating that, from the very beginning of the life of Jesus, the facts of His life, and Jesus as the great fact, were interpreted authoritatively as constituting glad tidings of salvation. One may freely acknowledge, then, that his interest is theological and christological since his entire message is presented in terms of divine action and revelation, and is occupied with the proclamation of Jesus as the divine Messiah. But it is crucial to a proper estimate of the Lucan philosophy of history not to regard the christological and the historical as mutually exclusive. Though he does not write as a secular historian, Luke gives evidence at every point of being concerned with historical fact and takes great pains to assure his readers that he is qualified to provide them with reliable information concerning what had taken place. The concept of Messiahship is historical as well as theological; the Anointed of the Lord is One whose *coming* into the world constitutes the single theme of the revelation of both covenants, and it is that aspect of the manifestation of the Christ which is the very foundation of the gospel.

CHAPTER IV

PREACHING AND CONFLICT AT NAZARETH

THE appearance of Jesus in Nazareth 'where he was brought up,' and his rejection there on the part of his fellow townsmen, comprise one of the most arresting features of the entire Lucan portrayal of the public ministry. This narrative, in view of its position at the very beginning of the story of the Galilean activity, as the first concrete report of the message of Jesus and of the impact which He made upon His hearers, is somewhat plausibly regarded by many students of Luke as deliberately chosen to present the leading motifs of the Gospel. The message is solemnly introduced in the prophetic words of Isaiah:

'The Spirit of the Lord is upon me,
Because He anointed Me to preach good tidings to the poor:
He hath sent Me to proclaim release to the captives,
And recovering of sight to the blind,
To set at liberty them that are bruised,
To proclaim the acceptable year of the Lord.'

(iv. 18, 19.)

The realization of the gospel in history is announced by Jesus in completely unambiguous terms: 'Today this scripture is fulfilled in your hearing!' Although 'the words of grace which proceeded out of His mouth' are not set down in detail, the text quoted from the Old Testament and its immediate historical application are so specific that this first Lucan report of the proclamation of Jesus appears to serve as an inaugural address. But hard upon the completion of the address comes the denouement in terms of rationalizing doubt, offence, rejection, wrath and murderous hate. Thus Luke at once discloses that the good tidings of grace and liberty tragically failed to win the universal acclaim and acceptance which their intrinsic meaning and validity justified and demanded.

Nor is the originality of the Lucan introduction of Jesus qualified decisively by the consideration that Matthew and Mark also contain vivid accounts of the rejection at Nazareth. Indeed, in spite of the broad correspondence of the three synoptic accounts, and to an extent because of this very correspondence, the distinctive features in Luke tend to emphasize, rather than to detract from, the novelty of his narration. Matthew and Mark wait until near the close of their accounts of the Galilean ministry to introduce the story of the unbelief of His fellow Nazarenes (Mt. xiii. 53 ff.; Mk. vi. 1 ff.). In contrast Luke appears very bold in sounding this sombre note at this very early point, even before he has dwelt triumphantly upon the favour with which Jesus was received by many. Moreover, the message of Jesus at Nazareth is expressed in distinctive terms. Here surely he is not following a stereotyped pattern which had been formed by earlier evangelists. No one will dispute the conclusion, accordingly, that Lk. iv. 16-30 provides a most fascinating instance of the distinctiveness of Luke, and that it has most important bearings upon one's understanding of the public ministry as a whole.

As a background for the study of this incident, one may note with advantage the modern critical estimate of Luke's procedure at this point. Generally speaking, his treatment of the episode at Nazareth has not served to commend his Gospel to modern historical critics. The charge is frequently made that Luke betrays here a lack of historical objectivity. Either deliberately or unconsciously he is thought to have revealed his own special insights and to have disclosed his peculiar bias. The modern exponents of the two-document theory of Gospel origins, in particular, view these materials as proof of a radical manipulation of the Christian tradition. J. M. Creed, for example, maintains that Luke took the narrative found in Mark vi as the foundation 'for a representative and symbolic scene to open the public ministry of Jesus,' and that Luke himself 'is mainly responsible for the section as it stands.' He further says:

> 'The narrative must not be pressed. Its real function is to introduce the main *motifs* which are to recur throughout the Gospel and the Acts, and this it does with great effect: the gospel to the poor is preached by Jesus in His home and rejected. The rejection by Nazareth foreshadows the rejection by the Jewish people and the subsequent universal mission of the Church.'[1]

[1] Op. cit., pp. 65, 66. Cf. also R. H. Lightfoot, *History and Interpretation in the Gospels*, pp. 182 ff., 196 f., 199 f., 202.

Other students of Luke, like Easton and William Manson, though regarding the evangelist as essentially an editor rather than as the creator of new forms of tradition, likewise disparage Luke's account. The evangelist is thought, on their view, to have elaborated upon the incident recorded in Mark. Both the position which the incident occupies within the framework of the ministry of Christ and the distinctive formulation of the message of Jesus are thought to demonstrate that Mark is more reliable.[1]

THE HISTORICAL SETTING

The question why Luke begins the narration of the public ministry with the incident at Nazareth must be examined because of its bearing upon the larger question of the distinctiveness of Luke's witness to Christ. One aspect of the problem is whether Luke actually intended to present the address at Nazareth as an inaugural discourse or as programmatic, and thus as indicative of his special interests and emphases.

These matters require an examination of the historical setting of the incident in relation to the Matthaean and Marcan data. We shall help to clear the atmosphere if, first of all, we face the question whether there may not have been two appearances in Nazareth, one near the beginning of the Galilean ministry, reported by Luke, and a second near its close, recorded by Matthew and Mark. Mark indeed says nothing of a visit to Nazareth until the account in chapter vi, and he may appear to centre the earliest activity in Capernaum. Nevertheless, in view of the summary description of activity in Galilee in Mk. i. 14 f. ('Now after that John was delivered up, Jesus came into Galilee, preaching the gospel of God, and saying, The time is fulfilled, and the kingdom of heaven is at hand: repent ye, and believe in the gospel'), and the episodic character of Mark's narrative as a whole, the possibility of a ministry in Nazareth before the activity in Capernaum cannot be excluded.[2] Matthew indeed solemnly indicates that Capernaum was the centre of Jesus' early activity, but he explicitly mentions a stay in *Nazara* (the same

---

[1] In the Commentaries, ad loc.
[2] William Manson, MC, p. 40, is not on solid ground when he avers that 'Mark definitely locates the earliest activities of Jesus in Capernaum. . . .' Mark does not speak of 'the earliest activities' in point of time.

PREACHING AND CONFLICT AT NAZARETH 71

distinctive form that Luke employed in iv. 16) before He went to Capernaum, without, however, relating anything that happened in Nazara, or stating what occasioned His departure (Mt. iv. 13 ff). So far as the pertinent evidence in Matthew and Mark go therefore, it is entirely possible to maintain that Luke reports here a significant incident not mentioned by the other evangelists, and that he may have omitted reference to a later rejection at Nazareth in the interest of brevity and in view of his earlier inclusion of a similar narrative.[1]

To allow for the possibility of two distinct instances of rejection at Nazareth, however, is not tantamount to the conclusion that the evidence requires us to assume two such incidents, or that it encourages us, on the whole, to accept that as a solution of the problem. If attention is now turned to the Lucan data which bear upon the decision, we may determine whether this Gospel allows of, and perhaps even suggests, the conclusion that the appearance in Nazareth which it describes may legitimately be regarded as having taken place considerably after the commencement of the public ministry in Galilee.

Most illuminating is the observation that, prior to the narrative reporting what occurred at Nazareth, Luke speaks quite independently of the Galilean ministry:

> 'And Jesus returned in the power of the Spirit into Galilee: and a fame went out concerning Him through all the region round about. And He taught in their synagogues, being glorified of all' (Lk. iv. 14 f.).

He tells, therefore, quite without reference to Nazareth, of a period of activity in Galilee, in which Jesus was busy teaching in the synagogues, and became well known.[2] It appears therefore

[1] Advocates of the Four-document Theory maintain approximately this same viewpoint, except for the significant difference that they regard all the narratives as pointing back to a single historical event. They assert that the final editor of the Gospel, when he came to interpolate portions of Mark into Proto-Luke, did not introduce Mk. vi. 1-6, because an account of the rejection at Nazareth already occupied a position at the beginning of the narrative of activity in Galilee as found in Proto-Luke, which he was principally following. Cf. Streeter, op. cit., pp. 209 f.; Taylor, *Behind the Third Gospel*, p. 142, p. 192.

[2] Cf. also iv. 16, where Luke reports that Jesus came to Nazareth, and 'entered, as His custom was, into the synagogue on the sabbath day.' The reference must be to His custom of entering the synagogues of Galilee on the sabbath day.

that the entrance into the synagogue at Nazareth, like His ministry in Capernaum reported in Lk. iv. 31 ff., is presented as an instance, but not necessarily the first instance, of preaching in Galilee. When, following the survey of activity in Capernaum, Luke reports Jesus as saying, 'I must preach the gospel of the kingdom to other cities also' (iv. 43), and follows this with the intimation that, as a matter of fact, 'Jesus was preaching in the synagogues of Judæa' (iv. 44) we have further evidence that Luke does not intend to supply his readers with an itinerary of Jesus' mission in Galilee. The activity in Nazareth and in Capernaum are presented as illustrative of the preaching and healing ministry of Jesus as a whole. In effect, therefore, he does not say more than that, *in the course of Jesus' ministry in the synagogues of Galilee, He also preached in the synagogue at Nazareth.* He by no means says or implies that the Galilean ministry began at Nazareth, or that the address there was His inaugural proclamation.[1]

The general contextual considerations, accordingly, allow definitely for the possibility that the incident at Nazareth took place relatively late in the Galilean ministry, but do not bring to a decision what Luke actually thought on the matter. The question appears to be settled once for all, however, by a reference to Capernaum in the discourse of Jesus at Nazareth. In reply to the exclamation, 'Is not this Joseph's son?' Jesus said:

> 'Doubtless ye will say unto Me this parable, Physician, heal thyself: Whatsoever we have heard done at Capernaum, do also here in Thine own country' (iv. 23).

How can these words be understood unless all the while Luke has been presupposing a previous period of activity in Capernaum? The plain implication seems to be that his hearers at Nazareth are understood by Jesus as being informed concerning his previous activity in Capernaum.[2]

---

[1] The only detail which might appear to establish chronological sequence between the appearances in Nazareth and in Capernaum is the use of the verb κατῆλθεν in iv. 31, which would appropriately describe a journey from the higher ground at Nazareth to Capernaum on the sea shore. But this may not be pressed. It may mean merely 'arrive'. See MM; Liddell and Scott, *Greek-English Lexicon*, 1940; cf. Plummer, ad loc.

[2] Cf. Augustine, *Harmony of the Evangelists*, II, xliii (90): Migne, *Pat. Lat.* xxxiv. 1121 f.; Easton; Creed; Greijdanus.

But even this specific mention of Capernaum is thought by Wellhausen not to clinch the matter.[1] According to Wellhausen, Luke represents the residents of Nazareth as manifesting a positively favourable attitude toward Jesus at first, and that only the final remarks provoked them to wrath. The favourable attitude is thought to be displayed particularly in the words that 'all bare him witness, and wondered at the words of grace which proceeded out of his mouth' (v. 22).[2] Their question, 'Is not this Joseph's son?' on this view merely indicates surprise, not a basic scepticism or hostility. And Jesus' words that follow (verses 23 ff.) are judged by Wellhausen to intimate that He cannot rejoice in their present favourable attitude since He knows that *at some future time* their attitude will change. When Jesus says, 'Doubtless *ye will say* unto Me this parable, Physician, heal thyself: whatsoever we have heard done at Capernaum, do also here in Thine own country,' He is speaking of a future attitude to be disclosed in what they would say to taunt and ridicule Him. The implication of Luke's report is, accordingly, that Jesus anticipates a future activity in Capernaum and beyond that another visit to Nazareth when He would be mocked. Wellhausen also implies that Luke's use of traditional materials at this point provides a particularly crass example of the failure of an editor to observe the full consequence of a transposition, for Luke is supposed to anticipate the narrative of Mk. vi and yet to retain the thought of its futurity.

Although the passage admittedly is not without exegetical difficulty due largely to the problem of reaching certainty concerning continuity and transition in thought and reaction, the view of Wellhausen must be rejected as raising grave difficulties and as offering no really satisfactory solution of detailed questions. In general his view attributes extreme clumsiness to Luke, and presupposes that the constituent elements of the Lucan narrative can be harmonized with each other only on the assumption that there has been profound confusion concerning the actual facts. Thus the difficulty of arriving at an integrated interpretation is greatly exaggerated. Moreover, Wellhausen's view is itself beset by insuperable exegetical obstacles.

[1] *Evangelien, Das Evangelium Lucae*, 1904, pp. 8 ff. Cf. also Klostermann, HBNT, ad loc.
[2] The RSV translates: 'And all spoke well of him, and wondered at the gracious words which proceeded out of his mouth.' Cf. J. W. Bowman, *The Intention of Jesus*, 1943, pp. 92 ff.

The decision will turn mainly about the question of the propriety of interpreting the future 'ye will say' of a reaction of His hearers at some future date when Jesus would return to Nazareth. Even the general tone of the address, with its note of urgency and timeliness, suggests that Jesus is concerned with the immediate response of His hearers, rather than, more casually, with an eventual and rather remote situation. Moreover, the Lucan account is perfectly clear in disclosing that the reaction of hostility is not remote, for a most conspicuous feature of his narrative is that they were filled with murderous wrath before He had concluded speaking (v. 28). *When the prediction of hostility finds immediate fulfilment, is it not far-fetched to insist that Luke has in mind a remote outbreak of opposition in Nazareth, concerning which Luke actually reports nothing?*

Moreover, the view that the hostility manifested at the end of Jesus' discourse constitutes a reversal of an earlier positively favourable attitude is open to serious question. The wonder at the words of grace spoken by Jesus may seem indeed to point in that direction. But their state of wonder may not be isolated from the question, 'Is not this Joseph's son?' which immediately follows and is presented as a further disclosure of their reaction. This question is shown to manifest an attitude which Jesus felt called upon to rebuke. The continuity of question and answer demonstrates that Jesus anticipates that they are about to demand a display of miraculous power. And to this demand He was unwilling to respond. The transition from the words of His hearers to Jesus' own reply is therefore somewhat abrupt, but the attentive reader is given a sufficient intimation of the tone of their reply by Jesus' own interpretation of it.

The parallelism with Mark, moreover, is greater than appears at first sight, and serves to set the reaction of the Nazarenes in a clearer perspective. Mark also reports their wonder at His teaching: 'many hearing him were astonished, saying, Whence hath this man these things? and, What is the wisdom that is given unto this man, and what mean such mighty works wrought by his hands? Is not this the carpenter, the son of Mary, and brother of James, and Joses, and Judas, and Simon? and are not his sisters here with us?' (vi. 2, 3; cf. Mt. xiii. 54-56). But Mark immediately adds, 'And they were offended in Him' and soon adds that

Jesus 'marvelled because of their unbelief' (vi. 4-6; cf. Mt. xiii. 57). If Mark regards the astonishment evoked by the teaching and deeds of Jesus as being quite consonant with the offence and unbelief that came to immediate expression, may Luke be confidently judged to have in view two divergent attitudes when he speaks of their wonder at His teaching and of their taunting and wrathful reaction? The offence and unbelief of which Mark speaks are quite as negative as the reactions indicated by Luke, and hence are introduced fully as abruptly.[1] But the general disposition of Mark's narrative shows that the abruptness is more semblance than reality. Jewish hearers might marvel and be astonished at Jesus' proclamation of the dawn of the messianic salvation, which they might well acknowledge to have significant points of contact with their own eschatological outlook, and yet they might take offence because of the more or less open claim of Jesus to be associated intimately with its manifestation. That the kingdom of which the prophets spoke was coming was a message which might strike a responsive chord; that Jesus, who seemed to them to belong to their everyday existence in Nazareth, should be somehow responsible for it was quite a different matter. At this point, as later, it was the place occupied by Jesus within the gospel of the kingdom that caused men to stumble; but in the happenings at Nazareth the offence was accelerated and aggravated by their arrogant assurance that He who was of their number could not possibly wear the mantle of God's special minister.

My general conclusion, therefore, is that there is no need to resort to Wellhausen's extreme exegetical and critical procedures, and that the reference to previous activity in Capernaum in Lk. iv. 23 is adequately and naturally accounted for by the broad characterization of the Galilean ministry with which Luke begins his narrative of the public ministry of Jesus (iv. 14 f.). The activity in Nazareth is not described as inaugurating the public activity, and the address in the synagogue there may not precisely be characterized as the inaugural address of Jesus. All that may be said firmly is that it is Luke's first detailed account of Jesus' ministry. When one once recognizes that Luke's aim is not to tell

[1] Creed says that Luke softens Mark's 'offence,' but adds that 'here too we are probably meant to discover an undertone of indignation to which Jesus replies in the following verses.' He adds that 'in any case a very awkward transition is involved.'

in exact detail how Jesus' ministry in Galilee began, but only to illustrate its beginnings, it is no longer possible to insist that Luke intended to imply that the activity in Nazareth preceded that in Capernaum.

Nevertheless, the question as to what dictated the order of presentation remains to be considered. The answer may well be that, from among the various instances of preaching in the synagogues of Galilee, Luke selected the preaching at Nazareth because it could serve to present in brief compass some of the most significant features of the claims of Christ. To say that it is programmatic is misleading because, in spite of the many facets of its contents, it does not serve to sum up the distinctive testimony of Luke to Christ. For example, the full impact of the positive disclosure of Jesus' messianic claims is not realized in the manifestation at Nazareth. Nor does the place occupied in the Gospel by the parousia of Christ and the distinctly eschatological manifestation of the kingdom of God come to expression here. Nevertheless, conspicuous elements of the estimate of Christ which Luke is concerned to publish come vividly to view in the arresting account of what happened at Nazareth.

THE MESSAGE OF THE KINGDOM

The consideration of the historical setting of the appearance of Jesus at Nazareth has inevitably involved reflection upon certain aspects of Jesus' teaching there. It has appeared that it was in the course of His preaching the good tidings of the kingdom of God that He came to Nazareth (iv. 43 f.), and hence the actual proclamation there may advantageously be considered in the larger perspective of the message of the kingdom of God. The reaction to this message, of which some notice has already been taken, indicates that there was a personal aspect to the message of Jesus which provoked strong personal antagonism. And thus, in addition to the theme of the coming of the kingdom in the narrower sense, the question as to who Jesus claimed to be and how He conceived of His relation to the coming of the kingdom —in short, the christological question—is thrust into the foreground. These two interrelated themes—the coming of the kingdom and the coming of the Christ—will serve to place the varied contents of the preaching at Nazareth in sharpest relief.

That Luke, himself a Gentile and presumably writing with the Gentile world chiefly in view, introduces Jesus as reading from the Old Testament and as indicating that He had come to proclaim the fact of its fulfilment offers convincing evidence that Christianity according to Luke was not a new religion, but rather one whose foundations were established in what stood written in the Scriptures. Shortly before the ascension the risen Christ is reported as declaring that 'all things must needs be fulfilled, which are written in the law of Moses, and the prophets, and the psalms, concerning me' (Lk. xxiv. 44). Here in Lk. iv, at the beginning of His public ministry, Jesus is introduced as teaching that the necessary fulfilment of the Scriptures had already begun, indeed that it was taking place at the very moment that they heard the Scripture read. Although in the birth narratives (as has been demonstrated in the preceding chapter), the accent falls upon revelation contemporaneous with the momentous event of the birth of Christ, Luke shows here, beyond the shadow of a doubt, that the Old Testament revelation formed an integral aspect of the gospel proclamation. Luke no more than any other New Testament writer allows for the judgment that the Old Testament was expendable. Nor is the basic thought merely that Christianity would be unintelligible apart from an understanding of the manner in which its historical environment had been conditioned by the history of Israel and the message of its prophets and wise men. The Old Testament Scriptures were viewed as being themselves divinely given and of divine authority. Moreover, solid ground is reached only when there is recognition of the fact that Luke shares the philosophy of the history of revelation and redemption which distinguishes between the divine action and word in the old and new covenants. Thus only is there a perception of the diversity of the old and the new orders, a difference expressed oftentimes and perhaps most simply as one of prophecy and fulfilment. And thus only is justice done to the fact that the two covenants are ultimately considered one, and that only one religion is revealed in the Scriptures, only one way of salvation, as there is but one God who deals with sinners, and has declared and accomplished his purposes of righteousness and grace, in the old order as well as in the new.

The passage read by Christ shares the eschatological perspective of the Old Testament, recognized pervasively in the New, which envisages the dawn of a new day through the intervention of God in history. This outlook finds expression within the Old Testament in various forms which converge in the New Testament historical revelation: it is described in terms of the coming of the Lord, or of the coming of the Lord's Anointed, or of the outpouring of the divine Spirit. The language quoted by our Lord from Isaiah gives vivid expression to the hope of a new order of righteousness to be established by God and proclaimed by One who should be qualified to proclaim it by an anointing of the Spirit of the Lord.

That Jesus here proclaims the arrival of the new order of righteousness prophesied by Isaiah is evident even from a superficial reading of Luke's narrative, and there is apparently widespread agreement among modern interpreters of the Gospel on this point. But when one proceeds from general characterizations to more particular delineations of the exact nature of the kingdom of God as taught in Luke, and in the other writings of the New Testament, one encounters profound differences of judgment, ranging all the way from the view that the kingdom is essentially a moral order realized through human co-operation to the position that it has no point of contact whatsoever with this world order, and is to be realized solely by divine action. The issue at stake here—what the kingdom of God really is, how it confronts us, what it demands of us—is most basic to an understanding of the message of Jesus, more basic than the question often asked prematurely as to *the time* of the coming of the kingdom. This issue must be faced now as we study Luke's first record of the preaching of Jesus: it is an issue that remains urgent right throughout the study of the Gospel.

Progress towards a solution can be expected only if the Isaianic language is construed in its larger context. That the prophet presents, in the language quoted by Jesus, a gospel for the poor, the prisoner, the blind and the oppressed; that he proclaims righteousness and deliverance to men in misery and distress—these facts are inescapable. But exactly what does Isaiah mean by the poor and the oppressed, and how does he conceive that their needs will be met? We have become familiar with the claims that the prophets, and Jesus as standing in their tradition, proclaimed a social gospel, a gospel designed for the poor and afflicted of this world and aiming at the amelioration of their conditions. And it is not surprising that the preaching at Nazareth should be cited as offering proof that the Jesus of 'the social gospel' is the Jesus of the Gospels. Is there, however, any actual basis for this far-reaching conclusion? Does not the Isaianic analysis of the need of men and how this need is supplied actually point in a different direction?

The beneficent acts which are proclaimed by the anointed of the Lord are not brought before the reader of Isaiah for the first time in chapter lxi, but have been mentioned before especially in contexts where the Servant of the Lord has been introduced. Thus the stately forty-second chapter which begins

> 'Behold my servant whom I uphold;
> My chosen, in whom my soul delighteth;
> I have put my Spirit upon him;
> He will bring forth judgment to the Gentiles.'
> (Is. xlii. 1.)

proceeds soon with the declaration

> 'I the Lord have called thee in righteousness,
> And will hold thine hand,
> And will keep thee,
> And give thee for a covenant of the people,
> For a light of the Gentiles;
> To open the blind eyes,
> To bring out the prisoners from the dungeon,
> And them that sit in darkness out of the prison-house.'
> (Is. xlii. 6 f.)

Previously Isaiah had predicted the deliverance of the people in these terms:

> 'And in that day shall the deaf hear the words of the book,
> And the eyes of the blind shall see out of obscurity and
>   out of darkness.
> The meek also shall increase their joy in the Lord,
> And the poor among men shall rejoice in the Holy One of
>   Israel.'
> (Is. xxix. 18 f.)

The words quoted from Is. lxi come therefore as a reiteration and reinforcement of the message of the redemption of the people of God which has been the dominant theme of the evangelical prophet.

Who, then, are the poor and how are they delivered from poverty? We must certainly avoid the extreme of supposing that Isaiah's contemplation of the poor disregards the social conditions of his time and has in view only the spiritual state of Israel. The truly pious man is emphatically not one who, though scrupulous with regard to all the formal observances of religion, neglects the requirements of mercy; the Lord is indignant with such and asks

> 'Is not this the fast that I have chosen?
> To loose the bonds of wickedness,
> To undo the bands of the yoke,
> And to let the oppressed go free,
> And that ye break every yoke?
> Is it not to deal thy bread to the hungry,
> And that thou bring the poor that are cast out to thy house?'
> (Is. lviii. 6, 7a.)

But it is, nevertheless, particularly the *poor of God's people* that are in view, and it is against those who have been appointed to rule righteously that the wrath of God is pronounced:

> 'The Lord will enter into judgment
> With the elders of his people and the princes thereof:
> It is ye that have eaten up the vineyard;
> The spoil of the poor is in your houses:
> What mean ye that ye crush my people,
> And grind the face of the poor?
> Saith the Lord, the Lord of hosts.'
> (iii. 14 f.; cf. x. 1, 2.)

These acts of unrighteousness, this grinding of the face of the poor, are, therefore, roundly condemned, and men are called upon to repent of their wicked exploitation and discrimination. But the analysis of the social situation is nevertheless not one which contemplates that a 'new deal' will be realized for the poor through a process of reform from within. On the contrary the gospel of the prophet points to the Holy One of Israel as the One who alone will effect a radical change in the fortunes of the poor. And the transformation that is promised is viewed as part of a radical and thoroughgoing renewal of the present order:

'The poor and needy seek water and there is none,
And their tongue faileth for thirst;
I the Lord will answer them,
I the God of Israel will not forsake them.
I will open rivers on the bare heights,
And fountains in the midst of the valleys:
I will make the wilderness a pool of water,
And the dry land springs of water.
I will plant in the wilderness the cedar,
The acacia tree, and the myrtle, and the oil tree;
I will set in the desert the fir-tree,
The pine, and the box-tree together:
That they may see, and know, and consider, and understand together,
That the hand of the Lord hath done this,
And the Holy One of Israel hath created it.'

(Is. xli. 17-20.)

As accomplished by the Lord who insists that men shall recognize that He and He alone has done it (cf. also xlviii. 5), this announcement of salvation inevitably cannot have in view that the poor of the earth, as such, simply because of their poverty, will be without want. The poor who ultimately will rejoice in the Holy One of Israel are the meek who shall increase their joy in the Lord, while 'they that watch for iniquity are cut off' (xxix. 19 f.). In short, the age of transformation will be the portion of a transformed people.

The one anointed with the Lord's Spirit next declares that He has been sent 'to proclaim release to the captives.' Here it is even clearer than in the instance of Isaiah's contemplation of the poor that compassionate concern is being shown for the covenant children of God. The captivity and bondage of Israel as God's people and their deliverance from their oppressors by the Mighty One of Jacob constitute one of the most significant aspects of the prophetic doctrine of the coming salvation.

'Awake, awake, put on thy strength, O Zion;
Put on thy beautiful garments, O Jerusalem, the holy city;
For henceforth there shall no more come into thee
The uncircumcised and the unclean.
Shake thyself from the dust;
Arise, sit on thy throne, O Jerusalem;
Loose thyself from the bands of thy neck,
O captive daughter of Zion.
For thus saith the Lord,
Ye were sold for nought;
And ye shall be redeemed without money.
For thus saith the Lord God,
My people went down at the first into Egypt to sojourn there;
And the Assyrian hath oppressed them without cause.
Now, therefore, what do I here, saith the Lord,
Seeing that My people is taken away for nought?
They that rule over them do howl, saith the Lord,
And My name continually all the day is blasphemed.
Therefore My people shall know My name;
Therefore they shall know in that day
That I am He that doth speak;
Behold it is I.'

(Is. lii. 1-6, A.R.V.; cf. xlix. 8-13; 22 ff., 24 ff.)

Though Isaiah stirs the consciences of the people to 'loose the bonds of wickedness' (lviii. 6), the proclamation of release to the captives cannot have precisely in view the plight of outcasts, and least of all the misery of men who are imprisoned because of their own iniquity. Not the suffering of sinful men as such is the basic cause of God's action, but its basis is rather His contemplation of the fact that the captivity of His people causes His enemies to blaspheme and His recollection of the covenant which He has mercifully established with Israel.

Following the text of the Septuagint, as the quotation in Luke rather closely does throughout, mention is next made of 'the recovering of sight to the blind.' This feature of Isaiah's gospel might be understood quite literally; so indeed our Lord has evidently understood it, as reported by both Luke and Matthew, when He alludes to this language assuring John the Baptist that

He was indeed the one that should come (Lk. vii. 22; Mt. xi. 5). But even in the Gospels the historical miracles are not viewed as merely isolated acts of mercy and beneficence, but as signs of the inbreaking of the promised rule of God. And there can be little doubt that Isaiah has pre-eminently in view the divine action in removing the spiritual blindness. This blindness is specifically ascribed to Israel as a nation:

> We look for light, but behold, darkness;
> For brightness, but we walk in obscurity.
> We grope for the wall like the blind,
> Yea, we grope as they that have no eyes:
> We stumble at noonday as in the twilight . . .
> We look for judgment, but there is none;
> For salvation, but it is far off from us.
> For our transgressions are multiplied before Thee,
> And our sins testify against us:
> For our transgressions are with us,
> And as for our iniquities, we know them:
> In transgressing and denying the Lord,
> And turning away from following our God,
> Speaking oppression and revolt,
> Conceiving and uttering from the heart words of falsehood.
> And judgment is turned away backward,
> And righteousness standeth afar off.
> For truth is fallen in the street,
> And uprightness cannot enter.'
>
> (Is. lix. 9-14.)

And considering Israel as the servant of the Lord, he says:

> 'Who is blind, but My servant?
> Or deaf, as My messenger that I send?
> Who is blind as he that is at peace with Me,
> And blind as the Lord's servant?
> Thou seest many things, but thou observest not;
> His ears are open, but he heareth not.'
>
> (Is. xlii. 19-20.)

When, therefore, the blessed future of the people of God is realized, when 'the ransomed of the Lord shall return, and come with singing unto Zion; and everlasting joy shall be upon their heads,' 'the eyes of the blind shall be opened, and the ears of the deaf shall be unstopped' (Is. xxxv. 5, 10). Its own eyes opened, Israel shall be 'for a light to the Gentiles' (xlii. 6 f., xlix. 6).

'To set at liberty them that are bruised' is derived from Is. lviii. 6, where it is mentioned among the things pertaining to true religion. But like the call to minister to the poor, it must be understood as ultimately realizable only through the divine action of salvation. Isaiah does not provide the specific linguistic background for the interpretation of this statement which has been observed in the other clauses. The verb appears to be used in addition only in Is. xlii. 4, but evidently in a different sense. Dt. xxviii. 33, speaking of the consequences of disobedience, states that 'thou shalt be only *oppressed* and crushed away' (the same verb is used in both the Hebrew and the LXX as in the texts of Is. lviii. 6), and thus serves to establish the antithesis of judgment and salvation. In spite of the absence within Isaiah of the exact terminology used in this clause, the contextual thought of breaking every oppressive yoke is not novel. For example, in Is. xiv. 25, the Lord of Hosts swears that 'I will break the Assyrian in My land; then shall his yoke depart from off them, and his burden depart from off their shoulder.' This thought is closely related to that of the release of captives.[1]

If any doubt remains that the prophetic message quoted by our Lord at Nazareth had in view the eschatological salvation of the new age to come, that vanishes when one takes note of the concluding feature of the proclamation: the annunciation of 'the acceptable year of the Lord.' Thus the enactment and observance of the year of Jubilee, when liberty should be proclaimed throughout the land unto all the inhabitants thereof, and old arrangements would be restored and new beginnings made (Lv. xxv. 10 ff.,

---

[1] Cf. Ezk. xxx. 18, xxxiv. 27, where the same word for yoke appears as in Is. lviii. 6, and reference is made to the Lord's breaking the yoke of the enemies of His people.

On the combination of Is. lviii. 6, with the opening words of Is. lxi, cf. I Abrahams, *Studies in Pharisaism and the Gospels*, First Series, 1917, pp. 8 f.: 'The right to "skip" while reading the prophets was well attested (*Mishnah, Megilla*, iv. 4). Being written on a Scroll, the two passages might easily be open together, and Jesus, in accordance with what at all events became a usual Rabbinic device, intended to use both texts as the key to His exposition.' The larger context in which 'The Freedom of the Synagogue' is discussed is also of interest.

xxvii. 24), is utilized to characterize the new order as a time of grace and liberty (cf. Je. xxxiv. 8-10; Ezk. xlvi. 17).

In general, then, Isaiah views the people as in a state of sin and misery, in poverty and oppression, in bondage and darkness. But a new day of salvation and deliverance is promised, a day when righteousness will reign supreme. Israel is implicated in the evil because of her perversity, and thus her state of misery constitutes a just judgment upon her and the deliverance in view demands that she turn her back upon her sin and return unto God. Nevertheless, the God who saves Israel is not like unto men that He should bargain with them, or await their response before manifesting His favour, but freely manifests His saving work, telling beforehand what He will do that none may take His work for granted or attribute it to an idol, and that all may acknowledge that God is sovereign in His saving acts.

Is not Isaiah's delineation of the coming kingdom of God the very pattern of the kingdom as it is proclaimed by our Lord and as it begins to come to realization through His mighty deeds?

THE KINGDOM AND THE ANOINTED ONE

In addition to the basic subject of the meaning of the coming of the kingdom of God according to Jesus Christ, the Lucan narrative brings before us a still more challenging question, perhaps the most controversial of all contemporaneous questions relating to the interpretation of the Gospels: What relation does Jesus Christ Himself sustain, according to His own claims, to the manifestation of the rule of God?

In general modern criticism has tended to reduce the role of Christ to that of a mere herald. The older liberalism affirmed in the words of Harnack that 'The gospel, as Jesus proclaimed it, has to do with the Father only and not with the Son,' thus excluding Him from an integral place within the gospel. Yet Harnack went on to say that 'He was its personal realization and its strength, and this He is felt to be still,'[1] thereby giving expression to the motif that, after all, the historic personality of Jesus was a factor which was indispensable to the liberals. On this view the historicity of the messianic consciousness of Jesus was affirmed

[1] *Das Wesen des Christentums*, 1901, pp. 91 f. (*What is Christianity?*, p. 144, p. 145).

in the abstract, but it was judged to possess mere formal and peripheral significance, if not to be an actual burden to Jesus, and thus in fact it was largely discounted. The later criticism of the present century has, on the whole, been more consistently sceptical or agnostic on the subject of the historicity of the messianic consciousness, and hence has also gone even further than the old liberalism in denying a place to Jesus within the gospel of the kingdom. Perhaps the extreme of scepticism in this regard is found in Bultmann's declarations to the effect that, while he himself is confident that Jesus Christ was an actual historical person and was the herald of a distinctive message, his own indifference to 'Christ according to the flesh' is such that he would be content, if any one should insist upon it, to place the name Jesus in quotation marks as an abbreviated designation of the historical phenomenon.[1]

We should be going far afield from our present purpose if we undertook here an analysis and critique of modern opinion which, proceeding from the dogmatic judgment that the Christ of the Gospels cannot be the Jesus of history, seeks to recover a supposedly earlier gospel, which inevitably is discovered to be a Christless gospel. But we may profitably take account of the critical exegesis in our effort to discover exactly what the Gospels themselves have to say.

Now when we consider the impact of Jesus' preaching and appearance at Nazareth, we cannot doubt that the Lucan narrative establishes an intimate and indissoluble connection between the activity of Jesus Himself and the coming of the kingdom. When Jesus declares, 'Today this scripture is fulfilled in your hearing,' He signifies that the promised manifestation of the new order was realized, at least incipiently, and the only evidence that this was so is that Jesus Himself was proclaiming it to be a fact.

Having considered the passage from Isaiah from the viewpoint of its testimony to the coming kingdom, it is vital to observe that it also contains a distinctly personal note, and it is the personal aspect of the quotation that forms the immediate background for an evaluation of Jesus' own claims. The Scripture reading began:

[1] See *Die Forschung der synoptischen Evangelien*, 2te Aufl., 1930, pp. 32 f.; *Jesus*, pp. 12 ff.; 'Zur Frage der Christologie,' in *Glauben und Verstehen*, 1933, pp. 100 f. Cf. my discussion in WThJ, I, pp. 29 f.

'The Spirit of the Lord is *upon Me*, because He hath anointed *Me* to preach good tidings to the poor; He hath sent *Me* to proclaim release to the captives.'

The fascinating but rather intricate question as to the exact place of Isaiah's reflections upon the anointed one in chapter lxi within the larger context of his messianic prophecies in general and his portrayal of the Servant of the Lord in particular need not be evaluated here, for the decisions reached as to the Lucan passage are not dependent upon reaching certainty regarding it. The anointed prophet who speaks in Is. lxi is not specifically identified as 'the Servant of the Lord' or as 'the Anointed of the Lord.' Yet it is surely not insignificant that the functions ascribed to him have been associated in large part with the ministry of the Servant of the Lord. And though the language used in Is. lxi need not be restricted to the Messiah, the fact is that the one who appears there is described as one who is chosen and appointed, and evidently qualified, to discharge a pre-eminent function in relation to the coming kingdom, and thus the language is supremely appropriate as a reference to the Messiah. Moreover, even if the flexibility of the prophetic language in general would prohibit taking the words as an exclusive prophecy of Jesus Christ, there could be no doubt that Jesus himself, according to Luke, refers the personal aspect of the prophecy directly to Himself, and that within the context of the Gospel as a whole the one upon whom the Spirit came is regarded as none other than the Messiah.[1] In brief, therefore, Jesus' quotation of Isaiah, and His declaration concerning its fulfilment, thrust His own person forward as an integral aspect of His message, and intimated the pre-eminence of His claim to declare the word and will of God.

In spite of the unmistakable personal note which Luke strikes here, however, it is highly necessary to avoid exaggerating the positiveness of the disclosure.[2] There are significant silences and

[1] See Lk. vii. 19 ff. (Mt. xi. 3 ff.).
[2] R. H. Lightfoot, *History and Interpretation*, p. 202, regards the personal note in Luke as at variance with Mark, 'our primary authority for the earliest teaching of Jesus.' This teaching, he says, 'seems to have in view a general call to repentance, in view of the great nearness of the kingdom of God,' and adds, 'We may say with some confidence that in its first stages it contained no reference to Himself.' Is Lightfoot prepared to argue that Mark ii. 10, 28, for example, constitute a later stratum of development in Jesus' teaching, or are such features rejected outright as due to the supposed dogmatizing of the early Church?

a marked note of reserve that may not be overlooked. Though Luke no doubt regarded Jesus as the Christ and as the Servant of the Lord, he does not represent Jesus as making such claims at this point in any direct fashion. The words, 'The Spirit of the Lord is upon Me,' are a quotation from Scripture, and are not in themselves, therefore, a personal avowal. It is only the declaration, 'This day is this scripture fulfilled in your hearing,' which immediately, but still somewhat obliquely, brings intimations of His personal implication and participation in the fulfilment of the divine plan.

Moreover, the reserve with which the messianic claim is being asserted at Nazareth is unmistakably evident from the absorption with the *prophetic* function, for the prophetic activity serves less compellingly than the kingly and priestly functions to establish the indispensability of the ministry of the Christ to the establishment of the kingdom. The scriptural quotation treats only of proclamation, not of the actual defeat of the enemies of God nor of the removing of the burdens of the oppressed. And in the proverb which He refers to Himself He implies that it is *as a prophet* that He is unacceptable in His own home. There is far from being a manifestation of the fullness of messianic prerogative. It appears, accordingly, that it is only with considerable exaggeration that one could characterize the Nazareth story as programmatic for the entire Gospel or as containing the leading motifs of the Gospel.

How shall one, then, evaluate the place of this narrative within the broader structure of Luke's portrayal of Christ's ministry? Perhaps there is more than one answer to this inquiry. It may be that Luke intends to illustrate the *earlier* preaching of Jesus, and, on the background of the reserve with which the Messiahship was disclosed at Nazareth, to point to the fact that it was revealed to men with greater and greater fullness and explicitness as the historical career unfolded. But, at any rate, a more conspicuous characteristic of the incident claims our attention. More basic than the factor of development from the partial and simple to the more comprehensive and complex is the observation that the evangelist regards the course of things at Nazareth as being *quite untypical* of the Galilean ministry as a whole.

Jesus was unwilling to perform cures at Nazareth and thus He does not disclose *by deed* that the kingdom of God had come upon them. At other points in the ministry of Jesus there is also considerable reserve with regard to the performance of miracles: there are injunctions to silence concerning cures that had been effected; there are withdrawals from scenes of healing activity. But nowhere, it seems, does He so deliberately refrain from performing miracles as here at Nazareth. The discourse of Jesus, which has already been considered in an earlier connection in some detail, shows that His fellow townsmen expected and desired a display of power, but that Jesus was unwilling to conform to their expectations. Here clearly He would not appear as a miracle worker, a thaumaturgist.

The point made most pervasively and emphatically by the entire narrative is missed if what happened at Nazareth is conceived of as disclosing a leading motif of Luke's Gospel as a whole. The opening words of Jesus may be regarded as generally indicative of the contents of His message, but the further actions and reactions of Jesus and His hearers are underscored as being completely unrepresentative. Although the working of miracles could easily lead to misunderstanding of the purposes of Jesus, He acknowledges that He has performed them at Capernaum, and He takes it for granted that these acts would have been widely reported, or at least that His fame would have reached His own city. There is no suggestion that Jesus wishes to conceal the fact that He had carried on a healing ministry elsewhere. But what He refuses emphatically to do is to perform such miracles *in His own patris.*

That the entire emphasis of the narrative falls upon what would not occur at Nazareth, but could be expected to happen elsewhere, is borne out further, in my judgment, by the concluding words of Jesus. Following the quotation of the proverb, 'No prophet is acceptable in his own country,' Jesus says:

> 'But of a truth I say unto you, There were many widows in Israel in the days of Elijah, when the heaven was shut up three years and six months, when there came a great famine over all the land; and unto none of them was Elijah sent, but only to Zarephath, in the land of Sidon, unto a woman that was a widow. And there were many lepers in Israel in the time of

Elisha the prophet; and none of them was cleansed, but only Naaman the Syrian' (Lk. iv. 25-27).

It is popular today to regard these words as pointing to another motif in Luke's Gospel, namely, the feature of universalism including specifically the Gentile mission. Thus Creed says:

'Jesus is represented as appealing to the precedents of Elijah and Elisha who worked miracles for aliens rather than for their own country-men, to explain why His own miracles performed at Capernaum had not been repeated at Nazareth ... the incidents cited from the careers of Elijah and Elisha provide good precedents for a mission to the Gentiles—and this no doubt was their real significance to the evangelist—but the implied analogy between the inhabitants of Capernaum and the heathen widow of Sarepta and Naaman is too remote to be original.

'The narrative must not be pressed ... Its real function is to introduce the main *motifs* which are to recur throughout the Gospel and the Acts ... The rejection by Nazareth foreshadows the rejection by the Jewish people and the subsequent universal mission of the Church.'[1]

Once again the insistence that Luke is freely shaping the tradition so as to introduce the leading motifs of the Gospel at the very beginning results in a forced and unnatural interpretation, which Creed himself is unwilling to attribute to Jesus on the ground that the analogy is 'too remote to be original.' A great deal is indeed being read into the allusions to the experience of the widow of Zarephath and Naaman when they are interpreted as intimations of the Gentile mission; if Luke were constructing a narrative with a view to centring attention upon the universalism of the gospel, would he not have done so with far greater explicitness and clarity? This view of Creed involves the judgment that Luke has introduced this motif in a very abrupt and awkward manner, for there has been nothing to suggest universalism in anything that precedes. Had that been Luke's intent it would have been easy for him, for example, to represent Jesus as including in the Scripture lesson intimations as to the dawn of light for the Gentiles. One must conclude, therefore, that the view that Luke

[1] Op. cit., p. 66; cf. Lightfoot, op. cit., p. 198.

is thrusting the motif of universalism into the foreground of his Gospel, regardless of the violence which is done to the tradition, is at the serious disadvantage of being both exceedingly abrupt and pitifully tenuous. If an interpretation not beset by these objections is available, it will have much to recommend it.

And exactly such an understanding of our Lord's references to the widow and to Naaman, perfectly prepared for in the preceding context and not taking us far afield, is at hand. Do not these allusions serve admirably to illustrate and establish the truth of the proverb that a prophet is not acceptable in his own country, which has been quoted because of its pertinence to the fact that Jesus had been rejected in His home city? Do not the references to the favour shown to a Sidonian and to a Syrian fulfil their purpose in expressing the thought that the power and grace of God had been manifested in unexpected places, not in the home of Elijah or of Elisha but rather beyond the area where, according to human expectations, their ministry would have made its impact? Sidon and Syria are contrasted with Israel solely to illustrate the fact that in Capernaum and in the remoter regions of Galilee Jesus had performed miracles and had been received favourably, whereas in the very place where He had been brought up He was unwilling to manifest His power and was rejected. The supposed allusion to the Gentile mission is accordingly left without basis in fact. The reactions of scepticism, wrath and murderous hate disclosed at Nazareth are viewed as exceptional and isolated within the developing Galilean ministry.

Although Luke presents the rejection at Nazareth as quite exceptional, it is nevertheless extraordinarily arresting that this discordant note is struck at the very beginning of his narrative of our Lord's public ministry. Its prominent position exhibits forcefully and even spectacularly the fact that Jesus would not win universal acclaim. And one may also recognize that, in the context of the entire Gospel, with the overpowering accent which it, in common with the other Gospels, places upon the passion and death of Christ, the rejection at Nazareth serves to prepare the way for the understanding of the more encompassing rejection which lay ahead. As Simeon had said, the Child was set 'for the falling and rising up of many in Israel; and for a sign which is spoken against' (ii. 34).

The question why Jesus was rejected by His own townsmen remains. Although Matthew and Mark place the story much later, they too do not suggest that the conflict is to be explained in terms of a long period of developing tension. On the contrary, they explain the results simply in terms of unbelief. Mark declares that Jesus 'marvelled because of their unbelief' (Mk. vi. 6; cf. Mt. xiii. 58). Such unbelief might indeed have certain historical antecedents, but the impression is given that, in the last analysis, the men of Nazareth failed to believe on Him because of the hardness of their hearts.

Although Luke's narrative does not make specific mention of their unbelief, the thrust of his account does not create an impression contrary to that given by Matthew and Mark. Jesus detects a basic scepticism in their attitude. But in Luke there is in addition the suggestion of another factor which centres in the divine purposes and actions. Jesus appears to perceive that there was a certain inevitability that His own people at Nazareth would not receive Him, that a mysterious, divine plan rather than a pattern of human expectations was being followed.

Yet the men of Nazareth are fully accountable. The gospel was preached to them. Nor does the consideration that no miracles were done in their midst alter the situation; to the extent that their being performed entered into the fulfilment of the good tidings it should have sufficed that miracles had been done in Capernaum and that the report of their occurrence had reached Nazareth. Thus 'the thoughts of many hearts' are revealed at Nazareth, and Jesus Christ is disclosed to be a stone of stumbling and a rock of offence.

Nevertheless, the proclamation of the divine word of promise and fulfilment gives assurance that the stone thus rejected of men would become the head of the corner (Lk. xx. 17 f.)

CHAPTER V

THE GALILEAN MINISTRY AS A WHOLE

THE consideration of the preaching of Jesus at Nazareth has served to centre attention upon certain aspects of the structure of Luke's narration of the public ministry. Although such questions lack the relevancy of profound issues like those pertaining to the message of Jesus concerning the coming of the kingdom of God, they demand an answer from serious students of the New Testament. Conclusions regarding them bear pointedly upon one's final judgments as to the essential character of the Gospels. The freedom with which Luke, for example, arranges his record of the ministry of Jesus as he tells of the unique experiences at Nazareth before relating the more typical incidents of the Capernaum cycle underlines the fact that he is not a mere chronicler but writes as an evangelist. As an evangelist he can allow himself considerable flexibility in the ordering of his materials. Nevertheless, there is no evidence that he is taking liberty with or doing violence to the facts at this point. In presenting the developments in Nazareth and Capernaum as illustrations of the ministry of Jesus in Galilee, he may not fairly be charged with arbitrarily fashioning a new chronological framework to suit his purposes of edification.

In the remainder of the record of the Galilean ministry there are no problems competing in interest and difficulty with that which has been already discussed. And one might be tempted, therefore, to pass over the comparatively tedious questions of structure in the interest of expediting the evaluation of what may appear to be more basic matters. But this temptation must be resisted. One cannot scrutinize too painstakingly the most minute details of the Gospel record, or take too much time in comparing the several accounts. As a matter of fact the Galilean ministry as a whole presents many fascinating questions in detail. And the problem of structure emerges with special acuteness in the middle chapters of Luke (leaving on one side for the moment the resurrection narrative), so that with regard to the evangelist's methods and aims one requires all the discernment that can be attained from the advance consideration of the earlier record.¹ It is my purpose therefore to deal rather broadly with the Galilean ministry in this chapter.²

CORRESPONDENCE WITH MARK

As one proceeds with an examination of Luke's portrayal of the public ministry, one is struck especially with the extent of his agreement with Mark. Matthew also is in close correspondence with Mark in the latter part of the Gospel narratives, but Luke's agreement is far more comprehensive. Luke includes nearly all the incidents found in Mark, and in such pervasive agreement of order that even many scholars who have not adopted the two-document theory of Gospel origins, or one of its variations, have come to regard the direct dependence of Luke upon Mark as demonstrated. The agreement with Mark is all the more remarkable because of the distinctiveness of Luke at many other points, a fact which has been brought to light in the sections of Luke which have already been evaluated. Nor does what looks like the interpolation of non-Marcan materials at a number of points within the Marcan framework serve otherwise than to place in sharper relief the parallelism of the corresponding sections.

There are three Marcan 'blocks' in the Lucan structure: (1) iv. 31-44 (cf. Mk. i. 21-39); (2) v. 12-vi. 16 (cf. Mk. i. 40-iii. 19); (3) viii. 4-ix. 17 (cf. Mk. iii. 20-vi. 44). In addition to the distinctive Lucan narrative of the ministry at Nazareth, there are three departures from the Marcan outline. The first is the insertion between the first two 'blocks' of the very brief episode of the miraculous catch of fish (Lk. v. 1-11). Of considerably greater moment are the materials in Lk. vi. 17-viii. 3, which contain many features that can be paralleled in Matthew. And finally

---

¹ Urgency is added to this examination by the significant evaluation of the framework of the gospel history in K. L. Schmidt, *Der Rahmen der Geschichte Jesu*, 1919, and in *Formgeschichte* generally.

² Lk. iv. 14, clearly marks the *terminus a quo*. The *terminus ad quem* is less definite. At any rate, it seems most convenient to draw the line at a point just before the confession of Peter rather than later when Galilee is finally left behind. Though the situation in Luke is somewhat more complex than in the other synoptic Gospels, here, as well as in Matthew and Mark, there emerges in connection with Peter's confession an occupation with the great climax of the ministry in Jerusalem that sets the middle section apart from the earlier delineation of the ministry in Galilee. Accordingly, we shall be concerned here with Lk. iv. 14-ix. 17.

THE GALILEAN MINISTRY AS A WHOLE   95

there is the observation of a different kind that Luke appears suddenly and sharply to leave off paralleling Mark following the third 'block,' and contains nothing corresponding to Mk. vi. 45–viii. 26. On the assumption that Luke used Mark there are therefore instances of borrowings from Mark but also of additions and omissions. A study of both these sections where Luke appears to be on his own and of the passages where he is dependent on Mark may be expected to illumine the question of his literary and historical method.

The agreement between Luke and Mark is perhaps most clearly exemplified in the first of the three parallel sections (iv. 31–44; Mk. i. 21–39; cf. Mt. viii. 14–17). Both relate in order Jesus' teaching in the synagogue in Capernaum, the astonishment because of His authority, the healing of a demoniac who was present and His resultant fame, His departure to the house of Simon where Simon's mother-in-law was healed of a fever, and the healing of many that evening. The accounts are also closely parallel in reporting next Jesus' retirement to a desert place and in relating in summary fashion a preaching ministry in the synagogues. Here there is certainly no lack of interest in the precise locality and time of the several incidents within this single cycle (cf. Lk. iv. 31, 38, 40, 42). On the other hand, neither Mark nor Luke indicates any concern to define more precisely the setting of this group of incidents within the broader framework of the Galilean ministry. As intimated above, the particular activity in Capernaum is evidently meant to illustrate the Galilean activity as a whole (cf. Lk. iv. 43).

There is, however, one interesting difference between Luke and Mark in this context. Whereas Mark concludes this section by describing in general terms Jesus' activity 'throughout all Galilee,' Luke, according to what appears to be the correct text, states that Jesus 'was preaching in the synagogues of *Judæa*' (Mk. i. 39; Lk. iv. 44; cf. Mt. iv. 23). It is true indeed that Tischendorf and some other modern editors accept the reading 'Galilee' rather than 'Judæa.' 'Galilee,' as a matter of fact, is found in Codex Bezae and the Latin versions, as well as in the mass of the cursives, and might seem to be required as the evident intention of the evangelist. However, the reading 'Judæa' is supported by powerful considerations. It is the text of the great uncials Aleph, B and L, of certain distinctive cursives, the Sinaitic Syriac, and the consensus of the Coptic versions. Moreover, the origin of the reading 'Galilee' is far easier to account for on the assumption that 'Judæa' is the original reading than, on the contrary assumption, to account for the origin of the reading 'Judæa.' The apparent incongruity of the reading 'Judæa' within the context of the Galilean ministry constitutes it as the harder reading. But is it actually intrinsically impossible? If Luke intended at this point suddenly to refer to a phase of activity in southern Palestine, he would be guilty of introducing confusion into his narrative. But the fact is, as a survey of Lucan usage easily demonstrates, that the designation 'Judæa' signifies 'the land of the Jews,' that is, Palestine as a whole.[1] There is, then, no contradiction or confusion in Luke. But there is the difference that at this point he does not confine the ministry of Jesus so strictly as Mark to the bounds of Galilee, but allows himself, in the midst of his narration of Jesus' ministry in Galilee, to take note of the broader sphere of His preaching. Luke is also interested in the specific location of Jesus' activity, but he appears to be somewhat less concerned than the others to mark off from the rest of His work a ministry confined to the north.

Lk. v. 1-11 interrupts the parallel course of the Lucan and Marcan narratives with the story of the marvellous draught of fishes, one of the six miracle stories peculiar to Luke.[2] But the

---

[1] Thus Herod is described as king of 'Judæa' in i. 5, and Galilee is specifically included within Judæa in xxiii. 5, and Acts x. 37. Cf. also vi. 17; vii. 17; Acts ii. 9.

There is no reason to suppose that the non-mention of Galilee is due to a dogmatic construction. It is noteworthy that R. H. Lightfoot is much more reserved in finding doctrinal implications in Luke's references to locality than in Mark's. He speaks of Galilee as having equal significance and worth with Samaria and Jerusalem, but maintains that the presentation of Jerusalem as the goal and the culminating scene of the Lord's activity 'rests not only on historical considerations but on the doctrinal conception that Jesus is primarily Messiah, the lawful King of Israel, who receives the throne of His father David, and will be King over the house of David for ever' (Lk. i. 32 f. *Locality and Doctrine*, p. 143; cf. pp. 134, 136, 137). Actually, of course, Lk. i. 33, says that He will reign over the house of *Jacob* for ever. As Messiah, the Son of David, He will therefore reign over the whole of Israel. Evidence is lacking, therefore, that the interest in Jerusalem expresses a messianic motif.

[2] The raising of the widow's son at Nain (vii. 11-17) is the only other one within the record of the Galilean ministry where thirteen of the total of twenty are found. Three peculiar to Luke are found in the middle section: the infirm woman

climax of the story is found in the word to Peter: 'Do not be afraid; henceforth you will be catching men' (verse 10 RSV). As regards the calling of the disciples, it may be recognized as having elements of correspondence with Mark's account of the call of the disciples from their nets to follow Jesus, especially in view of the summons: 'Come ye after me, and I will make you to become fishers of men' (Mk. i. 16-20; cf. Mt. iv. 18 ff.). Nevertheless, the stories are basically so divergent that few commentators take Luke's miracle story as a mere reconstruction of Mark's account. And even if Luke's story were an amplification of Mark's, no problem of chronological sequence would emerge, for Luke tells the story without establishing any connection with what precedes or what follows.

But the question whether there is an historical difficulty in Luke's story remains. This narrative is indeed the first to mention contact with Peter, James and John. But this is not to say that Luke views this incident as establishing the initial contact with the disciples. His entrance into Simon's boat presupposes acquaintance with him (v. 3); previously there has been a report of the healing of Peter's mother-in-law (iv. 38). And strictly speaking the story, unlike the accounts in Mark and Matthew, is not occupied with a summons to the three disciples. Here James and John figure only secondarily. Basically the story is concerned with a profound personal experience which Peter underwent as he came face to face with the supernatural, and through which he comes to acknowledge Jesus as transcendent Lord: 'Depart from me; for I am a sinful man, O Lord' (verse 8). There is, therefore, no difficulty in supposing that the call to become fishers of men was repeated for emphasis since Jesus had in view that they should leave *all things* and follow Him (verse 11).

The parallelism of Lk. v. 12-vi. 16 and Mark i. 40-iii. 19 (cf. Mt. ix. 18-xi. 30) is also pervasive, extending to the narratives of the healing of a leper and of a paralytic, the call of Levi and the controversy occasioned by Jesus' fellowship with publicans, the question about fasting, the dispute occasioned by the disciples' plucking of grain on the sabbath, and the healing of the withered hand.

(xiii. 10-17); the dropsical man (xiv. 1-6); the ten lepers (xvii. 11-19). The sixth Lucan miracle (the only miracle recorded in the section concerned with the ministry in Jerusalem) is the healing of the servant's ear (xxii. 51).

Only at the very end of these sections does a problem of arrangement emerge, for there seems to be a transposition of certain incidents. Whereas Mark first speaks of a great multitude of people gathering to listen to Jesus and of His healing activity, (iii. 7-12) and then reports the choice of the twelve (iii. 13-19), Luke recounts the latter immediately after the story of the healing of the withered hand (vi. 12-16) and only afterward speaks of the gathering of a large crowd (vi. 17-19). The difference here is, however, not one of mere transposition. For in distinction from Mark who reports the two incidents as isolated events, the healing activity being placed 'at the sea' and the call of the twelve 'on the mountain', Luke in reality omits the former incident and, having related the naming of the twelve apostles, tells of a gathering of crowds when, in the course of Jesus' descent, he came to 'a level place.' The crowd, he says, came to hear Jesus and to be healed of their diseases (vi. 17). He then speaks of Jesus' response to their desires, relating first briefly the healing activity and then more particularly Jesus' discourse. On the assumption that Luke is dependent on Mark, therefore, one might possibly maintain that Luke has omitted the contents of Mk. iii. 7-12 in view of his purpose to refer almost immediately to a similar situation. It is misleading, however, to regard this arrangement as a mere transposition in view of the distinctive contents of Lk. vi. 17-19 as the introduction to the discourse that follows.[1]

The correspondence of Lk. v. 12-vi. 16 and Mk. i. 40-iii. 19 is not restricted to the order of events. It extends also to the relative indifference to geographical and temporal setting. In this section, in contrast to the preceding one, there are few signs of a definite itinerary in Mark, and Luke shows even less interest in fixing the time and place of the incidents. No particular difference can be noted in the story of the leper, although Luke vaguely describes it as taking place 'in one of the cities' (v. 12). In the account of the healing of the paralytic, on the other hand, Luke omits any reference to the locality which Mark designates as Capernaum, and his temporal phrase 'on one of these days' is hardly more precise than Mark's 'after some days' (Lk. v. 17; Mk. ii. 1). In

[1] Huck, *Synopse*, and Cadbury, *Style and Literary Method of Luke*, p. 77, classify this as a transposition. Burton and Goodspeed's *Harmony* takes the position supported here.

reporting this incident, Luke seems to show a special interest in the wide geographical distribution of the effects of Jesus' ministry, for where Mark merely speaks of a concourse of many, Luke reports the gathering of Pharisees and scribes 'out of every village of Galilee and Judæa and Jerusalem' (v. 17). Nevertheless, it would be too bold to claim this as a Lucan tendency, and especially to charge that a severe strain is being put upon the Marcan framework,[1] for Mark only a little later, at a point that can hardly be regarded as marking a significant new stage in the expansion of Jesus' ministry, speaks even more comprehensively of the impact of His work. In Mk. iii. 7 f. we read:

> 'And Jesus with His disciples withdrew to the sea; and a great multitude from Galilee followed; and from Judæa, and from Jerusalem, and from Idumæa, and beyond Jordan, and about Tyre and Sidon, a great multitude, hearing what great things He did, came unto Him.'

Even in vi. 17 Luke does not include mention of Idumæa and the region beyond Jordan. Finally, as characteristic of Luke's topographical interest, we note that he says nothing concerning the place of toll from which Levi was called, although Mark has stated that it was 'by the seaside' (Lk. v. 27; Mk. ii. 13 f.). For the rest Luke and Mark are in close correspondence in this section.

DISCOURSES AND MIRACLES

Lk. vi. 17-19, as has been noticed, serves to introduce an extensive section not paralleled in Mark. The Marcan arrangement is not resumed again until Lk. viii. 4 is introduced. This section of 86 verses of non-Marcan materials is easily the longest within the narrative devoted to the Galilean ministry (the other two such sections together comprise only 26 verses). Though non-Marcan, in contrast to nearly all that has gone before, the section contains much that is not exclusive to Luke for at many points there is close agreement with gospel tradition reported by Matthew.

That Luke shares with Matthew the desire to report the message of Jesus much more fully than Mark has done appears especially from the sermon reported in Lk. vi. 20-49. The extent of its parallelism with Matthew's 'Sermon on the Mount'

---

[1] Thus Lightfoot, *Locality and Doctrine*, p. 134.

suggests the possibility that both evangelists are reporting the same discourse. There seem indeed to be no insuperable difficulties besetting this hypothesis. The location may well be the same: Luke does not designate it as the sermon of the 'plain' or 'field,' and the 'level place' mentioned in Lk. vi. 17 may well be located on the side of the mountain. Nor may the relative brevity of Luke's report or the differences in detail between the two be appealed to as decisive for a contrary view. The brevity of the reports, in Matthew as well as in Luke, distinctly allows for the judgment that both have made a selection from a discourse which, as originally spoken, would presumably have taken considerably more time than that required for the delivery of the Sermon on the Mount. Although one is not in a position to state positively what principles have guided such a selection, it is plausible that the different audiences the evangelists had in view affected the decision. Thus, for example, Luke, contemplating his distinctively Gentile audience, may have decided to omit the antitheses of Mt. v.

On the other hand, the elements of agreement and difference in the two discourses are congruous with the view that Luke is reporting a discourse delivered on another occasion. Quite irrespective of one's judgment as to the precise length of the ministry of Jesus, there can be no doubt that it was widespread, that His teaching and preaching must have been repeated in similar form again and again, and that the gospel tradition preserves for us only a small segment of the total. Nor may one assume that Luke's knowledge of the tradition was confined to meagre literary sources. The details regarding the transmission of the gospel tradition are not sufficiently well known to permit a dogmatic judgment on questions of this kind.[1]

In the remaining paragraphs of the section under consideration, there are other substantial agreements with Matthew in the choice of incidents, but also certain narratives peculiar to Luke. Following the discourse of Lk. vi. 20-49, two miracles are reported, the first common to Matthew, and the second found only in Luke. These are the healing of the centurion's servant at Capernaum (vii. 1-10; Mt. viii. 5-13), and the raising of the widow's son at Nain

[1] On the entire question see especially Plummer, pp. 176 f.; Greijdanus, KNT, pp. 282 ff.

(vii. 11-17). These are followed with incidents where the teaching element is prominent, the first again finding its counterpart in Matthew and the second likewise being peculiar to Luke. The materials parallel with Matthaean data are the closely connected group consisting of the impatient inquiry of the Baptist concerning Christ and the testimony of Jesus concerning John (vii. 18-35; Mt. xi. 2-19); the story distinctive of Luke concerns the anointing in the house of Simon the Pharisee (vii. 36-50). The whole is rounded off with a summary statement of a ministry of preaching and healing which took place 'soon afterwards,' and in which certain women ministered to them (viii. 1-3; cf. xv. 41; Mt. xxvii. 55).

The arrangement of these materials suggests that logical considerations rather than topographical interests or literary influences have dictated their order. Though there are some references to time and place, it is clear that Luke does not place the incidents within the framework of an itinerary. Capernaum and Nain are mentioned as the location of the first two incidents, but there is nothing to suggest that a circuit of the cities of Galilee is in view. The interest in the narrative of the healing of the centurion's servant appears to be less in its connection with Capernaum than in the fact that such faith as the centurion manifested had not been found 'in Israel.' The action at Nain is linked temporally with the preceding context in a general way, however, for Lk. vii. 11 states that it occurred 'soon afterwards.'[1] Still another feature which indicates that this event is not presented as a quite isolated instance of miraculous activity is that Luke closes the account by indicating that the profound impression of the presence of the power of God created by the miracle was by no means confined to that city. Its effects comprehended 'the whole of Judæa' and even the areas beyond the land of the Jews (vii. 16 f.).

The inquiry of the Baptist is introduced without reference to

---

[1] Some ancient MSS., perhaps in the interest of a more specific reference, through the change of but a single letter, set the time as 'the next day'. This reading of TR and AV is also supported by Huck. The external evidence does not submit a clear pattern, for the TR also has the support of Aleph, C D W, some Old Latin MSS., and the Bohairic Coptic, whereas the other reading is supported by A B L Theta, certain MSS. of the Old Latin, the Sahidic Coptic, and the Sinaitic Syriac. 'Soon afterwards' seems to conform to the Lucan pattern. Cf. viii. 1.

time or place (vii. 18 ff.). It does indeed follow upon a report of John's disciple to John concerning 'all these things' (vii. 18), but this appears to have in view the total impression of the activity of Jesus rather than just the miracle at Nain. The logical progression from miracle activity to teaching as to the meaning of Jesus' mission reappears in Lk. vii. 21, 22, for further healing acts 'in that hour' become the background for Jesus' reply to John concerning His works. Similarly, there is no indication as to exactly when and where the anointing of Jesus in the house of Simon took place. It is introduced quite casually with the words: 'And one of the Pharisees desired him that he would eat with him' (vii. 36). But this Lucan story, occupied as it largely is with the exposure of Pharisaic lack of genuine love, has perhaps been suggested by the previous reflection upon the unbelief and hostility of the Pharisees (cf. vii. 30 ff.). The summary statement concerning the tour through 'cities and villages' which took place 'soon afterwards' presumably has the cities and villages of Galilee in view, but it is of interest that no specific mention is made of this locality.

The final section of the Galilean ministry where Luke closely follows the same order as Mark comprises Lk. viii. 4–ix. 17 (cf. Mk. iii. 20–vi. 44). Within this section, however, there are a number of departures from the Marcan order which require examination and which must be explained. The differences are as follows: (1) Luke does not include the parabolic discourses of Mk. iii. 23-30, although at later points he introduces materials that correspond more or less closely (cf. Lk. xi. 14-23, xii. 10). (2) Luke records the narrative concerning true kindred after the parabolic discourses, whereas Mark puts it before (Lk. viii. 19-21; Mk. iii. 31-35). (3) Luke 'omits' certain parables and comment on this teaching, although he includes one of these parables at a later point (Mk. iv. 26-34; cf. Lk. xiii. 18-19). (4) He further omits the account of the rejection at Nazareth as found in Mk. vi, but this, as intimated above, must be evaluated in connection with his distinctive narrative of Jesus' preaching and reception there. (5) He omits the story of the death of the Baptist which, as noted above, is explained by his inclusion of the imprisonment of John within the section devoted to the Baptist's ministry (Mk. vi. 17-29; Lk. iii. 19, 20).

While these divergences of order, apart from the story of the reception at Nazareth, do not pose any serious problems, they nevertheless are significant for our understanding of Luke's method. In the first place, he is frequently more concise than Mark. Perhaps this is simply a matter of style. But another factor may be that Luke felt the need of conserving space for the treatment of other matters, and especially for the great middle section. In the second place, in considering those instances where discourses of Jesus are omitted here apparently because they find a place in a later phase of the ministry, one should avoid the dogmatic conclusion that Luke has simply transferred the setting of these discourses without regard for their original historical occasion. Such a conclusion would indeed be demanded if it could be proved that Jesus never repeated Himself in His preaching and teaching and that Luke could not have had access to any tradition independent of Mark. Both of these judgments would involve an unrealistic conception of the transmission of the gospel before it was committed to writing in the Gospels. As Burton Scott Easton says, 'We must think of hundreds of instructions delivered in dozens of places. So there must have been an almost infinite repetition of material.' He further observes that, while many of the parables and sayings would have been repeated in the same form, other saying and parables would have received different form and different grouping on different occasions.[1]

Finally, bearing in mind the matter with which this chapter is chiefly concerned, and which is of the most fundamental importance as one considers variations of order in the Gospels, we observe that the differences in order of the various incidents require no special explanation if only Luke's evident method is kept in view. In this section, no less than in those previously examined, Luke shows even less concern than Mark to fix the place and time of the several events. Whereas Matthew and Mark introduce the parabolic discourses by reporting that the crowd at the seaside compelled Jesus to sit in a boat, Luke merely reports the presence of a crowd after referring in general terms to a journey 'through cities and villages' which came to pass 'soon afterwards' (Lk. viii. 1, 4; Mt. xiii. 1 f.; Mk. iv. 1f). Mark opens the story of the storm at sea with the precise temporal reference 'on that day when even

[1] *The Gospel before the Gospels*, 1928, p. 39; cf. pp. 122 f.

was come,' but Luke merely says that it came to pass 'on one of those days' (Mk. iv. 35; Lk. viii. 22). In the other narratives of this group Luke closely agrees with Mark in the presence or absence of geographical and chronological details.

RETIREMENT TO BETHSAIDA

In the final story in this section, however—the story of the feeding of the five thousand—Luke supplies a specific geographical reference not found in the other Gospels. He mentions in ix. 10 a retirement 'to a city called Bethsaida.' If the other evangelists were merely silent on this particular, no weighty problem would present itself. As a matter of fact, however, a complication arises because the reference to Bethsaida is not so distinctively Lucan as a comparison of the accounts of this miracle might suggest. For in the very next section, in reporting the miracle of Jesus' walking on the sea (which is not found in Luke), Mark likewise refers to a journey by boat towards Bethsaida (Mk. vi. 45). It may appear then that Luke gets Jesus to Bethsaida considerably before Mark does.

Before proceeding to a clarification of this problem, it is necessary to deal with two preliminary points which bear upon the interpretation of the Lucan narrative, one which concerns the motive for referring to Bethsaida at this juncture, and the second dealing with the consistency of Luke's own account with itself.

Is there an adequate explanation of the reference to Bethsaida at this point in Luke? Or is the evangelist open to the charge that he has merely anticipated the Marcan reference to Bethsaida because he plans to omit that Marcan section and must prepare for Lk. x. 13, which presupposes an activity in Bethsaida? Easton, for example, supports the latter theory. He says:

> 'The interval between the departure of the Twelve and their return is filled up by verses 7-9. No other connection appears to exist and, in particular, nothing here in Luke suggests that Christ went to Bethsaida to avoid Herod. Bethsaida, as a matter of fact, lay outside of Galilee, just across Jordan, but Luke does not indicate this in any way and his readers would not have known it. So in Luke the only apparent motive for Christ's withdrawal is a search for quiet.

'Such a geographical reference is contrary to Luke's usual practice, and it can be explained only as a preparation for x. 13. The name is taken from Mk. vi. 45, proving that Luke's copy of Mark did not contain a lacuna after vi. 44; Mk. viii. 22 is too remote...'[1]

The appeal to Lk. x. 13 is not impressive, since Luke does not feel it necessary to prepare for the reference to Chorazin in the same verse. It is natural therefore to look for the motive in the immediate context. Now it is true, as Mark reports, that Jesus sought a period of rest (vi. 31); but the insertion of the account of Herod's sudden interest in Jesus, including specifically his desire to see Jesus, whose name stirred up uncomfortable reminiscences of his beheading of the Baptist (Lk. ix. 9), can hardly be intended for any other purpose than to throw light upon Jesus' own actions. When, therefore, in Lk. ix. 10 Luke says that Jesus withdrew apart privately into a city called Bethsaida, he would have indicated to readers for whom the other geographical references had meaning that Jesus had left the region under Herod's domain for that of Philip's, Bethsaida being on the north-east coast of the lake, just within the border of Philip's tetrarchy.

The second question relates to the self-consistency of Luke's own account. The evangelist is sometimes charged with handling his Marcan source so clumsily, because of his supposed anticipation of the Marcan reference to Bethsaida in vi. 45, that he left his own account of the miracle of the feeding of the 5,000 in self-contradiction. Creed, for example, declares that, whether 'village' or 'city' be read as the correct text in Lk. ix. 10, 'there appears to be an inconsistency between this verse and verse 12:' in the first instance he is said to be in a city or village; in the second the disciples and multitude are said to be 'in a desert place.' Creed adds that Luke's inconsistency is due to his modification of Mark, and that his 'introduction of Bethsaida at this point is probably a sign that he was acquainted with the Marcan material at the end of this paragraph.' Since the crowds were compelled to go to the villages and country round about for lodging and provisions, it appears improbable that they could have been

[1] *The Gospel according to St. Luke*, ad ix. 10, and p. 138. Cf. Schmidt, op. cit., pp. 189 f., 193.

thought of as being in a populated centre. The intrinsic difficulty would be removed if one could adopt the reading of the Textus Receptus, 'to a desert place belonging to the city of Bethsaida.' But this reading, and other similar readings with meagre support, evidently arose from a desire to overcome this very difficulty.[1] Still this is not sufficient reason for concluding that Luke would have contradicted himself so flagrantly within the compass of three verses. It is a basic canon of criticism that, particularly in the case of a conscientious writer, one must assume self-consistency until the contrary has been firmly established. In this case clearly one must avoid undue rigidity in the interpretation of terms. As Easton points out in his comment on this passage, ' "city" here can only mean "city state".' The usage in Lk. viii. 26, 27, 39 affords a good parallel, for there 'city' evidently has in view the *district* of the Gerasenes. If then, Luke had in mind to point out that Jesus retired to a place outside the borders of Galilee, which he designates rather generally as the district of Bethsaida, it was still possible for him, in describing the situation which occasioned the feeding of the multitude, to speak more precisely of the place as an isolated spot where no lodging or provisions were available.

The question of the harmony of Luke with Mark remains. How can both evangelists be accurate if one locates the arrival in the vicinity of Bethsaida after a journey which *preceded* the feeding of the five thousand (Lk. ix. 11-17) whereas the other tells of the command of the disciples to sail to Bethsaida *after the miracle* while he dismissed the multitude (Mk. vi. 45). Luke, as has been observed, seems to get Jesus to Bethsaida considerably before Mark does. In the older discussions a solution of the problem was often found in the conjecture, supposedly supported by Jn. i. 44 ('Philip was from Bethsaida, of the city of Andrew and Peter'), that there was another Bethsaida on the western side of the lake.[2] However, there does not appear to be any real foundation for this view.[3] Nevertheless, unless one prejudges the case by the assumption that Luke everywhere is characterized by a slavish dependence upon Mark, there is no adequate basis for the con-

---

[1] On the textual evidence, and some of the issues involved, cf. Streeter, op. cit., pp. 568 ff., and Creed ad ix. 10.
[2] So Alexander and Gould on Mark vi. 45.
[3] Cf. Dalman, *Orte und Wege Jesu*, p. 158.

THE GALILEAN MINISTRY AS A WHOLE

clusion that Luke has arbitrarily anticipated the arrival in Bethsaida. Matthew and Mark tell of a sea voyage to the scene of the feeding of the multitude, and Luke adds the information that this place was in the general vicinity of Bethsaida (Mt. xiv. 13; Mk. vi. 32; Lk. ix. 10). Luke does not tell what happened next; from a comparison with the other Gospels it appears that he here breaks off the narrative rather sharply. Matthew and Mark, on the other hand, report a sea voyage of the disciples which took them away from the place where the multitude was gathered, a voyage which began without Jesus and which soon ran into a fearful storm during which Jesus came walking to them upon the water (Mt. xiv. 22 ff.; Mk. vi. 45 ff.). After the storm they landed in Gennesaret on the western side of the lake (Mt. xiv. 31; Mk. vi. 53). So far there is a perfectly harmonious and consistent representation, quite in keeping with Luke's intimation that the multitude was fed at a point in the vicinity of Bethsaida near the northern end of the lake.[1]

Does not, however, Mark's report in vi. 45, that Jesus 'constrained His disciples to enter into the boat, and to go before Him unto the other side to Bethsaida,' introduce a contradiction? Actually, of course, Mark does not say anything of a voyage to Bethsaida, but only of an injunction of Jesus that they sail to, or towards, Bethsaida. It appears from the narrative that the storm may have prevented their ever reaching this destination; in any case we learn that they crossed over and landed in Gennesaret.[2] The ultimate issue, then, is whether, at a point in the general vicinity of Bethsaida (as indicated by Lk. ix. 10), Jesus could have contemplated a voyage of His disciples to the other side to, or towards, Bethsaida (as Mark states in vi. 45).[3] Cognate language

---

[1] Matthew's account does not contain the Marcan reference to Bethsaida. If his narrative is read without relation to Mark, one would naturally get the impression that the desert place was quite far removed from the vicinity of Gennesaret on the western side of the lake. It agrees well therefore with Luke ix. 10 ff. in placing the scene in the vicinity of Bethsaida.

[2] W. C. Allen, *Mark* (1915) ad vi. 53, however, on the basis of the western text, which reads, 'And having crossed over *thence* to the land, they came to Gennesaret and moored,' construes this as beginning a new paragraph, thus allowing for an interval between the events of Mk. vi. 45-52, and those introduced by verse 53. It is presumed then that the disciples actually arrived in Bethsaida; later they again crossed the lake and went to the land of Gennesaret.

[3] εἰς τὸ πέραν πρὸς βηθσαϊδάν.

is used on an occasion by Josephus in reporting a voyage of less than four miles.[1] Moreover, the Marcan account is highly congruous with the viewpoint that only a short voyage is contemplated, for evidently there is the expectation, which was frustrated by the storm, that Jesus would join them on the shore (cf. vi. 45 ff.).[2] Accordingly, Mark may well imply what Luke states explicitly, that the retirement of Jesus at this time was to a district bordering the lake on the north, of which Bethsaida was the centre.

The question of the so-called 'great omission' in Luke, that is the question why Luke closely agrees with the Marcan order as far as vi. 44, and resumes again at viii. 27, but passes over the materials found in Mk. vi. 45–viii. 26, is primarily a question of synoptic criticism, and not one that bears in any direct way upon the distinctive witness of Luke. On the assumption that Luke was familiar with this passage, it would not follow that he would think of its non-insertion as a great omission, for his very considerable independence of Mark at other points indicates that he would not have regarded his own plan as largely dictated by Mark's narrative. Hence, no dogmatic reply may be given as to the reasons why Luke does not follow Mark at this point. His interest in brevity and conciseness at various points, together with his intention of dealing at considerable length with other phases of Jesus' ministry, notably in the middle section, may have been a leading factor. Evidently Luke judged that he had set forth the basic features of the Galilean ministry with sufficient fullness and clarity in his selection of incidents and teaching, and that in particular it was not essential to his purpose to report several additional acts of healing and a second story of a miraculous feeding of a multitude. Nothing that may fairly be charged with being at variance with Luke's perspective appears in this section. At most one might say that such materials as the denunciation of the Pharisees (vii. 1-23; cf. viii. 11-21) would have appeared

---

[1] *Life*, 59 (304). Cf. G. A. Smith, *Historical Geography of the Holy Land*, 1902, pp. 457 f. Josephus says that, from Tiberias, 'he embarked and crossed over to Tarichaeae' (ἐμβὰς εἰς τὰς ταριχαίας διεπεραιώθην).

[2] Rawlinson, ad Mk. vi. 47, observes that '*In the midst of the sea* may mean "half-way across," but does not necessarily mean more than "a good way out from the shore".'

relatively inappropriate in a Gospel designed for Gentile readers.[1]

From the consideration of the early chapters devoted to the public ministry of Jesus, in which the parallelism with Mark, and to a lesser extent with Matthew, is so pervasive that we encounter comparatively little exclusively Lucan materials, we turn to the major problem of the middle chapters of Luke where the evangelist seems largely to go his own way. It may appear, however, that even in this section there is basic agreement with the perspective of the other evangelists.

[1] For the entire question cf. especially Hawkins, *Oxford Studies in the Synoptic Problem*, pp. 61 ff., 67; Streeter, op. cit., pp. 172 ff.; Taylor, *Behind the Third Gospel*, pp. 138 ff., 188 ff.

CHAPTER VI

FROM GALILEE TO JERUSALEM

ONE of the most extraordinary features of the canonical Gospels is their extensive occupation with the passion and resurrection of our Lord. Small wonder that in telling of the career of Jesus Christ the evangelists should have rounded off their narratives with the report of the stupendous and awe-inspiring fact of His resurrection, for the resurrection belonged in their thought to the age to come, and it was surely deserving of climactic treatment that for Christ that age had dawned. But the concentration upon the theme of the death of Christ, especially in writings which otherwise bear so little the mark of tragedy and indeed end on the note of glorious triumph and vindication, is a different matter. If other characteristics of the narratives, such as those which introduce Jesus to men as the divine Anointed and portray the astounding effects of His words and deeds upon men, had not already disclosed that the evangelists were not biographers telling the story of an historical figure of heroic dimensions, that would become luminously plain when once due weight was given to their overpowering interest in the theme of the passion. With very little exaggeration one might say that the Gospels are passion Gospels—with only so much space given to other details as are considered essential to the intelligible introduction of Him who was to go to the cross.

This evaluation of the Gospels applies most pointedly to Mark since its introduction of Jesus, like its taking leave of Jesus following the crucifixion, is exceedingly abrupt and since Mark's report of the teaching of Jesus is relatively brief. Mark may be said, like Paul, to know nothing save Christ and Him crucified. But if the disposition of materials in Mark excludes its categorization as biographical literature, but rather demands the recognition of a new and quite distinctive literary form, which cannot be more aptly named than simply by the use of the term Gospel, the situation is not essentially changed when one considers the other three. They may tell more of Christ's origin, His person, His message and the issue of His life, but they all likewise may be said to be absorbed above all with the story of the march to the cross and the meaning of that overwhelming event.

My purpose in this and the following chapters is to consider the place occupied within Luke's Gospel by the witness to the death and resurrection of Jesus Christ. So far as the concentration upon these closely integrated themes is concerned, Luke can hardly be said to be following a pattern different from that of Mark. His narrative of the resurrection is far more extensive; his narrative of the passion (in the narrower sense of the story of the events commencing with Christ's final entrance into Jerusalem and concluding with the crucifixion and the burial) is slightly briefer (about ten per cent); when both are combined Luke's account is somewhat, but only a little, longer than Mark's. If there is a difference in emphasis, then, between Mark and Luke, it is only because the latter is far longer than the former, somewhat more than half as long again.

INTRODUCTION OF THE PASSION THEME

The consideration of the broad disposition of the Gospels, while in itself not insignificant, serves chiefly to introduce the evaluation of the contents of the several narratives, and it will be my concern in what follows to deal with certain of the most remarkable features of Luke's representation. Before that, however, it is well to consider other evidence pertinent to the principal theme which confronts the reader well in advance of the narration of the climacteric events in the closing chapters. In Matthew and Mark the passion motif is introduced conspicuously in close connection with the withdrawal from Galilee, and is again and again brought into the focus of attention in their accounts of the journey to Jerusalem. The same or similar materials are also present in Luke. But in reading Luke the impression is sometimes received that there is quite a different perspective. Instead of the brief accounts of the journey from Galilee to Jerusalem found in Matthew and Mark, we encounter in Luke a section approximately three times as long as the corresponding sections in the other two synoptics, which frequently is thought to be occupied with a quite distinctive phase of the public ministry. I have chiefly in mind, of course, the great central section of Luke variously called 'The Lucan Travel Narrative' or 'The Great Interpolation,' comprising Lk.

ix. 51–xviii. 14. Although the special problem presented to students of the Gospels by this Lucan feature has too many facets to allow for a thorough evaluation here, it may not be ignored in view of its decisive bearing upon one's conception of the Gospel as a whole. And greater justice will be done to this problem, and to our basic theme, if this section is contemplated in the somewhat broader context introduced by the confession of Peter (ix. 18 ff.), and concluding with the actual arrival in Jerusalem (xix. 45).

Following the lead of Matthew and Mark, then, one may begin with a consideration of the manner in which the Confession of Peter became the occasion of the initiation of a solemn proclamation of the coming passion on the part of Jesus. When, however, Luke is compared with the other synoptics, one may receive the impression that Luke is less concerned than the others to mark this development as a new stage in the ministry of Christ. For Luke gives no intimation whatsoever of a withdrawal from Galilee to Caesarea Philippi which in Matthew and Mark sets the scene for the climacteric developments to come. Instead, he introduces the cycle of events in the most unobtrusive manner possible in the words: 'And it came to pass, as He was praying apart, the disciples were with him, and He asked them, saying, Who do the multitudes say that I am?' (ix. 18). If this evangelist were constantly and minutely concerned with the geographical and chronological framework of the gospel history, it would be difficult to overcome the impression that the confession of Peter and the events associated intimately with it were not intended to indicate a transition in the progress of events. Since, however, as the study of the Gospel as a whole demonstrates, such was not his aim, no special stress may be placed here upon the absence of any mention of a withdrawal from Galilee.

In spite of the absence of this feature, however, Luke no less strikingly centres the reader's attention upon the course of things to come. A comparison of Lk. ix. 18–50 with the closely corresponding narratives in Mk. viii. 27–ix. 41 and Mt. xvi. 13–xviii. 5 shows, in truth, that Luke marks the presence of the passion motif fully as emphatically as the others. In the first place, Luke is most explicit in noting the intimate connection between Peter's acknowledgment of Jesus' messiahship and the coming passion and resurrection (ix. 22). Whereas Matthew and Mark allow one

FROM GALILEE TO JERUSALEM

to infer that the acknowledgment of Jesus' messianic dignity and His command that He should not be made known provide the occasion of, and offer the explanation for, His solemn disclosure concerning the future programme of the Messiah (cf. Mt. xvi. 21; Mk. viii. 31), Luke alone explicitly joins these features:

> 'And Peter answering said, The Christ of God. But He charged them, and commanded them to tell this to no man; *saying*, The Son of Man must suffer many things, and be rejected of the elders and chief priests and scribes, and be killed, and the third day be raised up.' (Lk. ix. 20 ff.)

Evidently the official proclamation of the Christ had to await the consummation of the messianic death and resurrection.

Even more conspicuously does the passion motif appear in Luke's account of the transfiguration (ix. 28 ff.). The transfiguration as set forth in the other accounts likewise must be understood, not as an isolated disclosure of Jesus' exalted dignity, but as a manifestation of divine approval of the course of action upon which Jesus had entered.[1] But Luke adds the significant item that the topic of conversation between Moses and Elijah concerned 'His decease (or, 'departure') which He was about to accomplish at Jerusalem' (ix. 31). In spite, therefore, of the absence of any reference to a change of scene and activity in Lk. ix. 18 ff., Luke even more pointedly than the other evangelists demonstrates that a new cycle of events is under way, which must take Jesus to Jerusalem for the climax of His ministry. The close connection of the transfiguration with the preceding disclosures concerning the coming passion is confirmed by Luke's distinctive reference to the time that had elapsed: it was 'about eight days after these sayings,' says Luke, that Jesus 'took with Him Peter and John and James, and went up into the mountain to pray' (ix. 28). In a context where the chronological details are so meagre, this reference emphasizes the inner connection between the stupendous developments and the disclosures in this section. Why Luke says that the period was 'about eight days,' whereas Matthew and Mark speak of six days, has never been satisfactorily explained on the basis of the theories which regard Luke as slavishly dependent upon Mark. If Luke were trying to improve upon Mark, it is

[1] See WMMC, pp. 68 f., 237.

difficult to understand why he should have submitted an indefinite measure of time for a more precise one, especially since there is substantial agreement between the two expressions.[1] But even this measure of independence stresses the close connection between the passion and the transfiguration.

DISPOSITION OF THE MIDDLE CHAPTERS

When one turns from the comparison of the parallel sections to the extensive travel narrative of Lk. ix. 51–xviii. 14, one faces squarely the major question of Luke's historical method. The final decision on this matter is necessarily bound up with the positions taken on broader historical and literary questions, including the identity of the evangelist, his sources of information, and his trustworthiness. To enter fully upon their evaluation would take us beyond the scope of the present discussion, but some stock must be taken of the main problem as it bears upon the disposition of the Gospel.

According to the most consistent representatives of the two-document hypothesis (which at this point means those who regard the third evangelist as rather exclusively an editor of Mark and 'Q' who, therefore, where he departs from Mark and the reconstructed 'Q,' is hardly likely to be publishing solid historical tradition), this entire middle section is to be regarded as being, at least so far as its references to time and place are concerned, essentially a creation of the evangelist. Creed, for example, maintains that, although Luke purports to describe a direct journey through Samaria to Jerusalem, this is inconsistent with references to Jericho (xviii. 35; xix. 1) as well as with mention of thronging multitudes, sabbath day preachings, offended Pharisees, and reports of Herod's hostility, which are said to suggest the background of the Galilean ministry rather than a set journey through Samaria to Jerusalem. The supposed discrepancy between the contents of this section and the framework of the journey is to be explained, according to Creed, as a literary construction. Wishing to incorporate a large body of

[1] As Plummer says, ad loc., 'it looks as if he had not seen their expression.' Luke also notes the intimate connection of the events following the transfiguration, for he, alone of the evangelists, introduces the story of the healing of the youthful demoniac with the expression 'on the following day,' which perhaps implies that the transfiguration took place at night. Cf. Lk. ix. 37.

teaching from 'Q' and certain material associating Jesus with Samaria, and wishing to avoid disturbance of the essential framework of Mark, Luke has simply imposed the element of continuous narrative upon the materials he desired to present.[1]

A somewhat higher estimate of the historical character of Luke's central section comes to expression among the advocates of the Proto-Luke Theory which, in contrast to a view like Creed's, allows that Mark was a secondary rather than a primary source for the third evangelist. And since, furthermore, it is widely held that Luke himself constructed Proto-Luke on the basis of 'Q' and distinctive tradition to which he had access, the unique materials in Luke are not so readily set aside as due chiefly to his editorial operations. On this perspective, although Luke is still thought to have introduced some incidents that rightly belong in Galilee, and his account is judged to betray certain gaps in his information concerning this period, Luke's theory is thought to be more than a mere literary device.[2]

No definite preference is being indicated for either view. In my judgment the choice is by no means limited to these two possibilities. And in any case the decision must be sought by a testing of the data as a whole, not by the simple expedient of determining which of several theories credits Luke with greater trustworthiness. One may again recognize, however, that the latter theory represents a salutary emphasis not found in the former, namely, that it credits the evangelist with a considerable measure of independence from previous literary efforts, a point which the author makes with some force in the prologue, and which finds impressive confirmation from the testimony of Acts to the authorship of the double work. The brief summary of these two tendencies in synoptic criticism, which are in part opposed to each other, serves, however, to provide a background for a review of the data in Luke.

In this extensive middle section one rarely loses sight of Jerusalem as the final destination, where Jesus' decease was about to be 'accomplished.' The section begins with the solemn declaration that Jesus 'set His face' that is, reached the fixed determination, to

---

[1] Cf. Creed, op. cit., pp. 139 ff.; Schmidt, *Rahmen*, pp. 246 ff.
[2] Cf. Taylor, *Behind the Third Gospel*, pp. 234 ff. See also Streeter, op. cit., pp. 203 f.

go to Jerusalem when the days were well-nigh come that He should be received up (ix. 51).¹ He was received with hostility when he entered into a village of the Samaritans because it was known, perhaps from messengers who had gone ahead, that His destination was Jerusalem, the centre of the religious fellowship which was the object of their implacable hatred (ix. 52 f.). That He was journeying to Jerusalem is also stated in Lk. xiii. 22 (33 f.), xvii. 11, and xviii. 31; He reaches the vicinity of Jericho in xviii. 35 ff., approaches Jerusalem at xix. 28, sees the city at xix. 41, and enters into the temple at xix. 45. At a number of other points Jesus is described less definitely as being on a journey (cf. ix. 56 f., x. 1, 38, xiv. 25). Since, however, many incidents and discourses are introduced without reference to an itinerary or other connecting links, it is not legitimate to conclude that Luke represents Jesus as continuously en route to Jerusalem.²

A rather popular evaluation of the problem is that which conceives of Luke as setting the scene of this phase of Jesus' ministry in Peræa. The journeying in view is regarded as following the longer route through Peræa, often taken by pilgrims on their way to Jerusalem in order to avoid contacts with the hostile Samaritans. Thus Luke is thought to be setting forth in detail what Mark has stated summarily in x. 1, where reference is made to Jesus' coming 'to the borders of Judæa and beyond the Jordan.' Although such an approach offers a simple, and in some respects attractive, solution of the problem of harmonizing the Gospel accounts, it breaks down on the mention of Samaritan activity within this section. The reference to the entrance into a village of the Samaritans in Lk. ix. 52 indeed would not rule out the idea of a Peræan ministry, since it might be allowed that the hostility of the Samaritans, which erupted in the first village which was entered after crossing the border of Galilee, caused Jesus to take a longer route. But an insuperable obstacle is presented by Lk.

¹ This appears to mean, more precisely, that the period to be concluded by His 'assumption' was drawing to a close. On the verb, cf. the usage in Acts ii. 1; on the meaning of 'assumption', cf. Acts i. 1 where the ascension of Christ is plainly in view.

² For a classification of the materials, see Schmidt, op. cit., pp. 248 f. Plummer's idea that Luke narrates 'journeyings to Jerusalem' is accordingly not positively supported by the evidence. Lk. x. 38, may imply that Jesus was in the vicinity of Jerusalem, but this too is not directly established by the evidence in Luke. Cf. Ogg, op. cit., p. 24.

xvii. 11 which discloses that Jesus is not, even at this late point, beyond the Jordan, but still 'passing along the borders of Samaria and Galilee.' It appears, then, that it is plainly a misnomer to speak of this section as concerned with 'The Peræan Ministry.'

But if this phase of the ministry may not fairly be called Peræan, may it not be correct to regard it as Samaritan? This is the conclusion of R. H. Lightfoot who maintains that Luke presents in succession three theatres of activity: Galilee, Samaria and Judæa.[1] And Creed at least partially agrees, for he maintains that Luke represents Jesus as taking the most direct route to Jerusalem, through Samaria, but that, through the influence of Mark's itinerary, he introduces a discrepancy by telling of His journey through Jericho (xviii. 35; cf. Mk. x. 46). The pertinent data, however, do not justify the adoption of these conclusions. The two references to Samaria (ix. 52, xvii. 11) are quite insufficient to ground the judgment that Luke purposes to narrate a ministry to the Samaritans or even one confined to Samaria. The very silence of Luke is a weighty consideration. If he intended to describe a distinctly Samaritan phase of the ministry of Christ, is it not remarkable that he neglects so many opportunities to make that clear to his readers? He might easily, for example, have stated that he had Samaria in mind when he speaks in Lk. x. 1 of 'every city and place where He was about to come.'[2] But the most decisive consideration against these views is presented by the specific testimony of Lk. xvii. 11. If this passage referred only to Samaria, there would indeed be plausible support for the theory that the middle section of Luke is concerned with Samaria. The fact is, however, that this verse places Jesus and his followers as much within *Galilee* as within Samaria. The translation of the verse is somewhat difficult, as is suggested by the marginal reading of the Revised Version 'through the midst' for 'along the borders' in the text:

> 'And it came to pass, as they were on the way to Jerusalem, that he was passing along the borders of Samaria and Galilee.'

Actually, however, there can be little question that Luke places

---

[1] *Locality and Doctrine*, pp. 137 ff., 143; cf. Lohmeyer, *Galiläa und Jerusalem*, 1936, pp. 41, 42 f.
[2] Cf. also Lk. xiii. 22, where similar language is used.

Jesus on the frontier of Samaria and Galilee.¹ So far as the evidence in Luke goes, therefore, it is not safe to go beyond the conclusion that a ministry near the border of Samaria and Galilee is in view, a ministry which may well have taken Jesus into Samaria on several occasions besides the one mentioned in Lk. ix. 52 f., but which also may well have included several stops in cities and villages of Galilee.

But if Jesus remained so long near the southern border of Galilee, how is one to make intelligible the frequent references to a journeying to Jerusalem? Jesus is indeed often viewed as proceeding on His way to Jerusalem, but the explicit references to Samaria and Galilee (ix. 51, xvii. 11) are congruous with the evaluation that Jesus was journeying, evidently in rather leisurely fashion, making stops at various cities and towns near the border. The references to Jerusalem do not imply that He was determined to reach Jerusalem in the shortest possible time and by the most direct route: they serve not so much to mark the outward course of the journey as to call attention to the inner purpose of Jesus which centres in His determination to reach the goal of His 'decease' and of his 'assumption' (Lk. ix. 31, 51).

Luke indeed is so far from marking out the exact course of the journey that, in contrast to Mark and Matthew, he does not even note the arrival in Judæa. One might perhaps gather from the third announcement of the coming passion that Jerusalem is near (Lk. xviii. 31), but no specific confirmation is given until the arrival in the vicinity of Jericho is recorded in Lk. xviii. 35. Then, however, Luke provides considerable information concerning the ministry of Jesus. For in addition to the story of the healing of a blind man, he reports the distinctive narrative of Jesus and Zacchaeus and the parable of the ten pounds, spoken 'because he was near Jerusalem and they supposed that the kingdom of God was immediately to appear' (Lk. xix. 11).

JESUS' MESSAGE TO ANTIPAS

That the frequent mention of Jerusalem in this section is due not to a concern on Luke's part to mark the course of the journey to that city, but rather to disclose the inner conviction of Jesus that

¹ On the textual and exegetical questions, cf. especially Plummer and Creed. The RSV translates: 'He was passing along between Samaria and Galilee.'

the messianic task was unthinkable apart from the programme of suffering and death which awaited Him, is impressively corroborated by the episode reported only by Luke in which Jesus addresses Herod Antipas (xiii. 31-33):

> 'In that very hour there came certain Pharisees, saying to Him, Get thee out, and go hence: for Herod would fain kill thee. And He said unto them, Go and say to that fox, Behold, I cast out devils and perform cures today and tomorrow, and the third day I am perfected. Howbeit I must go on My way today and tomorrow and the day following; for it cannot be that a prophet perish out of Jerusalem.'

The message is so singular both as to its occasion and its content that it claims more than passing notice.

However unusual the situation, it is surely quite intelligible that Antipas should have expressed a desire to kill Jesus. Not that he had determined to arrest Jesus and put Him out of the way, for in that case he would have done more than talk. But he was acting quite in character in seeking to intimidate Jesus that He might leave his territory. For this Herod, though a wicked man who could be utterly ruthless to gain his own ends (as shown in his divorce of his own wife, his marriage with his brother's wife, his imprisonment of the Baptist, if not in his order to have him executed), seems to have acted chiefly out of fear. For besides the fears which developed out of his political insecurity (due to his rivalry with Philip, the changing moods of the people, and especially the necessity of pleasing a succession of emperors, his failure in which led ultimately in A.D. 39 to his banishment to Gaul), there were the fears of his bad conscience. Knowing that the Baptist was a holy and righteous man, he had feared to put him to death (Mk. vi. 20). Later, when reports of Jesus' activity reached his ears, his evil conscience produced the interpretation that John had risen from the dead and 'therefore do these powers work in him' (Mk. vi. 14; Mt. xiv. 1 f.). Only when Jesus was finally arrested, and Pilate sent Jesus to him, could the cowardly bully be more or less at ease. For, as Luke alone reports,

> 'When Herod saw Jesus, he was exceeding glad; for he was of a long time desirous to see Him, because he had heard

concerning Him; and he hoped to see some miracle done by Him. And he questioned him in many words; but He answered him nothing. And the chief priests and the scribes stood, vehemently accusing Him. And Herod with his soldiers set Him at nought, and mocked Him, and arraying Him in gorgeous apparel sent him back to Pilate. And Herod and Pilate became friends with each other that very day; for before they were at enmity between themselves.'

(Lk. xxiii. 8-12.)

Antipas, accordingly, was a man who was deeply disturbed by the presence and activity of Jesus within his realm, for Jesus was a threat to his own security and a disturber of his peace of mind. He was entirely capable of uttering murderous threats though he seemed to lack the courage to deal summarily with the situation.[1]

That the intimidating threat of Herod should have been conveyed to Jesus by the Pharisees is also quite singular but altogether credible. In view of the constant evidences of tension between them, the Pharisees can hardly be regarded as having suddenly become friends of Jesus. Moreover, Jesus does not thank them, but treats them as if they were agents of Herod, and sends them back to him as if to say that He recognized that they were virtually associated with Herod in wishing that He might be killed. In complete consistency with the testimony of the Gospels as a whole, they may be understood as urging Jesus to leave Galilee either to weaken His cause in Galilee or to secure the advantage of His presence in Judæa where their own hostile power could be marshalled more effectively against Him through the activity of the Jewish Sanhedrin.[2]

Consequently, at the very time that Jesus of set purpose was shaping His ministry in terms of its climax at Jerusalem, the hostile secular and religious forces combined to seek to hasten Him on His way. In that peculiar situation, if Jesus allowed His course of action to be interpreted as influenced in the slightest

---

[1] This narrative provides incidental confirmation of the conclusions reached with regard to Lk. xvii. 11, since Antipas ruled over Galilee and Peræa. Inasmuch as the Lucan testimony excludes Peræa, Luke is implying that Jesus was still in Galilee.

[2] See 'Who Crucified Jesus?' in WThJ, V. 2 (May, 1943), pp. 137 ff., a discussion of Zeitlin's book with that title.

degree by such pressure, there would have been an obscuring of the decisive consideration that He was to go to Jerusalem completely apart from any outward constraint, but only because He freely and sovereignly, as His Anointed, undertook to do so in submission to the will of God. Accordingly, the first portion of Jesus' reply to Herod takes the form of a calm defiance of his threat.

Characterizing Herod as 'that fox,' and displaying neither fear of nor respect for him, Jesus lays bare the subterfuge and craft which he was employing. He first invites Herod to consider His works, the works which must have been known to Herod, for they had led him to conjecture fearfully that John the Baptist had risen from the dead: 'Go and say to that fox, Behold I cast out demons and perform cures today and tomorrow.' These works, the more so because Herod was not prepared to deny their genuineness, should have led him to repentance and restrained him from his evil course of sinning against his conscience as he had done in the case of the Baptist. There may, therefore, have been in these words a rebuke which should have compelled Herod to recognize that Jesus had done nothing worthy of death. Their main impact lies, however, in a different direction. For Jesus is insisting particularly that *He has work to do and that, despite Herod's threats, His work will go on*, not only 'today' but 'tomorrow.' He will not bring His mission to an abrupt close or seek to flee from Herod's domain.

The sovereign self-assurance of Jesus expressed here is unintelligible apart from the recognition of His consciousness of messianic authority. His work is not done by Herod's leave. There is a compulsion that transcends political pressure and the constraint of expediency. One is reminded of the manner in which Jesus had previously centred attention upon His works as evidence of His messianic authority when the Baptist had inquired from prison whether he was the one that should come:

> 'Go and tell John the things which ye have seen and heard; the blind receive their sight, the lame walk, the lepers are cleansed, and the deaf hear, the dead are raised up, the poor have the good tidings preached to them' (Lk. vii. 22 f.; Mt. xi. 4 f.).

If Herod had had ears to hear, he would have acknowledged that He whom he would fain have killed had come with divine authority and power.

But besides the public activity, which Jesus says must go on, He also points to the consummation of His life when he adds, 'And on the third day I finish my course.'[1] The thought evidently is that there is assurance that He will reach the end, or goal, of His ministry. Though Herod would fain secure His death to bring a catastrophic end to His ministry, Jesus considers His death as a consummation which is to be reached at exactly the proper and determined time. To interpret the reference to the 'third' day literally of the interval before the death of Christ would place Luke in hopeless contradiction with himself in the rest of the Gospel. Moreover, since Jesus is evidently speaking figuratively in declaring that His work would go on 'today and tomorrow,' His further statement concerning the consummation of His ministry as finding place on the 'third' day may not be fairly forced into a precise chronological framework. This reference to future developments, in spite of its indefiniteness, nevertheless serves to express the thought that a definite, prescribed time is in view, which will not be abbreviated or modified by threats. But since the period is measured in terms of days, Jesus appears to be intimating that the consummation is not far distant. He will not arrive at His goal before the appointed time, but He is marching forward with firm and rapid pace to the end.[2]

The message of Jesus to Herod does not conclude, however, on

---

[1] The ARmg and RSV take the form as a middle, and translate as 'end my course' and 'finish my course' respectively. The RV has 'I am perfected.' The passive is somewhat less appropriate in the context, which stresses Jesus' *activity*.

One is reminded of Hebrews ii. 10 (cf. v. 9, vii. 28) where Jesus is declared to be made perfect through sufferings. To read the distinctive teaching of Hebrews into this saying of Jesus is surely too bold. Moreover, in Hebrews the 'perfecting' is viewed as a process of extensive duration, while here it relates only to the climax on 'the third day.' The notion that Hebrews and this Lucan passage alike have in view the idea of 'bringing Christ to the full moral perfection of His humanity,' as Plummer says in dependence upon Westcott, misses the point that Hebrews has in view the qualification of Christ to be a sympathetic priest. The New Testament nowhere supports the conception of a moral evolution of Jesus to a state of perfection.

[2] There is no necessity of resorting to the hypothesis of primitive textual corruption, as Wellhausen does, if the language is not construed in an unnecessarily literal fashion. Creed appears to share Wellhausen's outlook.

FROM GALILEE TO JERUSALEM

the note that Christ quite sovereignly and freely, regardless of human hatred and intimidations, will accomplish His mission and Himself write '*telos*' as the last word. For there is another motif in the Gospel, that of the necessity of the submission of the Servant of the Lord to the divine will. This motif receives somewhat distinctive expression when Jesus adds, 'Nevertheless I must go on My way today and tomorrow and the day following; for it cannot be that a prophet perish out of Jerusalem.' The Pharisees had said, 'Get thee out and go hence,' and Jesus had uttered His defiance. But now He admits that He must go to Jerusalem. The departure which the Pharisees suggested and Herod evidently had in view will inevitably take place but because of a stronger necessity than that of the decree or whims of tyrants.

This procession to Jerusalem must take place 'today, and tomorrow and the day following' and thus, like the carrying forward of His work to the appointed goal, will take place in the immediate future. Coincident with the active discharge of His mission there will be a constant facing towards the city where His decease would be accomplished.[1]

Although, then, the necessity of Jesus' march to Jerusalem as expressed at this time appears to echo other solemn utterances of the divine necessity of the passion, a somewhat different direction appears to be given to the argument in the words, 'For it cannot be that a prophet perish out of Jerusalem.' These words introduce an historical consideration as requiring His death at Jerusalem: not the working of an inexorable divine purpose, but rather an ironical and paradoxical consideration which centres attention upon the strange workings of the sinful heart of man. Jerusalem, the Holy City, the city where Jesus comes to manifest His glory and authority, over which He now pours out His heart in tender yearning, once again would have to experience its infamous distinction of being a murderer of the prophets! Not Galilee or Peræa, the domain of Herod, but Jerusalem, where a Roman procurator sits in judgment and where the Jewish Sanhedrin convenes, would be the scene of His death. There is therefore no mitigation of

[1] If Luke's language in verse 33 were meant to be taken literally he would apparently contradict his use of similar language in verse 32, for in the former instance He reaches His end on the third day and in the latter He is still going to Jerusalem on the day following 'today and tomorrow.' In both expressions Jesus is employing concrete but figurative language.

human guilt, no sanction of the action of those who would put Him to death, but a pointing to the inevitability that human sin should conspicuously display its own perversity. But even this perversity is subservient to the fulfilment of the divine purpose which compelled Jesus, in submission to Him who had sent Him, to go up to Jerusalem.

The recognition that the passion was to be explained basically in terms of the fulfilment of the divine plan, and yet in its historical realization would also manifest the enormity of human sin and guilt, came to even sharper focus later on. For at the last supper, in calling attention to the presence of the betrayer at the table, Jesus declared that 'the Son of Man goeth as it hath been determined; but woe unto that man through whom He is betrayed!' (xxii. 22). And Peter on the Day of Pentecost, in proclaiming Jesus of Nazareth, said: 'Him, being delivered up by the determinate counsel and foreknowledge of God, ye by the hand of lawless men did crucify and slay' (Acts ii. 23; cf. iv. 27 f.). But this perspective upon the messianic programme has been present from the beginning of explicit reflection upon the passion. It was conspicuously present in the solemn declarations concerning the necessity that the Son of Man should suffer many things and be betrayed into the hands of men, which, as has been noted, were intimately associated with the confession of Peter (ix. 22; cf. ix. 44). And even more vividly was it reiterated in the declaration of Lk. xviii. 31 ff., reported as having been uttered shortly before the arrival at Jericho:

> 'And He took unto Him the twelve, and said unto them Behold, we go up to Jerusalem, and all the things that are written by the prophets shall be accomplished unto the Son of Man. For He shall be delivered up unto the Gentiles, and shall be mocked, and shamefully entreated, and spit upon; and they shall scourge and kill Him: and the third day He shall rise again.'

In these sayings there appears, perhaps as an undertone, the note that the manner in which men treated Jesus, who as the Son of Man should have been accorded divine honours, was a shocking disclosure of the utter wickedness of the human heart.[1]

---

[1] Cf. G. Vos, *The Self-Disclosure of Jesus*, 1926, pp. 238 f.

COMPARISON WITH MARK

The survey of the middle chapters of Luke provides a useful background for the consideration of the harmony of the Lucan narrative with the data of Mark. In an earlier connection brief mention was made of the common judgment that Luke's distinctive middle section is reporting a Peræan ministry, to which Mark is thought to allude in x. 1. Since, however, as Lk. xvii. 11 particularly shows, Jesus is still at a late point on the borders of Samaria and Galilee, this evangelist cannot be thinking in terms of a Peræan ministry. Harmonization cannot be achieved, therefore, by the simple expedient of fitting this section into the framework of Mk. x. 1.

Do the Lucan references to Samaria, however, conflict with the Marcan representation concerning the transition from Galilee to Judæa? That might appear to be the case if Mark, as is often supposed, implies that the journey from Galilee to Judæa followed a route through Peræa along the eastern side of the Jordan. Though Mk. x. 1 may, as Swete says, have in view 'a considerable journey,' there is nothing to suggest that the journey was wholly or largely through Peræa; the passage teaches only that in connection with the journey he *arrived* in Peræa. This remains true also on the widely accepted western reading, 'Judæa beyond the Jordan,'[1] although the received text, in mentioning Judæa before Peræa, would add to the difficulty of construing the reference as a *journey through* Peræa. Actually Mark tells us nothing concerning the route by which Jesus travelled from Galilee to the South.[2]

Burkitt is particularly ingenious in suggesting a harmonization at this point.[3] Jesus is allowed, following Luke, to have travelled through Samaria, and it is supposed, in view of the mention of James and John in Lk. ix. 54, that they alone accompanied Him. But Peter and some other disciples took the eastern route through Peræa. And Mk. x. 1 was written from the point of view of Peter's observations (upon which Mark was dependent): he observes Jesus arriving in 'Judæa beyond the Jordan,' that is, on the *western* side of the river. Then the Peræan ministry would vanish

---

[1] E.g., by Wellhausen, Burkitt, *Gospel History and Its Transmission*, 1906, p. 96; Branscomb (MC).
[2] Cf. Rawlinson, ad loc.   [3] Op. cit., pp. 96 f.

in thin air. This theory, however, apart from its generally conjectural character, is under the severe burden of its assumption that 'beyond the Jordan' might well be understood of the area west of the Jordan.

Since, accordingly, Mark is silent concerning the course of Jesus' journey from Galilee to southern Palestine, the problem of the framework of the Lucan narrative is greatly relieved. But the question remains whether, assuming that Mk. x. 1 does not give the setting for Luke's middle chapters, this Gospel does not afford other points of contact with Luke. As a matter of fact, Mark's account does not fall simply into two sharply distinct divisions, the one Galilean and the other Judæan, without a transition from the one to the other. Although Galilee is finally left behind only at the end of Mk. ix, *the actual withdrawal begins much earlier.* The turning point in the narrative is found in the departure to the regions of Caesarea Philippi (Mk. viii. 27). Nevertheless, afterwards we hear of Jesus' passing through Galilee (ix. 30) and of activity in Capernaum (ix. 33 ff.). Lk. ix. 18-50 closely parallels Mk. viii. 27-ix. 50, and though Luke does not state where these events took place, the contents of the section, as noted above, indicate fully as emphatically as the Marcan account that they form a significant part of the story of the way to the cross at Jerusalem. Lk. ix. 51 ff. then provides us not so much with an account of a new phase and locality of Jesus' ministry as with a supplement to the meagre account found in Mark of the new stage inaugurated by Jesus' solemn pronouncement of His coming passion and resurrection. The activity on the way through Galilee, which Mark explicitly mentions in ix. 30, and the ministry along the borders of Samaria and Galilee, referred to by Luke in xvii. 11, may accordingly be viewed as parts of a larger whole, namely, the ministry in Galilee and northern Samaria which was undertaken in connection with the Lord's approach to the climactic events at Jerusalem.

On the background of these observations, one may observe how baseless the charge is that Luke has introduced Galilean materials into a non-Galilean framework. We have observed that, strictly speaking, there is no exclusively non-Galilean framework within this section. Therefore there is no good reason for doubting that reports of the hostility of Herod Antipas may have reached

Jesus as he was passing along the borders of Samaria and Galilee (Lk. xiii. 31, xvii. 11). Nor, unless it can be proved that the journey to Jerusalem was a direct one, without any stops in the cities and villages along the way, is there any improbability in the statement that 'He was teaching in one of the *synagogues* on the sabbath (Lk. xiii. 10). It might possibly be surprising to find contact with the Pharisees in the heart of Samaria, but no difficulty is created by the references in Lk. xi. 37 and xiv. 1 if Jesus was still on the Galilean frontier. The 'throngs' referred to in Lk. xi. 29, xii. 1, and xiv. 25, provide a picture which admittedly agrees ill with the notion that Jesus, accompanied only by the inner circle of disciples and perhaps a few others, went post-haste towards Jerusalem. Mark's account indeed concentrates one's attention so exclusively upon the passion of Christ, and upon the intimate disclosures to and reactions of the disciples, that there is little consideration of anything else.[1] Nevertheless, for Mark too, Jesus is not isolated from the crowds: they are about Jesus after the descent from the Mount of Transfiguration (Mk. ix. 14), and again there are crowds present when He teaches in Judæa (x. 1).[2]

---

[1] Cf. WMMC, pp. 37 f., 44 ff., 80, 118.

[2] Besides the charge that Luke creates discrepancies by introducing various situations that are not congruous with the notion of a journey, there is the more general claim that many of the discourses have been transported arbitrarily from 'Q' into this new framework. On the question of the existence of 'Q,' it is worthwhile to consider the viewpoint of Ropes, *The Synoptic Gospels*, pp. 37, 93, and Enslin, *Christian Beginnings*, 1938, pp. 431 ff.

The likelihood that Jesus frequently repeated His teaching in substantially the same form has been noted above. There is no compelling reason, for example, why Jesus would not have repeated at some later time His defence against the Beelzebub charge (cf. Mt. xii. 22 ff.; Mk. iii. 20 ff.; Lk. xi. 14 ff.).

CHAPTER VII

DEATH AND RESURRECTION

IN view of all that has gone before, as the preceding chapter particularly recalls, Luke's record of what actually happened at Jerusalem does not appear anticlimactic. The story of the passion and death of Christ, as of His resurrection, is presented as the accomplishment of the divine purpose. And Jesus Himself is not merely passive in the developments leading to the goal. Since the knowledge of the divine will controls His thought of His mission, He actively and self-consciously labours to bring about the destined consummation. In these respects, in spite of the different disposition of the Lucan narrative of the public ministry, there is profound agreement with the perspectives of the other Gospels. And, speaking broadly, there is basic agreement also in the records of what actually took place after Jesus had entered Jerusalem. Nevertheless there are features of Luke's closing chapters that have been viewed in modern times as pointing to a strikingly independent testimony concerning the actual course of events and their meaning for the understanding of Christianity. Their evaluation will chiefly occupy our attention in this chapter. Questions relating to structure will not be neglected, but the principal concern will be the meaning of the events themselves as that is disclosed by the teaching of Jesus.

By common consent Luke does not provide any specific knowledge as to the duration of the ministry in Jerusalem. Mark, and to a somewhat lesser extent Matthew, provide a rather clearer picture of the events of the several days of the week following the entry into the city. But even Mark does not indicate precisely the transition from day to day after the second day of the week, and he cannot fairly be regarded as aiming to offer a complete outline of the events of each day.[1] Nevertheless, the general vagueness of Luke is in remarkable contrast to the explicitness of Mark at many points.

Whereas Mark is careful to delineate the progress of events on the first day after the entry into the city, Luke virtually

[1] Cf. WMMC, p. 35.

supplies only a summary of the activity of Jesus there (Lk. xix. 47 f.). It is of moment that he omits altogether any reference to the incident of the cursing of the fig tree, and describes the cleansing of the temple with the utmost brevity (xix. 45 f.). Since Luke does not even refer explicitly to Jesus' entry into the city, it is unwarranted to state, as Creed does,[1] that on His entry Jesus 'proceeds at once' to the temple and expels the traders (cf. xix. 45). The casting out of the traders obviously presupposes Jesus' presence in the city, and it is the first incident mentioned by Luke which does so, but so far as the evangelist's own language is concerned this event might have occurred some time after His arrival.

The summary character of Luke's account is observed especially in the references to His teaching daily in the temple. The extensive record of the teaching given in Lk. xx and xxi, and described as delivered 'on one of the days, as He was teaching the people in the temple, and preaching the gospel' (xx. 1) finds close parallels to the teaching recorded in Matthew and Mark. But it is evidently intended to illustrate Jesus' teaching during the last days in Jerusalem, for it is presented as a kind of parenthesis between the references in Lk. xix. 47 and xxi. 37 to His custom of teaching daily in the temple.

An even more telling proof of Luke's relative lack of concern for a precise chronological outline of the events immediately preceding the crucifixion is disclosed by the manner in which the passion story is introduced. Whereas Matthew and Mark both begin with the intimation that the feast of the passover and of the unleavened bread was 'two days' away, Luke is content merely to state that it 'drew nigh' (Lk. xxii. 1; cf. Mt. xxvi. 2; Mk. xiv. 1). Omitting the anointing at Bethany, Luke centres attention upon the manner in which Judas, through Satanic inspiration, solved the problem confronting the Jewish rulers by promising to betray Jesus in the absence of the multitude (Lk. xxii. 2-6). Nevertheless, Luke as explicitly as the other Gospels associates the final developments with the celebration of the feast.

R. H. Lightfoot, in connection with his theory that, because of Luke's conception of Jesus as the Messiah, the lawful king of Israel, Jerusalem is viewed as the goal and culminating scene of

[1] Op. cit., p. 239.

activity, argues that the indefiniteness of Luke in such passages as xx. 1 and xxii. 1 offers further proof of his theory since the ministry in Jerusalem, rather than being marked off as lasting less than a week, thus appears to be of 'indeterminate duration.'[1] Apart from other objections to which this theory is subject, it seems particularly far-fetched to appeal to the indefiniteness of the duration of the activity of Jesus in Jerusalem in view of the accumulation of evidence that throughout the Gospel Luke again and again displays a remarkable lack of interest in chronological details.

So far as the rest of the passion narrative is concerned, no acute problems of order and locality present themselves. Luke continues at various points to be less definite than the other synoptics. The last supper begins 'when the hour was come,' not, as the other accounts state more explicitly, 'when it was evening' (Lk. xxii. 14; Mt. xxvi. 20; Mk. xiv. 17). Luke agrees with the others in stating that after the supper Jesus went unto the Mount of Olives (although Luke adds 'according to His custom'), but the particular place, identified by the other evangelists as Gethsemane, is left unnamed (Lk. xxii. 39 f.; cf. xxi. 37; Mt. xxvi. 30 ff.; Mk. xiv. 26 ff.). In the account of Jesus' appearance before Herod, reported only in Luke, the occasion is given as the charge before Pilate that Jesus 'stirreth up the people, teaching throughout all Judæa, and beginning from Galilee even unto this place' (Lk. xxiii. 5). But this provides no new information concerning the scope of the ministry in and around Jerusalem. Here as on other occasions 'Judæa' evidently means Palestine, the land of the Jews,[2] and 'this place' must be Jerusalem. The impact of the charge was to the effect that Jesus had created far more than a local disturbance, one that involved even Galilee.

THE MEANING OF CHRIST'S DEATH

There are two outstanding facts which are largely responsible for the judgment that Luke presents a perspective with regard to the significance of the death of Christ remarkably divergent from

---

[1] Cf. *Locality and Doctrine*, p. 141; cf. pp. 139 ff. I have shown that the theory is not well established so far as Mark is concerned. Cf. WMMC, pp. 38 ff. See also Chapter V, p. 96, note 1.

[2] See above, Ch. V, p. 96.

that found in the other synoptics. The first of these is that Luke fails to mention the 'ransom' saying reported in Mt. xx. 28 and Mk. x. 45, though in other respects he seems to parallel rather closely the contexts in which this saying is found. And the second fact is that Lk. xxii. 19b, 20, which contains the teaching that the cup is 'the new covenant in my blood which is poured out for you,' is judged by many textual critics today to be an interpolation.[1] Since it it these two passages which offer the most positive evidence that Jesus conceived of His death in terms of redemptive sacrifice, their omission from the Gospel according to Luke might point to a divergent view of the death of Christ or at least to a somewhat different emphasis with regard to it.

Evaluating these conclusions in relation to the other Lucan data, William Manson sums up the results by stating that 'on this view Luke's original text, following his Judæan source, made the Supper a prophecy of the Messianic banquet and a symbol of the disciples' fellowship with Christ, but not a representation of His sacrifice or a channel by which the results of that sacrifice are communicated.'[2] Recognizing the distinctiveness of the Lucan teaching in such terms, one might still allow that this evangelist supplements the other accounts rather than contradicts them. But in the modern situation one rarely encounters such a total judgment concerning the diversity of the witness of the records but rather an approach which is assured of basic discrepancies in the tradition and its interpretation and seeks to evaluate the origin of the various traditions within the development of Christianity as a whole. In this instance, that is characteristically true, for Luke is widely thought to display a distinctive theological point of view

---

[1] Hort's discussion in Westcott and Hort, *The New Testament in Greek*, 1882, Vol. II, Notes on Selected Readings, pp. 63 f., is the most basic argument for the view that Lk. xxii. 19b, 20 is an interpolation. The WH text, however, retains this passage as does RV, though the margin indicates that 'some ancient authorities omit' the passage. The RSV, on the other hand, omits the passage, and states in the margin that 'many ancient authorities add' it. The latter view is in keeping with the thrust of modern opinion, represented, for example, by Plummer, Easton, Creed, Wellhausen, B. Weiss, J. Weiss, Zahn and Klostermann. On the other side, cf. especially A. H. McNeile, *The Gospel according to St. Matthew*, 1915, pp. 385 f.; H. J. Holtzmann, *Die Synoptiker* (HC), 1901, p. 409; M. J. Lagrange, *Evangile selon Saint Luc*,[7] 1948, pp. 545 ff.; S. Greijdanus, *Lucas* (KNT), II, 1941, pp. 1045 ff.; *Lucas* (KV), II, 1941, pp. 217 f.

[2] Op. cit., p. 242.

and to present a quite independent conception of the origin of the Lord's Supper.[1]

The longer reading of Luke is omitted by Codex Bezae and certain manuscripts of the Old Latin versions, and thus belongs to a group of passages, mostly in the latter part of Luke's Gospel, which Hort grouped together as 'Western non-interpolations.' While recognizing the epochal significance of the work of Hort in the field of textual criticism, it is well to observe that the conclusions reached with regard to these passages as a group are not nearly so securely established as other basic features of that system, which themselves have been widely recognized as not allowing sufficiently for the weight of intrinsic considerations in individual cases. Streeter, for example, though still agreeing largely with the final conclusions of Westcott and Hort, challenged the propriety of setting as high a value upon any one form of text as they did, and in particular insisted that each of the so-called Western non-interpolations had to be judged on its own merits.[2] Accordingly, the fact of the absence of the words in question from D and certain allies cannot be regarded as particularly meaningful unless most weighty arguments compel the decision that the Western reading is the original.

It is precisely in the sphere of internal evidence, however, that many modern scholars judge that the case for the omission is particularly strong. In the first place, it is observed that the longer text involves the extraordinary situation that Luke has already in verse 17 referred to a dispensing of the cup, and thus the cup of verse 20, the passage in question, would be a second cup, and this reading is thought to be intrinsically difficult because of the resultant complexity of the representation of the course of events.[3] And in the second place, the origin of the longer reading is explained as due to the incorporation of language from I Cor.

[1] Creed, op. cit., p. 265, suggests that perhaps this element was 'not entirely congenial' to Luke himself; cf. pp. lxxi f., 261 ff. W. Manson, op. cit., p. xxv, regards the omission of the ransom saying as 'doubtless accidental'. He says further that 'theological interests were not paramount in the mind of Luke' and that 'his leaning is towards the emotional and practical aspects of religion, towards the elements of feeling and action.' Cf. also Cadbury, *Making*, pp. 280 f.

[2] Cf. op. cit., pp. 318, 330, 553 n. He does not express a final judgment on Lk. xxii. 19b, 20, though he seems sympathetic to Hort's conclusion. Cf. p. 553 n.

[3] Cf. Wellhausen, op. cit., p. 122: '. . . es kann doch nicht ein Mahl sofort auf das andere gesetzt und zweimal gegessen und getrunken werden.'

xi. 24, 25 at a time when the Lucan account would have been considered unsatisfactory as placing the cup before the breaking of the bread and defective because of the absence of the sacrificial feature. On the other hand, there is said to be no adequate explanation of the omission of the words on the understanding that the longer text was the original.[1]

These considerations do not, however, carry the weight, in my judgment, that is often assigned to them. In brief, my impression is that Luke's account, on the supposition that the longer text is Lucan, although containing some distinctive features, is characterized by intrinsic intelligibility and consistency. Such difficulties as appear are comparatively superficial and largely vanish in the light of exegetical and archæological investigation. On the other hand, the shorter text, though its divergences from the longer are commonly exaggerated, presents a substantially different conception of the Supper which is beset by insuperable exegetical and historical obstacles.

That the advocates of the shorter text generally stress the distinctiveness of Luke's representation of the Supper is hardly a matter of argument. This appears, for example, from the fact that the longer text is commonly regarded as the product of a process of harmonization which resulted when the need was felt of bringing Luke into line with records of the institution of the Supper. Creed, for example, holds that Luke did not think of the last Supper as 'a proclamation of the death of Christ according to a rite instituted by Jesus' but as simply one occasion among many of 'breaking bread.' Although Luke is thought not to reflect a primitive source, he is said to write 'in an age when Christian rites and institutions are still in a fluid state' and 'no fixed interpretation has become normative.'[2] There thus comes to expression a deep-seated scepticism with regard to the historicity of the

---

[1] Easton, op. cit., p. 321, makes the point that while the omission of verse 20 might be explained by its reference to a second cup, the omission of verse 19b would not thus be accounted for. R. Otto, *The Kingdom of God and the Son of Man*, n.d., c. 1938, says: 'The phenomenon is easily explained if these words were originally lacking, and were later supplied from the other accounts, especially from Paul; but if these words had stood originally in Luke, we cannot explain why they could have been omitted later by anyone, while all the other accounts were left uncontested. But that means that the original text of Luke did not contain these words.'

[2] Op. cit., p. 262.

institution of the sacrament of the Lord's Supper, as well as a judgment that it is quite credible that Luke should have published a representation of the last Supper sharply at variance with that of the other accounts.

Although the scepticism which comes to expression at this point is not isolated from a broader scepticism with regard to the testimony of the New Testament writings regarding Christ and the origins of Christianity, I must be content here with pointing out that it is hardly likely that a radical divergence of viewpoint with regard to the institution of the Lord's Supper would have developed in the early church. In particular, considering the association of Luke with the apostle Paul and his opportunities of information regarding the life of the church of his day, it is incredible that he would have been unacquainted with the practice of the church as Paul reports it in 1 Cor. xi. 23 ff., and would have published a contradictory version of it. For Paul's testimony, it should be observed, concerns not the observance of a segment of the church as that had developed several decades after the death of Christ, but a view which he must have taught and maintained throughout his Christian career and which he insists is clothed with the authority of the Lord Himself. Like the doctrine of the resurrection of Christ, this is hardly a matter on which Paul would have differed substantially from the other apostles (cf. 1 Cor. xv. 11). Quite apart from the common testimony of the Gospels, therefore, there is good reason to conclude that there must have been in the early church a normative tradition and interpretation. So if Luke's association with the apostle Paul were less intimate than the evidence appears to demand, and even if the Lucan authorship of this Gospel were rejected, it would still not follow that the author of Luke-Acts, who at so many points gives proof of his competence to report Christian tradition accurately, would have been likely to go astray on this feature of Christian worship.[1]

---

[1] *Didache* 9 mentions the cup before the broken bread, and does not specifically associate the death of Christ with the Eucharist. Thus it is thought to have points of contact with the Lucan representation according to the Western Text as well as to point to the flexibility of observance at the close of the first century. Cf. Creed, op. cit., pp. 262, 265.

The *Didache* account is indeed distinctive. As a matter of fact, the broken bread, as well as the cup, is not referred to the death of Christ, and hence it differs

Most earnest consideration must be given, therefore, to the possibility that the textual variation is the result of a scribal error of omission. The ancient scribes were not distinguished for their archæological knowledge or their exegetical penetration, and hence they often stumbled over superficial difficulties and fashioned 'easier' readings. May that not be the case here? May not the second reference to the cup have been confusing to a second century scribe who knew only of the single cup in the other accounts and of the single cup employed in the current Christian observance of the sacrament? That the double cup would have been disconcerting to some early Christians is shown from the fact that the Syriac Peshitto Version solves the problem by omitting verses 17 and 18, an excision which had the advantage of preserving essentially intact the Pauline form. But one can quite easily imagine that an early scribe, acting with less conscious deliberation, might rather clumsily have removed the reference to the second cup.[1]

That which might have confused a scribe would, however, have been altogether intelligible to one who was acquainted with the Jewish celebration of the passover. There can be no question that Luke is underscoring the fact that the Passover was the occasion of whatever was taught and done that was new and distinctive. Among modern scholars who have been concerned with the problem of the date of the death of Christ, there has developed the view that certain data of Matthew and Mark may best be understood on the supposition that the occasion was prior to the Passover. But no one can doubt that Luke is depicting the occasion as the Passover meal. For example, he reports Jesus as saying, after He had sat down with the apostles, 'With desire I

---

essentially from Luke at this point. But the testimony of the *Didache*, in spite of its claims, does not possess the historic or normative significance of Lucan tradition. On the credibility of its picture of the apostolic practice, cf. J. Armitage Robinson, *Barnabas, Hermas and the Didache*, 1920, pp. 97 ff., and my *The Apocalypse in the Ancient Church*, 1929, pp. 31 ff.

[1] This would not explain why the concluding words of verse 19 ('which is given for you. Do this in remembrance of me'), words which relate to the bread rather than to the cup, would also have been omitted. See note 3, p. 132. Nevertheless, it seems easier to suppose that a scribe did not make a smooth excision than that Luke, with his fine sense of language and style, would have left verse 19 in the abrupt and awkward state which is admittedly present on the interpolation hypothesis.

have desired to eat this passover with you before I suffer' (xxii. 15).[1] Matthew and Mark concentrate so fully upon the new transactions of the occasion—in stating that it was 'while they were eating' (Mt. xxvi. 26; Mk. xiv. 22) that Jesus instituted the Christian sacrament in His monumental declarations—that the traditional elements of the Jewish passover hardly come to view at all. But may not the greater detail of Luke's account be due to the fact that he is sketching in certain preliminary features of the occasion? As Billerbeck has shown, the first reference to thanksgiving and the giving of *a* cup may provide further evidence that the Lord's Supper was instituted in the course of the passover meal, which, judged by the rabbinic tradition, was by no means restricted to a single cup.[2] Luke, writing in the first century, with abundant opportunity to inform himself concerning the institution of the Supper in Jerusalem, as well as the contemporaneous practices of Judaism, could thus in his account reflect on the historical situation while scribes of a later day might have stumbled at the additional features which were not a part of the Christian observance.

An even more weighty argument concerns the state of the shorter text on the supposition that it was the original. Lk. xxii. 15-18 is beautifully integrated and symmetrical: Jesus speaks of His intense desire to eat the passover before He suffers, but then points to its fulfilment in the kingdom of God; He distributes a cup which He had received, and likewise points to a future action of like character when the kingdom should come. But 19a, which says, 'And He took bread, and when He had given thanks, He brake it, and gave to them, saying, This is my body,' followed by a reference to the presence of the betrayer at the table, leaves the mention of the breaking of the bread, and the reference to His body, hanging in the air. No wonder that several advocates of the interpolation hypothesis conjecture that verse 19a should be deleted, even though there is not a particle of external evidence favouring the omission.[3]

---

[1] E.g., Creed says that Luke 'gives a definitely Paschal colouring to the Supper itself.' Op. cit., p. 265.

[2] Cf. SBK, IV, p. 75. Pesahim X (*The Babylonian Talmud*, ed. by I. Epstein, 1938, p. 532; cf. pp. 560 ff.) declares that the participant should be given 'not less than four cups'.

[3] E.g. Wellhausen; Blass, op. cit., pp. 179 f. Klostermann allows for this view.

Creed's approach to this situation is most illuminating. He frankly admits that verse 19a 'undoubtedly makes an awkward and abrupt conclusion to the verses preceding' but chiefly because of its presence in all the MSS. and versions does not feel prepared to reject them as an addition.[1] The best argument that Creed can offer, however, in support of his view that Luke retained these words from Mark in spite of the fact that, on his construction, they do not fit easily into his account of the paschal meal, is that it was a part of the tradition from Mark that 'he was unwilling to disturb.' To say the least, it becomes exceedingly difficult on this basis to secure a clear picture of what Luke is supposed to be about. At one moment this Gospel is judged to be radically differing from Mark's version of the Last Supper, but the next so slavishly conservative that it retains a Marcan feature which deeply disturbs the unity of his main approach!

It might be somewhat easier to account for the retention of 19a if Luke were viewed as less exclusively dependent on Mark than is true on Creed's approach, and this condition is in fact fulfilled by advocates of the Four Document Theory. Vincent Taylor, for example, in dealing at length with this question, admits the abruptness of the shorter text and the distinctiveness of perspectives within Luke's account as a whole, as the result of his use of Mark and other sources, and maintains that first Luke added 19a to the original account found in his source (verses 14-18) and, later, copyists added verses 19b, 20, and these are regarded as 'successive attempts to bring the narrative into line with the Marcan and Pauline stories.'[2] But this remains at best a very doubtful hypothesis. If verse 19a represents Luke's own effort to conform his own special viewpoint to that of Mark and Paul, why did he fall so far short of conforming to them as to fail to include the cup which was identified as 'the new covenant in My blood, which is poured out for you'? Why would he have left his own narrative in such an awkward and unintegrated state?

---

[1] Op. cit., p. 264. He further argues that the position of 19a between verse 16 and verse 17 in the old Latin MSS. b and e does make the words suspect since this peculiar position may be accounted for as due to the desire to assimilate the Lucan account to the other texts (first the bread and then the cup). Moreover, since the words of 19a are in Mark, and Luke used Mark, there is no good ground to regard them as a gloss.

[2] Cf. *Jesus and his Sacrifice*, 1937, p. 176; *Behind the Third Gospel*, pp. 36 ff.

My conclusion, therefore, is that a compelling case for the omission of Lk. xxii. 19b, 20 has not been made. And the difficulties attached to the interpolation hypothesis are so considerable that the rejection of the witness of the type of text usually regarded as superior appears to be quite unjustified. On this view, then, Luke, in common with the other New Testament records which report the institution of the Lord's Supper, reports the teaching of Jesus that through the sacrifice of His body and the shedding of His blood there would be inaugurated a divine covenant transcending the covenant of Sinai, which was also ratified by a sacrifice in which blood was shed.

While the decision regarding the original text of Luke's narrative of the last supper is momentous, it remains doubtful whether, even on the supposition that the shorter text is the original, this Gospel presents an essentially different conception of its meaning. One gets the impression that most supporters of the shorter text have fallen so much under the spell of the impact made by the omission of the reference to the cup, and its redemptive significance, that they have neglected to reflect sufficiently upon the stupendous implications of what Luke is admitted to have set forth in the text which finds universal textual support. In Lk. xxii. 19a, we read that Jesus 'took bread, and when He had given thanks, He broke it, and gave to them, saying, This is My body.' Although, as has been observed, this statement is abrupt, and accordingly presents a serious obstacle to the advocates of the interpolation hypothesis, nevertheless it constitutes a most pregnant utterance concerning the meaning of the death of Christ. For the breaking of the bread, no less unmistakably than the pouring of the cup, points to the violent death which awaited Christ. And Luke is fully as explicit as Matthew and Mark in intimating this fact.

Moreover, Luke, as well as they, declares that Jesus *gave* them the broken bread, and thus discloses that Jesus looked upon His death as that which was undertaken for their sakes. It may not be overlooked that Matthew and Mark make this point without saying that the body of Christ was given on their behalf. Paul is more explicit in reporting that Jesus said, 'This is My body, *which is for you*,' but this does not say anything that is not implicit in the reports of the first two evangelists. And thus also, when the

DEATH AND RESURRECTION

longer text of Luke proceeds to say that the body was 'given for you,' it would be absurd to say that these words, which virtually only echo the declaration that Jesus *gave them* the broken bread, introduce any really new element. All the accounts agree, therefore, in understanding that Christ freely surrendered His body unto death, and that this gift of Himself in death constituted a sacrifice on behalf of His disciples. Regardless, then, of the decision reached with regard to the latter part of verse 19, it may not be affirmed that Luke has dropped the sacrificial language of Mark.[1]

Rudolph Otto, who accepts the shorter text of Luke at this point, must be given credit for recognizing substantially the point just made. Without doubt there are contributing factors bound up with his broader conclusions concerning Christ and the Gospels which affect the decision. These include both his general judgment as to the archaic character of the Lucan testimony and his conclusion that Jesus Himself interpreted His messiahship in terms of the Servant of the Lord concept. But even if these viewpoints are not everywhere acknowledged as salutary, and though one may find good reason for dissenting from other aspects of his construction, he has the merit of construing Lk. xxii. 19a in

---

[1] H. Lietzmann, *Messe und Herrenmahl*, 1926, p. 216, maintains that Luke pictures the supper merely as a breaking of bread and as being concerned with eschatological hopes. Cf. p. 239. See also Creed, op. cit., pp. 262, 265; Klostermann, p. 208. This conception of the supper is also thought to be reflected in Lk. xxiv. 30, 35, where Jesus is recognized in the breaking of the bread, and in Acts ii. 46, where the Christian fellowship is described as including 'breaking bread in their homes.' Lietzmann says that according to the latter passage, the characteristic cultic practice of the Church was the breaking of bread. Back of the final development of thought and practice concerning the Lord's Supper there stand, accordingly, various influences including the continuation of the table fellowship of Jesus and his disciples, represented particularly by Luke, and the specifically sacrificial conception found in the Pauline teaching.

In view of Lk. xxii. 19a, however, which Lietzmann accepts as original (cf. op. cit., p. 216, note 3 against his HB *I Cor.*[2], p. 60), the significance of the language cannot thus be reduced to the eschatological. Moreover, it is over bold to claim on the basis of Acts ii. 46 that, according to Acts, 'the breaking of bread' exhaustively and particularly describes the cultic practice of the Church. References to breaking of bread may on occasion reflect table fellowship with Jesus, but this would not imply that all do so, and still less that Luke is presenting a special version of the cultic practice. Cf. Lk. ix. 16; Acts xx. 7, 11, xxvii. 35. And in view of the fact that the Lord's Supper was evidently observed in intimate connection with the common meals (cf. I Cor. x and xi), one may not safely conclude that the table fellowship of Acts ii. 46, does not allow for the specific celebration of the sacrament in Pauline terms.

terms of Biblical data. He even states that 'the idea of the ransom for many was precisely the meaning of the distribution of the bread and by the act of distributing the meaning had just been fixed', and his general conclusion is that 'all the essential and constitutive elements of the other accounts are contained in the archaic account,' namely in Luke.[1]

The conclusion that Luke found the redemptive interpretation of the death of Christ uncongenial, or that he was indifferent to it, is also contradicted by Luke's report of Paul's address to the Ephesian elders in which he speaks of the church as 'the church of God which He purchased with His own blood' (Acts xx. 28). Cadbury dismisses the passage in a footnote on the ground that 'it is doubtful both in text and interpretation.'[2] Without minimizing the difficulties of the passage, it is my judgment that neither the textual variations nor the uncertainties of interpretation are such as to obscure the conclusion that the blood of Christ was the redemptive price paid for the church. It is not necessary to argue here in support of my view that 'the church of God' means the church of the divine Christ and that Paul means that Christ acquired the church for Himself at the price of His own blood. For even if 'the church of God' were not intended to designate the church as Christ's, we should still be required to understand that the church became God's possession at the price of the blood of His own Son. The reference to Christ is at least as clear if the reading 'Lord' be accepted.[3]

In the light of these facts and considerations, one may therefore not fairly charge Luke with a special bias against or a basic indifference to the subject of the atonement of Christ because of his failure to quote the ransom saying. He is not indeed writing a dogmatic treatise devoted to an exposition of the doctrine of the atonement as that was taught in the church of his day. The speeches in Acts, for example, while highly doctrinal, are basically summaries of public missionary preaching rather than of the instruction of converts. And in his two-volume work he is aiming to present, in broad strokes, the two main stages of the Lord's activity, and thus considerable stress falls upon the external course

---

[1] Op. cit., pp. 172, 175; cf. pp. 266 f., 296. Cf. also Dalman, *Jesus-Jeschua*, 1922. pp. 131 f.
[2] *Making*, p. 280, note 2.   [3] See WMMC, p. 166.

of history. But he would obviously have been quite out of sympathy with the modern notion of the Christian message which allocates to Christ and His history, with its climax in His death and resurrection, at best a peripheral place. He plainly believed not only that Christ brought the gospel but also that He was its principal content. For Luke, Christ was pre-eminently the Saviour who came to seek and to save the lost (xix. 9, 10; cf. ii. 11, i, 69, 71, 77; Acts xiii. 23, xvi. 17). He presents the view of radical intolerance with the thought that there is salvation in any other name (Acts iv. 12). And though there is little that explains exactly how men are saved by the cross of Christ and His glorification through the resurrection, the entire disposition of the Gospel, as well as the record of the preaching in Acts, shows that repentance unto remission of sins was preached to the nations only on the basis of the glad tidings of the crucified and risen Saviour (cf. Lk. xxiv. 46; Acts ii. 38, xiii. 38 f.).

THE RESURRECTION NARRATIVE

Although students of the passion narrative of Luke are divided sharply on the question of its dependence upon Mark, the account of the resurrection is so pervasively distinctive that its independence from Mark, except perhaps for the story of the empty tomb, is taken for granted. Indeed, the chief questions relating to Luke's last chapter rise from the fact that it appears to give a picture of the resurrection events utterly different from that of the other synoptics. Whereas Mark and Matthew centre their attention upon an appearance in Galilee, Luke seems to know only of happenings in Jerusalem and its immediate vicinity. The accounts are not as mutually exclusive as they are sometimes thought to be, for in both Mark and Matthew the scene of the stupendous miracle is Jerusalem, and there is in Matthew besides a record of an appearance to certain women after they had left the scene of the empty tomb.[1] Nevertheless, neither Mark nor

---

[1] Even more basic significance is attached to the belief that the Church originated in Jerusalem by representatives of the 'Jerusalem Hypothesis.' See especially J. Weiss, *Urchristentum*, 1917, pp. 10 ff., 17-71 (*The History of Primitive Christianity*, 1937, I, pp. 14 ff.) and F. C. Burkitt, *Christian Beginnings*, 1924, pp. 76 ff. For evaluation cf. W. P. Armstrong, 'The Place of the Resurrection Appearances of Jesus,' in BTS, 1912, pp. 329-332, and K. Lake in *Christian Beginnings*, II, pp. 170 f.

Matthew contains any intimation of an appearance to the eleven in Jerusalem.

As a corollary of the Galilean Hypothesis, it is commonly maintained that Luke's narrative is clearly secondary. It is thought to have originated some time after the tradition relating to an appearance in Galilee, and to owe its origin to nothing more than the belief that, since Christ was believed to have been raised from the dead, He must have appeared also near the scene of His death. This belief, it is thought, would have found confirmation, if it did not actually originate, from the fact that Jerusalem was regarded as the birthplace of the Christian church. The limits of our present discussion prohibit our undertaking a survey of the history of this hypothesis. It may be recalled, however, that Strauss acutely expressed the problem in the form that, according to one tradition, the disciples are told to go to Galilee in order to see Jesus, whereas, according to the other, they must tarry at Jerusalem.[1] And quite recently, almost exactly one hundred years later, R. H. Lightfoot has written that

> 'all the events narrated in Lk. xxiv between the visit of the women to tomb and the Lord's last parting from the eleven and those that were with them were represented by St. Luke as occurring in or near Jerusalem, and also, we may add, according to the strict letter of the narrative, upon one and the same day, so that as regards both place and time everything set forth in this chapter is brought into very close and intimate connection.... The possibility of manifestations of the risen Christ in Galilee is decisively excluded.'[2]

Does Luke in reality exclude the possibility of appearances of the risen Christ in Galilee? If Lk. xxiv is properly construed as Luke's representation of the history of Christ from the time of the resurrection to the ascension, activity in distant Galilee would seem to be beyond the realm of the conceivable. However, such a simple formulation of the disposition of Lk. xxiv fails to take into adequate account several important considerations. These involve the testimony of Paul, the witness of Luke's own narrative in Acts, and the manifest aims and methods of his own Gospel.

[1] *Das Leben Jesu*, 1840, II, pp. 588 f., 606 ff. (Eng. trans., III, pp. 327 f., 343 f.)
[2] *Locality and Doctrine*, pp. 78 f.

DEATH AND RESURRECTION 143

In the first place, the apostle Paul, in setting forth the gospel which he had received, indicates that according to the earliest known Christian tradition there were many appearances of the risen Lord. With this tradition in view it is unreasonable to suppose that Luke, or any other of the evangelists, was intending to list all the manifestations of the risen Christ which were generally known. The basic significance of the Pauline testimony to the resurrection of Christ is recognized by critics of the Gospel narratives, and it is often alleged that Paul proves some of the testimony of the Gospels to be in error. But is justice done to the impact of Paul's witness to the primitive tradition concerning the resurrection? If Paul were reporting his own individual faith and experience merely, or were only recording an isolated tradition, the situation would be different. But the fact is that he claims to present Christian tradition which was current as early as the days of his own first contacts immediately after his conversion with the Christian church, the church of the apostles, the church which recognized Jerusalem as its centre.[1] And since Luke was not isolated from Paul or that church, there is in advance a strong improbability in the supposition that his brief account in Lk. xxiv is presented as a summary of the known facts.

Nor, in the second place, has Luke's own account in Acts i been allowed its due weight by those who have insisted that Lk. xxiv excludes more than a single day's appearances at the scene of Christ's death. Although 'the former treatise' included in its scope 'all that Jesus began both to do and to teach until the day in which He was received up,' and the Acts is basically occupied with the activity of the exalted Lord through the Holy Spirit whom He sent forth on the day of Pentecost, the line is not drawn so sharply at the ascension as to exclude reflection within Acts upon the final events of the historical career of Christ upon earth. Thus the references to the resurrection and to the ascension of Christ in Acts i serve to centre attention upon the future programme of the Lord but also supplement in a significant manner the knowledge of the things which Jesus did 'until the day in which He was received up.' The ascension is given the briefest reference at the close of Luke, but is set forth with considerable explicitness in Acts. Similarly, the

[1] Cf. I Cor. xv. 1 ff., 11; Gal. i. 18 f.; ii. 1 ff.

testimony to the resurrection in Acts i, supplements in important particulars the Gospel narrative. In Acts i, in keeping with its generally forward look, prominence is given to the future significance of the apostles, and it was appropriate in this connection to mention their election and commission as a kind of recapitulation of the history of their association with Christ. Of utmost significance for their qualifications was the fact that Christ had 'showed Himself alive after His passion by many proofs, appearing unto them by the space of forty days, and speaking the things concerning the kingdom of God' (Acts i. 3). Since Luke here intimates that there were forty days of contact between Jesus and His disciples between His resurrection and ascension, and he moreover does not restrict the appearances to any particular locality, it would be surpassing strange if Lk. xxiv were intended to be understood as restricting this history to a single day in Jerusalem.

Those who nevertheless interpret Lk. xxiv in such terms are certainly not completely oblivious to the force of the testimony of Acts i. But they are compelled in this exigency to maintain that Luke, perhaps under the influence of a written source or a tradition which came to his attention after he had completed the Gospel, contradicted his earlier record. If Luke and Acts could be shown to be two sharply isolated works, separately conceived and definitely demonstrating independent influences in their execution, such an explanation might possess a degree of plausibility. In the light of the facts, however—that Luke and Acts, as the research of recent decades has emphatically confirmed, not only are demonstrably in remarkable agreement in form and outlook, but also may most satisfactorily be viewed as constituting not two separate treatises but a single work—the view that Luke would introduce at the beginning of Acts a flagrant contradiction of the narrative in the final chapter of the Gospel is most improbable. In continuing his narrative to Theophilus concerning 'those matters which have been fulfilled among us,' Luke makes no apology for mistakes or misrepresentations in his former treatise. Consequently, it would be most unscientific to dismiss the testimony concerning the forty days in one's interpretation of Lk. xxiv, unless the evidence in support of the charge of discrepancy were actually overwhelming.

When one finally turns to examine Lk. xxiv, one encounters another basic defect in the modern approach. This amounts virtually to a failure to take seriously into account at this point what one should observe as to the evident aims and methods of the evangelist in the preceding twenty-three chapters. As attention is directed to the framework of Luke's Gospel in comparison with that of the other synoptics, it appears again and again that the third evangelist is least concerned with the chronological and topographical setting of the incidents and teachings which he reports. He is not, as has been shown above, indifferent to the matter of framework, but he is content frequently to introduce discourse or narrative material without reference to time or place, and hence it is impossible to speak in terms of a definite itinerary or an established sequence of events in most contexts. There is cause for wonder whether recent critics of the Lucan narrative have been fully emancipated from the older view that the evangelists were intending to set forth the precise historical framework of Jesus' life or, on a lower view of their trustworthiness, that they aimed to construct a precise framework of their own. Whatever the factors may be that are responsible for such views of the intent of the evangelists, it is my judgment that the more closely one attends to Luke's method in narrating all that precedes the resurrection story, the less ready one will be to conclude that in chapter xxiv he definitely meant to narrate the events of but a single day.

Although the considerations just reviewed suggest the propriety of caution, the question remains to be considered how Lk. xxiv may be understood as allowing for a longer interval than one day between the resurrection and the ascension. There can be no question that the resurrection itself and the interview on the way to Emmaus are placed on the first day of the week (Lk. xxiv. 1-35; cf. verse 13). The appearance to the disciples recorded in Lk. xxiv. 36-43 is also intimately associated with what precedes, and can hardly be thought of as having occurred later than at evening or during the night at the close of that first day. On the other hand, the charge not to depart from Jerusalem until after the outpouring of the Holy Spirit (Lk. xxiv. 49; cf. Acts i. 4) appears decisively to exclude any later journey to Galilee. Such a journey and the other events of the forty days apparently must fall between Lk. xxiv. 43 and xxiv. 49. Here various possibilities are suggested. Plummer, for example, thinks the entire contents of the section including verses 44-49 are to be regarded as *a summary* of the teaching of Jesus to His disciples during the period following His resurrection. On this view, while Luke is recognized as being aware of the fact that Jesus associated with the disciples over a period of forty days, the evangelist is seen to be content to narrate briefly the first and final appearances to the disciples and to indicate the nature of the message which He taught within this period. Other interpreters allow for the events of the forty days by finding a point of transition at verse 44 or verse 45, or at still other points. The most plausible of these is that verse 44 introduces a new paragraph, and is not meant to be immediately associated with what precedes.[1] Luke himself does not mark out the sequence of events or indicate points of transition, but with an eye upon his characteristic literary method one may infer that he does not rigidly exclude a flexible construction of the course of events.

Although, therefore, the resurrection narrative in Luke is selective and compressed, it remains true that the Gospel places a remarkable emphasis upon the fact of the resurrection. Since the death of Christ is constantly proclaimed in connection with the resurrection, the evaluation of the peculiar stress upon the resurrection will also have implications for our understanding of the subject of the death of Christ which has been so largely before us in this chapter. And indeed this evaluation will bear significantly upon our total thought with regard to Luke's proclamation of the gospel.

The solemn pronouncements concerning the approaching passion and death of the Son of Man, as reported by the other evangelists as well as Luke, point to the resurrection as an act by which the One who was to be set at nought of men would be exalted by God. But this motif comes to much fuller and more explicit expression in Luke's treatment of the resurrection than in the other accounts.

---

[1] The particle δέ might conceivably link the contents of verse 44 closely with that which precedes, but its use in Luke illustrates the fact that it may introduce a new situation and new disclosures. Cf. Lk. ii. 1, iii. 1, ix. 1, xvi. 1, xvii. 1. See also Plummer, Klostermann and Creed on Lk. xxiv. 44.

This appears strikingly in his narrative concerning the developments at the empty tomb. The women are not left in doubt as to the true interpretation of what had occurred, for divine messengers explain that the One they were seeking was not to be found among the dead, because He had risen (xxiv. 5 f.). Essentially the same message is reported in Matthew and Mark, but Luke alone intimates that the message recalled the repeated solemn utterances concerning the messianic programme.

'Remember how He spoke unto you when He was yet in Galilee, saying that the Son of Man must be delivered up into the hands of sinful men, and be crucified, and the third day rise again. And they remembered His words, and returned from the tomb, and told all these things to the eleven, and to all the rest' (Lk. xxiv. 6-8).

Luke, therefore, far more explicitly than the others, calls attention to the fulfilment of the prophecies of Jesus concerning His passion and resurrection, and thus indicates the integration of the ministry of Christ in its various phases. And the recollection of the prophecies just as this point serves to focus attention upon the conviction that the resurrection of Christ was the goal of His ministry as of Luke's narrative. The resurrection story is in no sense an afterthought, an appendix, to the story of the cross, but rather forms the inevitable climax of the course of events with which Luke was concerned. While there was a divine necessity which underlay the march to the cross at Jerusalem, it was unthinkable that the divine Servant should not triumph over death.

The silence of Luke with regard to a reunion with the disciples in Galilee, recorded by both Matthew and Mark, is striking. He is, of course, completely self-consistent on this point, for he also omits any reference to Christ's prophecy concerning the reunion spoken on His way to Gethsemane.[1] In considering this silence, one is faced with the alternative that the evangelist had never heard of an appearance there—an intrinsically difficult hypothesis —or that he decided to omit that tradition and to confine his account to manifestations in and about Jerusalem. The question would still be an open one on the latter alternative whether or not the difference in the scene of the appearance involves on

[1] Mt. xxvi. 32, xxviii. 7, 10, 16; Mk. xiv. 28, xvi. 7.

Luke's part a deliberate rejection of the Galilean tradition and an effort to establish, or confirm, a tradition which confined Jesus' post-resurrection activity to Judæa. It is quite possible that Luke, without doctrinal and historical bias, chose to select, from the many appearances of the risen Christ known to the Christian church, certain manifestations of which he personally could testify on the basis of his contacts with Christians in Judæa.

While, then, Luke might remain silent on the Galilean tradition without prejudice to its historicity, the fact remains that the content of the message to the women as reported by Luke contains unique elements. R. H. Lightfoot speaks of the Lucan form as involving 'a very daring change.'[1] Luke is thought to have freely manipulated the traditional material as found in Mk. xvi. 7 by the substitution of Lk. xxiv. 6 f. When it is argued in support of this view that the mention of 'Galilee' in Lk. xxiv. 6 is due to his knowledge of Mark and a compulsion to be faithful to the older tradition, or, as Creed says, that it 'is no doubt an echo of the Marcan source,' the reasoning is particularly implausible. If Luke is as radically independent of Mark as is assumed at this point, how can he have been so slavishly dependent upon him as is implied here? Moreover, the Lucan words in xxiv. 6 f. to which exception is taken are not Luke's version of the message for the disciples. On the contrary they form a supplement to the words spoken to the women in explanation of the empty tomb. And in view of the integration of this message with the pronouncements concerning the approaching passion and resurrection, they do not form an excrescence upon the tradition or constitute a bold change. If there is a surprising feature in this connection, it is that Matthew and Mark fail to include specific recollection of the fulfilment of the solemn pronouncements of Jesus.

The extensive Lucan story concerning the encounter with the two disciples on the way to Emmaus sounds the same note as the angel's message to the women at the tomb. The disappointed disciples who had supposed that Jesus was the One who should redeem Israel, and who were bewildered by reports that had reached them that He was alive, are told:

'O foolish men, and slow of heart to believe in all that the

---

[1] See *History and Interpretation*, pp. 166 f.; *Locality and Doctrine*, pp. 80 ff.

prophets have spoken! Behoved it not the Christ to suffer these things, and to enter into His glory?' (Lk. xxiv. 25 f.).

Reflection upon the sufferings and death of Christ, apart from contemplation of His glory, left men in despair and disillusionment. But so to think of Jesus was not to recognize Him as the Christ. For the Christ, the Anointed of the Lord, there could be no supposition of failure and defeat. Consequently, in the historical situation, the resurrection rather than the crucifixion is in the foreground of attention.

Finally, in Luke's report of the message of Jesus to His disciples, the resurrection is seen to be the goal of His ministry to which the Scriptures and Christ's own teaching pointed:

'These are My words which I spoke unto you, while I was yet with you, how that all things must needs be fulfilled, which are written in the law of Moses, and the prophets, and the psalms, concerning Me. Then opened He their minds, that they might understand the scriptures; and He said unto them, Thus it is written, that the Christ should suffer, and rise again from the dead the third day . . .' (Lk. xxiv. 44 ff.).

It does not come as a surprise, therefore, that Luke's record of the apostolic preaching in the Acts is occupied to a large extent with the resurrection of Christ, while the passion of Christ is introduced more succinctly. The apostolic message thus reflects basically the perspective of Jesus' own outlook upon the climax of His career, and in turn the message serves to illumine the origin of the formation of the written Gospels. One must allow for differences of emphasis in the Gospels, as in the reports of the apostolic preaching, taking account of the somewhat different historical occasions of the utterances and the individuality of the spokesmen. Thus the stereotyped character of the proclamation of the gospel of Jesus Christ must not be exaggerated. There is even somewhat of a difference in emphasis between the final chapters of Luke and his reports of the early preaching, which suggests that the first preaching of the Christian missionaries gave great prominence to the evidential significance of the resurrection of Christ for the understanding of Christ and Christianity, while the more finished publication of 'the things fulfilled among us' in the Gospel as appropriately dwelt more fully upon the saving significance of Christ's passion. But it must be reiterated that in all the real goal is the exaltation of Christ through the resurrection, and the full realization of this fact has left its impact upon the disposition of Luke's Gospel.

That Luke somewhat distinctly accents the glory of Christ through His exaltation receives confirmation from a quite different angle. Luke alone of the evangelists brings his Gospel to a close with a real departure of Jesus from His disciples; he alone reports the ascension. The words 'and He was carried up into heaven' are lacking in certain manuscripts, and they are omitted in certain modern editions of the New Testament. But even if they are a gloss, they represent an entirely correct understanding of what Luke meant when he said that 'while He blessed them, He parted from them' (xxiv. 51). That Luke has the ascension in mind is clear, in the first place, from the testimony of Acts, which not only narrates the ascension in some detail as the event which marked His departure (Acts i. 9 ff.), but explicitly views the ascension as the *terminus ad quem* of Luke's Gospel, concerned as it was with 'all that Jesus began both to do and to teach, until the day in which He was received up' (Acts i. 1 f.). But, even without the benefit of this testimony, it would have been quite clear that in xxiv. 51 Luke had in mind far more than a casual departure of Jesus; it was a departure which caused them to return to Jerusalem with great joy, evidently to await the fulfilment of the promise that, tarrying in the city, they would be clothed with power from on high (xxiv. 49). In their exultant joy as they awaited that great event, they 'were continually in the temple, blessing God.' The Father's promise was to be fulfilled, and they recognized in Jesus' parting the event which would hasten the further manifestation of the divine action on their behalf. The Gospel according to Luke, therefore, ends on a triumphant note, a note of fervent joy, and of praise at the contemplation of the marvellous works of God.

To some extent the Acts promotes understanding of this distinguishing feature of the Gospel. Luke was an author whose literary goal comprehended the Acts as well as the Gospel. The exaltation of Christ through the resurrection and ascension did not merely serve him to round off the publication of the Gospel. As his occupation with these events in the first chapter of Acts especially intimates, they are viewed pre-eminently as the great foundational facts which undergird the new order. They are historical events, but with eschatological significance, ushering in a new era marked by the extraordinary manifestation of the Holy Spirit whom the exalted Lord at God's right hand had sent forth. Hence, even Luke's literary goal helps to explain the accent upon Christ's exaltation.

But in his case, without doubt, the literary aims were rooted in his outlook upon the unfolding of history according to the divine plan. As a Christian man Luke shared the faith which joyfully acknowledged Jesus as Lord and Christ, who had entered upon a new and victorious phase of His messianic ministry through His exaltation to the right hand of God (Acts ii. 35 f.). A still more glorious phase of His messianic activity would be ushered in by His return (cf., for example, Acts i. 11, iii. 21); and it had been preceded by his ministry as the Servant, the Holy and Righteous One, the Christ of God (cf., for example, Acts iii. 13, 14, 18). In these distinctions with regard to the ministry of Jesus—past, present and future—there was implicit a broad conception of the unfolding of the divine action in Christ. But the Christ who was invoked, confessed and worshipped by the faithful, was the living Lord. Though He was remembered as the One who on their behalf had surrendered His life unto death, and had ratified the new covenant in His blood, and though there was a sober realization that the perfect consummation was to be manifested only in the future manifestation of the rule of God, their present faith in Him as the Lord bound the elements of remembrance and hope together and afforded a present assurance of grace and righteousness through faith in His name. That living, abiding, dynamic faith of Luke gives perspective to his entire undertaking in proclaiming Jesus as the One 'that died, yea rather was raised from the dead' (cf. Rom. viii. 34).[1]

[1] Cf. my *The Areopagus Address*, pp. 48, 12 f., Tyndale Press, London, 1950.

CHAPTER VIII

THE KINGDOM AND THE MESSIAH

IN this concluding chapter our attention will centre upon the message of Christ according to Luke. As in the other Synoptics that message may be most concisely summed up in terms of the coming of the kingdom of God.[1] But there also emerges, in the context of the evangelical proclamation of the Messiah, Jesus' own claims of messiahship expressed in word and deed. These are not two messages, however, but one; and hence there is no more significant question of interpretation than that of the relation of the coming of the Christ to the manifestation of the kingdom.

To a considerable extent this theme has been evaluated in the preceding chapters. The discussion of the passion narrative and of its climax in the resurrection of Jesus has thrust into the foreground the Christological question, and has demonstrated that, though the gospel might be formulated tentatively in terms of the coming of the kingdom, that kingdom is so indissolubly bound up with the ministry of Christ, and even identified with His person, that the gospel comes to find expression in distinctly personal terms. The decisive work of salvation is Christ's, the action of the Son of Man who 'came to seek and to save the lost' (Lk. xix. 10). This work itself has such transcendent significance that its accomplishment by the Messiah implies that He is thought of in transcendent terms, and since He is none less than the divine Messiah there is a guarantee that the kingdom will come to realization as He fulfils His ministry.

The leading issues involved in the subject of the Messiah and the kingdom have been in view at least as early as the Lucan narrative of the appearance and rejection at Nazareth, which was considered at length in chapter IV. The Christological aspect of the message is distinctly present, for it is evident that the coming of a new order coincides with the presence and activity of Christ. Nevertheless, this aspect is presented with considerable reserve,

---

[1] Cf. Lk. iv. 43 ('I must preach the good tidings of the kingdom of God to the other cities also: for therefore was I sent'), viii. 1, ix. 11. See also Lk. ix. 2, 60.

and the accent falls at this point upon the dawn of the new age of righteousness and grace rather than upon the coming of the Messiah. Utilizing one of the climactic prophecies of Isaiah, the Lord discloses by His extraordinary comment that the eschatological age, when injustices and other consequences of sin would be overcome and which was proclaimed as realizable and assured of realization only because of the free, sovereign grace of the Holy One of Israel, was in process of fulfilment. Here, too, there is restraint in presenting the theme of the establishment of the divine rule. No account is taken at Nazareth of the final consummation of the kingdom associated with the coming of the Son of Man on the clouds of heaven. And it remains expressed basically in the prophetic language of the Old Testament rather than in the more didactic language of the New Testament which has been fashioned within the crucible of the development of stupendous and momentous historical events. Hence the teaching at Nazareth is not programmatic for the Gospel; it does not summarize the teaching of Jesus. It serves, rather, effectively to introduce it. Reflection upon Isaiah's delineation of the coming kingdom indicates the pattern of the kingdom as proclaimed by Christ and as it begins to come to realization through His deeds. But one must undertake an examination of the actual teaching of our Lord within the entire Gospel to take in its entire sweep and to bring the whole into sharp focus.

Advantage may be taken here of the results arrived at in the study of the teaching as recorded in Mark and Matthew. Particularly on the basis of the data in Matthew, it appears that various aspects of the manifestation of the kingdom must be distinguished. The kingdom is one, and it may be recognized as being basically 'eschatological' in view of its consummation through divine interposition. But no contradiction is involved in recognizing that, prior to the consummation at the end of the age, there have been significant preliminary manifestations of the kingdom which are also the consequence of decisive divine action in history. The divine action in view is in and through Christ, and thus the stages of the coming of the kingdom correspond with the stages of the ministry and activity of Christ. The action of the returning Son of Man ushers in the kingdom in its final glory and power. His exaltation to God's right hand also constitutes a most signal triumph of God in the accomplishment of His purposes of redemption, and hence a specific historical turning point in the work of making actual the divine rule. But even prior to this development the very presence of the Son of Man upon earth, and His victory over the works of Satan, signalizes that the kingdom has actually come.[1]

THE COMING OF THE KINGDOM

Do not the Lucan data require the same three-fold distinctions? In most instances where Luke refers to the kingdom, the question of stages of manifestation is left quite unsettled. When Jesus says, for example, 'Blessed are ye poor, for yours is the kingdom of God,' the kingdom of consummation may be in view but quite as well also its prior realizations in history.[2] There are, however, other utterances which unambiguously have in view a coming that is future from the point of view of Jesus' utterance. The kingdom is announced as having drawn nigh (Lk. x. 9, 11, xxi. 31); the disciples are taught to pray, 'Thy kingdom come (Lk. xi. 2). Such references need not indeed be restricted to the final consummation. But the expectation of the future also includes the hope of the establishment of a new and final order in which the pious dead will participate. Jesus looks forward to a fulfilment of His eating and drinking with the disciples in the kingdom of God (Lk. xxii. 16, 18, 29 f., xiv. 15), and teaches that Abraham, Isaac and Jacob and all the prophets will be seen therein (Lk. xiii. 28 f.; cf. xxiii. 42 f.).

Although, then, the strictly eschatological aspect of the kingdom is plainly in view, there is a remarkable emphasis upon the phase of the kingdom which has been realized in the history of Christ. Since Lk. vii. 24 ff., 28, xvi. 16 and xi. 20 closely parallel Mt. xi. 7 ff., 12, xii. 28 in showing that through the work of Christ the kingdom had come, and men were entering it, this perspective does not find its original expression in Luke.[3] Nevertheless, as the preaching at Nazareth has shown, it is placed in the foreground in this Gospel. Most pointed of all is the distinctive

---

[1] This subject, especially as it is presented in Matthew, has been treated at some length in WMMC, Chapter VIII.
[2] Lk. vi. 20. Cf. viii. 10, ix. 62, xix. 16 f., 24 f., xiii. 18 f., 20 f.
[3] On the interpretation of the passages in Matthew see WMMC, pp. 244 ff.

saying of Lk. xvii. 21, 'The kingdom of God is in your midst.' Here Jesus points to the radical misunderstanding of the nature of the kingdom displayed by the Pharisees. While they supposed that its manifestation was completely future, and conceived of it as so much a part of the present world-order that one might calculate the time of its coming, Jesus taught that it was of such an utterly different nature that it would come only through a sudden divine act, and indeed was even then in their very midst.[1]

In view of the plain testimony to the kingdom as realized, at least incipiently, through the ministry of Christ upon earth, it is remarkable that there is little or no explicit reflection upon the fashion in which the kingdom of God was to enter upon a new stage of realization through the exaltation of Christ. That this thought is dwelt upon in Matthew may well be explained by its teaching concerning the establishment of the Church.[2] Nevertheless, in other ways the same basic perspective appears. Luke, too, pointedly emphasizes the supreme dignity and power which the Son of Man will occupy at God's right hand (Lk. xxii. 69). He also stresses the fact that through the resurrection the Son of Man would enter into His glory (Lk. xxiv. 26; cf. ix. 22, xviii. 31 ff., xxiv. 46). And he points forward to the new era which would be inaugurated by the Spirit when He was sent forth by the exalted Christ (Lk. xxiv. 49; cf. Acts i. 8, ii. 33). Moreover, it is clear from the place which the church occupied in Acts as the new people of God constituted through the redemption of Christ and the eschatological manifestation of the Spirit (Acts xx. 28, ii. 1 ff.)

[1] Bultmann, *Jesus*, 1926, p. 39; *Die Geschichte der synoptischen Tradition*, 2te Aufl., 1931, pp. 24, 128, interprets ἐστίν as a prophetic present in the interest of conforming the passage to the 'consistent' eschatological view of the kingdom. K. L. Schmidt in TWNT, I, p. 587 says it has nothing to do with the question of time, but only with the rejection of omens. On the other side, cf. R. Otto, op. cit., pp. 131 ff. If there were no other evidence in the teaching of Jesus that the kingdom was regarded as already significantly present, and if in the present context there were intimations that a future coming were as a matter of fact clearly in view, this interpretation of the present tense might be allowable. However, the use of the present rather than the future creates a definite presumption in favour of understanding it as an actual present. And that a future meaning cannot have been in Jesus' mind is shown most simply from the consideration that the words 'The kingdom of God will be in your midst' would be pointless as a reply to the question of the Pharisees concerning the time of the coming of the kingdom.

[2] Cf. WMMC, pp. 234 ff.

that, in the last analysis, Luke also looked upon the church as a climactic carrying forward of the kingdom that appeared in the very midst of the Jewish people through the presence and activity of Christ. In view of these considerations, it is not at all incongruous to judge that the church may be included within the kingdom in the words, 'But I tell you of a truth, There are some of them that stand here who shall in no wise taste of death until they see the kingdom of God' (Lk. ix. 27).[1]

On the background of this survey of the structure of the historical realization of the kingdom of God according to Luke, one may evaluate the charge that Luke tones down the earlier Christian emphasis upon the imminence of the kingdom.[2] Appeal is made particularly to Lk. ix. 27, xxii. 69, xix. 11, and xxi. 8 to substantiate this judgment, but obviously there is presupposed a certain judgment as to the eschatological perspective of Mark and other early witnesses. And it is my conviction that, apparently because of the vogue obtained by the 'consistent' eschatological viewpoint, extremely one-sided opinions have developed. On the basis of the dogma that Christ and the early Christian Church acted on the assumption that the end of the world was necessarily to come momentarily, thoroughgoing reconstructions of the origins of Christianity have been undertaken. There have been confident assertions that at first there could have been no interest in external organization, in a written expression of the faith, and in the formation of the New Testament Canon. Such theories have been spun out of most inadequate interpretations of the pertinent data. Broadly speaking, indeed, the outlook was eschatological. One encounters frequent admonitions to be found watchful and waiting. But the warning to live in expectation of the return of the Son of Man because He would come as a thief in the night (1 Thes. v. 2) does not imply that He would necessarily return so soon that provision for earthly needs and eventual wants would be of no concern. In fact the very insistence upon the uncertainty of the time of His return would stand as a constant warning not to determine in advance precisely when the hour would strike. The position of 2 Thessalonians may not therefore be held to disclose a modified eschatological perspective. It

[1] On these passages and their synoptic parallels cf. WMMC, pp. 238 ff.
[2] E.g. Creed, op. cit., pp. lxxii f. Cf. also Cadbury, *Making*, pp. 291, 293 f.

protests against certain foolhardy and disastrous deductions from what had been taught, and intimates that there would be events of catastrophic proportions in the midst of the present world before the return of Christ (2 Thes. ii. 1 ff.). But this implies only that some Christians had drawn wrong inferences from Paul's teaching, not that Paul had altered his own position.

Nor does the teaching in Mark support the one-sided conception of the imminence of the kingdom. For Mark also contains the teaching that the 'end' will by no means come before the fulfilment of certain highly significant prophecies, including that concerning the proclamation of the gospel to all the nations (Mk. xiii. 7, 10). And in general Mark places such an emphasis upon the transforming meaning of the ministry of the Son of Man upon earth and upon the resurrection as the goal of His ministry that his testimony gives far greater prominence to eschatology that is realized before the end than to that which awaits realization through the parousia.[1]

Creed cites Lk. ix. 27 and xxii. 69 in declaring that 'the more striking Marcan prophecies of the *imminence* of the kingdom are softened.'[2] It is not self-evident, however, that Mark's 'until they see the kingdom of God come with power' (ix. 1) stresses imminence more than Luke's 'until they see the kingdom of God' (Lk. ix. 27). Coming 'with power' may quite well be distinguished from coming 'with great power and glory' (Mk. xiii. 26). And in view of the use of the word 'power' for the miracles of Christ for example in Mk. vi. 2, 5, 14), and its application to the resurrection in Mk. xii. 24, it would be quite appropriate to characterize the preliminary manifestations of the kingdom as a coming 'in power.' The appeal to Lk. xxii. 69 is somewhat more impressive since Luke, as distinguished from Matthew and Mark (Mt. xxvi. 64; Mk. xiv. 62), omits at this point any reference to the coming of the Son of Man on the clouds of heaven. Since, however, he includes frequent references to the coming of the Son of Man in glory (Lk. ix. 26, xvii. 24, 26, 30, xviii. 8, xxi. 27, 36), great care must be exercised not to overstress the significance of the omission at this point. Mark does not say or imply that the coming with the clouds of heaven would follow immediately upon the 'sitting at

[1] On the eschatological perspective of Mark cf. WMMC, pp. 109 ff.
[2] P. lxxii.

the right hand of Power,'[1] and so Luke's omission may be merely in the interest of simplicity and clarity of expression. It was sufficient for his purpose to report merely the statement concerning Christ's exaltation to God's right hand as indicative of His vindication and victory.

Creed contends that Lk. xix. 11 and xxi. 8 'betray an attitude of some suspicion towards those who look for an immediate fulfilment of the hope.'[2] In the former passage, where Luke says that Jesus proceeded to tell the parable of the pounds 'because He was nigh to Jerusalem, and because they supposed that the kingdom of God was immediately to appear,' there is indeed an implied disagreement with an eschatological outlook which is in danger of losing sight of tasks to be accomplished on earth while men were waiting for the coming of the kingdom. But this is hardly distinctive of Luke. And though Lk. xxi. 8 disapproves of false Christs who say, 'The time is at hand,' the polemic is more basically directed against the false Christs than against the words as such. Though the words employed are not given in Mark, that Gospel quite as definitely as Luke warns in this discourse against those who would lead the disciples astray with premature and erroneous reports concerning the appearance of Christ (cf. Mk. xiii. 5 ff.).

There does not therefore appear to be a solid case for the contention that Luke has softened the prophecies of the imminence of the kingdom in the interest of adjusting the eschatological perspective of primitive Christianity to historical developments. The conception of the kingdom of God is by no means restricted to the final consummation, but is in view also when earlier aspects of the realization of the rule of God through the decisive action of Christ are being reflected upon. And in all the records there is a powerful accumulation of testimony to the effect that God's purposes of grace, whereby His rule would be established, His name would be hallowed and His will would be done, did not have to remain merely prospective until the day of the return of the Son of Man on the clouds of heaven, but were decisively, though somewhat preliminarily, realized through the ministry of the Son of Man upon earth and through His entrance upon His glory by the resurrection on the third day.

[1] Cf. H. B. Swete, *Mark*, ad loc. ,and WMMC, pp. 240 ff. [2] P. lxxii.

THE NATURE OF THE KINGDOM

Of even deeper significance than the question of the time and times of the manifestation of the kingdom is that of its basic meaning: what it reveals concerning God and His relations to men. In a word the kingdom of God may be said to be God-centred and God-given, and thus there are in view the same characteristics which have been observed in connection with our evaluation of the prophetic Scripture read by our Lord in the synagogue at Nazareth.[1] As God-centred, it is basically viewed as the realization of the rule of God, involving the glorification of His holy name and the performance of His righteous will on the part of men; only then can it be a kingdom or realm in which men participate in divine blessings. In congruity with its God-centred character it is God-given; it depends for its realization upon the sovereign grace of God. If God's rule is to be established, He must mercifully bring it to pass. Because it is a reign of righteousness it can never be brought about through the initiative and as a co-operative action of men.[2]

Luke contains a few distinctive sayings that pointedly bear out these characterizations of the kingdom. He reports the saying of Jesus: 'Fear not, little flock; for it is your Father's good pleasure to give you the kingdom' (Lk. xii. 32). Here the non-political, non-worldly character of the kingdom is strikingly disclosed: it belongs to the true disciples of Christ, a little flock, who receive it only because of a disposition of sovereign grace. That the kingdom is constituted by the disposition of God also appears from the saying recorded in Lk. xxii. 29 f. There, according to the rendering of the RV, Jesus declares, 'I appoint unto you a kingdom, even as my Father appointed unto me.' If, as is more probable, as the RV margin and the RSV reflect, the word 'kingdom' is to be construed with the second use of the verb 'appoint,' the passage may be rendered: 'I appoint unto you, as my Father hath appointed unto me a kingdom, that ye may eat and drink at my table in my kingdom.' But the substance remains

---

[1] See above, pp. 76 ff.
[2] On the basic questions concerning the nature of the kingdom of God see especially G. Vos, *The Teaching of Jesus concerning the Kingdom of God and the Church*, 1903, pp. 90 ff.

the same, for on the second rendering the disciples are assured the blessings of participation in the kingdom because of the fact of Christ's appointment. The choice of the verb translated 'appoint' accents the freedom of the appointment. It may have in view the idea of a testamentary bequest, and then the unilateral character of the action would be stressed. More probably, however, it reflects covenantal bestowal of blessing since the Father would hardly have been spoken of as 'bequeathing' a kingdom to the Son. And then it has all the rich significance bound up with the biblical conception of the covenant established by God with His people, a conception which wonderfully serves to describe the fellowship between God and man, and yet never loses sight of the fact that its establishment is a marvel of divine grace.[1]

Although Luke sets forth the message of the kingdom in absolute terms as God's rule and as God's gift, it is significant that he by no means avoids the use of traditional Jewish language in reporting its expectation. The messianic hope of the disciples on the way to Emmaus, a hope seemingly shattered by the crucifixion, was expressed in the form that Jesus was the one who 'was about to redeem Israel' (Lk. xxiv. 21). And after the restoration of the disciples' confidence in Jesus, the question is still raised whether He would now 'restore the kingdom to Israel' (Acts i. 6). And in speaking of the blessings of His kingdom, Jesus includes the promise that the disciples would 'sit on thrones judging the twelve tribes of Israel' (Lk. xxii. 30; cf. Mt. xix. 28). The formulation of the messianic hope in these terms is misconstrued, however, if it is taken as pointing to a particularistic, essentially Jewish, kingdom in distinction from or alongside of the eternal kingdom. He is not speaking in these connections of a particular phase of the kingdom, but of the kingdom as a whole.

The birth narratives eloquently establish the fact that such language is meant to designate the eternal kingdom inaugurated by the appearance of the Messiah. There it appears that the distinctive terminology is chosen because, quite in keeping with the tenor of the narratives as a whole, the hope is expressed from the point of view of the promises of the Old Testament. Thus the message of the angel to Mary which tells of the significance of His

---

[1] Cf. also Lk. xvii. 21, which intimates the non-secular character of the kingdom and Lk. i. 33, which characterizes the rule as eternal.

birth relates, in terms of 2 Sa. vii. 12 ff. and Dn. vii. 13 f., the promise that God would give Him the throne of His father David, and emphatically asserts that His reign will be eternal (Lk. i. 32 f.). The pious Simeon was waiting for 'the consolation of Israel' when the Holy Spirit revealed that he would live to see the Anointed of the Lord. And Luke goes on to tell in the words of the *Nunc Dimittis* how Simeon, having seen the babe and received Him into His arms, exults in the fact that His eyes have seen the salvation of God, a salvation which, as Isaiah had prophesied, would be for the Gentiles as well as for the Jews (Lk. ii. 25 ff.). And Anna, the prophetess, having seen Christ in the temple, 'spake of Him to all them that were looking for the redemption of Jerusalem' (Lk. ii. 38). And even at the close of Acts Paul's faith in Christ which had brought him into prison is formulated as 'the hope of Israel' (Acts xxviii. 20). Accordingly, the expectation could be expressed concretely in Old Testament terms as the hope of Israel, the restoration of the kingdom to Israel, the redemption of Israel, the consolation of Israel, and the like, and yet clearly not signify a particularistic manifestation of the kingdom.

Closely associated with the question whether the kingdom is particularistic is that raised by the use of earthly terms in describing the prerogatives of its participants. Notice has been taken of the description of its fellowship and privileges in realistic terms, of eating and drinking at a table and of sitting on thrones (Lk. xxii. 29 f.; cf. xiv. 15 ff.). How are such data to be construed, and what bearing do they have upon the understanding of the nature of the kingdom? On the one hand, it must not be forgotten that biblical eschatology presupposes the doctrine of the creation of the world by God in envisaging a transformed world. It is not a gnostic, spiritualizing doctrine which would find abhorrent the idea of a new heaven and a new earth. The world to come is the world of the resurrection of the dead, in which men, constituted of soul and body, will dwell. On the other hand, that world is a transformed world, suited to the existence of transformed men. Hence care must be taken not to construe the realistic language employed in describing the blessings of the kingdom in a severely physical sense. Account must be taken of the fashion in which within the Bible the glories and blessings of the age to come are characteristically depicted in terms of the restoration of original glories and the repetition of covenant blessings, though it is understood all the while that the world to come, in which the curse has been removed and Christ is seen face to face, is a new world so transcending the glories that have been revealed that it cannot be adequately described in human language. Appropriately then, the language describing the table fellowship of Christ and His disciples is employed to intimate the fellowship of the future age. Similarly the privilege of reigning with Christ is intimated in language drawn from the history of the kingdom upon earth. As the messianic prerogative takes the form that Christ should occupy the throne of His father David, the privilege of those who enjoy the most intimate fellowship with Him in His reign is appropriately expressed in the form that they should sit on thrones judging the twelve tribes of Israel. There is no implication that their thrones were to be physical thrones in a reconstituted theocracy any more than that His throne is conceived in such terms.

While then Luke clearly envisages the kingdom of God as a transcendent new reality, and gives prominence to the universalism of its historical manifestation, it is remarkable how fully Luke retains the Christian sense of continuity with the old order. Only after the most drastic surgery, as Marcion saw, can Luke be appealed to in support of a view of Christianity as a creation out of nothing, as a new beginning in history completely isolated from the Jewish religion. Luke's comprehensive historical work does indeed demonstrate in impressive fashion that Christianity was irreconcilable with the particularism and legalism of contemporaneous Judaism. Nevertheless, as clearly as the other records, he manifests the historical perspective which recognizes that the particularism of the old covenant no less than the universalism of the new was of divine appointment, and that the historical realization of the kingdom through the appearance of Christ by no means relaxed the authority of the law and the prophets. Although Luke perhaps does not fully share Matthew's concern with the theme of the place of Christ in the history of divine revelation, it is clear that his appraisal of the stupendous meaning of the coming of Christ, no less emphatically than Matthew's, presupposed and involved the affirmation of the

THE KINGDOM AND THE MESSIAH

divine character of the Scriptures of the Jews. The Jesus of Luke, in affirming that 'the law and the prophets were until John' (Lk. xvi. 16), insists also that 'it is easier for heaven and earth to pass away, than for one tittle of the law to fall' (Lk. xvi. 17), and that 'all things must needs be fulfilled, which are written in the law of Moses, and the prophets, and the psalms, concerning Me' (Lk. xxiv. 44). In view of this sense of solid continuity between the action of God under the old covenant and under the new, the formulation of the messianic hope and its realization in Christ and His kingdom in terms of 'the hope of Israel' and of Israel's consolation and redemption does not appear anomalous.

Another question that arises as one gives consideration to the question of the meaning of the kingdom of God for Luke is that of its significance for the world. Since the kingdom of God, as set forth in Luke's record of Jesus' message, is emphatically an historical reality signified as present through the appearance of Christ himself, this matter is of intensely practical concern. Luke has been regarded as presenting essentially a message for the poor and afflicted of this world, and thus a message with strong social implications. Jülicher, for example, maintaining that there is nothing distinctively Pauline in Luke's work, and that the features which show closest agreement with Paul—the universality of salvation and the limitless grace of God—ultimately go back to Jesus himself, finds his own estimate in close agreement with Wellhausen's. This was to the effect that, because of an outspoken sympathy for delinquents and outcasts, Luke commends the Saviour to the sympathy and trust of Greek readers, including particularly the lowest classes.[1] Jülicher further characterizes Luke's religious attitude as one of world-flight, which led to the utilization of a source bearing an Ebionite-Jewish character, and views the future glory as the recompense which will be the portion of those who have hungered and suffered here below.[2] Burkitt similarly speaks of 'a tinge of asceticism' and of 'communism' (by which he seems to mean 'voluntary poverty') as characteristic of Luke.[3]

It is true indeed that Jesus proclaims at Nazareth the message

---
[1] J. Wellhausen, *Einleitung in die drei ersten Evangelein*, 1905, pp. 69 f.
[2] *Einleitung in das N.T.*[7], 1931, pp. 315 ff.
[3] *The Gospel History and its Transmission*, pp. 210 ff.

that the kingdom of God brings glad tidings to the poor and afflicted (Lk. iv. 18). Moreover, the Gospel gives great prominence to Jesus' friendship with publicans and sinners[1] and His pronouncements of woe upon the rich.[2] But these data provide exceedingly precarious support for the conclusion that the gospel of Jesus was, according to Luke, characterized by an Ebionite social slant or a tendency towards asceticism and communism. There is no glorification of poverty as such and no assurances to the poor that, because they are poor, they will necessarily find happiness. If a state of poverty were being idealized there could hardly be place for the commendation of the rich Zacchaeus for his almsgiving and of almsgiving in general (Lk. xix. 2, 8, xi. 41, xii. 33).[3] The issue is seen to be basically religious rather than basically social. Jesus is not so much concerned to assure the publicans and sinners of the love of God as to rebuke the self-righteous pride of the Pharisees and the complacency of the rich.[4] The advantage which the poor and the publican enjoyed over the rich and the Pharisee was not a positive one, which assured him of the divine favour in this world or in the world to come. It was rather the negative advantage that he was likely to be more ready to receive the kingdom of God because he lacked the self-righteousness and complacency of those who trusted in their religious pre-eminence or material wealth.

In stressing the essentially religious character of this message, however, one must avoid the impression that the kingdom of God as proclaimed by Jesus was without profound social implications. The kingdom is a gift of the Father's good-pleasure, but as it comes in the midst of the world it comes as a rule of righteousness, demanding absolute righteousness of its subjects, and this includes the application, in a thoroughgoing fashion, of the principle of stewardship in all of one's social relationships. It is necessary to stress, however, that this feature is somewhat inferential and secondary. The primary feature of the gospel, without which

---

[1] Lk. vii. 34; cf. vii. 37, 39, xv. 1, xviii. 10-13, xix. 7.
[2] Lk. vi. 24; cf. xiv. 12, xvi. 1, 19 ff.
[3] The development in the Church at Jerusalem reflected in Acts ii. 44 f., iv. 32 ff., v. 1 ff., vi. 1, was not communism or voluntary poverty. It is described in terms of a voluntary sale and distribution of proceeds to meet the needs which arose. Cf. Acts ii. 34, iv. 34 f., v. 4.
[4] On this point cf. Cadbury, *Making*, pp. 258 f.

the other is meaningless, concerns the tidings of the crucified and risen Saviour in whose name repentance and remission of sins were to be proclaimed (cf. Lk. xxiv. 46, 47). The realization of the kingdom was therefore inconceivable without the accomplishment of the Messiah's task, and the fulfilment of the messianic mission gave assurance of the coming of the kingdom.

THE PERSON OF THE MESSIAH

This brings us to a consideration of the person of Christ in Luke's Gospel. One has no difficulty in recognizing that Luke is presenting the very same Jesus who has been portrayed in the other Synoptics. In all three He is pre-eminently *the divine Messiah*.

A rather extraordinary feature of the modern radical criticism of the Gospels, which may serve well to introduce the discussion of this subject, is that Wrede appealed to a statement recorded by Luke as presenting a Christology more primitive than that contained in Mark itself. The passage is Acts ii. 36 where Peter says: 'Let all the house of Israel therefore know assuredly that God hath made Him both Lord and Christ, this Jesus whom ye crucified.' However, for Wrede's view that according to the earliest form of the Christian messianic faith Jesus became the Messiah only through the resurrection, as also for the view of Schweitzer that Jesus Himself contemplated only a future messiahship, the testimony of Luke as a whole offers no support. The resurrection is marked indeed as the point of Jesus' entrance upon a glorious and triumphant exercise of His lordship, as Christ sat at God's right hand, but there is also a clear recognition of a manifestation of His divine messiahship within the days of His flesh.[1]

Though Luke writes from the point of view of the Christian belief that Jesus entered into His messianic glory through His exaltation, he clearly shared also the conviction of the other evangelists that Jesus had claimed to be and was recognized as being the Messiah from the beginning of His ministry. As in the

---

[1] Cf. Vos, *The Self-Disclosure of Jesus*, pp. 87, 120. On the self-concealment of Jesus' messiahship, cf. WMMC, pp. 50 ff.; WThJ, Nov. 1947 .X), pp. 83 ff.; Vos, op. cit., pp. 67 ff.; H. N. Ridderbos, *Zelfopenbaring en Zelfverberging*, Kampen, 1946. Ridderbos, pp. 62 f., observes that though the element of concealment is less prominent in Luke than in Mark no different tendency can be detected.

other Gospels, Jesus acknowledged the confession of Peter that He was the Lord's Anointed as being a fitting response to the disclosure of His person and work through His previous activity (Lk. ix. 20). This acknowledgment was also made the occasion for Christ's pronouncements as to the programme of suffering and of the glory that would follow. But Luke alone adds the report that after the resurrection the risen Jesus pointed to the testimony of the Scriptures that the Christ should suffer and enter into His glory (Lk. xxiv. 26, 46; cf. Acts iv. 26, xvii. 3, xxvi. 23). That Jesus was condemned by the Jewish leaders, was crucified, and received the taunts of men because of His claims to be the Messiah (and not merely the prospective Messiah) is abundantly clear (cf. Lk. xxii. 67, xxiii. 2 f., 38, xxiii. 35, 37, 39). Luke, moreover, alone records the acclaim of the crowds at His entry into the city in the precise form, 'Blessed is the King that cometh in the name of the Lord' (Lk. xix. 38). Perhaps the most explicit evidence, however, that Luke views Jesus as the Messiah from the beginning is to be found in the birth narratives. For there the angelic glad tidings tell of the birth in the city of David of 'a Saviour, who is Christ the Lord' (Lk. ii. 11) and Simeon receives the revelation that he should not see death before he had seen the Lord's Christ (Lk. ii. 26).

That Luke believed in Jesus Christ as a supernatural Person will not be disputed, although there exists some difference of opinion as to the exact nature of Jesus' transcendence above mankind. The names and titles which express that superior dignity of Jesus are admittedly somewhat flexible in their meanings. It is therefore necessary to judge their precise connotations in the light of the contexts in which they are found.

So far as the name 'the Son of God' is concerned, the usage coincides so largely with that in Matthew and Mark that it may suffice to treat the evidence merely by way of summary.[1] Satan's use of the name in addressing Jesus (Lk. iv. 3 ff.) and perhaps also that of the demoniacs (Lk. iv. 41, viii. 28) appear to fall short of the level of ontological Sonship. On the other hand, the divine acclamation at the baptism and transfiguration involves a relationship to God that evidently obtains prior to and independently of the Son's mission in the world (Lk. iii. 22 f., ix. 35; cf. xx. 13).

[1] Cf. WMMC, pp. 16 ff.; 211 ff.

THE KINGDOM AND THE MESSIAH

For Luke, too, it appears that the Jewish rulers, though representing to Pilate Jesus' claim of messiahship as a threat to the sovereignty of Rome, actually reacted as they did to Jesus' claim, not because of the claim of messiahship as such, but because they understood it as involving a presumption of superhuman dignity (Lk. xxii. 67, 70). Most clearly of all perhaps, the claim to divine Sonship in a form excluding subordination altogether is found in Lk. x. 22, which closely parallels Mt. xi. 27. The Son's knowledge of the Father and the Father's knowledge of the Son are set forth with such exact correspondence and reciprocity, and are moreover made the foundations of their respective sovereign revelational activity, that all subordination is excluded, and the passage constitutes an unambiguous claim of deity on the part of the Son.

To these passages, none of which is completely distinctive of Luke, must now be joined the testimony of Lk. i. 32 and 35. In virtue of the overshadowing of the Holy Spirit which effected the conception of Jesus, He is designated as 'Son of God.' The supernatural conception of Jesus does not by itself, as an isolated fact, establish the deity of Christ. He was divine from all eternity; He could not become more so because of the virgin birth. And it would be appropriate to regard the titles 'Son of God' and 'Son of the Highest' in this context as appropriately given in view of His supernatural conception rather than as precise intimations of deity. On the other hand, it is evident that Luke is witnessing to one who did not have to await any transformation of character to become Son of the Highest (cf. Lk. vi. 35), or even His appointment to, or entrance upon, His office to be designated in this manner, but who from the very outset of His entrance into the world sustained a unique relationship to God. By no means all of the instances of the use of the name 'Son of God' in Luke, accordingly, may be construed as unequivocally signifying equality of the Son with the Father in power and glory. This supreme evaluation is definitely present in the record, however. And without it all the rest would remain inexplicable inasmuch as it is only on the background of a full acknowledgment of His deity that His supernatural entrance into the world and His appointment to perform transcendent religious functions become intelligible. All of these designations of Jesus as Son of God agree in witnessing to Luke's pervasively supernatural view of Jesus' person and activity, and therefore also present an insuperable obstacle in the path of the construction that Luke is a witness to an exclusively future exercise of Christ's messiahship.

It remains true that for Luke Jesus was also the Son of David. There is even an insistence upon the fulfilment of the messianic hope in terms of the Old Testament, which is bound up with previous observations as to the expectation of the coming of the kingdom in Old Testament terms. Although Luke, in distinction from Matthew, is patently not concerned especially to commend Christ to the Jew, his recognition of Jesus as the Son of David provides still another emphatic testimony of the indispensable place which the Old Testament and its formulation of the messianic hope occupied within the faith and life of early Christianity. The question of Jesus in Lk. xx. 41, 'How say they that the Christ is David's Son?' has been understood as a polemic against the interpretation of messiahship in these terms, but without justification. Jesus appeals to Ps. cx in order to sustain His transcendent view of messiahship as involving His lordship over David, but this does not imply that He was not also the Son of David. The firm place which the title occupies in the Christian tradition, including Luke, is proof that the acknowledgements of Him as both Lord and Son of David were considered entirely consistent with each other.[1]

Of special significance in this connection is Luke's description of the messianic hope in Lk. i. 32, 33: 'The Lord God shall give unto Him the throne of His father David: and He shall reign over the house of Jacob for ever; and of His kingdom there shall be no end.' Jesus is introduced as One whose mission could be significantly characterized in terms of the Son of David expectation. The context does not perhaps quite determine when the Son of David was thought of as beginning His reign. Since the context is concerned with the blessed significance of the birth of Christ it would seem more congruous to connect the beginning of His rule with His earthly life than with a future activity connected with the consummation of history. Moreover, in view of the acknowledgement of Jesus as Son of David recorded in Luke (Lk. xviii. 38 f.),

---

[1] Cf. WMMC, p. 223. For the tradition in Luke see Lk. i. 27, 69, iii. 31, ii. 4, 11; Acts ii. 29 f., xiii. 23; cf. Acts xiii. 34, xv. 16.

THE KINGDOM AND THE MESSIAH 169

and the testimony to Him as the anointed King (Lk. xix. 38), it is hardly plausible to view Lk. i. 32 f. as referring to a distantly prospective kingship. Regardless, however, of one's interpretation of this passage so far as the inception of His reign is concerned, there can be no question that the kingship attributed to Him transcends every political and other merely temporal category. The kingship is *eternal*, and therefore it possesses a transcendent character that corresponds with the view of messiahship which Jesus, by implication, claimed when He taught that the Christ is not merely Son of David but also his Lord.

A transition is thus provided for the consideration of the lordship of Jesus as that appears in Luke. Broadly speaking, there is close agreement with the usage in the other Synoptics.[1] It is employed with considerable reserve in the description of the public ministry. As a title or as a predicate it appears only in the sayings concerning lordship over the sabbath, the Lord's need of the colt, and in the teaching concerning the Messiah's lordship over David.[2] But it is also highly meaningful for the understanding of Jesus' own claims that He was frequently addressed as 'Lord' by disciples who were committed to Him, by those seeking supernatural aid as well as in certain eschatological parables.[3] These data demonstrate that, though Luke records the word of Peter that Jesus had been constituted both Lord and Christ by the resurrection (Acts ii. 36), he likewise regarded Jesus as exercising exalted sovereignty through His messianic activity on earth before the exaltation.

The reserve with which Luke, in common with the other Gospels, designates Jesus as Lord within the public ministry is the more remarkable when the testimony of the birth narratives is recalled. As has been observed in chapter III, even before the birth of Christ Mary is hailed by Elizabeth as 'the mother of my Lord' (Lk. i. 43). And the angelic announcement of the birth to the shepherds takes the form that a Saviour has been born who is 'Christ the Lord' (Lk. ii. 11). Since Luke frequently employs the

---

[1] See WMMC, pp. 253 ff.
[2] Lk. vi. 5, xix. 31, 34, xx. 42 ff. The instances in the eschatological parables are also significant. Cf. Lk. xii. 41 ff., xiii. 25-28.
[3] It is noteworthy that Luke sometimes uses the word ἐπιστάτα (v. 5, viii. 24, 45, ix. 33, 49, xvii. 13), and that the Semitic forms 'rabbi' and 'rabbouni' do not occur.

name Lord as the designation of God, as for example in recording the prophecy of Simeon that he would live to see 'the Anointed of the Lord' (Lk. ii. 26), it is impossible to avoid the impression that the evangelist is conscious of setting forth the profound mystery that He who was born as the promised Anointed of the Lord was Himself the Lord, and therefore possessed divine sovereignty quite apart from and prior to the establishment of His messianic kingdom.

Another distinctive feature of Luke, which also bears upon one's understanding of his perspective, is that he, as narrator, speaks of Jesus as Lord very frequently, no fewer than fourteen times in fact.[1] That this is characteristically Lucan appears from the observation that Matthew and Mark never refer to Jesus in this way and John does so only two or three times, besides the instances in the resurrection narrative.[2] In view of Luke's reserve elsewhere in his Gospel narrative, he evidently does not aim to create the impression that Jesus frequently spoke of Himself as Lord or was frequently thus addressed during His ministry before the resurrection. He apparently uses the name proleptically to conform to the usage which prevailed in the church when he wrote and to which he may have been somewhat partial. Nevertheless, one cannot fairly exclude the possibility that such a use was fostered by the belief that even before His exaltation to God's right hand, in the days of His ministry upon earth, Jesus was a supernatural person who acted with divine authority and at least occasionally applied the designation to Himself.

The Lucan delineation of Christ also includes the witness that he was the Son of Man. In this Gospel, as in the others, it is consistently used as a self-designation. In Acts, on the other hand, there is a single instance of its use, where Stephen is reported as seeing a heavenly vision of 'the Son of Man standing at the right

---

[1] Lk. vii. 13, 31, x. 1, 40, xi. 39, xii. 41, 42, xiii. 15, xvii. 5, 6, xviii. 6, xix. 8, xxii. 61 (bis); cf. xxiv. 3. In several of these instances there is some manuscript support, chiefly in the versions, for the omission of this title. It seems more likely, however, that the name was omitted by scribes in the interest of conformity to the customary usage than that it was introduced from liturgical motives. Cf. Creed on vii. 13.

[2] Jn. iv. 1 (where several witnesses including Aleph read 'Jesus'); vi. 23, xi. 2; cf. Jn. xx. 2, 20, xxi. 7, 12.

hand of God' (Acts vii. 56). Although this constitutes a formal exception to the rule that the title is found exclusively on Jesus' lips, the appropriateness of its use is evident when one considers the fact that Stephen's vision corresponds to Daniel's: like Daniel he is beholding the heavenly glory of this exalted figure as He shares the sovereignty of God, and is not speaking of an earthly advent of the Son of Man.[1]

In Luke, as in the other synoptic Gospels, the name appears in every stage of the career of Christ, and further confirmation is provided of the conclusion that there is intimate relationship between the various phases of the coming of the kingdom and the stages of the ministry of Christ. The distinctly eschatological coming of the Son of Man is clearly represented, in part in utterances represented in the Matthean and Marcan narratives, in part in references not closely paralleled in the other accounts.[2] These passages, however, represent only about one-third of the total number in which the title appears. In Lk. xxii. 69 the exaltation of the Son of Man to a place of glory and power at God's right hand is in view, and Luke is silent at this point concerning the return on the clouds of heaven. But in all the rest the predications made concerning the Son of Man relate to His appearance and mission on earth. Most of these, including especially the pronouncements concerning the suffering and humiliation which would precede the exaltation through the resurrection, correspond with utterances found in either Matthew or Mark or both.[3] If one leaves out of account Lk. vi. 22 and xxii. 48 as being only relatively unique,[4] it is discovered that only one utterance is exclusively Lucan. That is the saying at the close of the story of Zacchaeus, 'For the Son of Man came to seek and to save that which was lost' (Lk. xix. 10).

[1] Cf. WMMC, pp. 249 ff.
[2] For the first group cf. Lk. ix. 26, xii. 8, 40, xvii. 24, 26, xxi. 27; for the second group Lk. xvii. 30, xviii. 8, xxi. 36.
[3] Cf. Lk. v. 24, vi. 5, vii. 34, ix. 22, 44, 58, xi. 30, xii. 10, xviii. 31 f., xxii. 22, xxiv. 7.
[4] Lk. vi. 22 pronounces blessing upon those who are hated and reproached and whose names are cast out as evil 'for the Son of Man's sake.' Mt. v. 11 speaks similarly of those who are persecuted 'for my sake.' In Lk. xxii. 48 Judas is asked, 'Betrayest thou the Son of Man with a kiss?'. This also has no parallel, but Luke xviii. 31, xxii. 22, and their synoptic parallels deal with the betrayal of the Son of Man.

The purpose of bringing salvation to the house of Zacchaeus, which is grounded in Jesus' broad declaration of the goal of His mission, confirms emphatically the view of the meaning of the title as intimating the heavenly, supernatural character of the Messiah. Jesus is not a mere man, but a heavenly Being who came to effect supernaturally the salvation of men. He was born indeed as a man, but even His human nature He owed to a supernatural act. And though He lived a life of privation and ignominy, did not have a place to lay His head, brought offence when He joined others in social intercourse, was mocked and insulted, betrayed by one of the twelve, and finally nailed to the cross, we are never allowed to lose sight of the fact that these human experiences were in the last analysis of startling incongruity because of His rightful claim of glory as the Son of Man. These experiences were endured therefore only as required by the divine plan of salvation and as a prelude to His own vindication and glory through the power of God. His essentially supernatural and glorious nature was to manifest itself through His resurrection, His session at God's right hand, and His coming on the clouds of heaven, but even in His earthly career He acted in the consciousness of His supreme dignity and power.

So supernatural indeed is Luke's pervasive presentation of Christ that the charge is sometimes levelled at him that, owing to his reverence for Jesus' person, he has been reluctant to leave traces of human emotions or expressions of stern and violent feeling.[1] Much is made, for example, of the fact that in reporting the stories of the healing of a leper and the feeding of the five thousand Luke is silent concerning the 'compassion' of Jesus where Mark makes mention of it (Mk. i. 41, vi. 34; Lk. v. 13, ix. 11 f.). Besides Luke does not include the story of the feeding of the four thousand where the third instance of mention of the compassion of Jesus is found (Mk. viii. 2). This charge rests, however, on a quite inadequate induction of the facts. If Luke omitted the reference to Jesus' compassion in these stories because such an emotion seemed to conflict with his views of the transcendence of Christ, why does he use the very term in motivating Jesus'

---

[1] Cf. Cadbury, *Style and Literary Method of Luke*, pp. 90 ff.; *Making*, p. 266; M. S. Enslin, *Christian Beginnings*, 1938, pp. 405 f. On a similar charge against Matthew, cf. WMMC, pp. 82 f., 219 f.

action in raising the widow's son at Nain (Lk. vii. 13)? Nor can one readily set aside as irrelevant two other instances of the word in Luke. Both the characterization of the good Samaritan in Lk. x. 33 and of the father of the prodigal son in Lk. xv. 20 as moved with compassion, though of course they do not describe Jesus' own emotional life, are evidently approved as actions by which men would demonstrate their divine sonship (cf. Lk. vi. 35) or even, in the second case, the nature of the divine love for the lost. How then can it be supposed that Luke regards compassion as incongruous with divine dignity! Moreover, it is a highly hazardous procedure to draw far-reaching conclusions from the silence of Luke as to certain details, especially since his narrative is marked by brevity of characterization.[1]

The mere fact, moreover, that Luke, in reporting the cleansing of the temple, omits any reference to His overturning of the tables and seats is taken as evidence of Luke's desire to suppress intimations that Jesus acted with violence.[2] Mark's narrative does in fact present vivid details of Jesus' wrathful and stirring action which are not found in Luke (Mk. xi. 15-18; cf. Lk. xix. 45 ff.). But it is far-fetched to conclude that Luke presents an essentially different picture of Jesus' emotional reactions. If Luke were concerned to avoid the impression that Jesus acted with violence and spoke with vehemence against the occupants of the temple, why should he include the pregnant statement that 'He began to cast out them that sold' and the unmild charge that they had made the house of prayer a den of robbers (Lk. xix. 45 f.)?[3]

The sternness of Jesus as portrayed by Mark is often contrasted with the gentleness of Jesus in Luke's Gospel, and this seems to find its chief support in the absence from Luke of various refer-

[1] Cadbury himself makes this observation. *Style and Literary Method*, pp. 79 ff., 127 f.
[2] Cf. Cadbury, *Style and Literary Method*, pp. 90 f.; Enslin, op. cit., p. 406.
[3] Luke is also sometimes said to have been influenced in his treatment of the story by his concern to soften the impression of hostility to Judaism. Luke does indeed show in the Gospel as well as in the Acts that Christians were not hostile to the worship of the temple as such. But the zeal of Jesus for the worship of God in the temple is revealed in its greatest intensity precisely through the strength of His emotional reaction to its abuse on the part of certain contemporaries. On the other hand, in the Gospel and Acts, no more than in the other Gospels, is there any evidence of a tendency to relieve the tension between Jesus and His disciples, on the one hand, and the representatives of current Judaism, on the other. Cf., e.g., Acts ii. 22 f., iii. 13.

ences to Jesus' anger, His rebuke of Peter and the like (cf. Mk. iii. 5, viii. 33).[1] Since in Mark also, as has been noticed, Jesus is motivated in His actions towards men by love and compassion, the sternness displayed there is by no means unrelieved. And so far as Luke is concerned, though certain expressions which might seem severe are missing, others are conspicuously present. For all of His gentleness and kindliness the Jesus of Luke is absolutely uncompromising in His demands. Although the rebuke of Peter is not mentioned, Luke alone tells of the rebuke of James and John when they requested that they be permitted to bid fire come down from heaven to consume the Samaritans who did not receive Jesus (Lk. ix. 51 ff.). Only the Jesus of Luke charges the disciples that, if a brother sin, they should rebuke him (Lk. xvii. 3). And in none of the Gospels is Jesus' demands for self-sacrifice as a condition of discipleship expressed as absolutely as in Luke:

'If any man cometh unto Me, and hateth not his own father, and mother, and wife, and children, and brethren, and sisters, yea, and his own life also, he cannot be My disciple' (Lk. xiv. 26).

'So therefore whosoever he be of you that renounceth not all that he hath, he cannot be My disciple' (Lk. xiv. 33).

It may be recalled that it was these sayings which Renan especially appealed to in support of his construction that Jesus, now no longer under the spell of the sunshine and green hills of Galilee, had ceased to be 'the delicate and joyous moralist of earlier days' but was rather 'the sombre giant whom a kind of sublime presentiment was casting more and more beyond the pale of humanity.'[2] Renan's construction is, to be sure, quite unscientific. The double image of Christ which he finds in the Gospels, amounting virtually to implications of schizophrenia, and the extremely arbitrary forcing of the data into a scheme of development, will satisfy the historian and the psychologist no more than the man of faith. Nevertheless, his reconstruction has served the useful purpose of concentrating attention upon features of the Gospel witness which all too commonly are overlooked or under-

[1] Cf. Cadbury, *Style and Literary Method*, p. 91; Enslin, op. cit., pp. 405 f.; Creed, op. cit., pp. lxii f.
[2] E. Renan, *Vie de Jésus*, 1863, p. 312.

estimated. In particular, Renan's characterization reminds us at this point that the Lucan portrait is by no means divested of the traits of firmness. Christ demands an exclusive devotion to Himself, one that requires the subordination of all other affections to one great overpowering affection for Himself. In this Gospel, then, the elements of firmness and gentleness, of severity and graciousness are blended together to create an overwhelming impression of One who was constantly controlled in His actions no less by the demands of righteousness than by those of love.

Another feature of the Lucan portrayal which ill agrees with the notion that this evangelist was concerned to depict Jesus as free from human infirmity is the place given to the prayers of Jesus. The other records likewise speak of Jesus' practice of prayer,[1] but Luke does so far more often. He not only described the prayer in the garden (Lk. xxii. 41 ff.) and on many other occasions such as the baptism and transfiguration (Lk. iii. 21, ix. 28 f.), but also indicates that Jesus' praying was habitual and prolonged (cf. Lk. v. 16, vi. 12, ix. 18, xi. 1). It is hardly an exaggeration therefore to state that, according to Luke, the entire ministry of Jesus was carried out in a spirit of dependence upon God. If Luke were deliberately recasting the gospel tradition with a view to the obliteration of features which might seem to represent Him as sharing human emotions and attitudes, we should be at a loss to understand the prominence given to Jesus' practice of prayer.

The Christ of Luke is not a new Christ. One who turns from the portraits of Matthew and Mark to contemplate that of Luke will immediately recognize the identity of the Person. Prolonged and painstaking attention to details will serve only to confirm the judgment gained from first impressions.

There are indeed notable differences in the testimony of the three evangelists. In Mark we discover a figure who, for all of the mystery that surrounds Him, stands out in rugged simplicity as the Son of God who unwaveringly marches to the cross to give His life as a ransom for many. The Matthaean portrait is more complex. The central motif of Mark is present, but in Matthew there is much besides. Jesus is disclosed as being a divine Person, and one also contemplates the lonely act of self-humiliation to

[1] Mk. i. 35, vi. 46, xiv. 32, 35, 39; Mt. xiv. 23, xxvi. 36, 39, 42, 44.

the death on the cross. But now the figure of Jesus appears in less severe isolation. A richer background is drawn and the future is more sharply delineated, and thus one comes to a fuller understanding of Christ's place in history. Matthew's witness is wonderfully suited for instruction and meditation. It lends itself to a contemplation which rests upon one feature and then another until the whole is seen in its wealth of detail.

Luke like Matthew contains the message of Mark. He appears to have left it largely undisturbed. And much of the distinctive contents of Matthew may be paralleled in Luke. But there are also extraordinary supplementary features in Luke, many of which have been dwelt upon in the foregoing chapters. Much of the colour of Luke is derived from the singular and fascinating contents of the birth narrative, the parables and other teaching in the middle chapters, and the account of the resurrection and the ascension of Christ.

In taking account of the supplementary character of Luke, however, one is far from doing full justice to the individuality of this Gospel. It is by no means to be gauged simply in terms of additions or omissions, for it has a unity and coherence of its own. The gospel was in a most important sense the common property of the Christian Church. No matter who proclaimed it, there was the necessity of faithfulness to what had been handed down. But it was proclaimed by different evangelists at different times and in different situations. In explaining the individuality of Luke, accordingly, one must consider various historical factors. These must have included Luke's own special aptitudes and qualifications as a writer, his opportunities for securing information, and his estimate of the needs of those for whom the finished work was intended. His unusual skill as a writer is evident from beginning to end. His personal contacts with Christians in centres like Jerusalem and Caesarea explain many of his unique contributions to our knowledge of Jesus' life and message. The choice of materials and manner of presentation were also influenced by his aim to provide such an exposition and defence of the origins of Christianity as would be most conducive to the establishment of the faith of persons like Theophilus. Theophilus was evidently a Gentile, and he must have been viewed as a representative of the Gentile world to which Luke, the Greek writer, could with peculiar insight and sympathy address the Gospel. His avoidance of Semitic forms and his silence on some points which would have been peculiarly obscure to persons uninstructed in Jewish beliefs and practices may be explained on this basis.

It remains most remarkable, however, that for all of the distinctiveness and individuality of Luke, it is impossible to single out perspectives that may be characterized as constituting *tendencies* of the Gospel. In the modern literature there have indeed been frequent allegations that Luke has edited the tradition and manipulated it in the interest of setting forth, consciously or unconsciously, his own special viewpoints. As the evidence has been examined, however, it has been found that it is impossible to set Luke sharply over against Matthew and Mark in regard to such matters as the lordship of Jesus and His atoning death or the coming of the kingdom of God.

Though there are unique features and special interests and emphases, there is nothing to disturb the unity of the testimony. The beauty and charm of the whole seem to be due to a skilful blending of a wealth of detail into an inspiring single impression. Luke did not believe that religious devotion flourished in the absence of earnest meditation upon historical truth, and we should therefore prove untrue to his approach to his subject if the suggestion were made that one might be indifferent to the details of Luke and yet gain a true appreciation of it. Our impression is rather that, though the details grip our attention, none is so conspicuous that we can long contemplate it without observing that it blends into the total representation. Luke's witness to Christ is therefore a superb work of devotion and adoration. And it is most appropriate that the first and last scenes of the Gospel find their setting in the temple at Jerusalem.

INDEXES

I. NAMES AND SUBJECTS

ABRAHAMS, I., 84
Acts of the Apostles, the; aim and scope of, 13, 26 f.; the apostles in, 27 ff., 149; the ascension in, 150 f.; the Church in, 155 f.; the resurrection in, 143, 149; significance for the Gospel, 10 f.; speeches in, 17; the Spirit in, 13, 14, 27, 151; 'we'-sections in, 15 ff., 36
Alexander, J. A., 106
Allen, W. C., 107
Anti-Marcionite Prologue, the Lucan, 14
Aristarchus, 19
Atonement, the, 130 ff., 138, 151
Augustine, 72
Augustus, 58 f., 65

BAUR, F. C., 21
Bethsaida, 104 ff.
Billerbeck, P., 136
Blass, F., 26, 30, 37, 38, 41, 136
Bowman, J. W., 73
Branscomb, H., 125
Bultmann, R., 86, 155
Burkitt, F. C., 125, 141, 163
Burton, E. de W. and Godspeed, E. J., 98

CADBURY, H. J., 11, 15, 16, 17, 18, 20, 22 f., 26 f., 28, 30, 34 ff., 40 f., 42 f., 98, 132, 140, 156, 164, 172, 173, 174
Caspari, E. C., 60
Colson, F. H., 39, 43 f.
Creed, J. M., 11, 17, 20, 21, 23, 30, 34 37, 39, 40, 69, 72, 75, 90, 106, 114, 115, 118, 122, 129, 131, 132, 133, 136, 137, 139, 146, 156, 170

DALMAN, G., 106
Dibelius, M., 30, 40
Didache, the, 134 f.

EASTON, B. S., 22, 40, 70, 72, 103, 104 f., 131, 133

Enslin, M. S., 127, 172
Eschatology, 156 f., 161
Eusebius, 26, 31

FORM-CRITICISM, 21, 25, 29, 94
Four-document Hypothesis, the, 22, 71, 115, 137

GALILEAN HYPOTHESIS, 142
Goguel, M., 60
Gospel of Jesus Christ, the, 14, 27, 44 f., 47 ff., 51 ff., 67, 85, 149
Gospel Criticism; see Form-criticism, Four-document Hypothesis, Marcan Hypothesis, Two-document Hypothesis
Gould, E. P., 106
Greijdanus, S., 41, 72, 100, 131
Grosheide, F. W., 30

HARNACK, A., 9, 15, 19 f., 30, 86
Hawkins, J. C., 15, 109
Herod the Great, 59, 65, 97
Herod Antipas, 64, 118 ff.
Hobart, W. K., 19 f.
Holtzmann, H. J., 131
Hort, F. J. A., 131, 132
Huck, A., 98, 101
Humanity of Jesus, the, 172 ff.

IRENAEUS, 14, 15, 30

JAMES, the apostle, 18
Jerusalem, 115 ff., 123, 127, 147
Jerusalem Hypothesis, 142
Jesus Christ, the career of; birth, 46 ff.; baptism, 59, 63; public ministry 65 ff. and *passim*; calling of disciples, 96 f.; events in Caesarea Philippi, 112 f., 126; transfiguration, 113; passion and death, 110 ff., 122 f., 128 ff. rejection, 55 f., 68 ff., 91 f.; last supper, 131 ff.; resurrection, 110,

INDEX TO NAMES AND SUBJECTS

Jesus Christ, (continued); 122, 141 ff., 149; ascension and exaltation, 14, 27, 150 f., 155; return, 76, 151. See also Atonement, Humanity, Teaching, Works, Lord, Messiah, Messiahship, Servant of the Lord, Son of David, Son of God, Son of man
John the Baptist, 47, 51, 56 ff., 119, 121
John, the Gospel according to, 46
Josephus, 11 f., 108
Judaism, 162, 173
Judaea, 95 f., 130
Jülicher, A., 40, 45, 163

Kenyon, F., 10
Klostermann, E., 41, 45, 73, 131, 136, 146

Lagrange, M. J., 131
Lake, K., 141
Liddell, H. G., and Scott, R., 72
Lietzmann, H., 139
Lightfoot, R. H., 69, 87, 90, 99, 117, 129, 130, 142, 148
Lohmeyer, E., 117
Loisy, A., 60
Lord, the, 50, 62, 151, 169 f.
Luke, the evangelist; author of Luke-Acts, 14 ff.; historical sense, 14; Physcian, 19 ff.; and Paul, 16 ff., 134, 143; predecessors, 25 ff., 31 ff.; qualifications, 33, 93, 110, 176
Luke, the Gospel according to:
Contents of; prologue, 11 ff., 24 ff.; birth narratives, 46 ff.; Galilean ministry in, 72, 88, 94 ff., 102, 117 f. 120, 126 f.; middle section, 93 111 ff., 114 ff.; passion narrative in 110 ff., 122 f., 128 ff., 146; resurrection narrative in, 110, 122, 141 ff.
Characteristics of; comparisons with Mark, 34, 46, 68 f., 70, 74, 92, 94 ff., 105, 108, 110, 113, 125 ff., 137 f. 141, 156, 171, 175; comparisons with Matthew, 46 f., 48, 68 f., 70, 92, 153, 141, 162, 171, 175; concern with chronology and topography, 59, 65, 92, 95, 97, 103; critical views of, 21 ff.; disposition of, 10, 111; language and style, 9, 17, 19, 40 f., 103; supposed biographical and secular interests, 47 f., 61, 63 f., 66 f.; readers, 77, 176 f.; reflection on revelation, 47 ff.; summary evaluation, 175 ff.; universalism, 90 f., 162. See also Acts of the Apostles, and Luke-Acts
Luke-Acts, 10 ff., 20, 144

Machen, J. G., 18, 60, 65, 66
Manson, W., 22, 42, 70, 131, 132
Marcan Hypothesis, the, 21
Marcion, 21, 162
Mark, the Gospel according to: see *sub* Luke
Mark, the evangelist, 19, 37 f.
Mary, 47, 56, 62
Matthew, the Gospel according to; see *sub* Luke
McNeile, A. H., 131
Messiah, the, 50, 67, 87 f., 112 f., 121 f., 129 f., 149, 151, 152 f., 160, 165 f., 169, 172
Messiahship; the messianic hope, 48, 60, 77 ff., 85 ff., 160 ff., 168 f.; reserve in disclosure of messiahship, 88, 152 f., 165, 169, 170. See also Messiah, Servant of the Lord, Son of God, Son of Man
Meyer, W. A. H., 40
Moulton, J. H. 2nd Milligan, G., 32, 72

Ogg, G., 58, 60, 66, 116
Old Testament, Jesus' view of the, 77, 160, 162 f.
Oral tradition, 25, 29 f., 103. See also Form-criticism
Otto, R., 133, 139 f., 155

Paul, 16 ff., 134, 143
Peræa, 116 f., 120, 125 f.
Peter, 94, 97, 112 f.
Pharisees, 120, 127
Philip, 18
Piper, O., 27
Plummer, A., 20, 66, 72, 100, 114, 116, 118, 122, 131, 146
Prayers of Jesus, 175

Quirinius, 65

Rawlinson, A. E. J., 108, 125

Renan, E., 9, 174 f.
Ridderbos, H. N., 165
Robinson, J. A., 135
Ropes, J. H., 14, 35, 37, 127

SAMARIA, 116, 117 ff., 125
Schmidt, K. L., 40, 66, 94, 105, 115, 116, 155
Schweitzer, A., 165
Sermon on the Mount, 99 ff.
Servant of the Lord, the, 87 f., 147, 151
Simeon, 51 ff., 64, 91, 161
Smith, G. A., 108
Son of David, 50, 96, 161, 162, 168
Son of God, 50, 141, 166 ff.
Son of Man, 124, 146 f., 153 f., 155, 156, 170 ff.
Strauss, D. F., 142
Streeter, B. H., 18, 22, 23, 30, 42, 71, 106, 109, 115, 132
Swete, H. B., 125, 158

TAYLOR, V., 22, 71, 109, 115, 137
Teaching of Jesus, the; concerning the kingdom, 76 ff., 152, 154 ff.; concerning His relation to the kingdom, 75, 76, 85 ff., 152 ff., 165 ff. See also Messiahship and Sermon on the Mount.
Theophilus, 33, 35, 36, 41 f.
Tiberius, 58
Timothy, 19
Tischendorf, C., 95
Titus, 19
Turner, C. H., 59, 66
Two-document Hypothesis, the, 114

Vos, G., 124, 159, 165

WEISS, B., 131
Weiss, J., 42, 131, 141
Wellhausen, J., 21, 73 ff., 122, 125, 131, 132, 136, 163
Westcott, F. B., 122
Wieseler, K., 60
Windisch, H., 15 ff., 19, 21
Works of Jesus, the, 72 ff., 88 f., 92, 97, 101 ff.
Wrede, W., 21, 165

ZAHN, T., 11, 19 f., 42, 66, 131
Zeitlin, S., 120

II. SCRIPTURE REFERENCES

LEVITICUS	
xxv. 10 ff.	84
xxvii. 24	85

DEUTERONOMY	
xxviii. 33	84

II SAMUEL	
vii. 12 ff.	161

PSALMS	
cx	168

ISAIAH	
i. 9	56
iii. 14 f.	80
x. 1 f.	80
x. 22 f.	56
xiv. 25	84
xxix. 18 f.	79
xxix. 19 f.	81
xxxv. 5, 10	84
xl. 1 f.	51
xl. 5	54
xli. 17–20	81
xlii	84
xlii. 1	79
xlii. 6	55
xlii. 6 f.	79, 84
xlii. 19–20	83
xlviii. 5	81
xlix. 6	55, 84
xlix. 8–13	82
xlix. 13	51
xlix. 22 ff.	82
xlix. 24 ff.	82
li. 3	51
lii. 1–6	82
lii. 10	54
liii. 3, 11	56
lviii. 6	82, 84
lviii. 6 f.	80
lix. 9–14	83
lxi. 2, 3	51 f., 78 ff., 84

JEREMIAH	
xxxiv. 8–10	85

EZEKIEL	
xxx. 18	84
xxxiv. 27	84
xlvi. 17	85

DANIEL	
vii. 13 f.	161

MATTHEW	
ii. 1, 23	48
iv. 12	64
iv. 13 ff.	71
iv. 18 ff.	97
iv. 23	95
v. 11	171
viii. 5–13	100
viii. 14–17	95
ix. 18–x. 30	97
x. 34 ff.	55

INDEXES

xi. 2–19	101	iii. 7–12	98	xiv. 17	130
xi. 3 ff.	87	iii. 7 f.	99	xiv. 22	136
xi. 4 f.	121 f.	iii. 13–19	98 f.	xiv. 26 ff.	130
xi. 5	83	iii. 20–vi. 44	94, 102 f.	xiv. 28	147
xi. 7 ff.	154	iii. 20 ff.	127	xiv. 32	175
xi. 12	154	iii. 23–30	102	xiv. 35	175
xi. 15	58	iii. 31–35	102	xiv. 39	175
xi. 27	167	iv. 1 f.	103	xiv. 62	157
xii. 22 ff.	127	iv. 26–34	102	xvi. 7	147, 148
xii. 28	154	iv. 35	104		
xiii. 1 f.	103	vi. 1 ff.	69, 73, 103	**LUKE**	
xiii. 17	52	vi. 2	157	i. 1–4	12 f., 24 ff.
xiii. 53 ff.	69	vi. 2, 3	74	i. 5–25	47, 49
xiii. 54–56	74	vi. 4–6	75	i. 5	59, 65, 96
xiii. 57	75	vi. 5	157	i. 6	160
xiv. 1–12	64	vi. 14–29	64	i. 7	49
xiv. 1 ff.	119	vi. 14	119, 157	i. 13–17	49
xiv. 13	107	vi. 17–29	102	i. 17	50, 57, 61
xiv. 22 ff.	107	vi. 20	119	i. 18	57
xiv. 23	175	vi. 31	105	i. 19 f.	49
xiv. 31	107	vi. 32	106	i. 19	48, 57
xvi. 13–xviii. 5	112	vi. 34	172	i. 20	51
xvi. 21	113	vi. 44	105	i. 24	62
xix. 28	160	vi. 45–viii. 26	95, 108	i. 25	57
xx. 28	131	vi. 45 ff.	107 f.	i. 26–38	47, 49
xxvi. 2	129	vi. 45	104 f.	i. 28	49
xxvi. 20	130	vi. 46	175	i. 30–33	49
xxvi. 26	136	vi. 47	108	i. 31	27, 168
xxvi. 30 ff.	130	vi. 53	107	i. 32 f.	48, 50, 161,
xxvi. 32	147	vii. 1–23	108		168, 169
xxvi. 36	175	viii. 2	172	i. 32	167
xxvi. 39	175	viii. 11–21	108 f.	i. 33	160
xxvi. 42	175	viii. 22	105	i. 34	62
xxvi. 44	175	viii. 27–ix. 41	112	i. 35	49, 50, 167
xxvi. 64	157	viii. 27–ix. 50	126	i. 36 f.	62
xxvii. 55	101	viii. 27	126	i. 39–56	49
xxviii. 7	147	viii. 31	113	i. 42–45	49, 62
xxviii. 10	147	ix. 1	157	i. 43	49, 50, 169
xxviii. 16	147	ix. 14	127	i. 45	57
		ix. 30	126	i. 46	49, 55
MARK		ix. 33 ff.	126	i. 47	51
i. 14 f.	70	ix. 52	116	i. 54 f.	51
i. 14	64	x. 1	116, 125, 126, 127	i. 56	62
i. 16–20	97	x. 45	131	i. 57–80	47, 49
i. 21–39	94, 95 f.	x. 46	117	i. 58	57
i. 35	175	xi. 15–18	173	i. 68	51
i. 39	95	xii. 24	157	i. 69	48, 51, 53,
i. 40–iii. 19	94, 97, 98 f.	xiii. 5 ff.	158		141, 168
i. 41	172	xiii. 7	157	i. 71	53, 141
ii. 10	87	xiii. 10	157	i. 72 f.	51
ii. 13 f.	99	xiii. 26	157	i. 76	57, 61
ii. 28	87	xiv. 1	129	i. 77	51, 141

i. 79	53	iv. 31–44	94, 95 f.	viii. 10	154
i. 80	60 f., 66	iv. 31	72, 95	viii. 19–21	102
ii. 1–7	47, 49	iv. 38	95, 97	viii. 24	169
ii. 1 ff.	48, 59, 65	iv. 40	95	viii. 26	106
ii. 4	168	iv. 41	166	viii. 27	106
ii. 8–20	49	iv. 42	95	viii. 28	166
ii. 10–12	49	iv. 43 f.	76	viii. 39	106
ii. 10	48, 57	iv. 43	58, 72, 95, 153	viii. 45	169
ii. 11	50, 51, 61, 141, 166, 168, 169	iv. 44	72, 75	ix. 2	152
ii. 14	49	v. 1–11	94, 96	ix. 9	64, 105
ii. 21	49, 50	v. 3	97	ix. 10	104 ff., 107
ii. 22–38	49, 51 ff.	v. 5	169	ix. 11–17	106
ii. 25 ff.	161	v. 8	97	ix. 11 f.	172
ii. 25	51	v. 11	97	ix. 11	152
ii. 26	49, 50, 52, 61, 166	v. 12–vi. 16	94, 97, 98 f.	ix. 12	105
		v. 13	172	ix. 16	58, 139
ii. 27 f.	52	v. 16	175	ix. 18–50	112 f., 126
ii. 29 f.	53	v. 24	171	ix. 18	112, 175
ii. 29	50	v. 27	99	ix. 20 ff.	113
ii. 30	51	vi. 5	169, 171	ix. 20	166
ii. 34	50, 55	vi. 12–16	98	ix. 22	112, 125, 155
ii. 35	50, 56	vi. 12	175	ix. 26	157, 171
ii. 38	50, 51, 161	vi. 17–viii. 3	94	ix. 27	156, 157
ii. 39 f.	40	vi. 17–19	98, 99 f.	ix. 28 ff.	113
ii. 41–52	50	vi. 17	96, 99, 100	ix. 28 f.	175
ii. 49	50	vi. 20–49	99 f.	ix. 30	126
iii. 1 f.	58 ff., 59, 66	vi. 20	154	ix. 31	118
iii. 3 ff.	63	vi. 22	171	ix. 33	169
iii. 6	53	vi. 24	164	ix. 35	166
iii. 10–14	57	vi. 35	167, 173	ix. 37	118
iii. 16	63	vii. 1–10	100 f.	ix. 44	124, 171
iii. 18	57	vii. 11–17	101	ix. 49	169
iii. 19 f.	102	vii. 13	170, 173	ix. 51–xviii. 14	111 f., 114 ff.
iii. 21 f.	63, 175	vii. 17	96		
iii. 22 f.	166	vii. 18–35	101	ix. 51 ff.	127, 174
iii. 22	66	vii. 18 ff.	64, 102	ix. 51	115 f., 118
iii. 23	65, 66	vii. 19 ff.	87	ix. 52 f.	116, 118
iii. 31	168	vii. 22 f.	121 f.	ix. 52	117
iv. 3 ff.	166	vii. 22	58, 83, 104	ix. 54	125
iv. 14–ix. 17	94	vii. 24 ff.	154	ix. 58	171
iv. 14 f.	71, 75	vii. 28	64. 154	ix. 60	152
iv. 14	94	vii. 30 ff.	102	ix. 62	154
iv. 16–30	68 ff., 152 f.	vii. 31	170	x. 1	117, 170
iv. 16	48, 71	vii. 34	164, 171	x. 9, 11	154
iv. 18 f.	68	vii. 36–50	101	x. 13	104 f.
iv. 18	58, 165	vii. 36	102	x. 22	167
iv. 21	26	vii. 37	164	x. 33	173
iv. 22	73	vii. 39	164	x. 38	116
iv. 23	72 ff.	viii. 1–3	101	x. 40	170
iv. 25–27	90 ff.	viii. 1	58, 103, 152	xi. 1	175
iv. 28	74	viii. 4–ix. 17	94, 102 f.	xi. 2	154
		viii. 4	103	xi. 14–23	102

INDEXES

xi. 14 ff.	127	xviii. 31 ff.	124, 155, 171	xxii. 67		166, 167
xi. 20	154	xviii. 31	116, 118	xxii. 69	155, 156, 157, 171
xi. 29	127	xviii. 35 ff.	116	xxii. 70		167
xi. 30	171	xviii. 35	114, 117, 118	xxiii. 2 f.		166
xi. 37	127	xviii. 38 f.	168	xxiii. 5		96, 130
xi. 39	170	xix. 1	114	xxiii. 8–12		119 f.
xi. 41	164	xix. 2	164	xxiii. 35		166
xii. 1	127	xix. 7	164	xxiii. 37		166
xii. 8	171	xix. 8	164, 170	xxiii. 38		166
xii. 10	102, 171	xix, 9 f.	141	xxiii. 39		166
xii. 32	159	xix. 10	152, 171	xxiii. 42 f.		154
xii. 33	164	xix, 11	118, 156, 158	xxiv		142 ff.
xii. 40	171	xix. 16 f.	154	xxiv. 1–35		145
xii. 41, 42	170	xix. 17 f.	129	xxiv. 3		170
xiii. 10–17	97	xix. 24 f.	154	xxiv. 6–8		147
xiii. 10	127	xix. 28	116	xxiv. 6 ff.		148
xiii. 15	170	xix. 31	169	xxiv. 7		171
xiii. 18 f.	102, 154	xix. 34	169	xxiv. 13		145
xiii. 20 f.	154	xix. 38	166, 169	xxiv. 21		160
xiii. 22	116 f.	xix. 41	116	xxiv. 25 f.		149
xiii. 28 f.	154	xix. 45 ff.	173	xxiv. 26		155, 166
xiii. 31–33	119 ff., 123	xix. 45 f.	129, 173	xxiv. 30		139
xiii. 31	127	xix. 45	112, 116, 129	xxiv. 35		139
xiii. 33 f.	116	xix. 47	129	xxiv. 36–43		145
xiv. 1–6	127	xx. 1	58, 129, 130	xxiv. 43–49		146
xiv. 1	127	xx. 13	166	xxiv. 44 ff.		148, 163
xiv. 12	164	xx. 17 f.	92	xxiv. 44–49		146
xiv. 15 ff.	161	xx. 41	168	xxiv. 44		77
xiv. 15	154	xx. 42 ff.	169	xxiv. 45 f.		147
xiv. 25	127	xxi. 8	156, 158	xxiv. 46 f.		165
xiv. 26	174	xxi. 27	157, 171	xxiv. 46	141, 151, 166
xiv. 33	174	xxi. 31	154	xxiv. 49	145, 150, 155
xv. 1	164	xxi. 36	157, 171	xxiv. 51		150
xv. 20	173	xxi. 37	129, 130			
xv. 41	101	xxii. 1	129, 130		JOHN	
xvi. 1	164	xxii. 2–6	129	i. 44		106
xvi. 16	58, 154, 163	xxii. 14–18	137	iv. 1		170
xvi. 17	163	xxii. 14	130	vi. 23		170
xvi. 19 ff.	164	xxii. 15–18	136	xi. 2		170
xvii. 3	174	xxii. 15	136	xx. 2		170
xvii. 5 f.	170	xxii. 16	137, 154	xx. 20		170
xvii. 11–19	97	xxii. 17	137	xxi. 7		170
xvii. 11	116 f., 118, 120, 125, 127	xxii. 18	154	xxi. 7, 12		170
		xxii. 19 f.	131 ff.			
xvii. 13	169	xxii. 22	124, 171		ACTS	
xvii. 21	155, 160	xxii. 29 f.	154, 159 f., 161	i		143
xvii. 24	157, 171	xxii. 30	160	i. 1 f.		150
xvii. 26	157, 171	xxii. 39 f.	130	i. 1		26 f., 116
xvii. 30	157, 171	xxii. 41 ff.	175	i. 3		144
xviii. 6	170	xxii. 48	171	i. 4		145
xviii. 8	157, 171	xxii. 51	97	i. 8		155
xviii. 10–13	158	xxii. 61	170	i. 9 ff.		150

i. 11	151	xiii. 23	141, 168	ix–xi	55
i. 21 f.	28	xiii. 24	61, 63	ix. 6	55
i. 22	29, 61, 63, 66	xiii. 34	168	xiv. 5	26
ii. 1 ff.	155	xiii. 38 f.	141		
ii. 1	116	xv. 16	168	I CORINTHIANS	
ii. 9	96	xv. 28	45	iv. 1	38
ii. 22 f.	173	xv. 36	38	xi. 23 ff.	134
ii. 23	124	xv. 37 ff.	19	xi. 24 f.	132 f.
ii. 29 f.	168	xvi. 10–17	15 ff.	xv. 1 ff.	143
ii. 32 ff.	164	xvi. 17	141	xv. 11	134, 143
ii. 33	155	xvii. 3	166		
ii. 34	164	xx. 4	19		
ii. 35 f.	151	xx. 5–xxi. 26	15 ff.	GALATIANS	
ii. 36	165, 169	xx. 7	139	i. 18 f.	143
ii. 38	141	xx. 11	139	ii. 1 ff.	143
ii. 44 f.	164	xx. 28	140, 155		
ii. 42	29	xxi. 8–12	18	COLOSSIANS	
ii. 46	139	xxi. 18	18	iv. 10 f.	19
iii. 13	151, 173	xxi. 21	43	iv. 14	19
iii. 14	151	xxi. 24	43		
iii. 18	151	xxi. 33 f.	43	I THESSALONIANS	
iii. 21	151	xxi. 34	43	v. 2	156
iv. 12	53, 141	xxii. 30	43, 44		
iv. 26	166	xxiii. 1 ff.	44	II THESSALONIANS	
iv. 27	124	xxiii. 26	42	ii. 1 ff.	156 f.
v. 1 ff.	164	xxiv. 3	42		
v. 4	164	xxv. 26 f.	43, 44	II TIMOTHY	
vi. 1	164	xxvi. 4	28	iv. 5	26
vi. 4	29, 38	xxvi. 16	38	iv. 11	15, 19
vi. 14	29	xxvi. 23	166	iv. 17	26
vii. 11–17	96	xxvi. 25	42		
vii. 56	171	xxvii. 1–xxviii. 16	15 ff.	PHILEMON	
x. 37	28, 61, 63, 66, 96	xxvii. 35	139	24	19
x. 38	63	xxviii. 20	161		
xi. 28	15	xxviii. 28	53	HEBREWS	
xii. 12, 25	19			ii. 10	122
xiii. 5	37 f.	ROMANS		v. 9	122
xiii. 13	19	viii. 34	151	vii. 28	122

twin brooks series — BOOKS IN THE SERIES

THE ACTS OF THE APOSTLES	Richard B. Rackham
APOSTOLIC AND POST-APOSTOLIC TIMES (Goppelt)	Robert A. Guelich, tr.
THE APOSTOLIC FATHERS	J. B. Lightfoot
THE ATONEMENT OF CHRIST	Francis Turrettin
THE AUTHORITY OF THE OLD TESTAMENT	John Bright
BACKGROUNDS TO DISPENSATIONALISM	Clarence B. Bass
BASIC CHRISTIAN DOCTRINES	Carl F. H. Henry
THE BASIC IDEAS OF CALVINISM	H. Henry Meeter
THE CALVINISTIC CONCEPT OF CULTURE	H. Van Til
CHRISTIAN APPROACH TO PHILOSOPHY	W. C. Young
CHRISTIAN PERSONAL ETHICS	Carl F. H. Henry
COMMENTARY ON DANIEL (Jerome)	Gleason L. Archer, Jr., tr.
THE DAYS OF HIS FLESH	David Smith
DISCIPLING THE NATIONS	Richard DeRidder
THE DOCTRINE OF GOD	Herman Bavinck
EDUCATIONAL IDEALS IN THE ANCIENT WORLD	Wm. Barclay
THE EPISTLE OF JAMES	Joseph B. Mayor
EUSEBIUS' ECCLESIASTICAL HISTORY	
FUNDAMENTALS OF THE FAITH	Carl F. H. Henry, ed.
GOD-CENTERED EVANGELISM	R. B. Kuiper
GENERAL PHILOSOPHY	D. Elton Trueblood
THE GRACE OF LAW	Ernest F. Kevan
THE HIGHER CRITICISM OF THE PENTATEUCH	William Henry Green
THE HISTORY OF CHRISTIAN DOCTRINES	Louis Berkhof
THE HISTORY OF DOCTRINES	Reinhold Seeberg
THE HISTORY OF THE JEWISH NATION	Alfred Edersheim
HISTORY OF PREACHING	E. C. Dargan
LIGHT FROM THE ANCIENT EAST	Adolf Deissmann
NOTES ON THE MIRACLES OF OUR LORD	R. C. Trench
NOTES ON THE PARABLES OF OUR LORD	R. C. Trench
OUR REASONABLE FAITH (Bavinck)	Henry Zylstra, tr.
PAUL, APOSTLE OF LIBERTY	R. N. Longnecker
PHILOSOPHY OF RELIGION	D. Elton Trueblood
PROPHETS AND THE PROMISE	W. J. Beecher
REASONS FOR FAITH	John H. Gerstner
THE REFORMATION	Hans J. Hillebrand, ed.
REFORMED DOGMATICS (Wollebius, Voetius, Turretin)	J. Beardslee, ed., tr.
REFORMED DOGMATICS	Heinrich Heppe
REVELATION AND INSPIRATION	James Orr
REVELATION AND THE BIBLE	Carl F. H. Henry
ROMAN SOCIETY AND ROMAN LAW IN THE NEW TESTAMENT	A. N. Sherwin-White
THE ROOT OF FUNDAMENTALISM	Ernest R. Sandeen
THE SERVANT-MESSIAH	T. W. Manson
STORY OF RELIGION IN AMERICA	Wm. W. Sweet
THE TESTS OF LIFE (third edition)	Robert Law
THEOLOGY OF THE MAJOR SECTS	John H. Gerstner
VARIETIES OF CHRISTIAN APOLOGETICS	B. Ramm
THE VOYAGE AND SHIPWRECK OF ST. PAUL (fourth edition)	James Smith
THE VIRGIN BIRTH	J. G. Machen
A COMPANION TO THE STUDY OF ST. AUGUSTINE	Roy W. Battenhouse, ed.
STUDIES IN THE GOSPELS	R. C. Trench
THE HISTORY OF THE RELIGION OF ISRAEL	John Howard Raven
THE HISTORY OF CHRISTIAN DOCTRINE (revised edition)	E. H. Klotsche
THE EPISTLES OF JUDE AND II PETER	Joseph B. Mayor
THEORIES OF REVELATION	H. D. McDonald
STUDIES IN THE BOOK OF DANIEL	Robert Dick Wilson
THE UNITY OF THE BOOK OF GENESIS	William Henry Green
THE APOCALYPSE OF JOHN	Isbon T. Beckwith
CHRIST THE MEANING OF HISTORY	Hendrikus Berkhof